Strategic Management and Policy in the Global Aviation Industry

Salim Kurnaz
Istanbul Aydın University, Turkey

Antonio Rodrigues
Instituto Superior de Gestão, Portugal

Anıl Padhra
West London University, UK

A volume in the Advances in Logistics, Operations, and Management Science (ALOMS) Book Series

Published in the United States of America by
    IGI Global
    Business Science Reference (an imprint of IGI Global)
    701 E. Chocolate Avenue
    Hershey PA, USA 17033
    Tel: 717-533-8845
    Fax: 717-533-8661
    E-mail: cust@igi-global.com
    Web site: http://www.igi-global.com

Library of Congress Cataloging-in-Publication Data

Names: Kurnaz, Salim, 1978- editor. | Rodrigues, António, 1973- editor. |
  Padhra, Anil, 1983- editor.
Title: Strategic management and policy in the global aviation industry /
  edited by: Salim Kurnaz, António Rodrigues, Anil Padhra.
Description: Hershey PA : Business Science Reference, [2024] | Includes
  bibliographical references. | Summary: "The book will include research
  results, authoritative overview articles, high-quality analysis trends,
  comparative studies, and analysis of particular cases in aviation"--
  Provided by publisher.
Identifiers: LCCN 2023050920 (print) | LCCN 2023050921 (ebook) | ISBN
  9798369309087 (hardcover) | ISBN 9798369309094 (ebook)
Subjects: LCSH: Aircraft industry--Management. | Strategic planning.
Classification: LCC HD9711.A2 S767 2024 (print) | LCC HD9711.A2 (ebook) |
  DDC 387.7068/4--dc23/eng/20231207
LC record available at https://lccn.loc.gov/2023050920
LC ebook record available at https://lccn.loc.gov/2023050921

This book is published in the IGI Global book series Advances in Logistics, Operations, and Management Science (ALOMS) (ISSN: 2327-350X; eISSN: 2327-3518)

British Cataloguing in Publication Data
A Cataloguing in Publication record for this book is available from the British Library.

For electronic access to this publication, please contact: eresources@igi-global.com.

Advances in Logistics, Operations, and Management Science (ALOMS) Book Series

John Wang
Montclair State University, USA

ISSN:2327-350X
EISSN:2327-3518

MISSION

Operations research and management science continue to influence business processes, administration, and management information systems, particularly in covering the application methods for decision-making processes. New case studies and applications on management science, operations management, social sciences, and other behavioral sciences have been incorporated into business and organizations real-world objectives.

The **Advances in Logistics, Operations, and Management Science** (ALOMS) Book Series provides a collection of reference publications on the current trends, applications, theories, and practices in the management science field. Providing relevant and current research, this series and its individual publications would be useful for academics, researchers, scholars, and practitioners interested in improving decision making models and business functions.

COVERAGE

- Finance
- Marketing engineering
- Networks
- Computing and information technologies
- Organizational Behavior
- Information Management
- Political Science
- Production Management
- Decision analysis and decision support
- Services management

IGI Global is currently accepting manuscripts for publication within this series. To submit a proposal for a volume in this series, please contact our Acquisition Editors at Acquisitions@igi-global.com or visit: http://www.igi-global.com/publish/.

Titles in this Series

For a list of additional titles in this series, please visit: http://www.igi-global.com/book-series/advances-logistics-operations-management-science/37170

Convergence of Industry 4.0 and Supply Chain Sustainability
Muhammad Rahies Khan (Bahria University, Karachi, Pakistan) Naveed R. Khan (UCSI University, Malaysia) and Noor Zaman Jhanjhi (Taylor's University, Malaysia)
Business Science Reference • copyright 2024 • 491pp • H/C (ISBN: 9798369313633) • US $275.00 (our price)

Drivers of SME Growth and Sustainability in Emerging Markets
Sumesh Dadwal (Northumbrian University, UK) Pawan Kumar (Lovely Professional University, India) Rajesh Verma (Lovely Professional University, India) and Gursimranjit Singh (Dr. B.R. Ambedkar National Institute of Technology, Jalandhar, India)
Business Science Reference • copyright 2024 • 308pp • H/C (ISBN: 9798369301111) • US $250.00 (our price)

Navigating the Coaching and Leadership Landscape Strategies and Insights for Success
Andrew J. Wefald (Staley School of Leadership, Kansas State University, USA)
Business Science Reference • copyright 2024 • 306pp • H/C (ISBN: 9798369352427) • US $295.00 (our price)

Strategies for Environmentally Responsible Supply Chain and Production Management
Yanamandra Ramakrishna (School of Business, Skyline University College, Sharjah, UAE) and Babita Srivastava (William Paterson University, USA)
Business Science Reference • copyright 2024 • 309pp • H/C (ISBN: 9798369306697) • US $275.00 (our price)

Industry Applications of Thrust Manufacturing Convergence with Real-Time Data and AI
D. Satishkumar (Nehru Institute of Technology, India) and M. Sivaraja (Nehru Institute of Technology, India)
Engineering Science Reference • copyright 2024 • 353pp • H/C (ISBN: 9798369342763) • US $365.00 (our price)

Utilization of AI Technology in Supply Chain Management
Digvijay Pandey (Department of Technical Education, Government of Uttar Pradesh, India) Binay Kumar Pandey (College of Technology, Govind Ballabh Pant University of Agriculture and Technology, Pantnagar, India) Uday Kumar Kanike (Independent Researcher, USA) A. Shaji George (Crown University International, Saudi Arabia & Chartered International Da Vinci University, Nigeria) and Prabjot Kaur (Birla Institute of Technology, Mesra, India)
Business Science Reference • copyright 2024 • 336pp • H/C (ISBN: 9798369335932) • US $395.00 (our price)

A Critical Examination of the Recent Evolution of B2B Sales
Joel G. Cohn (Everglades University, Boca Raton, USA)
Business Science Reference • copyright 2024 • 276pp • H/C (ISBN: 9798369303481) • US $255.00 (our price)

701 East Chocolate Avenue, Hershey, PA 17033, USA
Tel: 717-533-8845 x100 • Fax: 717-533-8661
E-Mail: cust@igi-global.com • www.igi-global.com

Table of Contents

Detailed Table of Contents

Chapter 1
Ali Davut Alkan, Niğde Ömer Halisdemir University, Turkey
Osman Nuri Sunar, İstanbul Aydin University, Turkey

The fact that the civil aviation sector has a multicultural structure by nature and assimilates this structure is a situation that has both advantages and disadvantages. This situation reveals the importance of human resources management in the civil aviation sector. The fact that personnel working in the civil aviation sector have the opportunity to work worldwide, provided they meet certain conditions, provides freedom of movement for these employees. Especially in developed countries, as a result of the decrease in the young population and the tendency to leave jobs that require intense physical strength and have relatively low wages to immigrants, it has become possible to see immigrant workers in most of the business lines. Strategic human resources planning is extremely important to keep this situation under control and to train human resources in every field that may be needed in the civil aviation industry in the future. An understanding of human resources management, which specializes in the field of civil aviation, knows the needs and deficiencies of this field, and guides decision makers by offering the right solution suggestions, is deemed essential.

Chapter 2
Fatma Gül Karaçelebi, Niğde Ömer Halisdemir Üniversitesi, Turkey

The study focuses on the importance of human relations and why employee relations should be given importance in the aviation industry. In this context, first of all, information is included about the changes in the perspective of human beings throughout the development of management thought. Information about the service profit chain and employee service quality model in organizations is included. In employee relations management, the concept of the internal customer and its importance are emphasized, and the hierarchical process of the internal customer concept is included. Information is provided on what organizational managers should do to improve employee relations, ensure employee satisfaction, and retain employees. The strategic importance of employee relations for organizations is revealed by including the results of previous research on employee satisfaction and relations. Various suggestions are included for the development and sustainability of employee relations management in the aviation industry.

Chapter 3

Ümit Deniz Göker, Department of Solar Physics, Astronomical Institute of Czech Academy of Sciences, Czech Republic

This chapter gives the internal and external factors affecting the mental and physical activities of aircrew personnel by examining a wide range of aspects, from aviation psychology to solar physics. The author mentions the cognitive effects, mental activities, nervous system, neurophysiology, and physical activities as internal factors while solar activity, geomagnetic storms, and meteorological effects as external factors. Firstly, the consequences of the design of an air traffic management system as system capacity and throughput, progress time and/or ongoing work, efficiency and cost-effectiveness, flexibility, and complexity to performance evaluation and optimization; secondly, the results of geomagnetic storms over 115 years of aircraft accidents for latitudes between $\pm 10° \leq \varphi \leq \pm 90°$ in the northern and southern hemispheres of Earth, which is a very important space weather event and could be the main reason for most aircraft accidents are investigated on the mental and physical health conditions.

Chapter 4

Carolina Baptista, Instituto Superior de Educação e Ciências, Portugal
Rui Castro Quadros, Instituto Superior de Educação e Ciências, Portugal & Escola Superior de Hotelaria e Turismo do Estoril, Portugal

The COVID-19 pandemic has profoundly impacted various sectors, notably the aviation industry, where travel restrictions and reduced demand for flights led to significant challenges. This study examines the pandemic's financial implications on European companies during the period from 2018 to 2021, utilizing quantitative comparative analysis. The findings reveal a substantial decline in revenues for these companies, resulting in adverse effects on both their operational and net performance. Faced with the pandemic's uncertainty, these companies prioritized liquidity, resorting to external financing for support. Notably, the study highlights that TAP, the Portuguese airline, received significantly more state support compared to its European counterparts. Plus, TAP appears to encounter greater difficulties in servicing its financial debt, standing as the sole entity with an excessive debt burden among the analysed companies. This research contributes valuable insights into the aviation sector's challenges during the pandemic, encouraging a broader European-level dialogue on the subject.

Chapter 5

Rui Castro Quadros, Instituto Superior de Educação e Ciências, Portugal
Ana Barqueira, Instituto Superior de Educação e Ciências, Portugal
Jorge Abrantes, Estoril Higher Institute for Tourism and Hotel Studies, Portugal & Universidade Aberta, Portugal

Madeira airport is the main gateway responsible for the entry of passengers into the Autonomous Region of Madeira (ARM). Is tourism in ARM heavily dependent on Air Transport? The specific objective is to establish, through Pearson's correlation analysis, the observed behavior of some indicators (in 2919 and 2020) on tourist activity and its relationship with air traffic. Several tourist indicators and their influence on tourism were studied, as well as the evidence that air transport is central to the tourist development of Madeira Island. The information collected and the correlations results shows a crucial importance of air transportation for the tourism activity in ARM. The existence of flights to the island means more capacity to generate traffic, more tourists, more occupation of hotels and greater economic development.

Chapter 6

António Rodrigues, ISG - Business & Economics School, Lisboa, Portugal
Jorge Abrantes, Estoril Higher Institute for Tourism and Hotel Studies, Portugal &
Universidade Aberta, Portugal
Rui Quadros, Estoril Higher Institute for Tourism and Hotel, Portugal & Instituto Superior
de Educação e Ciências, Portugal
Salim Kurnaz, Istanbul Aydın University, Turkey

The objective of this chapter is to analyze the main sustainability and green financing challenges for the airline sector. Qualitative research, based on a literature review and mainly on official sustainability and green financing documents, was used. The methodology is suitable for collecting information within the scope of the study of subjective phenomena, which, in the opinion of Yin, favors a more critical position on the part of the researcher. The conclusion reached is that regulatory changes and society's greater focus on environmental issues lead to changes in the aviation industry, although they cannot be immediately applied to all flights and by all airlines. It is not enough to modernize planes and operations. Aviation support activities must also be part of the sustainability equation. Without adequate financing, it is not possible to reinvent the business. Financing through mixed financing agreements with public and private resources is one of the alternatives discussed in academia and the financial market. Capital needs to find good projects.

Chapter 7

Miguel Centeno Moreira, Atlântica Instituto Universitário, Portugal

This investigation reports on the recent evolution of a regional aviation/aerospace cluster in Portugal, located in Ponte de Sor, a small city in the region of Alentejo. Recognized as one of the driving forces of the cluster´s significant growth, the municipal aerodrome anchors the local and regional development in the last decade in this sector. In this chapter, recent and future investment cycles and their socioeconomic impacts are analyzed, the growing diversity and complementarity of activities are presented, and the municipal strategy is discussed going forward. The investigation, based on a Porter´s diamond model analysis, leads us to the conclusion that the Ponte de Sor cluster is set to become one of Portugal´s major aviation/aerospace keystones in future years.

Chapter 8

Carolina Correia Vieira, Instituto Superior de Educação e Ciências, Portugal
Rui Castro e Quadros, Instituto Superior de Educação e Ciências, Portugal & Escola
Superior de Hotelaria e Turismo do Estoril, Portugal

These perspectives are primarily reflected on a global scale for 2050 with individual perspectives of the continuation of current technology, advancement in technology and operations, aggressive development of sustainable fuels and a technologically aggressive perspective. Where is considered the average annual percentage of air traffic growth, technology development, improvements in operations and infrastructure, sustainable fuels (SAF – sustainable aviation fuel), and use of offsetting. These scenarios will allow an analysis of the developments studied, with reference to the relationship between CO2 emissions from air transport and the volume of passengers transported, use of new more sustainable models for short and long-distance routes, discrepancies in the development of countries and consequently in achieving the targets. It also enables an overview of the aeronautical industry in the face of various barriers at political, social, economic, and technological level.

Chapter 9

  Beyzanur Cayir Ervural, Department of Aviation Management, Necmettin Erbakan University, Turkey

The critical and strategic position of the aviation industry has increased the interest in research studies on aviation topics. Particularly, determining the ideal preferences for aircraft is a complete decision problem because it contains many complex and qualitative/quantitative elements. The purpose of this study is to highlight the missing points by presenting a more comprehensive analysis for airline companies to choose the ideal aircraft model by using analytical models from a holistic perspective. Some technical, economic, and environmental criteria should be considered to identify the most proper aircraft. The selection of the most suitable aircraft in line with the characteristics determined as a result of the opinions received from aviation experts and extensive literature research is evaluated with recently developed multi-criteria decision-making (MCDM) methods such as complex proportional assessment (COPRAS), emergency descent arrest systems (EDAS), and weighted aggregated sum product assessment (WASPAS), then sensitivity analysis is applied to demonstrate the reliability of the methods after comparing the results obtained with each other.

Chapter 10

  Marcelo Martins, Instituto Superior de Educação e Ciências, Portugal
  Rui C. Castro e Quadros, Instituto Superior de Educação e Ciências, Portugal & Escola Superior de Hotelaria e Turismo do Estoril, Portugal
  Ana Barqueiro, Instituto Superior de Educação e Ciências, Portugal

The personalization of services is a crucial element in full-service airlines, as they seek to meet the needs of their passengers. This work aimed to analyze the personalization strategies adopted by the main airlines with the largest number of passengers at Lisbon Airport and to evaluate the level of passenger satisfaction in relation to these strategies. The research was carried out through a questionnaire survey applied to passengers, so that it was possible to assess the level of customer satisfaction in relation to the strategies adopted by the full-service airlines under study. Data were analysed quantitatively. The results revealed that the personalization strategies adopted by the studied airlines are similar, contrary to the initial hypothesis that there would be significant differences between them. In addition, the level of passenger satisfaction regarding these strategies was also similar, indicating that airlines are responding equally satisfactorily to the individual needs and preferences of passengers.

Chapter 11

Kübra Nur Cingöz, Gaziantep University, Turkey
Vildan Durmaz, Eskisehir Technical University, Turkey

The aviation industry is evolving, driven by advanced techology like autonomous systems, machine learning, and data analytics. Artificial intelligence (AI) applications, including predictive maintenance, flight planning, and air traffic management, are transforming operations and safety. However, integrating these technologies poses challenges and ethical dilemmas explored in this chapter. The authors analyze AI's impact on safety, efficiency, customer service, and cost-effectiveness in the airline industry. Through a systematic examination, the authors seek to offer insights into the pivotal question of whether the preference should lean towards a fully automated AI-driven system, human operation, or a harmonious AI-human partnership within the airline industry. By weighing the pros and cons of each approach, the authors aim to shed light on the path that holds the greatest promise for the future of aviation, ultimately ensuring the industry's continued excellence and sustainability.

Chapter 12

Diogo Andrade Belejo, Universidade Lusófona, Portugal
José Carlos Rouco, Universidade Lusófona, Portugal
Lúcia Silva Piedade, Universidade Lusófona, Portugal

Nowadays, when it's a priority to support the recovery of the civil aviation industry, it is essential to consider the role played by technology, specifically artificial intelligence. The goal of this study is to dissect how this powerful tool can contribute to the growth of the airport sector, starting by raising the research question, "How can artificial intelligence add value to an airport?". It is within the scope of its application that the concept of performance is highlighted, based on measuring the efficiency level of operational activities, through principles such as consumer trust, service quality and opportunity for organizational cost reduction, driving the investment to critical value-creating elements for airport management. By exposing the presently known cases of AI application, it becomes necessary to address their level of expansion across the world, outlining their relationship with the responsible factors for value growth, and enabling the development of forecasts, regarding the investment in airport security, which is currently limited to only certain segments.

Chapter 13

Jorge Abrantes, Estoril Higher Institute for Tourism and Hotel Studies, Portugal &
Universidade Aberta, Portugal
Rui Castro e Quadros, Instituto Superior de Educação e Ciências, Portugal & Escola
Superior de Hotelaria e Turismo do Estoril, Portugal
António Rodrigues, ISG - Business & Economics School, Lisboa, Portugal

Seasonality is a reality in leisure tourist destinations such as the Mediterranean and the Algarve (Portugal) Region in Europe. The objective of the present investigation is to evaluate the seasonal effects on passenger air operations to/from Faro airport (Algarve), based on a comparative analysis that takes into account a period of low season (February) and a period of high season (August). In methodological terms, the analysis will be exploratory, descriptive, and qualitative although based on quantitative elements, taking into account the origin destinations of the traffic, the airlines and their operations and the respective number of flights. The results obtained show the strong incidence of seasonality at Faro airport, both with an increase in the number of flights operated in high season, as well as a greater number of airlines and destinations (some of them operated exclusively seasonal).

Chapter 14
Fırat Cem Doğan, Hasan Kalyoncu University, Turkey
Mehmet Hanifi Aslan, Hasan Kalyoncu University, Turkey

The study aims to reveal the possible economic, social, and technological consequences of these activities and make projections and evaluations regarding the space economy for the future of humanity. It also aims to create a futuristic perspective on what space could bring to humanity, which has been a subject of great curiosity. Within this study, space and space economy will also be evaluated in terms of addressing the problems that may arise from the depletion of natural resources on Earth in the future. The study examines the space activities of both the public sector and private enterprises in various countries using numerical data. For example, the budget of the (NASA) of the United States alone reached $57.69 billion in 2022, more than two and a half times the amount in 2009. It is estimated that the size of the global space economy will reach approximately $641.2 billion by 2030. As activities related to all components of the space economy continue to increase through public and private initiatives, the dream of a future in space for humanity is closer than ever before.

Preface

A large portion of aviation companies and airports are still managed by governments although the aviation industry is handled in the field of business management. In addition, most of the general airlines and airports operating in the aviation sector are owned by the states. So, the aviation sector is closely followed by public administrations, especially due to its economic size, great investment need and taking up a large place in the country's economies. For this reason, the development and sustainability of the aviation industry is supported and encouraged by the administrations. It is also for this reason that when the aviation activities, which came to a standstill during the Covid-19 pandemic which greatly affected the sector, the governments could not remain unresponsive to this situation. During the pandemic process, the aid and support efforts of many governments to national aviation companies have revealed the importance of the sector in the eyes of governments and administrations. For this reason, a more in-depth investigation of the relationship between governments and aviation companies will guide the future of the industry.

Another important issue in front of governments regarding aviation activities is ensuring the sustainability of increasing aviation activities. In this context, compliance with the sustainability targets determined by the UN is the main target of aviation enterprises. The achievement of these targets will be shaped by the regulations to be implemented by the governments and the willingness of aviation enterprises to participate.

Finally, the digital transformation in the aviation industry is increasing day by day. While this change provides comfort and convenience to passengers' aviation experience, it makes the aviation industry the first point where new technologies enter our lives. So, it will be useful to examine the new technologies implemented in the aviation sector.

Artificial intelligence (AI) is revolutionizing the airline industry by improving operational efficiency, increasing safety, reducing costs and delivering improved experiences for both airlines and passengers.

Data management through AI can have a positive impact to address some of the sector's great challenges in different areas. Aircraft production and maintenance, air traffic management, airport security or security risk management will be affected by the emergence of AI.

There are numerous practical applications of AI, it can represent a great opportunity for the optimization of flight trajectories in the search for reduction of emissions, time and fuel consumption. In airport management, you can introduce improvements in the detection of FOD's (Foreign Object Debris/Damage) on the runway or improve security systems. It can also contribute to risk analysis and management both in security management systems and to detect cybersecurity threats.

AI will redefine how the air transportation industry will function in the future.

For this reason, this book focus on the modern research on government interaction with aviation companies, sustainability in aviation and digital transformation in aviation.

The book includes research results, authoritative overview articles, high-quality analysis trends, comparative studies, and analysis of cases in aviation. It draws attention to the aviation industry's current situation and future expectations by focusing on stakeholders, gender issues in aviation, e-aviation, and various other industry trends in the context of full-service network carriers, low-cost airlines, charter, regional, cargo, and hybrid airlines; aviation education and management, highlighting the use of digital technology in the aviation sector and the various communication technologies available.

Editors hope that this book will reach its target audience of researchers, scholars, academics, post-graduate and undergraduate students, and professionals in the areas of philosophy, ethics, sociology, development studies, economics, political science, cultural studies, the entire humanities, and social sciences family, as well as the public. Academics, researchers, and aviation students will find this book helpful in furthering their research exposure to pertinent topics and assisting in further promoting their research efforts in this field.

Editors would like to thank the authors of all chapters for their invaluable efforts and contributions to our book. The geographical diversity of the authors has certainly enriched the discussion of Strategic Management and Policy in the Global Aviation Industry, so without their efforts it would be impossible to finish this book.

ORGANIZATION OF THE BOOK

The book is organized into fourteen chapters. A brief description of each of the chapters follows:

Chapter 1 by Alkan & Sunar focuses on the importance of human resources management in the civil aviation sector. The fact that personnel working in the civil aviation sector have the opportunity to work worldwide provides freedom of movement for these employees. Especially in developed countries, as a result of the decrease in the young population and the tendency to leave jobs that require intense physical strength and have relatively low wages to immigrants, it has become possible to see immigrant workers in most of the business lines. Strategic human resources planning is extremely important to keep this situation under control and to train human resources in every field that may be needed in the civil aviation industry in the future.

Chapter 2 by Karaçelebi focuses on the importance of human relations and why employee relations should be given importance in the aviation industry. In this context, first of all, information is included about the changes in the perspective of human beings throughout the development of management thought. Information about the service profit chain and employee service quality model in organizations is included. In employee relations management, the concept of the internal customer and its importance are emphasized, and the hierarchical process of the internal customer concept is included. Information is provided on what organizational managers should do to improve employee relations, ensure employee satisfaction, and retain employees. The strategic importance of employee relations for organizations is revealed by including the results of previous research on employee satisfaction and relations. Various suggestions are included for the development and sustainability of employee relations management in the aviation industry.

Chapter 3 by Göker focuses on the internal and external factors affecting the mental and physical activities of aircrew personnel by examining a wide range of aspects, from aviation psychology to solar physics. The author mentions the cognitive effects, mental activities, nervous system, neurophysiology, and physical activities as internal factors while solar activity, geomagnetic storms, and meteorological effects as external factors.

Chapter 4 by Bastista & Quadros examines the pandemic's financial implications on European companies during the period from 2018 to 2021, utilizing quantitative comparative analysis. The findings reveal a substantial decline in revenues for these companies, resulting in adverse effects on both their operational and net performance.

Chapter 5 by Quadros, Barqueira & Abrantes tried to explain the specific objective is to establish, through Pearson's correlation analysis, the observed behavior of some indicators (in 2919 and 2020) on tourist activity and its relationship with air traffic. Several tourist indicators and their influence on tourism were studied, as well as the evidence that air transport is central to the tourist development of Madeira Island. The information collected and the correlations results shows a crucial importance of air transportation for the tourism activity in ARM. The existence of flights to the island means more capacity to generate traffic, more tourists, more occupation of hotels and greater economic development.

Chapter 6 by Rodrigues, Abrantes, Quadros & Kurnaz tries to analyze the main sustainability and green financing challenges for the airline sector. Regulatory changes and society's greater focus on environmental issues lead to changes in the aviation industry, although they cannot be immediately applied to all flights and by all airlines. It is not enough to modernize planes and operations. Aviation support activities must also be part of the sustainability equation. Without adequate financing, it is not possible to reinvent the business. Financing through mixed financing agreements with public and private resources is one of the alternatives discussed in academia and the financial market. Capital needs to find good projects.

Chapter 7 by Moreira focus on the recent evolution of a regional aviation/aerospace cluster in Portugal, located in Ponte de Sor, a small city in the region of Alentejo. Recognized as one of the driving forces of the cluster´s significant growth, the municipal aerodrome anchors the local and regional development in the last decade in this sector. In this chapter, recent and future investment cycles and their socioeconomic impacts are analyzed, the growing diversity and complementarity of activities are presented, and the municipal strategy is discussed going forward. The investigation, based on a Porter´s Diamond Model analysis, leads us to the conclusion that the Ponte de Sor cluster is set to become one of Portugal´s major aviation/aerospace keystones in the next three to four years.

Chapter 8 by Vieira & Quadros focus on the global scale for 2050 with individual perspectives of the continuation of current technology, advancement in technology and operations, aggressive development of sustainable fuels and a technologically aggressive perspective. Where is considered the average annual percentage of air traffic growth, technology development, improvements in operations and infrastructure, sustainable fuels (SAF – Sustainable Aviation Fuel) and use of Offsetting. These scenarios will allow an analysis of the developments studied, with reference to the relationship between CO_2 emissions from air transport and the volume of passengers transported, use of new more sustainable models for short and long-distance routes, discrepancies in the development of countries and consequently in achieving the targets. Also enables an overview of the aeronautical industry in the face of various barriers at political, social, economic, and technological level.

Chapter 9 by Ervural attempts to highlight the missing points by presenting a more comprehensive analysis for airline companies to choose the ideal aircraft model by using analytical models from a holistic perspective. There are some technical, economic and environmental-based criteria that should be considered in order to identify the most proper aircraft. The selection of the most suitable aircraft in line with the characteristics determined as a result of the opinions received from aviation experts and extensive literature research will be evaluated with recently developed multi-criteria decision-making methods such as COPRAS, EDAS, and WASPAS, then sensitivity analysis will be applied to demonstrate the reliability of the methods after comparing the results obtained with each other.

Chapter 10 by Martins, Quadros & Barqueiro aims to analyze the personalization strategies adopted by the main airlines with the largest number of passengers at Lisbon Airport and to evaluate the level of passenger satisfaction in relation to these strategies. The research was carried out through a questionnaire survey applied to passengers, so that it was possible to assess the level of customer satisfaction in relation to the strategies adopted by the full-service airlines under study. Data were analyzed quantitatively. The results revealed that the personalization strategies adopted by the studied airlines are similar, contrary to the initial hypothesis that there would be significant differences between them. In addition, the level of passenger satisfaction regarding these strategies was also similar, indicating that airlines are responding equally satisfactorily to the individual needs and preferences of passengers.

Chapter 11 by Cingöz & Durmaz intends to analyze AI's impact on safety, efficiency, customer service, and cost-effectiveness in the airline industry. Through a systematic examination, authors seek to offer insights into the pivotal question of whether the preference should lean towards a fully automated AI-driven system, human operation, or a harmonious AI-human partnership within the airline industry. By weighing the pros and cons of each approach, we aim to shed light on the path that holds the greatest promise for the future of aviation, ultimately ensuring the industry's continued excellence and sustainability.

Chapter 12 by Belejo, Rouco & Piedade focused on deepening the understanding of technological innovation, which has gained importance in the aeronautical industry over the past few years. It is within the scope of its application that the concept of performance is highlighted, based on measuring the efficiency level of operational activities, through principles such as consumer trust, service quality, and opportunity for organizational cost reduction, driving to the investment in critical value-creating elements for airport management. By exposing the presently known cases, described throughout this project, it is also necessary to address their level of expansion across the airports, outlining their relationship with the factors responsible for the value growth, and enabling the development of forecasts, regarding the investment in airport security, which is currently limited to certain segments of its entirety.

Chapter 13 by Abrantes, Quadros & Rodrigues tries to evaluate the seasonal effects on passenger air operations to/from Faro airport, based on a comparative analysis that takes into account a period of low season (February) and a period of high season (August). The results obtained show the strong incidence of seasonality at Faro airport (Algarve), both with an increase in the number of flights operated in high season, as well as a greater number of airlines and destinations (some of them operated exclusively seasonal).

Chapter 14 by Dogan & Aslan aims to reveal the possible economic, social, and technological consequences of these activities and make projections and evaluations regarding the space economy for the future of humanity. It also aims to create a futuristic perspective on what space could bring to humanity, which has been a subject of great curiosity. Within this study, space and space economy will also be evaluated in terms of addressing the problems that may arise from the depletion of natural resources on Earth in the future.

Salim Kurnaz
İstanbul Aydın University, Turkey

António Augusto Baptista Rodrigues
ISG-Business and Economics School, Portugal

Acknowledgement

The editors would like to acknowledge the help of all the people involved in this project and, more specifically, to the authors and reviewers that took part in the review process. Without their support, this book would not have become a reality.

First, the editors would like to thank each one of the authors for their contributions. Our sincere gratitude goes to the chapters authors who contributed their time and expertise to this book. The geographical diversity of the authors has certainly enriched the discussion of Strategic Management and Policy in the Global Aviation Industry, so without their efforts it would be impossible to finish this book.

Second, the editors wish to acknowledge the valuable contributions of the reviewers regarding the improvement of quality, coherence, and content presentation of chapters. Most of the authors also served as referees; we highly appreciate their double task.

Salim Kurnaz
İstanbul Aydın University, Turkey.

António Augusto Baptista Rodrigues
ISG-Business and Economics School, Portugal.

Chapter 1

Human Resources Management in the Civil Aviation Sector:
A General Overview

Ali Davut Alkan

https://orcid.org/0000-0002-9463-8683

Niğde Ömer Halisdemir University, Turkey

Osman Nuri Sunar

https://orcid.org/0000-0003-4405-1945

İstanbul Aydin University, Turkey

ABSTRACT

The fact that the civil aviation sector has a multicultural structure by nature and assimilates this structure is a situation that has both advantages and disadvantages. This situation reveals the importance of human resources management in the civil aviation sector. The fact that personnel working in the civil aviation sector have the opportunity to work worldwide, provided they meet certain conditions, provides freedom of movement for these employees. Especially in developed countries, as a result of the decrease in the young population and the tendency to leave jobs that require intense physical strength and have relatively low wages to immigrants, it has become possible to see immigrant workers in most of the business lines. Strategic human resources planning is extremely important to keep this situation under control and to train human resources in every field that may be needed in the civil aviation industry in the future. An understanding of human resources management, which specializes in the field of civil aviation, knows the needs and deficiencies of this field, and guides decision makers by offering the right solution suggestions, is deemed essential.

INTRODUCTION

Air transportation has become more accessible worldwide in recent years, and it is preferred by more and more passengers every day because it is fast, safe and economical. Walker & Cook (2009: 378),

DOI: 10.4018/979-8-3693-0908-7.ch001

states that the international airline passenger transportation capacity has tripled in the last 25 years and this expansion is expected to be at the same pace in the next 25 years.

Aviation is a labor-intensive industry that requires experience (Çiçek et al., 2023: 366). The aviation industry provides qualified employment in the world; It shows itself as an area where unqualified, uneducated or inexperienced employee candidates cannot find a place for themselves in this sector. Harvey & Turnbull (2020: 553), states that qualified human resources in aviation are rare, inimitable and irreplaceable. Due to these characteristics, it has been outlined in which units the employees will work in the aviation sector, especially in the operational departments, according to the human resources and education/experience. Since these standards are set on a world scale, aviation education around the world must be planned to meet certain standards. Lyssakov & Lyssakova (2019: 131-132), draws attention to the importance of training to be received in a dangerous sector such as the civil aviation sector.

There are institutions operating on a global scale and setting standards in various fields related to civil aviation (freight transport, passenger transport, airport etc.). Eilstrup-Sangiovanni (2022: 293), emphasizes the importance of implementing international regulations, although the existence of these institutions is sometimes viewed with a negative approach, as it reduces the functions and effectiveness of governments. Brief information is given below about the institutions that set the standards for education and practice in the civil aviation industry around the World.

International Air Transport Association (IATA); it is an international trade standard setting organization to which airline and ground handling companies can become members. It is aimed to provide safe, secure and economical air transportation.

International Civil Aviation Organization (ICAO); it is the United Nations agency responsible for the sustainable development of international civil aviation activities all over the world without compromising safety and security.

European Civil Aviation Conference (ECAC); The European Civil Aviation Conference is an intergovernmental organization established by the International Civil Aviation Organization and the Council of Europe. Established in 1955 with 19 member countries, ECAC has had 44 members since 2008.

Joint Aviation Authorities Training Organisation (JAA TO); it is a sub-organization of ECAC and aims to provide training services needed to ensure European aviation safety. 44 countries that are members of ECAC are also members of this organization.

European Union Aviation Safety Agency (EASA); it is the civil aviation agency formed by the member states of the European Union[1]. It is aimed to control the creation and implementation of legislation related to all kinds of aircraft, flight, production and inspection, and to ensure flight and ground safety.

Airports Council International (ACI); Representing the interests of governments and international organizations and airports, it aims to develop standards, policies and recommended practices at airports, to raise standards in the world, and to increase information and training opportunities.

The training and implementation standards of the civil aviation sector are determined worldwide by the above-mentioned institutions. Stedmon et al. (2017: 976), states that the aforementioned institutions have an increasing regulatory role in the field of civil aviation. Employee candidates who are trained in these standards can also apply for job positions in the civil aviation sector in almost every country in the world, if they prove that they are reliable and do not have a criminal history, in the absence of other obstacles. With this feature, the civil aviation sector stands out as an international business area that offers the opportunity to work for people from different countries around the World. This situation makes it important for people from different cultures to work in harmony. As a result of Coşkun's (2020: 605) research, it was concluded that the necessary conditions for person-group harmony are provided by building relationships between working individuals and that the goals and objectives of the organization and the goals and objectives of the individual are reconciled with socialization tactics. Similar findings are also revealed by Şahin & Çona (2019).

However, possible disruptions in communication between employees in the operation departments can lead to accidents. Differences in accent and intonation in communication between air traffic controllers and pilots can cause potential accidents (Tiewtrakul & Fletcher, 2010: 229). Because one of the deadliest accidents in the history of civil aviation is considered to be the collision of two Boeing 747 planes in Tenerife, Spain in 1977 due to a simple lack of communication in foggy weather (Landry, 2021: 1672). For these reasons, as well as the necessity of standardization of the education to be received in the civil aviation sector, a training that can be understood worldwide and that has not only theoretical but also daily use, covering the basic terms, definitions and features required by aviation terminology is also a must.

HUMAN RESOURCES MANAGEMENT CONCEPT

Although human resources management has not been called by this name throughout history, it has been applied in many different civilizations and business lines. In this context, every business has tended to choose the human resources that will help it to achieve its expectations and goals, and to employ the best employee candidate. Especially since the 1990s, with the internet becoming more widespread and accessible, one of the channels that brings together candidate employees and employers has come to the fore as the internet. Over time, as a result of the increase in job and employee search parties, it has become possible to perform a more detailed and effective employee candidate-employer matching with job search sites that serve over the internet.

Özgen & Yalçın (2018: 6), defined human resources management as a process consisting of the analysis and design of the work done by the personnel working in the organizational structure, the collection and selection of personnel applications, the training and development, evaluation, remuneration, rewarding, and policies and practices related to human resources activities. It is also emphasized that human resources management is a strategic and holistic approach that contributes individually and collectively to the achievement of organizational goals.

Sadullah (2018: 4-6), defines human resources management as all of the functions and studies that ensure the effective and efficient management of existing human resources in any organizational or environmental environment in a way that will be beneficial to the environment, the organization and the individual, in accordance with the law. Human Resources Management; labor-related costs are gaining increasing importance due to problems such as productivity, changes, signs of negativity in the workforce and globalization.

Özgen & Yalçın (2018: 16-24), some of the external environmental factors affecting human resource management activities; law and legislation, society, unions, technology, economy, labor market, customers, stakeholders, competitor businesses, while some of the internal environmental factors are; vision-mission-goals, organizational policies, management approach, organizational culture, quality of business life.

Sabuncuoğlu (2018: 3), defines human resources as one of the most valuable business inputs called 5M (Machine, Money, Material, Management and Man) and defines two basic philosophies on which human resources management is built; the company's objectives in the direction of efficient use of manpower and employee expectations / ensuring the development of employees. Bingöl (2016: 28), activities carried out within the scope of human resources management;

- Human resources planning
- Staffing (provision, selection, placement)
- Training and development
- Performance evaluation
- Career development
- Remuneration and rewarding
- Industrial relations
- Classifies as employee protection

In today's market conditions, although brutal practices such as low wages, high workload and cuts in social rights are implemented by some companies, human resources management is a business area that aims to continue its activities in an ethical framework. Ertürk (2018: 22-25), principles of human resource management;

- Impartiality principle
- Competence principle
- Efficiency principle
- Assurance principle
- Openness principle
- Principle of respect for people
- Privacy policy
- It lists it as the principle of participation in management.

The main objective of human resources management is; To increase the creative contributions of the employees with the awareness of moral and social responsibility and to contribute to the realization of the strategic goals of the enterprise (Bingöl, 2016: 25). In this respect, it can be said that human resources management requires long-term planning and cannot be considered separately from the strategic goals of the business. Because, businesses prepare strategic plans for the future in order to maintain their earnings and competitive advantages and create strategic goals and targets within these plans. While reaching these goals and targets, qualified human resources emerge as perhaps the most important determinant. Özgen & Yalçın (2018: 35), states that strategic human resources management provides a vertical integration between human resources management policies and practices and the business strategy of the organization, and also contributes to the harmonizing of the elements that make up the scope of the human resources strategy with each other through horizontal integration.

Sadullah (2018: 7), Some of the positive results for companies, especially the cost, of using human resources effectively and efficiently are listed in the following items,

- Decreased labor turnover rate
- Decrease in absenteeism rate
- Reduction of losses caused by work accidents
- Decrease in faulty production
- Increasing product quality and general quality
- Increasing morale and motivation in the workplace environment
- Reduction of employee-employer conflict.

Dessler (2013), defines strategic human resources management as the process in which human resources policies and practices that enable the organization to achieve its strategic goals are formed, organizational performance is improved and a flexible and innovative organizational structure is created with the developed organizational culture. In the process of determining the strategies, the activities of the companies with a competitive advantage can be informative. At this point, two prominent actors in the civil aviation sector in the world, the U.S. and appears as Europe.

It is accepted that Europe is the most active continent in the world in terms of air traffic. In this regard, it can be said that the aviation activities carried out in Europe are of great importance both as a transfer point and as a center. Possible deficiencies and disruptions in the European aviation industry are likely to disrupt all world aviation activities (Alkan, 2022: 234). For this reason, Europe and U.S. are two important actors who are accepted as the authority for the accreditation and equivalence processes of aviation education institutions worldwide, it can be said that. It is known that developing and underdeveloped countries benefit from these two actors when establishing their aviation education systems, and in some cases, they carry out the process of creating educational institutions and curricula completely or for a while under the control of these two countries. In this way, it is possible to provide a uniformity in the education standard of the candidates who will work in the aviation sector around the World. It is considered that ensuring this uniformity will make a positive contribution to the civil aviation sector, although it is at the disposal of the countries.

CHANGE AND TRANSFORMATION OF HUMAN RESOURCES IN THE AVIATION SECTOR

Human resources are extremely important in the aviation industry and more than half of the accidents (approximately 70%-80%) in this sector are caused by human errors (Lyssakov & Lyssakova, 2019: 130; Tiftik & Yakupoglu, 2023: 140). Pizziol et al. (2014: 319), states that human-machine incompatibility and inadequate automation design are the most important causes of possible accidents in the civil aviation sector. In this respect, it is of great importance to choose the human resources correctly, to make the job descriptions correctly, and to make adequate automation designs in the required areas.

Harris & Stanton (2010: 145); defining aviation as an upper system formed by systems, that all procedures applied in aviation are carried out by organizational, technical and human elements, and the elements constituting this upper system; operational independence of components, managerial independence of components, development to a large extent, behavior required by the situation, and geographical distribution of components. Considering that organizational work and operations cannot be considered separately from human resources and technical operations are still carried out to a certain extent in today's technology, it can be said that human resources are indispensable in aviation, as in many other sectors. Similarly, Landry (2021: 1667) and Foster et al. (2023), considers aviation as a complex sociotechnical system by its nature. Do not forget the weaknesses of human resources, fatigue, insomnia, hunger etc. In addition to the weaknesses of technological devices such as the need for a continuous power supply and software support while they are physical needs, perhaps the most important weakness is the lack of reasoning ability. While accidents can be caused by humans, accidents caused by technical foreign matter damage are also encountered.

The Airbus A320-214 incident, which successfully landed on the Hudson River, located in the Manhattan area of New York City, where perhaps the highest human density, as a result of a bird entering its engine, on January 15, 2009, just 90 seconds after taking off from LaGuardia Airport in New York City, shows that civil aviation It is extremely important to determine the course of action and the procedures to be followed in emergency events in the sector. This event later became the subject of the movie "Sully" in 2016 and was brought to the big screen.

U.S. Air Force, On October 30, 1945, Dayton, Ohio held a competition among aircraft manufacturers for the next-generation long-range bomber it was planning to purchase at Wright airport. In this competition, the Model 299 produced by Boeing company stood out among other designs and proved with preliminary tests that it has much more than the specified features. For the test flight of this aircraft, the U.S. Major Ployer Peter Hill, one of the most experienced pilots in the Air Force, was assigned. In this test flight, the plane burst into flames shortly after take-off and two of the five crew members, including the pilot, died. No mechanical malfunction was found in the examination, and the cause of the accident was determined as pilot error. The reason for the pilot error is that the Model 299, which is more advanced and therefore more complex than the aircraft of the period, has the same working principle as the aircraft of the period, but due to its features and size, it has been reported that the pilot forgot to open the new locking mechanism of the elevator and rudder controls. Thereupon, U.S. decided to buy the plane after a while. Air Force has created a simple checklist for pilots and technicians. As a result of this practice, the Model 299 flew 1.8 million miles without a single accident (Gawande, 2009: 32-34). As can be seen in this example, many sectors, especially the aviation sector, have become too complex to rely on human memory as a result of technological developments, and an application that seems quite simple like a checklist can provide much greater contributions than expected. From time to time, these deficiencies can be overcome with devices and software developed by the joint work of people and technology

Bingöl (2016: 28), It draws attention to the fact that the job description should be made within the framework of these principles by revealing the qualities, quantities, requirements, responsibilities and working conditions of every job done in the organization through job analysis studies. Some developments have been made recently in areas where human resources are not as efficient as machines. Wan et al. (2021: 8), proposes a model for the systematic evaluation of human resource performance in the aviation sector and thus preventing possible accidents. Kallus et al. (2010: 246), proposes a model for the systematic evaluation of human resource performance in the aviation sector and thus preventing possible accidents. Banks et al. (2019: 250), states that the design and implementation of automation systems in the areas needed in the aviation industry increases the operational safety, reduces the probability of human error and accordingly the accident rates.

It is extremely important to use English as a universal language and standards valid all over the world in the aviation industry. Tiewtrakul & Fletcher (2010: 229), states that the English language has been used as the international aviation language since 1951, and that international aviation institutions conduct their proficiency tests in English. Tajima (2004: 451), It draws attention to the fact that possible disruptions in the English language proficiency of human resources operating in the field of air traffic control can lead to fatal and irreparable situations.

It is extremely important for airline companies to attract personnel in the human resources procurement process, or in other words, to be attractive to employee candidates. In this context, the aviation industry's having global standards and using a universal language brought along a very wide and deep human resource candidate pool. The selection process from a candidate pool of this size brings quality along with it. In addition, the fact that the flight personnel working in the aviation sector have the opportunity to see various countries of the world and the opportunity to work in a multicultural business environment are some of the factors that make the sector attractive for employees. Employees who live in countries where currencies with lower exchange rates are used against the US Dollar or Euro and earn income from this currency may also be very willing to join the aviation industry from all over the World. This situation leads to an increase in employee quality by expanding and deepening the candidate pool from which they will select potential employees of the aviation industry. The increase in quality also leads to better and faster services provided by human resources, and accordingly, customer satisfaction is provided and increased. Fisher & Marciano (1997: 287), It emphasizes the necessity of effective human resource management especially in periods when human resources are limited. It is possible to say that the depth of human resource supply is more limited than before due to various reasons, especially security, in a process where the civil aviation sector experienced a serious paranoia about security and this doubt continued even though it decreased afterwards.

However, the attacks that hit the World Trade Center in New York on September 11, 2001, which is considered a milestone in the history of world aviation security, and simultaneously a part of the US Department of Defense (Pentagon) buildings, have made the history of human resources candidates to work in the aviation sector much more highlighted the need for a detailed study. Juvan et al. (2021: 410), argues that new security measures have been determined in the civil aviation sector in order to prevent possible future threats as a result of events related to the security vulnerability experienced in the past years, and that some of these criteria have caused serious negative social reactions. Gemici & Yilmaz (2019: 15), states that the only condition for ensuring security in the civil aviation sector is the creation of a security strategy required by aviation sector stakeholders, including human resources, and environmental conditions. Walker & Cook (2009: 378), mentions the importance of environmental NGO and civil aviation sector in providing a balance strategy in the sustainable development of the civil aviation sector. It is known that devices and methods that cause/may damage the environment, especially air pollution, are frequently monitored and criticized by environmental organizations and governments. It is considered extremely important for sustainable aviation to act sensitively and in accordance with the determined rules regarding the environment.

In this context, it is known that candidates who have the same name as the terrorists who carried out the attacks, were born in the same or neighboring countries, and belong to the same religion, are subject to discrimination for a certain period of time. This situation creates inequality of opportunity and can cause employees to feel resentment towards the companies they are rejected or the aviation sector. In addition, employee candidates who try to understand the victims from time to time and give them rights may also lead to a decrease in the depth of the human resource pool. Gemici & Yilmaz (2019: 15), states that the companies in the civil aviation sector are the representatives of the countries they belong to, and therefore, the probability of being targeted for terrorist acts is with gas.

Sharma & Kaur (2019: 6875), argues that the civil aviation sector is one of the most rapidly changing and most affected by environmental conditions among all other sectors and worldwide. Ward et al. (2010: 257), stated that the civil aviation maintenance sector is a complex and competitive field that operates with extremely sensitive standards, where safety is critical, and states that a comprehensive and developed system in accordance with environmental requirements should be established in this field. Van Rooyen et al. (2021: 39), He states that the well-being levels of the employees are decisive in the implementation of the safety and security protocols that are indispensable in the civil aviation industry and that are constantly applied, and that the selection of employees with good well-being and the provision of workplace-based well-being conditions will increase the service quality and reliability of the enterprise.

Harris & Stanton (2010: 147), It predicts that research on the human factor in the field of aviation focused on safety and security benefits in the first 60 years, and in the second 60-year period, while safety-enhancing practices continue, at the same time, it will focus on increasing organizational efficiency and individual performance by applying ergonomics principles.

As a natural result of the increasing competition conditions, civil airline companies have adopted a short-term, cost-conscious, rational approach in all kinds of expenditures. However, employee health and safety remained relatively in the background. The strategies pursued by the civil aviation industry manifest themselves as an approach that aims to minimize operational costs and increase production capacity in the short term, in short, placing profits above employee health and safety (Boyd, 2001: 438). Solanki (2020: 1), Etihad Airways, in a study examining the human resources practices of the company, states that civil aviation businesses operate in the service sector, the development of the profitability and performance of the enterprise in this sector depends on the human resource that provides the service, and employee motivation is a key element for business success, productivity and performance.

Emirates Airlines is one of the official sponsors of the UEFA Champions League tournament. In this context, in each competition held in the said tournament, a female and a male Emirates Airline employee are positioned on the sides of the field exit tunnel during the teams' take-off. This shows that airline companies are not only recognized with their logos and emblems, but also try to increase their awareness through their personnel and clothes by making their personnel, representing human resources, visible in the said organizations.

However, even if it becomes visible, it is also known that employees in the civil aviation sector take actions such as slowing down or quitting work from time to time. The common point of most of these strikes is high working hours and low wages. Although the resolution of this conflict differs from country to country, unions appear as an important actor.

It is known that civil aviation unions make efforts to establish alliances with international regulatory bodies and especially passenger groups that protect determined working conditions, and to ensure the implementation of rigorous international standards regarding safety. In the case of the establishment and healthy operation of these new collaborations, the joint and coordinated movement of the workforce, which is expected to become organized, may become possible, which may emerge as an important element in shaping the future of the global civil aviation industry (Blyton et al., 2001: 459-460). Eraslan & Balcı (2022: 176), reminds the importance of the balancing role of trade unions in the relatively unfair employment relationship between the employee and the enterprise. Similarly, Boyd (2001: 452) states that unions related to the civil aviation sector are of vital importance.

Carrig (1997: 287), in parallel with the events that bring radical changes in the social field such as COVID-19 and the developments in technology, it points to the ability of deep analytical thinking and individual leadership as the two most fundamental characteristics that human resources managers operating in the civil aviation sector should have in the future. At the same time, it is stated that these managers should be chosen from people who are able to discover/experiment new ways to meet the needs of the organization, and to find new ways to mobilize the organizational structure and employees. There are many sub-fields in the civil aviation sector and the employee profile required by each field differs from each other. For example, air cargo transportation, which is a sub-branch of the aviation industry, is an area that is preferred especially for the transportation of high-cost and perishable products and has a relatively smaller share in the goods transportation market. Air cargo transportation provides competitive advantage and significant time savings to its local and global customers. In order to maintain this competitive advantage and to be preferred by air cargo transportation companies, it has become a necessity to select and employ the appropriate human resources (Tiftik & Yakupoglu, 2023: 125).

FUTURE RESEARCH DIRECTIONS

Especially in developed countries, especially in the United States and European countries, it is becoming increasingly difficult to find workers who are willing to do jobs that require physical strength. For this reason, in the aforementioned countries, the admission of migrants for the purpose of performing jobs that require physical labor continues in line with different criteria. While this multicultural working environment is more rapidly accepted in sectors that are inherently multicultural in nature, such as civil aviation, it can also bring some threats.

The first and perhaps the most important of these potential threats is the possibility that some immigrants, who work in a wide range of main and auxiliary service units of the civil aviation sector, which is one of the primary targets of terrorist attacks, and who have relatively limited information about their background in the country where they live, may serve terrorist acts.

In this context, it may be advisable to conduct research to determine how to implement practices and controls to identify migrants working in these countries or citizens of these countries with extremist ideologies or ideas. In addition, even though there is such a possibility in a very small number of them, it is thought that it would be useful to conduct research to establish an information gathering mechanism with the civil aviation authorities in the country of origin and the security institutions of the states, if any, taking into account the possibility that those who sympathize with extremist ideologies and views among immigrants working in the civil aviation sector may be involved in a possible terrorist attack in the future. For this information sharing, a database or information pool should be established within the international civil aviation institutions, where information entry and the accuracy of the information entered is verified by the institutional authority in each country, and a registry or tracking system should be established for the personnel operating in every field in the civil aviation sector.

DISCUSSION AND CONCLUSION

It can be said that human resources in the aviation industry underwent a security-oriented transformation, especially after the September 11, 2001 attacks. In this context, it is known that after September 11, 2001, migration movements increased around the world and human communities had to move to other countries as a result of various social events, especially the Arab Spring. This unusual mobility of human resources and the inclusion of people who have had to change countries into the human resource pool in the areas where they are needed in the countries they live in have been a factor that has increased security concerns. Juvan et al. (2021: 410), In order to maintain the legitimacy of the civil aviation sector, it is necessary to show sensitivity to social issues such as privacy, human rights and health in the implementation of new additional measures taken to increase its security.

Santana et al. (2019: 10), mentions that crisis and austerity practices are more common than ever in this period in which the world is going through, and emphasizes the importance of understanding the reasons for the decline of civil aviation companies and implementing human resources practices in an effective and efficient manner in this troubled period. Alola & Alafeshat (2021: 8), draws attention to the fact that careful and accurate human resource selection process in the civil aviation sector is as important as regular training and development, that the employees selected under these conditions contribute to the organizational success of civil aviation companies and that the organizational success achieved in this way contributes positively to the job satisfaction and retention of the employees. . As can be seen, the process and cycle that starts with the right selection of human resources results in job satisfaction and retention of human resources.

In the strategic management approach, it is seen as a necessity for businesses to try to gain competitive advantage in order to survive in the long term. Competitive advantage is possible with value-creating strategies. Human resource management practices that will support the general business strategies of businesses are essential at this point. In particular, the civil aviation sector in the transportation and service sector can be considered in this context, applications that will create value will follow a course directly proportional to the service provided and inevitably the quality of human resources. Harvey & Turnbull (2020: 564), states that human resources are a very important factor in providing competitive advantage in the civil aviation sector. Çiçek et al. (2023: 368), states that the aviation personnel who died in the accident/destroyed aircraft by Turkish Airlines were accepted as "aviation martyrs" and that a relative of the deceased personnel was employed in the company. These and similar practices increase the level of organizational belonging, organizational citizenship and trust in the organization of the employees. However, it is known that the relatives of the personnel who died due to this disease during the COVID-19 period in the same company were not recruited. Kurnaz & Rodrigues (2022: 235) stated that with the Covid-19 pandemic, serious declines in passenger and freight transportation have occurred worldwide.

The works to be done in the civil aviation sector are complementary to each other. Every job is as important and vital as the other and has a similar function to the links that make up a chain. From time to time, misconceptions are encountered in the aviation industry, such as giving more importance to some tasks than others. So to speak, working in the aviation industry is a team game, and the employees of this industry need to be good team players in addition to their technical competencies. Although it is not considered independent of the human factor, it is another necessity for employees to be skilled and trained in the operation and use of new devices, methods and equipment brought by technology. Kurnaz (2022: 255) point out that the civil aviation industry stands out as one of the priority sectors in terms of the employment it creates worldwide.

Since the first years of aviation history, equipment and methods used in this field continue to change and develop in parallel with technological developments. This change is most evident in the field of automation and it is expected that the need for human beings will decrease day by day. However, until now, it has been seen that a civil aviation sector completely independent of the human factor cannot be considered, except for limited areas.

Appelbaum & Fewster (2003: 56), draws attention to the specialization and strict division of the civil aviation sector. In this context, it is a necessity for the civil aviation sector to train its current and future human resources in a way that will adapt to current developments, to specialize in certain/considered areas with future projections, and to bring technology literacy competence to human resources. Özgen & Yalçın (2018: 26), It indicates that human resources management has proactive features such as taking necessary precautions and making preparations before problems arise. In addition, job descriptions in the aviation sector should be re-evaluated in the light of these developments, human resource training curricula should be implemented in accordance with the requirements of the new job descriptions, and training should be provided in line with the developments envisaged with a proactive approach through vocational training institutions. In this regard, the strategic plans and future predictions of states and international NGO institutions can be benefited from, as well as the fair organizations where companies that provide equipment to the aviation industry exhibit their activities.

Volatile and competitive market conditions have drastically changed the rules in the civil aviation industry around the world, with multiple price-cutting strategies eroding health and safety standards in the industry (Boyd, 2001: 451). In a business area that requires the highest level of occupational safety, such as the civil aviation sector, it is highly likely that these disruptions will result in accidents. Aviation practices around the world are seen as one of the most important business areas where safety rules are/ must be applied most sensitively. It seems possible to close these gaps in health and safety with technology to some extent. Edelman et al. (2022: 1129), states that human factors associated with prominent technological business systems and processes are prioritized and clearly separated from the measurement of the task outputs of civil aviation personnel and the adaptation of certain standards. Kaynak (2021: 652), In his research on civil aviation sector employees, she found that employees who are faced with time pressure experience disagreements and conflicts with their colleagues and superiors.

Chan & Li (2023: 1), In his research on employees in the civil aviation sector, it was found that employees with high experience tend to attribute faults and deficiencies to senior managers and find less ways to establish relationships with other units, while employees with less experience tend to be more willing to establish relationships with other units and are more affected by stress and uncertainty conditions showed. At this point, while the experience period of the employees is often seen as an advantage, it can also show itself as a disadvantage from time to time. In particular, the behavior of attributing faults to top managers seems likely to lead to conflicts between employees and managers. Çiçek et al. (2023: 368), evaluates that the leadership style adopted by the managers during the crisis periods will have a reducing effect on the negative effects of the crisis, especially the intention to leave.

ACKNOWLEDGMENT

This research received no specific grant from any funding agency in the public, commercial, or not-forprofit sectors. We would like to thank the editors of this book for their contributions and support. We would also like to thank the referees for their valuable contributions that made our work better.

REFERENCES

Alkan, A. D. (2022). The effects of COVID-19 on human resource management in aviation companies: The case of Europe. Digitalization and the Impacts of COVID-19 on the Aviation Industry (Eds. S. âurnaz & E. Argin), pp. 225-243. doi:10.4018/978-1-6684-2319-6.ch012

Alola, U. V., & Alafeshat, R. (2021). The impact of human resource practices on employee engagement in the airline industry. *Journal of Public Affairs*, *21*(1), 1–12. doi:10.1002/pa.2135

Appelbaum, S. H., & Fewster, B. M. (2003). Global aviation human resource management: Contemporary employee and labour relations practices. *Management Research News*, *26*(10-11), 56–69. doi:10.1108/01409170310784069

Banks, V. A., Plant, K. L., & Stanton, N. A. (2019). Driving aviation forward; Contrasting driving automation and aviation automation. *Theoretical Issues in Ergonomics Science, 20*(3), 250–264. doi:10.1080/1463922X.2018.1432716

Bingöl, D. (2016). *İnsan kaynakları yönetimi*. Beta Basım Yayım Dağıtım A.Ş.

Blyton, P., Lucio, M. M., McGurk, J., & Turnbull, P. (2001). Globalization and trade union strategy: Industrial restructuring and human resource management in the international civil aviation industry. *International Journal of Human Resource Management, 12*(3), 445–463. doi:10.1080/09585190122137

Boyd, C. (2001). HRM in the airline industry: Strategies and outcomes. *Personnel Review, 30*(4), 438–453. doi:10.1108/00483480110393394

Carrig, K. (1998). Reshaping human resources for the next century? Lessons from a high flying airline. *Human Resource Management, 36*(2), 277–289. doi:10.1002/(SICI)1099-050X(199722)36:2<277::AID-HRM8>3.0.CO;2-U

Chan, W. T.-K., & Li, W.-C. (2023). Development of effective human factors interventions for aviation safety management. *Frontiers in Public Health, 11*, 1–12. doi:10.3389/fpubh.2023.1144921 PMID:37213611

Çiçek, B., Bilkay, S., & Aktaş, K. (2023). Pandemi döneminde havacılık çalışanlarının tutumları. *Alanya Akademik Bakış, 7*(1), 355–374. doi:10.29023/alanyaakademik.1136478

Coşgun, M. (2016). Avrupa Birliği'nde genişleme süreci. In A. Ayata & M. Ercan (Eds.), *Avrupa Birliği ve Türkiye ile İlişkileri: İlişkilerin Siyasi, Askeri, Ekonomik ve Kültürel Çerçevesi* (pp. 21–33).

Coşkun, Ö. F. (2020). Örgütsel sosyalleşme sürecinde kişi-iş uyumundan kişi-örgüt uyumuna yönelik bir model önerisi. *Mustafa Kemal Üniversitesi Sosyal Bilimler Enstitüsü Dergisi, 17*(46), 605–625.

Dessler, G. (2013). *Human resource management* (13th ed.). Pearson.

Edelman, D. A., Duggan, L. V., Lockhart, S. L., Marshall, S. D., Turner, M. C., & Brewster, D. J. (2022). Prevalence and commonality of non-technical skills and human factors in airway management guidelines: A narrative review of the last 5 years. *Anaesthesia, 77*(10), 1129–1136. doi:10.1111/anae.15813 PMID:36089858

Eilstrup-Sangiovanni, M. (2022). Ordering global governance complexes: The evolution of the governance complex for international civil aviation. *The Review of International Organizations, 17*(2), 293–322. doi:10.1007/s11558-020-09411-z PMID:35722452

Eraslan, E., & Balcı, A. İ. (2022). İnsan kaynakları yönetimi ve endüstri ilişkilerinin çatışması noktasında değişen toplu pazarlık düzeylerinin karşılaştırmalı bir analizi. *Niğde Ömer Halisdemir Üniversitesi Sosyal Bilimler Enstitüsü Dergisi, 4*(2), 164–180. doi:10.56574/nohusosbil.1209232

Ertürk, M. (2018). *İnsan kaynakları yönetimi* (2nd ed.). Beta Basım Yayım Dağıtım A.Ş.

Fisher, E. G., & Marciano, V. (1997). Managing human resource shortages in a unionized setting: Best practices in air traffic control. *Journal of Labor Research, 18*(2), 287–314. doi:10.1007/s12122-997-1040-5

Foster, C. J., Plant, K. L., & Stanton, N. A. (2023). Maladaptation in air traffic management: Development of a human factors methods framework. *Human Factors and Ergonomics in Manufacturing*, *33*(1), 118–146. doi:10.1002/hfm.20974

Gawande, A. (2009). *Checklist manifesto* (7th ed.). Domingo.

Gemici, E., & Yılmaz, H. (2019). Güvenlik stratejileri ve yönetimi açısından havacılık güvenliği. *Journal of Aviation*, *3*(1), 15–27. doi:10.30518/jav.550123

Harris, D., & Stanton, N. A. (2010). Aviation as a system of systems: Preface to the special issue of human factors in aviation. *Ergonomics*, *53*(2), 145–148. doi:10.1080/00140130903521587 PMID:20099170

Harvey, G., & Turnbull, P. (2020). Ricardo flies Ryanair: Strategic human resource management and competitive advantage in a single european aviation market. *Human Resource Management Journal*, *30*(4), 553–565. doi:10.1111/1748-8583.12315

Juvan, J., Prezelj, I., & Kopač, E. (2021). Public dilemmas about security measures in the field of civil aviation. *Security Journal*, *34*(3), 410–428. doi:10.1057/s41284-020-00240-8

Kallus, K. W., Hoffmann, P., Winkler, H., & Vormayr, E. M. (2010). The taskload-efficiency-safety-buffer tringle-development and validation with air traffic management. *Ergonomics*, *53*(2), 240–246. doi:10.1080/00140130903199897 PMID:20099177

Kaynak, İ. (2021). İş stresinin örgüt içi çatışmaya etkisi: Sivil havacılık çalışanları üzerine bir araştırma. *Anemon Muş Alparslan Üniversitesi Sosyal Bilimler Dergisi*, *9*(3), 647–658. doi:10.18506/anemon.835175

Kurnaz, S. (2022). Bibliometric analysis of articles published in the field of aviation: Dergipark academic example. *Management Theory and Studies for Rural Business and Infrastructure Development*, *44*(3), 354–361. doi:10.15544/mts.2022.36

Kurnaz, S., Rodrigues, A., Kholiavko, N., Panchenko, O., & Tarasenko, A. (2022). The perspectives of the air transport market in Turkey during Covid-19 pandemic. *Management Theory and Studies for Rural Business and Infrastructure Development*, *44*(2), 235–243. doi:10.15544/mts.2022.24

Landry, S. J. (2021). Human factors and ergonomics in aviation. In G. Salvendy (Ed.), *Handbook of Human Factors and Ergonomics* (pp. 1667–1688)., doi:10.1002/9781119636113.ch55

Lyssakov, N., & Lyssakova, E. (2019). Human factor as a cause of aircraft accidents. *Advances in Social Science, Education and Humanities Research, 321*, 130-132.

Özgen, H., & Yalçın, A. (2018). *İnsan kaynakları yönetimi: Stratejik bir yaklaşım* (4th ed.). Akademisyen Kitabevi A.Ş.

Pizziol, S., Tessier, C., & Dehais, F. (2014). Petri net-based modelling of human-automation conflicts in aviation. *Ergonomics*, *57*(3), 319–331. doi:10.1080/00140139.2013.877597 PMID:24444329

Sabuncuoğlu, Z. (2018). *İnsan kaynakları yönetimi*. Bursa: Aktüel 16 Basım Yayım Dağıtım Ltd. Şti.

Sadullah, Ö. (2018). İnsan kaynakları yönetimine giriş: İnsan kaynakları yönetiminin tanımı, önemi ve çevresel faktörler. In *İnsan Kaynakları Yönetimi* (8th ed., pp. 1–50). Beta Basım Yayım Dağıtım A.Ş.

Şahin, M., & Çona, A. (2019). İnsan kaynakları yönetimi rol belirizliği-rol çatışması. In M. Sağır (Ed.), *İnsan Kaynakları Yönetimi ve Örgüt İçi Etkileşim* (pp. 219–246).

Santana, M., Valle, R., & Galan, J.-L. (2019). How national institutions limit turnaround strategies and human resource management: A comparative study in the airline industry. *European Management Review*, *16*(4), 923–935. doi:10.1111/emre.12177

Sharma, V., & Kaur, P. (2019). A study on HR practices in Indian aviation sector. *Think India Journal*, *22*(14), 6875–6882.

Solanki, K. (2020). Analysis of Etihad Airlines human resource management practices & factors that lead to employees motivation. *International Journal of Entrepreneurship*, *24*(1), 1–14.

Stedmon, A., Lawson, G., Lewis, L., Richards, D., & Grant, R. (2017). Human behaviour in emergency situations: Comparisons between aviation and rail domains. *Security Journal*, *30*(3), 963–978. doi:10.1057/sj.2015.34

Tajima, A. (2004). Fatal miscommunication: English in aviation safety. *World Englishes*, *23*(3), 451–470. doi:10.1111/j.0883-2919.2004.00368.x

Tiewtrakul, T., & Fletcher, S. R. (2010). The challenge of regional accents for aviation English language proficiency standards: A study of difficulties in understanding in air traffic control-pilot communications. *Ergonomics*, *53*(2), 229–239. doi:10.1080/00140130903470033 PMID:20099176

Tiftik, C., & Yakupoğlu, E. (2023). The importance of aviation safety in terms of human resources management in air cargo transportation. [USBED]. *Uluslararası Sosyal Bilimler ve Eğitim Dergisi*, *5*(8), 125–146.

Van Rooyen, J., Shrestha, P., & De Beer, E. (2021). Crisis on human resources: Airline companies in Thailand. *Journal of Human Resource Management*, *9*(2), 39–42. doi:10.11648/j.jhrm.20210902.12

Walker, S., & Cook, M. (2009). The contested concept of sustainable aviation. *Sustainable Development (Bradford)*, *17*(6), 378–390. doi:10.1002/sd.400

Wan, M., Liang, Y., Yan, L., & Zhou, T. (2021). Bibliometric analysis of human factors in aviation accident using MKD. *IET Image Processing*, *15*(12), 1–9. doi:10.1049/ipr2.12167

Ward, M., McDonald, N., Morrison, R., Gaynor, D., & Nugent, T. (2010). A Performance improvement case study in aircraft maintenance and its implications for hazard identification. *Ergonomics*, *53*(2), 247–267. doi:10.1080/00140130903194138 PMID:20099178

ADDITIONAL READING

de Brito, A. P., & Sousa, M. J. (2023). HR analytics in the commercial aviation sector: a literature review. *19th European Conference on Management Leadership and Governance (ECMLG 2023)*, (pp. 512-519). IEEE.

Harvey, G., Williams, K., & Probert, J. (2012). Greening the airline pilot: HRM and green performance of airlines in the UK. *International Journal of Human Resource Management*, *24*(1), 152–166. doi:10 .1080/09585192.2012.669783

Khan, S. (2022). An efficient human resource management system model using web-based hybrid technique. *Problems and Perspectives in Management*, *20*(2), 220–235. doi:10.21511/ppm.20(2).2022.18

Mızrak, F. (2023). Strategies for effective human resource management in the aviation industry: A case-based analysis. *Beykoz Akademi Dergisi*, *11*(2), 82–109. doi:10.14514/beykozad.1346605

Mızrak, K. C., & Mızrak, F. (2020). The impact of crew resource management on reducing the accidents in civil aviation. *Journal of Aviation Research*, *2*(1), 1–25.

Muñoz-Marrón, D. (2018). Human factors in aviation: CRM (crew resource management). *Papeles del Psicólogo*, *39*(3), 191–199. doi:10.23923/pap.psicol2018.2870

Peksatici, O. (2018). Crew resource management (CRM) and cultural differences among cockpit crew – the case of Türkiye. *Journal of Aviation/Aerospace Education Research*, *27*(2), 1–39. doi:10.15394/ jaaer.2018.1742

Shaikh, A. B. S., Habib, F., Hadi, M. Z., & Ahmed, O. (2021). *Applying singapore airline's human resource management strategy for service excellence at Pakistan International Airline*. [Unpublished graduate research project, Institute of Business Administration, Pakistan]. https://ir.iba.edu.pk/research-projects-mba/266

Warhurst, R. (1995). Coverging on HRM? Changing and Continuity in European Airline's relations. *European Journal of Industrial Relations*, *1*(2), 259–274. doi:10.1177/095968019512005

ENDNOTE

[1] For detailed information about European Union members and the enlargement process; Coşgun, M. (2016). *Avrupa Birliği'nde genişleme süreci*. In <u>Avrupa Birliği ve Türkiye ile İlişkileri: İlişkilerin Siyasi, Askeri, Ekonomik ve Kültürel Çerçevesi</u> (Eds. A. Ayata & M. Ercan), pp. 21-33.

Chapter 2
Employee Relations Management in Aviation

Fatma Gül Karaçelebi

(ID) https://orcid.org/0000-0001-8165-0491

Niğde Ömer Halisdemir Üniversitesi, Turkey

ABSTRACT

The study focuses on the importance of human relations and why employee relations should be given importance in the aviation industry. In this context, first of all, information is included about the changes in the perspective of human beings throughout the development of management thought. Information about the service profit chain and employee service quality model in organizations is included. In employee relations management, the concept of the internal customer and its importance are emphasized, and the hierarchical process of the internal customer concept is included. Information is provided on what organizational managers should do to improve employee relations, ensure employee satisfaction, and retain employees. The strategic importance of employee relations for organizations is revealed by including the results of previous research on employee satisfaction and relations. Various suggestions are included for the development and sustainability of employee relations management in the aviation industry.

INTRODUCTION

Establishing relationships is the most basic human need. Other people's presence, interest, and support constitute the essence of relationships. Quality relationships enable people to develop. It also strengthens people's sense of meaning, purpose, and belonging (Doğan, 2005). Human relations provide information on topics such as what a person is, how a person acts, the reasons for a person's behavior and actions, and how to benefit from other people in the best way. Having healthy relationships in business life, as well as in social life, is very important. Relationship management provides significant benefits for both organizations and employees. Joint effort in organizations is indispensable for a job to be done. Joint efforts are possible with healthy relationships (Karavardar, 2012). Establishing and maintaining sincere

DOI: 10.4018/979-8-3693-0908-7.ch002

relationships in interpersonal relationships, trying to understand different perspectives, aiming for mutual benefit, and including others in their emotional worlds increase the competence of relationships.

Nowadays, the increase in competition and the advancement of technology continue very rapidly and intensively. Another issue as a result of modern society is that people now establish relationships with more people. To maintain their competitiveness, organizations now strive to motivate their employees, increase their performance, and maintain their relationships with customers and other stakeholders. A comprehensive relationship management developed with internal and external stakeholders is an indispensable element for the organization's future (Çağlar & Türk, 2023).

Employees in workplaces develop many relationships from different departments on different subjects and intensities to achieve common goals. Weak relationships can lead to disagreements and as a result, it is not possible to achieve common goals. When the issue is examined from this perspective, it is of great importance that employee relations are established on a healthy basis. When organizational managers understand the wishes of each employee and try to meet their needs, they create employees who focus on the goals of the organization. Managers' determination to keep relations with their employees on a healthy basis increases the motivation of employees and facilitates the emergence of quality service for their customers (Brhane & Zewdie, 2018).

The aviation sector, which has many economic, social, and cultural benefits, is one of the most globalized sectors today. With the development of technology, increasing globalization has caused aviation to develop and become more widespread (Kurnaz, 2022). Competition in the aviation industry increases its intensity. More people now prefer air transportation because it is cheap and fast (Alkan, 2022). Keeping existing customers and gaining new customers is now more challenging for organizations. As important as providing cheap, safe, and fast transportation for customers is, a service approach that understands their interests, respect, courtesy, and wishes has become equally important. Developing good relationships where all customer demands can be met is a requirement for survival in sectors where competition increases, such as the aviation industry.

This situation requires airline companies to establish more intense and friendly customer relationships. Considering that organizations can develop such relationships through employees, the strategic importance of employee relations management emerges (Bulgarella, 2005). In sectors such as aviation, which are dynamic, sensitive, fast, and have a low tolerance for error, the management of employee relations is an issue that the management must focus on to not only ensure that things run smoothly but also to prevent any negativities.

In general, managing relationships is a systematic way of connecting the organization's employees, customers, and the entire society by using all its communication capabilities. Considering employees as the first customers is seen as a smart move for organizations. The organization will be able to develop a mutually productive relationship to the extent that it convinces its employees about the potential and excellence of the organization (Shen, 2009). Otherwise, it will damage the employee's trust in the organization. It is known that risk tolerance in the aviation industry is extremely low. Research has shown that accidents or poor service quality occur due to socio-technical reasons such as management, employee motivation, decision-making, and inadequate communication rather than technology. Such reasons can lead to loss of customers, loss of organizational assets, and, more importantly, loss of life (Appelbaum & Fewster, 2003). When we look at the issue from this perspective, it is predicted that the error rates of organizations whose relations with their employees are not developed will increase and therefore the organization will be negatively affected.

The aviation industry has a structure that employs workers in different fields such as ground and flight services. There are many different units in airline companies with different needs, interests, and priorities. Considering the error-free nature of the industry, establishing good relationships with employees and therefore customers is very important to prevent possible problems. The fact that employees have a close relationship with customers shows that they have more up-to-date information about customers. The loss of an employee can be as costly as the loss of a customer for the organization, and it also causes loss of information and time (Çağlar & Türk, 2023). Based on this, this study includes the importance of relationship management and employee relations management and offers suggestions for employee relations management in the aviation industry.

BACKGROUND

When we examine the literature on the aviation industry, we find that the studies primarily focus on topics such as customer satisfaction, loyalty, and customer relations. Given that customer demands and needs determine service quality and the competitive structure of the aviation industry, it is quite normal for there to be a high level of research in this field. In the aviation sector, it is crucial for organizations to effectively introduce themselves to their employees and communicate their brand and values through the appropriate channels, especially in a highly competitive environment. Establishing long-term healthy relationships with customers depends on employees. Therefore, it is crucial for the organization to manage its relationships with its employees, who should be regarded as internal customers, in addition to external customers.

The social exchange theory, introduced by Blau (1964), posits that people form relationships in which they have not only economic but also social obligations (Johnson & O'leary-Kelly). The organizational support theory, which was developed based on this theory also discusses how organizational support influences employee behavior. According to the theory, the more employees feel supported by the organization, the more likely they are to reciprocate in kind (Dasgupta, Suar & Sing, 2013). The aforementioned theories highlight the significance of employee relations.

Employee relations management is defined as the set of policies and practices aimed at minimizing potential conflicts within an organization and fostering employee loyalty (Bauer, Derwall & Hann, 2009). Generally speaking, organizations cannot achieve their goals without the support and creativity of employees. The way to achieve this is to create an environment where employees' desires and requirements are fulfilled. Effective employee relations aim to cultivate a highly motivated and productive workforce (Brhane & Zewdie, 2018). Studies also indicate that positive communication and support can enhance employees' emotional connection to their organizations and decrease negative outcomes such as absenteeism (Dasgupta et.al., 2013).

MANAGING EMPLOYEE RELATIONS

It has been a long time since it was understood that employees are an indispensable element of organizations. With the Hawthorne research conducted by Elton Mayo and his friends in Western Electric Companies, it was accepted that employees are social beings and the view of people in organizations was thus moved to a different dimension. The human relations approach has revealed that the most important and distinctive power of organizations is their employees. At the same time, proponents of this view emphasize the creation of supportive leadership models, employee motivation will increase employee productivity, and the importance of improving communication and relationships between people. The system approach, which later emerged with modern management thought, offered a different way to understand organizations and management processes. The systems approach argues that organizations consist of interconnected subsystems and therefore require high communication. It has revealed that subsystems are the building blocks of processes, the importance of communication and cooperation for an effective workflow, the need for two-way communication for the continuity of the system, and the importance of the feedback process (Eichorn, 2004a). The complex relationships created by inter-connected but independent subsystems in organizations have brought about many changes, such as the development of open communication channels and a flexible approach to differences (Demirel & Güner, 2015). While employees were previously seen as just a tool to get the job done, they have become the core competencies of the organization in the information age. Employees who produce and disseminate information in organizations and ensure the production of new information in the process are now an essential part of organizations.

Internal Customers

Dynamic business environments understand that the success and development of organizations are closely related to the development of their employees. Factors such as technology, globalization, and competition force organizations to establish closer relationships with their employees. Organizations can now achieve meaningful business results that add value through employee satisfaction and participation (Harter, Schmidt & Hayes, 2002).

Another reason why employees can work efficiently and effectively for their organizations is that employees are seen as internal customers. To establish better relationships with their customers, organizations must first harmonize their employees and their brands. This helps increase employee loyalty and retain employees. Organizations cannot continue where they are without the support of their employees (Demirbaş & Özek, 2021; Shen, 2009). It is a strategic approach developed to organize social relations between employees, departments, and management in internal customer organizations, facilitate information sharing, and increase cooperation. In this way, there may be an improvement in the attitudes and behaviors of managers and employees towards their customers. As a result, the organization can maintain its competitive position (Eichorn, 2004b). With a successful application, open communication, employee satisfaction and established relationships at all levels of the organization can be achieved and a customer-oriented structure can be created (Brhane & Zewdie, 2018).

All employees, including senior managers who carry out work related to the organization and new employees, are internal customers of the organization. Internal customers are all employees involved in the process from the emergence of the organization's product or service as an idea to its presentation to the customer (Doğan, 2005). As seen in Figure 1, internal customers are located in a hierarchical order within the organization. Seeing employees as internal customers and creating organizational strategies in this direction makes a positive contribution to the employee's performance, desire, and commitment by putting employee relations into action, starting from the recruitment of an employee.

As seen in Figure 2, it is emphasized that in order to achieve service profit in organizations, internal service quality must first be established and thus employee satisfaction and loyalty must be increased.

Figure 1. Internal customer hierarchy
Source: *Doğan (2005)*

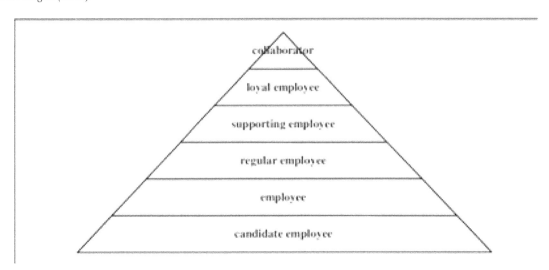

As a result of the satisfaction and loyalty that can occur through the correct management of employee relations, organizations will be able to make profits through customer satisfaction and loyalty.

A study conducted in Oxford also reveals the importance of the internal customer. In the study, managers were asked what the most important factors are to facilitate total quality management. Managers stated that understanding customer demands correctly can improve quality, and understanding employee needs plays an important role in providing quality to customers (Lukas & Maignan, 1996). Being aware of the demands and needs of employees, which allows for determining quality in organizations, has an important place in obtaining information about the preferences of external customers. At the same time, the importance given to the internal customer leads to permanent changes in the attitudes and behaviors of employees.

Competing in the aviation industry is possible with human resources having technical knowledge and skills. Considering the competition in the sector, retaining employees with sufficient knowledge and competence becomes extremely challenging. Overcoming this difficulty is possible by ensuring internal customer satisfaction. Ensuring the satisfaction of the internal customer not only contributes to employee retention but also contributes positively to all processes of the organization (Çağlar & Türk, 2023).

Yoon, Hyun Seo, and Seog Yoon (2000) explained the antecedents of employee service quality with a model in their study of employee satisfaction. According to the model, perceived organizational support (whether the organization values the employee's contributions and cares about his or her well-being), supervisor support (trust, helpfulness, and friendliness; meaning that important socio-emotional resources

Figure 2. The service profit chain
Source: *Gibert (2000)*

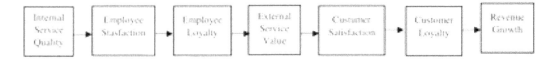

Figure 3. Antecedents of employee service quality model
Source: *Bulgarella (2005)*

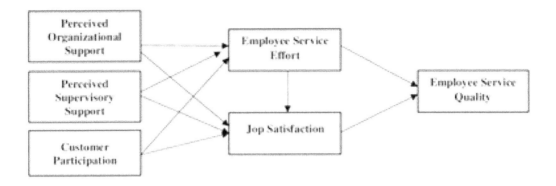

are readily available in the work environment) and customer involvement (the customer's physical, mental and emotional involvement in the presentation of the product) affects the employee's service performance and job satisfaction, thus resulting in a change in the employee's service quality (Bulgarella, 2005).

Bulgarella (2005), also makes various suggestions that managers can implement to improve employee relations and thus increase satisfaction.

- Determining the root causes of dissatisfaction among employees
- Developing satisfaction measurement systems that can be used throughout the organization and periodically measuring employee satisfaction levels
- Employees are seen as the primary source of the organization in providing competitive advantage.
- Caring about the general well-being of employees
- Ensuring employee participation and creating effective communication channels
- Establishing accountable management systems for people management (Bulgarella, 2005)

The results obtained as a result of the studies carried out to manage human resources and relationships in organizations are often collected under five headings. 1- the importance of employee attitude surveys, 2- being able to address employees by name and appreciating their performance, 3- paving the way for employees to communicate with senior management, 4- establishing relationships between management and employees and enabling employees to make meaningful contributions to their work, and 5- Establishing a practical leadership structure to participating in lower-level activities (Appelbaum & Fewster, 2003).

As can be understood from the studies, regulating employee relations and introducing the right communication channels not only affect the effective and efficient progress of organizations but also form the basis of the relationship they will establish with their customers. With employee relations management, organizations can not only establish solid relationships with their customers but also become structures that can compete in the long term (Brhane & Zewdie, 2018).

In general, employee relations management (ERM) is a tool and a strategic process used to continuously improve individual relationships between managers and employees and therefore increase work motivation (Wargborn, 2008). Employee relations are developed to create a suitable working environment by improving employee morale, loyalty, and a sense of trust. With this relationship formed between the manager and the employee, it is aimed for the employees to make maximum effort to achieve organizational goals (Bajaj, Sinha & Tiwari, 2013).

Many times in organizations, employees need to know the organizational culture and the differences of the sector to which the organization is affiliated to communicate effectively and efficiently. Ensuring information flow through open communication and training creates the perception that employees are supported. At the same time, feeling that their wishes and needs are understood will make it easier for the employee to establish a bond with the organization. Organizing employee relations ensures that every employee behaves with the same dedication, demonstrates high performance, and increases customer relations to the next level (Huang, 2020).

Success and failure are determined by employees who develop resources such as finance, technology, information, and production systems that provide a competitive advantage to organizations. For organizations to achieve goals, employees need to establish good relationships with other employees and management (Brhane & Zewdie, 2018). ERM is based on more collaborative collective relationships in which both parties (managers and employees) are motivated to add value to the organization. Such relationships are based on 1) employees' belief in trust, commitment, and cooperation, 2) employees' satisfaction with their jobs, 3) employees' right to influence and participate in decisions, and 4) increasing the productivity, profitability, and efficiency of the organization (Gennard & Judge, 2005).

ERM APPLICATIONS AND RECOMMENDATIONS IN AVAITION

It is seen that airline companies in Turkiye and around the world develop and implement projects to improve employee relations.

Turkish Airlines (THY) organizes training for its employees where basic concepts and field experiences about volunteering are shared by expert academics and experienced people (THY, 2023). *Sabiha Gökçen International Airport (İGS)* provides training to its employees regarding the services to be provided to disabled people. With the training, employees gain knowledge about how to communicate with disabled customers at the airport and transfer processes (İSG, 2010). *Pegasus Airlines* brings its employees together with social activity groups and activities outside the busy work schedule. It also collects the ideas of its employees through the Fyldea (employee suggestion system) platform and selects and rewards the most innovative ideas (Pegasus, 2024).

Lufthansa Airlines supports its employees with flexible working time models. In this way, employees can determine their working hours and establish a better work-life balance. *Air France-KLM* carried out the compassionate behavior project in 2018. The project includes employees in various units receiving coach training and leadership development training. The organization's digital learning portal is accessible to all employees, allowing them to receive training in line with their interests (Çağlar, 2021).

Employees are at the key point in a business's relationship with its customers. From this perspective, employees are at least as important as the product it produces or the service it offers in determining the structure, strategy, and culture of an organization (Appelbaum & Fewster, 2003). Every airline company has material elements such as aircraft, computer systems, and ticket sales offices. However, it is their employees who give airline companies their corporate personality and differentiate them from other airline companies (Ağraz, 2006).

The stronger the relationship established through the employee, the more it will increase the competitiveness of these organizations. Happy employees perform better within the organization and treat customers better. As a result, greater customer satisfaction occurs (Eichorn, 2004a). In a service-intensive sector such as aviation, the relationship between employees and customers is as important as the opportunities (cheap, etc.) provided by organizations to retain their customers or attract new customers to the organization. Considering the intense competition in the aviation industry, the relationships established by the organization with employees who are in direct contact with the customer are of critical importance.

REASONS FOR THE NEED FOR ERM IN AVAITION AND RECOMMENDATIONS

With globalization, transportation to all parts of the world has become easier. Countries can provide all kinds of commercial and economic transportation to other countries safely and comfortably. With the development of civil aviation, people prefer airline companies as a means of transportation. As a result of this increasing interest in air transportation, the employment volume in the aviation sector is gradually increasing. The sector supports approximately 87.7 million jobs worldwide, directly and indirectly (the tourism sector where aviation is active, and the provision of the supply chain with the aviation sector). 11.3 million people (airport operators, flight and cabin crews, managers, ground services, training-maintenance personnel, engineers, designers, and traffic controllers) are directly employed in the aviation industry (Aviation Benefits, 2020).

The increasing volume of data highlights the growing significance of the human factor in the aviation industry. Human resources are a key element in all sector processes, and effective and efficient outputs can be achieved by managing this resource correctly. When the issue is examined in this context, effective management of human relations will ensure the creation of the working environment that employees desire in organizations. However, there are challenges in recruiting and retaining human resources in the aviation industry.

- Employees work intensely during working hours and frequently work overtime, which poses a security risk and places excessive responsibility on them.
- Long working hours create negative impacts on the family and social lives of employees. Irregularities in this area cause psychological stress for the employee.
- Inadequate wages lead to employee dissatisfaction in this regard.
- Failing to provide sufficient vocational training. Lack of training in technical, psychological, or language subjects (Macit & Macit, 2017).

Appelbaum and Fewster (2003) asked employees at airline companies, "Which of the following topics do new employees receive information about?" The question was asked and the answers the employees gave (yes answer the percentage of 50% and above) were respectively about rules and regulations, social benefits, job-related information, wage information, and the organization's mission. The answers below 50% were about subjecting new employees to an orientation program regarding employee relations, conducting exit interviews, conducting employee opinion surveys, and communicating the results to employees. The research results can be interpreted as employee relations management not being fully achieved. Employees appear to be mostly informed of official policies and procedures. However, it is seen that the orientation program, which is extremely important to establish the relationship and communication between the organization and the employee when the job starts, has not been fully carried out. Ignoring the surveys in which employee opinions are taken or not providing feedback is seen as another obstacle to the development of the relationship between the organization and the employee.

The fact that there are many employees in the aviation industry in different positions such as pilots, cabin crew, and ground staff reveals that each of them has different needs, priorities, and problems waiting to be solved. First, the management must accept the differences and offer solutions to each unit (Siddiqui & Bisaria, 2018). Below are some suggestions within the scope of ERM applications in the aviation industry;

- *Having more flexible working hours for personnel:* Flexible working hours for all personnel, especially flight personnel, will help minimize the risk in security-sensitive sectors such as aviation. At the same time, the existence of flexible working hours instead of regular flights will make positive contributions to ERM. In this way, the staff will feel valued and will perceive that they are cared for (Gillet & Tremblay, 2021).

- *Increasing qualified employment by prioritizing education and training activities and thus preventing the attrition of existing employees*: Aviation is among the sectors with high work intensity and work stress. This situation may cause the employee to wear out in a shorter time. To prevent this, education and training activities, and especially the participation of qualified personnel within the organization should be ensured. In this way, it is anticipated that current employees will be free from the effects of attrition for a longer time (Wargborn, 2008). Training activities will also have a positive impact on the employee's performance.

- *Providing sufficient resources to employees to do their jobs:* Having sufficient resources while doing business is very important for the employee. In addition to sufficient resources, a fair distribution of resources will positively affect the employee's relationship with the organization. Studies show that employees who say there is justice in their organizations develop greater organizational commitment (Bulgarella, 2005). Another issue that affects the employee's bond with the organization is promotion delays and the establishment of an appropriate salary structure. Justice in these matters also has a significant impact on organizational commitment. All employees must be treated fairly and without prejudice.

- *Organizing social events that will bring together employees and management:* Relationships established through social activities outside of business life can enable personnel to establish more meaningful relationships with their managers and therefore with the organization. In organizations, human-to-human relations can positively affect business life (Çağlar, 2021).

- *Increasing employee commitment:* Improving trust and the ability to work together strengthens teamwork. Resolving conflicts, and improving problem-solving and communication skills can have a positive impact on teams' motivation to work together. The exemplary behavior of senior managers on these issues will set an example for employees (Lloyd, 2000).

- *Strengthen communication with employees:* Communication is important in establishing good relationships with employees, improving existing relationships and solving problems. Its importance is quite great. In this regard, it is necessary to pay attention to the language used in communication with employees. Because healthy relationships are the key to organizational success.

- *Organizations should carry out social responsibility activities that will enable employees to have a better image of the company (Çağlar, 2021).*

In addition to offering numerous benefits, the presence of risk in the aviation industry is a fact. Unintended accidents and even fatalities may occur due to technical or human errors. As a result, security is one of the foremost concerns in the aviation industry. Given that aviation is a critical component of global transportation, security should be the top priority in all related endeavors (Erceylan & Atilla, 2022).

Given that security can be upheld by employees at all levels of the organization, it becomes evident once again that relations and communication with employees must be effectively managed. Adhering to correct practices in this regard will make it easier to maximize security. It is important to communicate to all employees that senior management values security, welcomes feedback and criticism, and is open to different opinions. Employees should be informed about potential hazards and receive training on the consequences of unsafe actions. Employees should be encouraged to communicate safety-related information. Blaming employees for mistakes reduces feedback. Creating an environment of open communication, rather than blaming, will encourage employees to communicate more (Erceylan & Atilla, 2022; Flannery, 2001).

FUTURE RESEARCH DIRECTIONS

It is crucial to gather input from employees in service-oriented industries, such as the aviation industry. For this reason, effectively managing the relationships between the organization and its employees, as well as among the employees themselves, is one of the factors that determine the quality of service. From this perspective, it can be seen that managing employee relations is extremely important for the aviation industry.

This study is a theoretical examination of employee relations management in the aviation industry. It is recommended that future studies investigate the impact of employee relations management on the aviation industry using quantitative methods. The impact of employee relations management on the aviation industry is believed to be more evident through this approach. In this way, organizational managers will receive clearer information about what they need to do to cultivate healthy and proper relationships with employees.

CONCLUSION

Progress and technological developments in the aviation industry have made traveling by air transportation a part of daily life. Reasons such as the fact that people travel more, the increase in the world population, the increase in international trade, globalization, the spread of consumer culture, the increase in airline companies, and cheaper costs are among the reasons for traveling by air (Önen, 2022).

When examined globally, the aviation sector employs approximately 87.7 million people, and approximately 60% of this employment is concentrated in airports. Although there has been a slight decrease in these rates due to reasons such as the COVID-19 (Kurnaz & Rodrigues, 2022) pandemic and the Ukraine-Russia war, there is a recovery according to the results of the recent analysis of the aviation sector (Lioutov, 2020). Similar results were obtained in the research conducted by FlightGlobal on pilots in 2023. The research states that pilot employment rates are generally a reflection of rising and falling trends in air travel. The previous year's results of the same research show that the pilot employment rate was 62% and this rate will be 77% in 2023 (Flight Global, 2023).

Research results show that despite all the negativities experienced globally, people prefer air transportation when traveling. This situation brings about increasing competition among airline companies. The fact that people are both service providers and service recipients is an indication that the way to achieve competitive advantage in the aviation industry can be achieved through human-oriented approaches.

Becoming a preferred airline is possible by developing healthy relationships with customers. Organizations that best describe the organization and the brand and understand customer needs most accurately can take one step ahead of the competition. Considering that customer needs and demands are constantly changing, retaining customers and reaching new customers is achieved through good communication. As a result, organizations can manage customer relations to the extent that they can manage employee relations and therefore maintain their competitive advantage.

Employees are the secret weapon of organizations. Seeing the employees as individuals with basic desires and needs such as being understood and supported, rather than seeing them as just a tool to get the job done, forms the basis of establishing good relationships. Organizations that are aware of this are aware that their ability to compete is thanks to their employees.

Considering the dynamic and fast structure of the aviation industry, service quality must be continuous. The fact that the service quality provided to customers is directly proportional to the internal service quality indicates that organizations should regard their employees as internal customers. The internal customer perspective, which is a part of employee relations management, increases employee loyalty and trust and paves the way for the same increase in the service quality of the organization. Employee relations management in organizations aims to develop relationships that care about the cooperation of managers and employees, have the belief in joint effort, and allow the development of a sense of mutual trust and commitment.

Low service quality and accidents in the aviation sector occur due to socio-technical reasons such as employee motivation, management weakness, lack of communication, and lack of decision-making, rather than technical reasons (Appelbaum & Fewster, 2003). When viewed from this perspective, the importance of employee relations management becomes evident. Employee relations management helps provide a working environment in which employees are empowered to make decisions, their ideas are taken into account, information flow is carried out bi-directionally through open communication channels, and employees are made to feel valued. In short, with employee relations management, employees are strengthened; thus, possible bad consequences can be prevented in organizations, especially in times of crisis.

The fact that service quality is a factor that determines the degree of competitiveness reveals the importance of training, and development activities of employees in the aviation sector. Investments in these areas help to increase employee quality, internal service quality, and the service quality of the organization, respectively.

The increase in passenger numbers, airline companies, and airports shows that the volume of the aviation sector is gradually growing. Considering that customer demands and needs are constantly changing, responding to and even exceeding these changes are the issues that organizations focus on the most. Communicating well with customers, making them feel special, and doing this constantly requires a great deal of effort. Considering that competition is increasingly intense, the importance of strategies to be developed in this direction increases. While developing their strategies, organizations should not forget that the way to customers passes through their employees. Awareness that employees are also customers will enable the understanding that customer satisfaction is a situation that can arise as a result of improving the internal processes of the organization. Practices such as support, resource adequacy, healthy communication, respect, kindness, etc. that will help strengthen employees' ties to their jobs and organizations are seen as elements that will move organizations forward in the service sector.

ACKNOWLEDGMENT

This research received no specific grant from any funding agency in the public, commercial, or not-forprofit sectors.

REFERENCES

Ağraz, S. (2006). Havayolu işletmelerinin istihdama katkısı. [Çalışma Ekonomisi ve Endüstri İlişkileri Anabilim Dalı PhD, İstanbul Üniversitesi, İstanbul].

Alkan, A. D. (2022). The Effects of COVID-19 on Human Resource Management in Aviation Companies: The Case of Europe. In S. Kurnaz & E. Argın (Eds.), *Digitalization and the Impacts of COVID-19 on the Aviation Industry*. IGI Global. doi:10.4018/978-1-6684-2319-6.ch012

Appelbaum, S. H., & Fewster, B. M. (2003). Global Aviation: Human resource management: Contemporary employee and labour relations practies. *Management Research News*, *26*(10/11), 56–69. doi:10.1108/01409170310784069

Aviation Benefits. (2020). Employtment. *Aviation Benefits*. https://aviationbenefits.org/economic-growth/supporting-employment/

Bajaj, R., Sinha, S., & Tiwari, V. (2013). Crucial factors of human resource management for good employee relations: A case study. *International Journal of Mining, Metallurgy &. Mechanical Engineering (New York, N.Y.)*, *1*(2).

Brhane, H., & Zewdie, S. (2018). A literature review on the effects of employee relation on improving employee performance. *International Journal in Management and Social Sience*, *6*(4).

Bulgarella, C. C. (2005). Employee satisfaction& customer satisfaction: Is there a relationship? Retrieved from Çağlar, Ç. (2021). Havacılıkta kurumsal sosyal sorumluluğun iç müşteri tatmini ile ilişkisi: Sektörel bir uygulama. [Havacılık Yönetimi Anabilim Dalı Master, İstanbul Gelişim Üniversitesi, İstanbul].

Çağlar, Ç., & Türk, A. (2023). Understanding the role of corporate social responsibility on internal customer satisfaction for sustainable business strategy; A qualitative research in the aviation industry. *Journal of Aviation*, *7*(1), 141–146. doi:10.30518/jav.1246801

Dasgupta, S. A., Suar, D., & Singh, S. (2013). Impact of managerial communication styles on employees' attitudes and behaviours. *Employee Relations*, *35*(2), 173–199. doi:10.1108/01425451311287862

Demirbaş, E., & Özek, H. (2021). Does feedbaack play a role during the construction of internal customers' psychological capital? *Journal of Global Strategic Management*, *15*(2), 89–106. Advance online publication. doi:10.20460/JGSM.2022.305

Demirel, Y., & Güner, E. (2015). İç müşteri İlişkileri yönetiminin örgütsel vatandaşlık davranışı üzerine etkisi. *International Journal of Alanya Faculty of Business*, 7(2), 1–14.

Doğan, S. (2005). *Çalışan İlişkileri Yönetimi*. Kare Yayınları.

Eichorn, F. L. (2004a). *Applying internal customer relationship management (intcrm) principles for improving business / IT integration and performance.* [Doctoral Thesis, University of Maryland].

Eichorn, F. L. (2004b). Internal customer relationship management (Int-CRM): A framework for achieving customer relationship management from the inside out. *Problems and Perspectives in Management*, 1, 154–177.

Erceylan, N., & Atilla, G. (2022). Aviation safety and risk management during COVID-19. In S. Kurnaz & E. Argın (Eds.), *Digitalization and the Impacts of COVID-19 on the Aviation Industry*. IGI Global., doi:10.4018/978-1-6684-2319-6.ch007

Flannery, J. A. (2001). *Safety culture and its measurement in aviation*. University of Newcastle.

Flight Global. (2023). *The pilot survey 2023*. Flight Global. https://www.flightglobal.com/download?ac=91648

Gennard, J. (2005). Employee relations. London: CIPD publishing.

Gibert, G. R. (2000). Measuring internal customer satisfaction. *Managing Service Quality*, 10(3), 178–186. doi:10.1108/09604520010336704

Gillet, A., & Tremblay, D.-G. (2021). Working in the air: Time management and work intensification challenges for workers in commercial aviation. *Open Journal of Social Sciences*, 9(1), 272–290. doi:10.4236/jss.2021.91020

Harter, J. K., Schmidt, F. L., & Hayes, T. L. (2002). Business-unit-level relationship between employee satisfaction, employee engagement, and business outcomes: A meta-analysis. *The Journal of Applied Psychology*, 87(2), 268–279. doi:10.1037/0021-9010.87.2.268 PMID:12002955

Huang, Y.-T. (2020). Internal marketing and internal customer: A review, reconceptualization, and extension. *Journal of Relationship Marketing*, 19(3), 165–181. doi:10.1080/15332667.2019.1664873

İSG. (2010). *Sabiha Gökçen Havalimanı çalışanlarına engelli eğitimi*. ISG. https://www.sabihagokcen.aero/basin-odasi/basin-kupurleri/sabiha-gokcen-havalimani-calisanlarina-engelli-egitimi

Johnson, J. L., & O'leary-Kelly, A. M. (2003). The effects of psychological contract breach and organizational cynicism: Not all social exchange violations are created equal. *Journal of Organizational Behavior*, 24(5), 627–647. doi:10.1002/job.207

Karavardar, G. (2012). Çalışan ilişkileri ve bilgi paylaşımı: Bankacılık sektöründe bir uygulama. *Çankırı Karatekin Üniversitesi İktisadi ve İdari Bilimler Fakültesi Dergisi, 2(1), 145-156.*

Kurnaz, S. (2022). Bibliometric analysis of articles published in the field of aviatıon: Dergipark academic example. *Management Theory and Studies for Rural Business and Infrastructure Development*, 44(3), 354–361. doi:10.15544/mts.2022.36

Kurnaz, S., Rodrigues, A., Kholiavko, N., Panchenko, O., & Tarasenko, A. (2022). The perspectives of the air transport market in Turkey during COVID-19 pandemic. *Management Theory and Studies for Rural Business and Infrastructure Development*, *44*(2), 235–243. doi:10.15544/mts.2022.24

Lioutov, L. (2020). *COVID-19: People risk in the airport industry*. ACI. https://blog.aci.aero/covid-19-people-risk-in-the-airport-industry/

Lloyd, D. (2000). *Improving employee commitment*. [Department of Education Doctoral Thesis, Concordia University].

Lukas, B. A., & Maignan, I. (1996). Striving for quality: The key role of internal and external customers. *Journal of Market Focused Management*, *1*(2), 175–187. doi:10.1007/BF00128689

Macit, D., & Macit, A. (2017). Türkiye'de sivil havacılık sektöründe istihdamın mevcut durumu, sorunları ve sorunların çözümüne yönelik öneriler. *Journal of Emerging Economies and Policy*, *2*(2).

Önen, V. (2022). İnsan faktörleri eğitimi sorunsallarının tespiti ve buna yönelik geliştirilmiş eğitim modeli ve iyileştirme önerileri. *Journal of Aviation Research*, *4*(1), 25–56. doi:10.51785/jar.953657

Pegasus. (2024). *Olanaklarımız*. Pegasus. https://www.flypgs.com/kariyer-pegasus/olanaklarimiz

Shen, H. (2009). *Organization-employee relationships model: A two sided story*. [Doctoral Thesis, University of Maryland].

Siddiqui, N. N., & Bisaria, G. (2018). Innovative techniques of motivation for employee retenteon in aviation industry. *Anveshak International Journal of Management*, *7*(1), 136. doi:10.15410/aijm/2018/v7i1/119882

THY. (2023). *Kurumsal sosyal sorumluluk*. THY. https://www.turkishairlines.com/tr-int/basin-odasi/sosyal-sorumluluk-projelerimiz/

Wargborn, C. (2008). Managing motivation in organizations: Why employee relationship management matters. [Master of International Management Master, ISCTE Business School].

ADDITIONAL READING

Altındağ, D. (2013). *Türkiye'de sivil havacılık sektöründe çalışan uçuş personelinin çalışma koşullarına yönelik bir alan araştırması* [Master's thesis, Pamukkale Üniversitesi].

Başar, P., & Arkan, G. (2023). The relations between digitalization and employee satisfaction in aviation. *Journal of Aviation*, *7*(3), 388–992. doi:10.30518/jav.1307693

Gennard, J., & Judge, G. (2005). *Employee Relations*. Chartered Institute of Personnel and Development.

Jones, E. (2014). An investigation into the true drivers of employee engagement. A case study within the aviation industry. [Human Resource Management Master, National College of Ireland, Ireland].

Kaps, R. W., Hamilton, J. S., & Bliss, T. J. (2012). *Labor Relations in the Aviation and Aerospace Industries*. Southern Illinois University Press.

Leggett, C. (2013). Workforce development and employment relations. *Employment Relations Record, 13*(1), 2.

Lutte, R. K. (2019). *Women in Aviation: A Workforce Report*. Aviation Institute Faculty Publications. https://digitalcommons.unomaha.edu/aviationfacpub/6

Northrup, H. R. (1983). The new employee-relations climate in airlines. *Industrial & Labor Relations Review, 36*(2), 167–181. doi:10.1177/001979398303600201

Şenol, L., & Üzüm, B. (2021). Havacılık Sektöründe Psikolojik Sahiplenme ve Devamsızlık İlişkisi. *İstanbul Gelişim Üniversitesi Sosyal Bilimler Dergisi, 8*(1), 67-78. doi:10.17336/igusbd.566559

Yadav, R., Panday, P., & Sharma, N. (Eds.). (2021). *Critical Issues on Changing Dynamics in Employee Relations and Workforce Diversity*. IGI Global. doi:10.4018/978-1-7998-3515-8

KEY TERMS AND DEFINITIONS

Flight Global: The primary source of news, data, insight, knowledge, and expertise for the global aviation community. It offers news, data, analysis, and consulting services to connect the global aviation community and assist organizations in shaping business strategies, identifying new opportunities, and making faster decisions.

Internal Custumer: Employees who perform tasks in a coordinated manner and in connection with the services offered and products produced in the workplace are considered internal customers.

THY: Turkish Airlines is the national flag carrier airline of Turkiye. Headquartered in Istanbul, the company's flight network extends to Europe, the Middle East, the Far East, North Africa, Central Africa, South Africa, and North and South America.

Chapter 3
Internal and External Factors Affecting the Mental and Physical Activities of Aircrew Personnel

Ümit Deniz Göker

Department of Solar Physics, Astronomical Institute of Czech Academy of Sciences, Czech Republic

ABSTRACT

This chapter gives the internal and external factors affecting the mental and physical activities of aircrew personnel by examining a wide range of aspects, from aviation psychology to solar physics. The author mentions the cognitive effects, mental activities, nervous system, neurophysiology, and physical activities as internal factors while solar activity, geomagnetic storms, and meteorological effects as external factors. Firstly, the consequences of the design of an air traffic management system as system capacity and throughput, progress time and/or ongoing work, efficiency and cost-effectiveness, flexibility, and complexity to performance evaluation and optimization; secondly, the results of geomagnetic storms over 115 years of aircraft accidents for latitudes between $\pm10^o \leq \varphi \leq \pm90^o$ in the northern and southern hemispheres of Earth, which is a very important space weather event and could be the main reason for most aircraft accidents are investigated on the mental and physical health conditions.

INTRODUCTION

Air transportation is the most customary, most convenient, and preferred transportation due to its large number of advantageous features such as fast and reliable services by shortening time independent of geographical barriers and accessibility around the world, and safety; and has become a high level of technical, administrative, and technological operations recently by the introduction and production of larger and faster aircraft, which largely includes advanced information management technologies (Göker, et al., 2021; Aksen et al., 2024). The fact that aircraft can carry people, cargo, mail, and similar at a more affordable price and in a shorter time has made aviation worthy in the sectoral meaning; furthermore,

DOI: 10.4018/979-8-3693-0908-7.ch003

air traffic control relates to teamwork, and it will be necessary to develop team structures and initiate optimization programs due to the increase in traffic volume (Riedle, 2006; Göker, et al., 2021). In addition to this, investigations and studies are carried out by many organizations to minimize the risk of accidents and maximize safety with developing technology.

The primary causes of accidents can be shown as human factors, mechanical/technical reasons, meteorology, bird strikes, lightning, etc., however, the human factors account for approximately 72-80% of all aircraft accidents shown from the accident reports. It can be said that accidents caused by mechanical/technical reasons have been replaced by an increase in the number of aircraft accidents caused by human-induced errors depending on the increasing manpower with the developing technology while the main causes of accidents in the first years of aviation were due to mechanical/technical reasons (Çetingüç, 2016; Göker, et al., 2021). Increasing aviation companies and developing accordingly getting larger traffic volume and demand for air transportation are caused by increasing competition; therefore, businesses that tend to overload employees for the sake of gaining more can cause increasing risks and aircraft accidents (Göker, et al., 2021; Aksen et al., 2024). Particularly, this overload and pressure on aircrew personnel who are much more exposed to the effects of external conditions such as space weather, meteorological events, and radiation will be much higher.

According to the "*Swiss-Cheese Model*", the cause of accidents is due to consecutive violations such as hardware or operational failures of multi-system defense, and all accidents are caused by a combination of both "*active*" which are errors that show expeditious effect are usually caused by principal personnel such as pilots, air traffic controllers, and aircraft maintenance technicians, and "*hidden*" errors that have been concealed due to a transaction or decision taken much earlier than accidents often caused by regulatory authorities and decision makers (Uslu and Dönmez, 2016). However, there are also meteorological and/or space weather events that may make it difficult to intervene in some "*sudden*" situations, and the reason why it is difficult to be concerned is that we suddenly get caught in this event during the flight. In this case, a different mechanism than the Swiss-Cheese Model must become a part of an activity related to space weather events, and it can be presented to different models connected with the "*Sun-Earth-Flight (SEF)*" connection. Particularly, it is impossible to predict geomagnetic storms (GSs) days in advance, like weather forecasts. The situation will be very difficult and complicated for the aircraft and the aircrew personnel and passengers on board if it encounters such a storm.

Based on all these explanations above, in the first part of this study, the internal factors that affect job performance depending on the air traffic management (ATM) system are mentioned and compared with the statistical analysis of human-induced errors, mechanical/technical system errors, and unknown reasons between the years 1918-2019 to establish a connection between aircraft accidents and mental and physical abilities of aircrew personnel. In the second part, the percentage distribution of meteorological reasons in addition to these errors above between the years 1908-2023 is determined while a comparison of the number of accidents that occur during the increasing and decreasing phases of the solar activity cycles (SACs) from the solar cycle (SC) 15 to SC 25 and their corresponding GSs are matched. In the same section, we revealed what kind of effects such storms will have on aircrew personnel in the short- and long-term periods, as well.

BACKGROUND

Air Traffic Management (ATM) System

Minimizing the arrival time of the passengers and goods is a common problem in ATM and operation management procedures are often based on a "*planning phase*" in which items are assigned according to capacity and other regulations, and a "*real-time*" is based on the idea of forcing the elements in the system and thus focuses on dealing with disagreements that may occur later in the chain of operations (Lucertini, Smriglio and Telmon, 1997; Göker, et al., 2021). The design of an "*air traffic flow management system*" mainly concentrates on the dynamic control of congestion problems; it can also be said that if it cannot make an exact number of take-offs and landings during an exact period due to limitations at the airport causes unacceptable delays and costs for airport and aviation companies (Lucertini, Smriglio and Telmon, 1997). Besides, raising the number of flights without making a good plan to protect these costs and surviving the contest leads to an increase in the number of aircraft accidents by employing airline personnel for more hours (Calderón, 2014). Unfortunately, with the use of large hulls of aircraft from the beginning of the 1970s, airline companies started to have excessive capacities, and many carrier companies have focused on the marketing concept that emphasizes shaping services to meet consumer needs instead of shaping the needs of the consumer to comply with existing services, and this profit-oriented situation has brought other problems (Wensveen, 2007). Performance evaluation and optimization are based on several key concepts: system capacity or throughput, progress time and/or ongoing work, efficiency and cost-effectiveness, flexibility, and complexity (Lucertini, Smriglio and Telmon, 1997).

Emotional deterioration causes a sudden, unpredicted, and traumatic event which is named "*crisis*"; we are forced by physical and physiological stresses such as hypoxia, barotrauma, pressure decompression, vertigo, jet lag, shift lag, acceleration (G forces), vestibular and visual illusions, cosmic radiation (CR), vibration, noise, fog, wind, rain, snow, cloud, cold, imaginary horizon starlight, ozone concentration, radiation, etc. when we enter the flight environment. Besides, the pilot's psychotic and personality disorders, suicidal tendencies, substance and alcohol abuse, dysfunction drugs, antipsychotic drugs, epilepsy drugs, self-mutilation and killing attempts, neuroses, loss of consciousness, and neurological progressive diseases are classified as accidents caused by human defects due to personality traits (Çetingüç, 2016); urbanization, industrialization, and technological developments also affect aviation operations (Göker, 2018). Pilots, aircraft maintenance technicians, air traffic controllers, and flight operation specialists responsible for every moment of flight are among those many people who directly contribute to the creation of airline transportation. The low-level performance of the human component within the system in communication, situational awareness, workload management, leadership, teamwork, decision-making, and stress management skills can lead to human errors and violations and thus low safety performance (Göker, 2018) because "*cognitive* (attention, memory, judgment, decision, focus, problem-solving)", "*emotional* (desperation, hopelessness, anger, crying, depression)", "*behavioural* (slowing down, loss of appetite, irritability)", and "*psychophysiological* (tremor, palpitation, nausea, sweating)" impairment leads to develop anxiety, fear, tension, confusion, depression, reduce problem-solving skills, helplessness, and disorganization (Çetingüç, 2016).

In addition to these internal factors depending on the ATM system which is the most important factors that affect job performance, the security focuses on the detection and prediction of rapidly changing convective weather conditions, icing, and fresh air turbulence, and providing better information to pilots and operations centre personnel about these external sources (Evans, 2001). Although attempts have been made to automate air traffic control and to replace control devices with machines or technical systems, airway personnel due to increasing competition and intense working conditions continue to experience psychological stress (Riedle, 2006) which has a direct impact on the safety of the aviation system and can result is a damaging outcome (Muller and Drax, 2014). When estimating hazards and planning controls, great care must be taken to estimate how often and how people make mistakes and how they interact with other components of the system by understanding physical (e.g., height, vision, strength), physiological (stress, fatigue, health), psychological (motivation, decision-making, risky altitudes), and psycho-social (personal financial issues, marital) factors (Stolzer, Halford and Goglia, 2008).

Geomagnetic Storms (GSs) in the Aviation Industry

Meteorological and/or space weather events, such as GSs that have disruptive effect on Earth's magnetosphere in certain periods, will cause negative effects, such as weakness, malaise and unspecified regional headaches, irregularity in movement functions, imbalance, heart infarction, undefined regional headaches, seizure situations, and mental disorders due to the nervous system of the pilot and cabin crew which will be experienced directly flying at high latitudes, on these organic processes (Göker, 2018; Aksen et al., 2024). The increased amount of radiation due to GSs and the effect of CR will be much more exhaustive in flights carried out in high latitudes and polar regions. The aircraft accident reports announced by The National Transportation Safety Board (NTSB) were based on weather conditions and only included meteorological effects such as rain, fog, low cloud height, snow, etc. (NTSB, 2005). Annex 3 also contains the research and results of the effects of meteorological effects such as rain, fog, snow, low cloud height, etc. on aviation activities and aviation psychology which is published by the International Civil Aviation Organization (ICAO) (Cannon et al., 2013a, b); the effects of GSs as a critical subject on aircraft accidents have begun to be taken into consideration since the mid-2000s.

It is thought that there will be a significant change in vision, hearing, and body senses in the brain cortex, especially during the process of being affected by GSs, because the parts of the body that require more sensitive behaviours and muscle coordination are possible by electrically stimulating different parts of the motor cortex and activating the parts corresponding to those parts of the body (Cüceloğlu, 2000; Carlson, 2014). Lesions caused by damage to the temporal cortex impair the ability to recognize distinctions between different perceptual stimuli and reduce the ability to perceive partial types of visual information (Carlson, 2014). If the incoming radiation has a significant effect only on the right brain cortex, considering that the right hemisphere is responsible for cognitive functions such as visual-locational-spatial material, the visual, locational, and spatial calculation ability, which is the main rule of flying, will be affected. It will also cause permanent damage in the long period.

We can classify short-term changes depending on GSs as decision-making and judgment problems, decreasing problem-solving abilities, organization capabilities, and instantaneous decisions, and abnormal attitudes such as anger, fearlessness, temerity, self-confidence, etc. However, in the long-term period, there will appear more dangerous problems such as cancers of the brain, testis, bladder, breast, colon, melanoma, and Hodgkin's type, in addition to Alzheimer's and dementia diseases, hypoglycaemia, stroke, epileptic seizures, insomnia, stomach bleeding, appendicitis, hernia, asthma, and severe spinal pains (Göker, 2023).

INTERNAL FACTORS

Serious headlines and constitute problems that affect the economic, social, psychological, and even political agenda are created by aviation accidents (Doviak, Mazur and Zrnic, 1999), even though, there is an increasing emphasis on security with the rapid development of civil aviation (Sun, Ma, Li and Shen, 2014). The historical development of the causes of aircraft accidents can be examined in three stages: (a) the period of technical factors (1900-1960); (b) the period of human factors (1970-1990); and (c) the period of organizational factors (1990-present) (Uslu and Dönmez, 2016). Air crash investigation (ACI) data involving the death from the beginning of 1918 to the end of 2019 for 3765 civil and commercial aviation accidents from the web pages https://www.planecrashinfo.com/database.htm (Plane Crash Info, 2022) and https://www.ntsb.gov/_layouts/ntsb.aviation/index.aspx (NTSB, 2005) are classified and analyzed in the paper of Göker et al. (2021). It is found that 58%, 27%, and 15% of aircraft accidents depend on mechanical/technical, pilotage, and unknown reasons, respectively from the classification of general causes of aircraft accidents according to 10-yearly intervals as seen on the right- and left-hand sides of Fig. 1.

It was shown in Fig. 1 that both the mechanical/technical and human-related accidents numerically followed this order of the years 1946-1956, 1968-1978, and 1935-1945. In the early 1970s, the introduction of jet engines, radar (both in the air and on the ground), autopilots, flight routers, advanced navigation and communication skills, and similar performance-enhancing technologies both for air and the ground have shown significant technological developments, this state caused focus on different phenomena such as team skills management (CRM), line-oriented flight training (LOFT), human-centred automation, and other interventions to human performance, as well as safety performance and human factors (Uslu and Dönmez, 2016).

"Aviation Psychology" is a branch of psychology that deals with the physical and mental effects of flight on aircrew personnel and passengers, if any, the performance and support of the flight crew, the administrators, and the control team in the air traffic control system, the airline personnel, and all other responsible people for all design and maintenance work related to the aircraft; and their behavioural skills

Figure 1. The percentage distribution of general causes of aircraft accidents between 1918-2019 (right), and the classification of general causes of aircraft accidents according to 10-yearly intervals (left)
Source: (Göker et al., 2021)

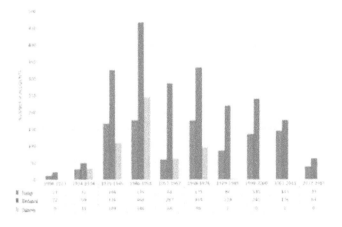
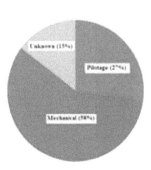

and limitations (Koonce, 1984). The organic processes work flawlessly in those who have successfully passed all the cognitive and personality psychology tests which will result in a strong commitment to their movements and ability to acknowledge the right steps to follow in their task and dangerous situations (Göker, 2018).

The definition of aviation psychology was first presented in Germany in 1915, and it focused mainly on the effects of altitude, G-force, noise, temperature, and other stresses on the pilot surrounded by the environmental changes in the first years (Göker, 2018). The first psychological tests related to a relationship between flight training performances, emotional stability, slope perception, and mental agility began in June 1917 at the Institute of Technology in Massachusetts, USA. It continued with establishing the National Research Council (NRC) for aviation psychology in 1939, and it carried on with a 19-volume series, called the "*Blue Book*" in 1947 by the American Air Force, USA; two years later, an aviation psychology laboratory has been opened, in the Ohio, USA. In Europe, the Western European Association for Aviation Psychologists (WEAAP) was established in 1956 while a more advanced aviation research laboratory was opened at the University of Illinois, USA and all this research was compiled into a book in 1971, and 1980, respectively (Koonce, 1984). Continuous improvements are being made in the aviation rules consisting of Annex 1-19 published by the ICAO at regular meetings, especially, since the study of the effects of meteorological events on aviation psychology has increased after the 1980s (Göker, 2018). Among all these annexes, Annex 3 includes the research and results of the effects of meteorological events such as rain, fog, snow, low cloud height, etc. on aviation activities and aviation psychology (Cannon et al., 2013a, b).

The most important causes of organic problems in aviation, such as headaches of unknown origin, irregularity in movement functions, and balance disorders mainly depend on the diseases in aviation medicine such as *"hypoxia"* (flying at high altitudes, hypoventilation, or lower than normal air inlet and outlet required to maintain the normal gas level of the blood, decrease in oxygen transfer from the atmosphere to the blood through the lungs due to respiratory lung problems), *"acceleration forces"* (change in the velocity vector and/or direction of the object due to gravity), *"spatial disorientation or volatile vertigo"* (the state of imbalance caused by false signals coming from the body's balance systems, that is, to the eyes, inner ears, neck, and spinal cord which send notifications to the cerebellum or misperception of correct signals), *"fatigue"*, *"shift-lag"* (a state of strain caused by the body's internal rhythm not being able to adapt to this new order in cases of geographical region changes, intense working hours, partial or complete displacement of the sleeping period), *"jet-lag"* (a series of mental and physical performance disorders caused by long-range and high-speed intercontinental journeys crossing longitudes and the incompatibility between the internal biological clock and the geographical clock of the destination region), *"thermal stress"* (an uncomfortable condition that occurs as a result of increased temperature), and *"dehydration or water loss"*. These problems will be much more effective in pilots who are much more exposed to the effects of GSs, especially flying at high latitudes (Göker, 2018).

When we consider the impact of these situations on pilots and flight personnel we have explained above, without including external environmental factors, the increase in the heavy working hours and sleepless periods that ATM imposes on flight personnel only within the competitive approach, will enable flight personnel to have a safer flight; reasons such as imposing coercive partnerships by ignoring crew recommendations, applying psychological pressure by airline companies regarding employment contracts or payments, enable the organic problems to become active more quickly for the cabin crew who enter the flight with these heavy psychological situations. As it is presented in the Swiss-Cheese

Model, this situation will affect not only the aircrew personnel but also all airline employees, following each other like a chain; in other words, it is from the bottom to the up and vice versa interaction.

Irregularity and balance disorder in movement functions will begin as the cerebral cortex is affected. In the case of *"hypoxia"*, volitional movements become difficult after altitudes of 3500-4000 meters (lack of muscle coordination), the tendency to cramp and contract increases, and the reflex slows down; intellectual activity (attention, memory, and judgment) decreases; physio-psychic chronic fatigue begins; cognitively, headache, depression, absent-mindedness, faulty decisions, and drowsiness occur, while decreasing insight, increasing self-confidence, unnecessary risk-taking, recklessness, stubbornness, and aggressive reactions occur, psychologically; visually unclear vision, decreased night vision and difficulty in colour differentiation occur; physically, lack of breath, hyperventilation (excessive breathing), dizziness, nausea, paraesthesia, tachycardia, and fatigue will be observed; there is a tendency to lack perception, irregularity of harmony and synergy in movements, and increase confidence (euphoria) which is called *"altitude drunkenness"* (Çetingüç, 2016).

In case of *"acceleration"*, visual field darkening, loss of consciousness and convulsive syncope may occur in pilots with an inadequate physical condition or who cannot properly perform anti-G manoeuvres. In jet aircraft, in situations that occur because of brain hypoxia, the withdrawal of blood from the brain to the tissues below and causes a decrease in blood pressure at the brain level, thus the pilot cannot control the aircraft for at least 15-30 seconds. In addition, cognitive disorders such as confusion, loss of awareness, euphoria, amnesia, and decision-making difficulty will be observed (Çetingüç, 2016). Somatic, cognitive, and psychological disorders occur in the case of *"jetlag"*. Somatically, abepithymia or feelings of hunger at unbecoming times, intestinal laziness (constipation), fatigue, insomnia, or sudden sleepiness are observed. Cognitively, concentration, attention, judgment-memory deficits, reaction time is prolonged, time and distance perception are impaired, and comprehension and learning functions are delayed. Psychologically, anxiety, irritability, depression, and sometimes euphoria are the prominent diseases. In the case of *"shift-lag"*, body temperature, blood sugar level, and mental working capacity are affected by changing the accustomed work-rest period; in this case, the digestive system and other somatic complaints and general malaise are observed (Çetingüç, 2016).

EXTERNAL FACTORS

The long-term statistics of ACI have shown that 70-80% of aircraft accidents are caused by human factors while meteorological events correspond to 20-30% of these accidents (NTSB, 2005), this is because the research on the damaging effects of GSs on flight instruments and human factors had not yet been considered in the aviation literature at this time (Aksen et al., 2024). Meteorological events such as wind, fog, snow, lightning, thunderstorms, mist, clouds, rainfall, sandstorms, in-flight and ground icing, dust, low visibility, turbulence, windshear, volcanic ash, aircraft wake vortices, and climate changes (Williams, 2017; Gultepe and Feltz, 2019; Aksen et al., 2024) effect aviation transportation significantly, and 70% and 23% of all delays and aviation accidents are controlled by meteorological events, respectively (Dan-Okoro et al, 2018; Schultz et al., 2018). Aircraft flight distributions are affected mostly by wind, turbulence (including gusts), and visibility rather than icing, pollution dust, and convection as mentioned by Gultepe and Feltz (2019). The occurrence of meteorological events on aircraft accidents such as bad weather conditions, fog, wind, storm, snowstorm, sandstorm, cloud, turbulence, icing, rain, oraj, lightning, hurricane, snow, volcano eruption, and volcano correspond to 20.44%, 25.40%, 4.91%, 8.84%,

4.35%, 0.80%, 6.64%, 6.36%, 9.36%, 5.57%, 2.81%, 1.54%, 0.84%, 1.78%, 0.28%, 0.09%, respectively (Aksen et al., 2024).

GSs are identified as electromagnetic fields of ionized radiation which is caused by two sources: (1) continuous background galactic CR outside the solar system that mostly affects the spacecraft and outer space missions; (2) charged energetic particles that come from explosions of the Sun toward the Earth from a few hours to several days cause ionospheric distributions and affect the air transportation directly (Mertens et al., 2010; Göker et al., 2018). However, estimating and modelling the formation of ionospheric disturbances (e.g., solar flares, solar energetic particle (SEP) events, and GSs are not easy because of the changing of the solar energy and ionosphere with location and time (Mertens et al., 2010; Göker et al., 2018). The formation of these disturbances is influenced by the seasons, geographical regions, solar activity (SA), and geomagnetic activity (GA) (Sağır et al., 2018). In the paper of Aksen et al. (2024), 7431 aircraft accidents involving death between the years 1908-2023 where 3835 (51.60%), 1459 (19.63%), and 2137 (28.76%) of these accidents were mechanical/technical and pilotage, unknown and meteorological reasons, respectively are classified and analyzed from the same web pages which we used above for the extended years and including meteorological effects as https://www.planecrashinfo. com/database.htm (Plane Crash Info, 2022) and https://www.ntsb.gov/_layouts/ntsb.aviation/index.aspx. (NTSB, 2005).

The classification and distribution of general causes of aircraft accidents that depend on GSs between the years 1908-2023 are given in Fig. 2(a). Here, it is seen that the mechanical/technical and pilotage reasons are higher between 1941-1950 and close to each other between 1951-1980 while the meteorological reasons are close to each other between 1941-1970 and 1971-2000. In Fig. 2(b), the classification and distribution of aircraft accidents due to different kinds of meteorological reasons according to 10-yearly intervals between 1908 and 2023 is given. Secondly, it is found that the accident rates of 1959 air crash events that might be related to GSs correspond to 68%, 22%, 8%, and 2% due to mechanical/ technical and pilotage reasons, unknown reasons, bad weather conditions, and turbulence are obtained for latitudes between $\pm 10^\circ \leq \varphi \leq \pm 90^\circ$ in the northern and southern hemisphere because the effects of the most severe storms have been seen to go as low as $\pm 10^\circ$ in the work of Aksen et al (2024).

The effect of GSs, which have been known for approximately 200 years, on military and civil aviation was revealed in a document published by the UK Aviation Industry in 2013 (Cannon et al., 2013a, b), since this date, progress has been made in research on the aviation psychology of GSs. Different intensities of GSs significantly affect brain activity and functions. Human orientation in space is achieved by the coordination of 4 systems (visual, auditory, vestibular, and proprioceptive). In balance and position perception, the allowance of visual perception, the deep sense, the vestibule, and the auditory system is 79%, %5, %15, and %1, respectively (Çetingüç, 2016).

The unbalanced pilot not only has a position understanding error; but also exhibits cognitive deficits in correctly reading and interpreting flight instruments and making correct decisions; reaction time becomes longer, mental confusion occurs, and incapacity occurs. This situation is called *"spatial disorientation"* (Çetingüç, 2016) where a significant change in vision, hearing, and body senses in the brain cortex, especially during the process of being affected by GSs will occur. During GSs, the parts of the body that require more sensitive behaviours and muscle coordination are possible by electrically stimulating different parts of the motor cortex and activating the parts corresponding to those parts of the body (Cüceloğlu, 2000; Carlson, 2014). Lesions caused by damage to the temporal cortex impair the ability to recognize distinctions between different perceptual stimuli and reduce the ability to perceive partial types of visual information (Carlson, 2014).

Figure 2. (a) The classification and distribution of general causes of aircraft accidents according to 10-yearly intervals between 1908-2023 (left); (b) The classification and distribution of aircraft accidents due to different kinds of meteorological reasons according to 10-yearly intervals between 1908 and 2023 (right)
Source: (Aksen et al., 2024)

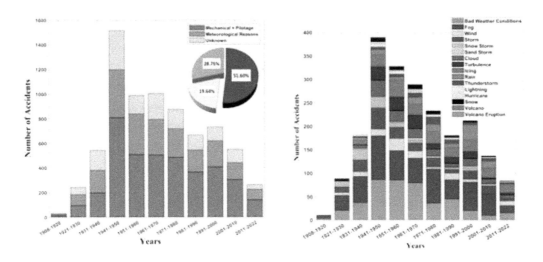

If the incoming radiation influences only the right brain cortex which is responsible for cognitive functions such as the visual, locational, and spatial calculation ability that is the main rule of flying will be affected, and during this situation, the pilot may forget important calculations, make incorrect calculations, and lose the ability to evaluate events carefully. However, this effect will be minimized individually, if the cognitive and personality characteristics of the pilot are sufficiently developed. If he/she does not have the emotional regulation capacity to overcome his/her fears, he/she may hesitate, panic, and fail to fulfil his/her task. At the same time, strong nervous tension can also distort the pilot's sense of time. This situation correlates with the different levels of passive-defensive reflexes (Gagarin and Lebedev,1984).

What happens if the nervous system, which brings information to the brain, is affected? We can list the results as follows: (**a**) heart infarction, seizures, and nervous system-related mental disorders are observed, and these disorganizations will become more disturbing as the duration of the effect of radiation increases; (**b**) urgent and sudden decisions will cause blood pressure and heart rate increase, respiratory rate increases, pupil dilation, sweating increases, salivation decreases, the amount of sugar blood increases resulting in excess energy, blood clotting increase, the digestive organs to direct towards the brain and striated muscles; (**c**) changes in vision, hearing, and body senses will be important in the cerebral cortex, especially during the process of being affected by GSs. In such instances, the motor cortex will be effective in parts of the body to control more sensitive behaviours and detailed muscle coordination; (**d**) lesions will harm the ability to realize distinctions between different perceptual stimuli and decrease the ability to perceive partial types of visual information when the temporal cortex is damaged (Göker, 2018). So, what kind of weather event, or more accurately, a space weather event has such a significant impact on the aviation industry?

The Impact of Geomagnetic Storms (GSs) on the Aviation Industry

A GS is a space weather event that interrupts the regularity of the Earth's magnetosphere at certain times, is a comet-like structure that encloses planets in a way that traps charged particles and deflects them and is expressed in [nT]. The shape of the magnetosphere is determined by the solar wind (SW) and the magnetic fields (MFs) of the planets (Göker, 2018). Solar-based effects that cause a GS are coronal mass ejections (CMEs) which generate high-energetic particles including electrons and coronal/ SW ions (mainly protons), coronal holes (CHs), the classes of solar flares as C-, M- or X-, the variable duration of the SC, and increasing and decreasing phases of the SC (Chapman et al., 2018), and the SWs propagating through shock wave that transmit these effects towards the earth. The geomagnetic field of Earth and the geospace environment with magnetospheric currents are given in Fig. 3. In this figure, the bow shock occurs if the magnetosphere depending on the high-energetic particles that come with the SW, and these particles move throughout polar cusps to produce auroral ovals. Magnetopause is the sudden and short-lived boundary between a magnetosphere and the surrounding plasma. High-energetic particles firstly pass the Earth's ionosphere that extends from 10 km to 1000 km and secondly, they move to Earth's atmosphere which is between 0-100 km. Magnetotail is the extended tail of the SW away from the Sun, and reconnection between MF lines in the Earth's magnetotail under disrupted geomagnetic conditions outcomes in the acceleration of electrons into the higher levels of the atmosphere, producing active and sometimes large-scale displays of the aurora. The molecular formation on surge which is generated in the auroral oval induces ionospheric storms from high to middle-latitude regions, and afterward, the horizontal neutral winds that appear from the pressure gradient force in the auroral oval and by ion drag in the polar cap expand these storms to lower latitudes. The expansion of solar MFs through the interplanetary medium to the orbit of the Earth and into the heliosphere is noticeably multi-variate at solar maximum rather than at solar minimum (Aksen et al., 2024).

The intensity of GSs that can be created by CMEs is classified as weak, moderate, or severe depending on the magnetic strength which is carried by the plasma of the SW coming from the Sun (Schieb and Gilson, 2011; Chapman et al., 2020a), and their intensities correspond to 45.47% (Weak-G1 class), 36.65% (Moderate-G2 class), 12.44% (Severe-G3 class), and 5.44% (Very severe-G4/G5 classes), respectively from 1919 to 2023 (Aksen et al., 2024). The most severe storms reach the Earth in one day after the eruption of CME while it takes two and six days for weak and moderate storms depending on the intensity of the GS which can be categorized as during the storm, after a week, and after a month. SWs continue to be effective after 24-36 hours as soon as they interact with the magnetosphere of Earth (Schieb and Gilson, 2011). GS advances throughout three phases such as the *initial* is completed in minutes to hours, the *main* might take 30 minutes to several hours, and the *recovery* from tens to hours up to weak phases which affect the infrastructure of the Earth when it reaches the Earth's MF (Tsurutani and Gonzalez, 1993), and effects power supplies, navigation, satellites, the aviation industry, monitoring, and radio communications to social and economic actions on Earth (Schieb and Gilson, 2011; Chapman et al., 2020a; 2020b). GSs can also cause bad weather conditions on Earth and turbulence in aviation which is irregular air movement that occurs with the change in atmospheric pressure depending on the differences in energy flux of the Sun as mentioned by Gultepe and Feltz (2019).

The thermal and kinetic energy of a multi-fluid medium produced by electrons, protons, and ions is increased by magnetic reconnection (MR) plays an important role in solar flares, coronal heating, and GSs (Göker, 2008) that leads to the production of reconnection outflow (Göker, 2012). During GSs, the mass, the energy, and the momentum in large quantities get into the polar regions of the Earth's magnetosphere.

Figure 3. The geomagnetic field and geospace environment with magnetospheric currents
Source: (NASA-CR-194800, 1993).

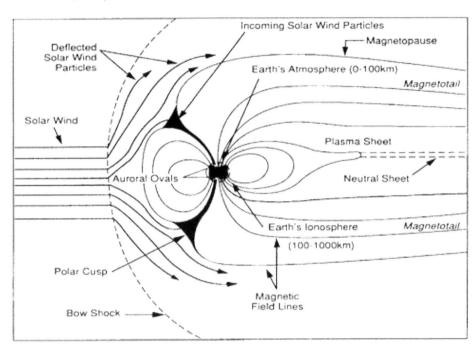

This energy input significantly modifies the chemical and the dynamical/electrodynamical processes of the ionosphere-thermosphere system at the polar regions, and higher ionospheric electron densities and total electron content (TEC) are observed. The radiation field at aviation altitudes is created in repeated interactions of the primary and secondary radiation with the constituents of the atmosphere as given in Fig. 4. The density and the time-dependent change of GSs vary at different latitudes and altitudes (Timoçin et al., 2018). Here, correspond to subatomic particle (neutral pion), neutron, subatomic particle (pion, down quark), proton, subatomic particle (pion, up quark), gamma- particle, positron, electron, anti-muon, and muon, respectively of radiation fields that affect different heights of the atmosphere.

Strong collisions are occurred in the ionosphere which is a partially ionized natural plasma while the magnetosphere plasma above 400 km is collision-free in general approximation (Mursula, Qvick, Holappa, Asikainen, 2022). In the low-latitude region, the ionospheric perturbations are produced by several processes, however, the warming in the high-latitude regions initiates equatorward wind fluctuations that drag the plasma across the MF lines to medium and low latitudes, and to higher latitudes. Uplift of the plasma in that region induces an increase in plasma density owing to the decrease in molecular gases (or decrease in O^+ loss rate) at higher latitudes as shown in Fig. 4 (Meier, 2020). To understand the dynamics of near-Earth plasma, electromagnetic field disturbances, aurora, plasma motion, ionospheric currents, and associated MF disturbances, and even the neutral atmosphere at high latitudes, it's essential to work in a reference frame that takes the geometry of the Earth's MF that is represented by the so-called magnetic elements, three of which are H, D, and z; where H is the horizontal field strength; D is the declination angle (angle with geodetic north, positive eastward); and z is the downward component of the field must be taken into account (Laundel and Richmond, 2016).

Figure 4. The radiation field at aviation altitudes is created in repeated interactions of the primary and secondary radiation with the constituents of the atmosphere
Source: (courtesy of Meier, 2020)

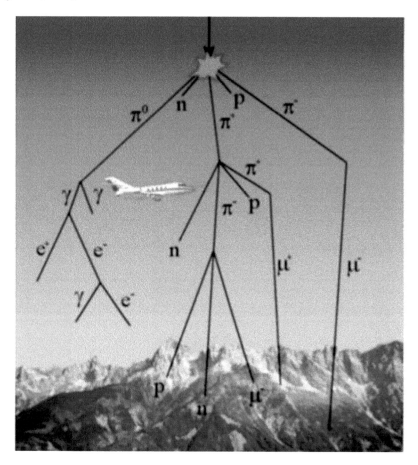

The distribution of GA indices varies both within and between SCs with its unique dominant distribution for different solar maximum and solar minimum (Chapman et al., 2018). The effective structure of the CHs causes to increase in the number of aircraft accidents in the decreasing phases of SACs rather than increasing phases, especially, since the highest number of accidents are determined in the equinoxes in March and September (and mostly at the beginning of October) while the lower number of accidents was seen in the solstices such as June and December; and they are followed from higher to lower as July, April, August, November, May, December, and February. The SC maximum intensity value that reaches a higher number, or even the duration of SC will not affect aircraft accidents directly; however, the number of GSs in the decreasing phase of SAC will affect the rate of accidents (Aksen et al., 2024). In Fig. 5, the comparison of the number of accidents that occurred during the increasing and decreasing phases of the SACs from SC 15 to SC 25 with the sunspot number (SSN) is given. SCs with the highest number of accidents are Cycles 18, 20, and 22; in the second it is followed by Cycles 19, 21, and 23; in the third Cycles 17 and 24 appear as seen in Fig. 5. It is also determined that aircraft accidents are more common both in the decreasing phase of the SA and in the equinoxes (Aksen et al., 2024).

The two most important structures leading to storms are the CMEs and the co-rotating interaction region (CIR) related to high-speed SW stream escape from large CHs (Mursula, Qvick, Holappa, Asikainen, 2022). CHs are regions of low-density and temperature plasma on the solar disk with MFs that open or extend into the heliosphere. The CH positions and lifetimes change significantly on time scales from months to years which is linked to the SAC. The lifetimes of low-latitude CHs are usually less than one rotation but may extend to almost 3 years. During minimum SA, large CHs cover the polar caps of the Sun while only small mid-latitude holes with shorter lifetimes exist in the solar maximum.

During the increasing and decreasing phases of an SC, CHs can exist at any latitude and can evolve into elongated structures stretching equatorward from the pole (Hewins, 2020). In Fig. 6, the comparison of the number of accidents that occurred during the increasing and decreasing phases of the SACs from SC 15 to SC 25 (left-hand side of the abscissa coordinate) with the GA intensities with the SSNs (right-hand side of the abscissa coordinate) is given. This figure shows that the number of aircraft accidents increased in the decreasing phases of SACs rather than increasing phases because the galactic CR flux enters the Earth's atmosphere at much larger scales in the minimum phase of SA (Rycroft et al., 2000). The reason for this higher flux in the minimum phase is the CHs tend to be fewer at high latitudes, but they are larger and longer-lived near the solar minimum. However, CHs tend to be more numerous at lower latitudes, but they are also much smaller and short-lived near solar minimum (Aksen et al., 2024). The other reason is that CHs are the dominant cause of recurrent GSs during the years of solar minimum (AFWAMAN 15-1, 2003).

Figure 5. Comparison of the number of accidents that occurred during the increasing and decreasing phases of the SACs from Cycle 15 to Cycle 25 with the SSN
Source: (Aksen, et al., 2024)

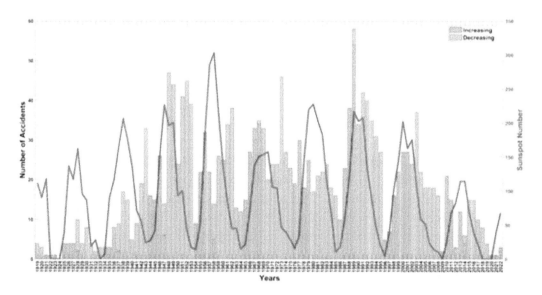

Figure 6. Comparison of the number of accidents that occurred during the increasing and decreasing phases of the SACs from Cycle 15 to Cycle 25 with the GA intensities
Source: (Aksen, et al., 2024)

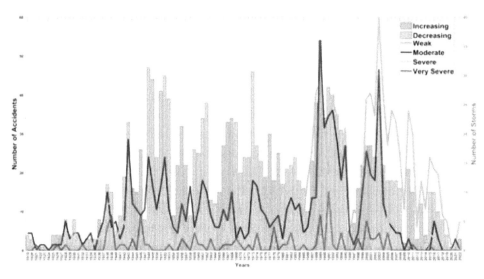

SOLUTIONS AND RECOMMENDATIONS

The mechanical/technical, pilotage, meteorological, and unknown reasons for accidents were higher between 1941 and 1950 while they were close to each other from 1951 to 1980; 1941-1970 and 1971-2000 for mechanical and pilotage; and meteorological reasons, respectively. The percentages of accidents for mechanical/technical and pilotage reasons, unknown reasons, bad weather conditions, and turbulence depending on GSs correspond to 68%, 22%, 8%, and 2% without including meteorological reasons for latitudes between $\pm10° \leq \varphi \leq \pm90°$ in the northern and southern hemispheres, respectively. The question here is what can be done to prevent these accidents? Is it possible to identify the effect of GSs to avoid aircraft accidents before they occur?

There could be some ways to prevent these accidents as mentioned by Meier et al. (2020): protecting from the radiation during such a solar storm is reducing the total time spent in high radiation zones as a result delaying non-urgent flights until the effect of the solar storm passes, and/or changing flight route depending on altitude and latitude effects, however, these protections cause more fuel consumption by changing the altitude, and it is possible to compensate this disadvantage by adjusting the flight speed according to altitude conditions. There will be some difficulties while bringing these suggestions to life as aircraft flow management at the airport causes undesired delays and costs if it cannot make a certain number of take-offs and landings during a certain period due to restrictions. Reasons for this limited capability include the rapid increase in customer demand, and the difficulty of increasing the capacity of the system by establishing new airport facilities or expanding existing ones, as well as excluding from existing analytical and simulation tools (Lucertini, Smriglio and Telmon, 1997). Increasing the number of flights without making a good plan to cover these costs and surviving the competition leads to an increase in the number of aircraft by employing airline personnel for more hours (Calderón, 2020).

The aircrew personnel and passengers flying at high latitudes will experience the effect of the GSs directly, whereas the response of the pilot, flight crew, and passengers flying in the middle latitudes, to these effects, can be measured only with tests in the laboratory environments, e.g., Electroencephalogram (EEG) technique which is the electrical recording of neuronal events (Aksen et al., 2024). In this paper, it is given some future suggestions below, but it mainly needs more progress and higher imaging techniques. Studies on the effects of GSs on military and civil aviation psychology started to gain momentum in 2013 mainly in the United Kingdom, however, a research laboratory has not yet been established for the possible effects of GSs on the volunteers and have not been investigated yet in many countries which are the members of ICAO. In addition, the countries located in the middle latitudes cannot be experienced directly the GS effect as it is experienced by pilots in high latitudes and polar regions, therefore laboratory studies should accelerate as soon as possible for the middle/low latitude regions (Aksen et al, 2024). This is the most acceptable way to understand the effects of GSs for countries where direct effects of GSs cannot be observed, such as the aircrew personnel and passengers flying at high latitudes.

FUTURE RESEARCH DIRECTIONS

The Volunteers Who Fly on Higher Geographic Latitudes (for $\geq 50°$)

1. It should be checked whether more pilot and aircrew personnel are coping with mental and physical complaints during the decreasing phase of the SAC than in the maximum phase of the cycle.
2. It should also be checked whether there are more pilot and aircrew personnel coming with mental and physical complaints during equinoxes in March and September (and mostly at the beginning of October). Moreover, it must be checked whether there is an increase in human-induced accidents during these months.
3. The volunteers should be taken to cognitive and personality psychological tests *directly* before and after the flight without creating a laboratory medium and subjected to tests for different categories as mentioned below. In addition to these experiments, physiological factors such as hypoxia, jetlag, shift-lag, etc. must also be considered that are faced during the flight.

The Volunteers Who Fly on Lower and Middle Geographic Latitudes (for $0° \leq \varphi < 50°$)

4. We need a laboratory medium that includes a low-pressure room, centrifuge, and air-conditioning room, cleansed with all dissipative effects that only include all physical conditions that are seen during the GSs, and a working team that consists of different disciplines.
5. The volunteers are chosen both from military and civil aviation pilots, and aircrew personnel, and are subjected to cognitive and personality psychological tests depending on their gender, age, physical conditions, etc. These volunteers are exposed to different levels of electromagnetic strength between 0 and 9 that correspond to the intensity change of GSs.
6. The volunteers are tested from a few hours to a few days depending on the intensity of GS and will be classified depending on these different time intervals.
7. The volunteers should always be taken to cognitive and personality psychological tests before and after the tests. In addition to these experiments, physiological factors such as hypoxia, jetlag, shift-lag, etc. must also be considered that are faced during the flight.

CONCLUSION

ICAO has lately started to emerge the influences of climate change on the aviation industry not just where we live on it, but also where we fly at 30000-40000 feet. Climate modelling studies have specified that depending on climate changes, the amount of moderate or major air turbulence in the transatlantic flight routes in winter flights will increase soon. Human-induced climate change is expected to build up perpendicular wind shears at aircraft cruising altitudes within the atmospheric jet streams. Such a reinforcement would increase the frequency of the shear instabilities that generate clear air turbulence (CAT). The mid-latitude jet streams in both the northern and southern hemispheres are anticipated to reinforce at aircraft cruising altitudes as the climate changes. In the coming decades, the prevalence of CAT may continue to increase due to climate change (Williams, 2017).

The impact of meteorological events on flights is so important is already known, however, the intense effects of high radiation on both technical and human factors must be taken very seriously which should be one of the leading causes of aircraft accidents at high latitudes both in the Northern and Southern Hemispheres of Earth. The research on the damaging effects of GSs on flight instruments as mechanical/technical and electronic accessories of aircraft, and the nervous system of the pilot and cabin crew, especially in high latitudes, had not been seriously placed in aviation literature until recently while GSs and the effects of climate change on ACI have been investigated nowadays, on the other hand, detailed research has not been done yet. However, it has already established a system of space weather centres for the solar radiation effects and advisors will be issued when certain levels of radiation are exceeded (Meier et al., 2020), and ICAO has started its studies on the effects of climate change and radiation levels on aircraft accidents.

Short-term changes ruin pilots meaning constant exposure to external forces, especially for pilots who fly long distances and continuously. Geographical latitudes have very important effects on flight as well, particularly pilots flying at high latitudes will be exposed to all these effects much more than flying pilots in the mid-latitudes or lower latitudes. These short-term effects are likely to cause serious brain and muscle diseases in the long-term periods, whether in civil aviation or military pilots. However, the effects of CR on pilots should not be confused with other basic flight diseases such as hypoxia, acceleration forces, spatial disorientation or volatile vertigo, fatigue, shift-lag, jetlag, thermal stress, dehydration or water loss, and altitude drunkenness. In the long term, short-term harmful effects will be more likely to develop cancers of the brain, testis, bladder, breast, colon, melanoma, and Hodgkin's type. It can even trigger Alzheimer's and dementia diseases. In addition, milder conditions such as hypoglycaemia, stroke, epileptic seizures, insomnia, stomach bleeding, appendicitis, hernia, asthma, and severe spinal pains can lead to it (Aksen et al., 2024).

FUNDING STATEMENT

This research received no specific grant from any funding agency in the public, commercial, or not-for-profit sectors.

ACKNOWLEDGMENTS

This paper was prepared during the author's scientific collaboration on the "Simulations of Shock Wave Propagation in the Solar Corona and Comparison with Observations" at the Astronomical Institute of Czech Academy of Sciences, Department of Solar Physics as a Sabbatical leave.

The author would like to thank the anonymous referee(s) for valuable comments and guidance.

REFERENCES

Aksen, U., Göker, Ü. D., Timoçin, E., Akçay, Ç., & İpek, M. (2024). The effects of geomagnetic storms on air crash events between the years 1919-2023. *Advances in Space Research*, *73*(1), 807–830. doi:10.1016/j.asr.2023.11.008

Calderón, D. J. (2021). Aviation Investment: Economic Appraisal for Airports, Air Traffic Management, Airlines and Aeronautics. England: Ashgate Publishing Limited.

Cannon, P. S., Angling, M., Barclay, L., Curry, C., Dyer, C., & Edwards, R. (2013a). Extreme space weather: impacts on engineered systems- a summary rep. Royal Academy of Engineering, London, UK.

Cannon, P. S., Angling, M., Barclay, L., Curry, C., Dyer, C., & Edwards, R. (2013b). Extreme space weather: impacts on engineered systems and infrastructure. Royal Academy of Engineering, London, UK. ISBN: 1-903496-96-9.

Carlson, N. R. (2014). Foundations of behavioural neuroscience [Lexical characteristics of Turkish language] (Trans. Ed. Muzaffer Şahin), Nobel Publications, İstanbul, Turkey.

Çetingüç, M. (2016). Havacılık ve Uzay Psikolojisi [Lexical characteristics of Turkish language], Nobel Publications, İstanbul, Turkey.

Chapman, S. C., Horne, R. B., & Watkins, N. W. (2020a). Using the aa index over the last 14 solar cycles to characterize extreme geomagnetic activity. *Geophysical Research Letters*, *47*(3), 1–10. doi:10.1029/2019GL086524

Chapman, S. C., McIntosh, S. W., Leamon, R. J., & Watkins, N. W. (2020b). Quantifying the solar cycle modulation of extreme space weather. *Geophysical Research Letters*, *47*(11), 1–9. doi:10.1029/2020GL087795

Chapman, S. C., Watkins, N. W., & Tindale, E. (2018). Reproducible aspects of the climate of space weather over the last five solar cycles. *Space Weather*, *16*(8), 1128–1142. doi:10.1029/2018SW001884

Cüceloğlu, D. (2000). İnsan ve Davranışı: Psikolojinin Temel Kavramları [Lexical characteristics of Turkish language]. Remzi Publications, İstanbul, Turkey.

Dan-Okoro, R., Musa, H. S., & Agidi, V. (2018). Seasonal effects of weather elements on flight operations at Nnamdi Azikiwe International Airport Abuja, Nigeria. *Current Journal of Applied Science and Technology*, *28*(6), 1–10. doi:10.9734/CJAST/2018/41590

Doviak, R. J., Vladislav, M. D., & Zrnic, S. (1999). Aviation Weather Surveillance Systems "Advanced Radar and Surface Sensors for Flight Safety and Air Traffic Management". United Kingdom: The Institution of Electrical Engineers.

Evans, J. E. (2001). Developments in US Aviation Weather R&D. In L. Bianco, P. Dell'Olmo, & A. R. Odoni (Eds.). New Concepts and Methods in Air Traffic Management (vol. 1, pp. 213-224). Berlin: Springer. doi:10.1007/978-3-662-04632-6_13

Gagarin, Y., & Lebedev, V. (1984). *Uzay ve Psikoloji* [Lexical characteristics of Turkish language]. (B. Konukman, Ed. & Trans.). İnkılap Publications.

Göker, Ü. D. (2008). The importance of heat conduction and viscosity in solar corona and comparison of magnetohydrodynamic equations of one-fluid and two-fluid structure in current sheet. *Sun and Geosphere, 3*(1), 52-56.

Göker, Ü. D. (2012). Magnetohydrodynamic study of shock waves in the current sheet of a solar coronal magnetic loop. *New Astronomy*, *17*(2), 130–136. doi:10.1016/j.newast.2011.06.010

Göker, Ü. D. (2018). Jeomanyetik fırtınaların pilotların kognitif durumlarına etkileri üzerine hipotez [Lexical characteristics of Turkish language]. *Journal of Defense Sciences, 17*(2), 116-138.

Göker, Ü. D. (2023). Short- and long-term changes in the neurophysiological status of pilots due to radiation exposure caused by geomagnetic storms. *Medical Research Archives*, *11*(9), 1–17. doi:10.18103/mra.v11i9.4395

Göker, Ü. D., Yazıcı, M., Balcı, G., Köksal, Ö., & Şengelen, H. E. (2021). The statistical analysis of air crash investigations from 1918 to 2019. *Journal of Defense Sciences*, *2*(40), 1–32. doi:10.17134/khosbd.1000317

Gultepe, I., & Feltz, W. F. (2019). Aviation meteorology: Observations and model. *Pure and Applied Geophysics*, *176*(5), 1863–1867. doi:10.1007/s00024-019-02188-2

Hewins, I. M., Gibson, S. E., Webb, D. F., McFadden, R. H., Kuchar, T. A., Emery, B. A., & McIntosh, S. W. (2020). The evolution of coronal holes over three solar cycles using the McIntosh archive. *Solar Physics*, *295*(11), 161–176. doi:10.1007/s11207-020-01731-y

Koonce, J. M. (1984). A brief history of aviation psychology. *Human Factors*, *26*(5), 499–508. doi:10.1177/001872088402600502

Laundal, K. M., & Richmond, A. D. (2016). Magnetic coordinate systems. *Space Science Reviews*, *206*(1-4), 27–59. doi:10.1007/s11214-016-0275-y

Lucertini, M., Smriglio, S., & Telmon, D. (1997). Network optimization in air traffic management. L. Bianco, P. Dell'Olmo, & A. R. Odoni (Eds.). Modelling and Simulation in Air Traffic Management Berlin. Springer. doi:10.1007/978-3-642-60836-0_5

Meier, M. M., Copeland, K., Klöble, K. E., Matthiä, D., Plettenberg, M. C., Schennetten, K., Wirtz, M., & Hellweg, C. E. (2020). Radiation in the atmosphere-A hazard to aviation safety? *Atmosphere (Basel)*, *11*(12), 1358–1389. doi:10.3390/atmos11121358

Mertens, C. J., Kress, B. T., Wiltberger, M., Blattnig, S. R., Slaba, T. S., Solomon, S. C., & Engel, M. (2010). Geomagnetic influence on aircraft radiation exposure during a solar energetic particle event in October 2003. *Space Weather*, *8*(3), S03006–S03022. doi:10.1029/2009SW000487

Muller, R., & Drax, C. (2014). Fundamentals and Structure of Safety Management Systems in Aviation. Aviation Risk and Safety Management Methods and Applications in Aviation Organizations. Switzerland: Springer International Publishing. doi:10.1007/978-3-319-02780-7_5

Mursula, K., Qvick, T., Holappa, L., & Asikainen, T. (2022). Magnetic storms during the space age: Occurrence and relation to varying solar activity. *Journal of Geophysical Research. Space Physics*, *127*(12), 1–36. doi:10.1029/2022JA030830

NASA-CR-194800 (1993). *The National Geomagnetic Initiative*. U.S. Geodynamics Committee Board on Earth Sciences and Resources Commission on Geosciences, Environment, and Resources National Research Council, National Academy Press.

National Transportation Safety Board. (2005). Risk factors associated with weather-related general aviation accidents. Safety Study NTSB/SS-05/01. National Transportation Safety Board.

Riedle, R. (2006). Importance of CISM in modern air traffic management (ATM). Critical Incident Stress Management in Aviation in Jörg Leonhardt and Joachim Vogt (Eds.). England: Ashgate Publishing Limited.

Rycroft, M. J., Israelsson, S., & Price, C. (2000). The global atmospheric electric current, solar activity and climate change. *Journal of Atmospheric and Solar-Terrestrial Physics*, *62*(17-18), 1563–1576. doi:10.1016/S1364-6826(00)00112-7

Sağır, S., Atıcı, R., & Dölek, İ. (2018). Investigation of the severe geomagnetic storm effects on ionosphere at nighttime through ROTI. *Journal of Science and Technology MSU*, *6*(2), 603–609. doi:10.18586/msufbd.493156

Schieb, P. A., & Gibson, A. (2011). Geomagnetic Storms. Multi-Disciplinary Issues International Future Programme [Lecture Notes], pp. 1-69. CENTRA Technology, Inc., on behalf of Office of Risk Management and Analysis, United States Department of Homeland Security, USA.

Schultz, M., Lorenz, S., Schmitz, R., & Delgado, L. (2018). Weather impact on airport performance. *Aerospace (Basel, Switzerland)*, *5*(4), 109–128. doi:10.3390/aerospace5040109

Stolzer, A. J., Halford, C. D., & Goglia, J. J. (2008). Safety Management Systems in Aviation. England: Ashgate Publishing Limited.

Sun, Z., Ma, C., Li, W., & Shen, C. (2014). Flight Operations Quality Assurance Based on Clustering Analysis. *Proceedings of the First Symposium on Aviation Maintenance and Management*. Berlin: Springer. 10.1007/978-3-642-54233-6_46

Timoçin, E., Ünal, İ., & Göker, Ü. D. (2018). A comparison of IRI-2016 foF2 predictions with observations at different latitudes during geomagnetic storms. *Geomagnetism and Aeronomy*, *58*(7), 846–856. doi:10.1134/S0016793218070216

Tsurutani, B. T., & Gonzalez, W. D. (1993). The causes of geomagnetic storms during solar minimum. NOAA/ERL/SEL.

Uslu, S., & Dönmez, K. (2016). Geçmişten günümüze havacılık kazalarının sebeplerindeki değişimler üzerine bir inceleme [Lexical characteristics of Turkish language]. *Journal of Social Sciences*, *3*(9), 222–239. doi:10.16990/SOBIDER.296

Wensveen, J. G. (2007). Air transportation: A management perspective. England: Ashgate Publishing Limited.

Williams, P. D. (2017). Increased light, moderate, and severe clear-air turbulence in response to climate change. *Advances in Atmospheric Sciences*, *34*(5), 576–586. doi:10.1007/s00376-017-6268-2

ADDITIONAL READING

An, H., Zhou, Z., & Yi, Y. (2017). Opportunities and Challenges on Nanoscale 3D Neuromorphic Computing System. Conference Paper, *2017 IEEE International Symposium on Electromagnetic Compatibility & Signal/Power Integrity (EMCSI)*. IEEE. 10.1109/ISEMC.2017.8077906

Babayev, E. S., & Allahverdiyeva, A. A. (2007). Geomagnetic Storms and Their Influence on the Human Brain Functional State. *Revista CENIC Ciencias Biológicas, 36,* 1-8.

Babayev, E. S., & Allahverdiyeva, A. A. (2007). Effects of geomagnetic activity variations on the physiological and psychological state of functionally healthy humans: Some results of Azerbaijani studies. *Advances in Space Research*, *40*(12), 1941–1951. doi:10.1016/j.asr.2007.02.099

Büyükgöze, S. (2019). *Non-invasive BCI Method: EEG-Electroencephalography*. Conference Proceedings Paper, International Conference on Technics, Technologies, and Education ICTTE 2019, Bulgaria.

Functional Areas of the Cerebral Cortex including Motor Cortex (Areas 3 and 12) and Temporal Cortex (Area 2), and the Cerebellum (2023). Accessed August 1, 2023. https://www.dana.org/article/neuroanatomy-the-basics/

Gurfinkel, I. I., Kuleskova, V. P., & Oraevski, V. N. (1998). Assessment of the effect of a geomagnetic storm on the frequency of appearance of acute cardiovascular pathology, *Biofizika. Journal of Biophysics*, *43*(4), 654–658. PMID:9783073

Introduction to Neurophysiology. (2023). Psysio-pedia. https://www.physio-pedia.com

Kay, R. W. (1994). Geomagnetic storms: Association with incidence of depression measured by hospital admission. *The British Journal of Psychiatry*, *164*(3), 403–409. doi:10.1192/bjp.164.3.403 PMID:8199794

Novik, O., Smirnov, F., & Volgin, M. (2019). Influence of Space Weather on the Bioelectrical Activity of the Human Brain. Electromagnetic Geophysical Fields. Springer Nature Switzerland AG. 91-103. doi:10.1007/978-3-319-98461-2_6

Pavlov, K. I., Syrtsev, A. V., Mukhin, V. N., Archimuk, A. N., Mikheeva, E. A., Nikolaeva, S. V., Andieva, N. M., Kamenskaya, V. G., & Petrenko, M. I. (2019). The effect of environmental factors on the cognitive functions of cadets at a military institute. *Izvestiya. Atmospheric and Oceanic Physics*, *55*(10), 1465–1487. doi:10.1134/S0001433819100086

KEY TERMS AND DEFINITIONS

Aviation Psychology: It is one of the branches of psychology that deal with all information relating to civil and military aviation, such as performances and support of aircrew and airline personnel, passengers, if any, air traffic control system administrators, and control team with all other responsible people, in addition to those in charge of all design and maintenance of the aircraft, includes the application of people based on their behavioural skills and limits in the face of all these information above. It also leads to tests and interviews to find the right people in the selection of flight candidates, finding solutions to the risky thoughts and behaviours of the flight candidate and their psychiatric disorders.

Cognitive Psychology: It is a branch of psychology that studies comprehension, memory, and intelligence processing periods, and it investigates the relationship between the class and structure of cognitive processes in the organism and the class and characteristics of observable behaviours.

Geomagnetic Storm: It is the temporary disturbance of Earth's magnetosphere caused by a shock wave that comes from the solar wind. The disturbances that cause geomagnetic storms may be a solar coronal mass ejection (CME-more severe) or a co-rotating interaction region (CIR-much less severe), a high-speed stream of solar wind originating from a coronal hole (CH). These disturbances change depending on the increasing and decreasing phases of the solar cycle.

Mental Activities: It is described as anything that encourages, activates, or strengthens the mind, and increases the flow of blood, oxygen, and nutrients to the brain. It is also called neurological stimulation which can be provided internally from thought or externally from the environment.

Meteorological Effects: They are observable weather events such as temperature, air pressure, water vapour, and mass flow on the Earth's atmosphere, and the variations and interactions of these variables over time are explained by meteorology. These effects can be classified as fog, wind, storm, snowstorm, sandstorm, clouds, turbulence, icing, shower/rain, oraj, lightning, hurricane, snow, volcano eruption, and bad weather conditions in aviation literature.

Nervous System: It transmits signals between the brain and the rest of the body, including internal organs to control the ability to move, breath, see, think, hear, and more. The nervous system has two main parts, the central nervous system which is made up of the brain and spinal cord, and the peripheral nervous system which is made up of nerves that branch off from the spinal cord and extend to all parts of the body.

Neurophysiology: It is a branch of physiology that deals with the functional properties of neurons, glia, and networks rather than the anatomy of the nervous system, and it also helps to diagnose and monitor the progress of nervous disorders *"for detail explanation about the short- and long-term changes in the neurophysiological status of pilots due to radiation exposure caused by geomagnetic storms, see the paper of Göker (2023)"*.

Physical Activities: The World Health Organization (WHO) defines physical activity as any movement function including immobile times, for transport to get to and from places, or as part of physical activity, produced by skeletal muscles that requires energy expenditure.

Solar Activity: Solar activity, which is strongly associated with magnetic fields, as measured by the number of sunspots, follows an 11-year cycle between two maxima, and a 22-year cycle depends on changing solar magnetic polarity. It is the collective term for all active phenomena on the Sun, including sunspots, faculae, active regions, plages, active prominences, and flares between the increasing and decreasing phases of solar cycles.

Chapter 4
European Airlines in Turmoil:
Post-Pandemic Challenges and Recovery Efforts

Carolina Baptista

Instituto Superior de Educação e Ciências, Portugal

Rui Castro Quadros

https://orcid.org/0000-0003-0685-259X

Instituto Superior de Educação e Ciências, Portugal & Escola Superior de Hotelaria e Turismo do Estoril, Portugal

ABSTRACT

The COVID-19 pandemic has profoundly impacted various sectors, notably the aviation industry, where travel restrictions and reduced demand for flights led to significant challenges. This study examines the pandemic's financial implications on European companies during the period from 2018 to 2021, utilizing quantitative comparative analysis. The findings reveal a substantial decline in revenues for these companies, resulting in adverse effects on both their operational and net performance. Faced with the pandemic's uncertainty, these companies prioritized liquidity, resorting to external financing for support. Notably, the study highlights that TAP, the Portuguese airline, received significantly more state support compared to its European counterparts. Plus, TAP appears to encounter greater difficulties in servicing its financial debt, standing as the sole entity with an excessive debt burden among the analysed companies. This research contributes valuable insights into the aviation sector's challenges during the pandemic, encouraging a broader European-level dialogue on the subject.

INTRODUCTION

The aviation industry has seen significant growth over the last century and has been understood as an integral part of global economic growth, being able to stimulate trade and cultivate tourism development (Lee, 2019). The increase in the capacity of this industry has increased the supply and decreased travel

DOI: 10.4018/979-8-3693-0908-7.ch004

time and travel costs, which has contributed to the increase in the number of tourists, and currently the act of traveling is considered as a lifestyle that more and more people share (O'Connell 2018).

The literature seems unanimous and suggests that the years 2018 and 2019 were very positive for the sector, mainly due to the growth of tourism and cargo transport around the world (Agrawal, 2021; Dube et al., 2021; Fontanet-Pérez et al., 2022; Pinto and Lucas, 2022).

Everything seemed to be going well in the sector until at the end of 2019, in the Chinese city of Wuhan, an outbreak of a disease caused by the SARS-CoV-2 virus emerged and quickly spread worldwide. In January 2020, the World Health Organization issued a Public Health Emergency of International Concern due to the speed of the spread of the disease worldwide, and on March 11, 2020, the situation was officially declared a pandemic (Henkes, 2021).

In addition to the obvious direct impact on health and mortality, the measures applied by governments to control the spread of the disease have caused major disruptions to global economic activity. However, the impact was not symmetrical in all sectors of activity. While high-tech industries related to online entertainment, online *shopping*, online medicine, *and* online *education seem to have* adapted quite well to social distancing requirements, other industries such as aviation have been particularly hard hit (Abate et al., 2020; Alfaro et al., 2020; Baker et al., 2020; Pagano et al., 2020; Martins & Cró, 2022). In this regard, the research of Dube and Nhamo (2020) and Suau-Sanchez et al. (2020) confirmed that the impact of the pandemic on the aviation sector as well as on other sectors of the tourism industry was very rapid and significant worldwide.

The main objective of this work is to determine the impact that the pandemic has had on the financial statements of European airlines. In addition, it will be analysed whether the size of state aid was very different between companies based on their size. Finally, the ability of companies to settle all their debt will be analysed, based on their operational performance before the pandemic.

LITERATURE REVIEW

The Impact of the Pandemic on Companies' Statements

The literature has given high prominence to the impact that the Covid-19 pandemic has had on airlines (He et al., 2020; Maneenop & Kotcharin, 2020; Kotcharin, 2020; Dube et al., 2021; Agrawal, 2021). In this way, this work aims to enrich the literature that focuses on this subject, since the discussion will also focus on the Portuguese reality, a fact that has been little analyzed compared to other European and even world countries. This will be followed by a historical contextualization of the sector, followed by an analysis of the studies of the impact of the pandemic on the financial statements of companies at an international level and, finally, an analysis of the Portuguese reality.

Historical Contextualization

The aviation sector has always been highly exposed to exogenous shocks, such as the terrorist attacks of September 11, 2001, the oil crisis of 2002, severe acute respiratory syndrome in 2003 and bird flu in 2006 (Sadi & Henderson, 2000; Yang 2007; Chung, 2015; Agrawal, 2021).

On the other hand, in 2006 the sector saw the entry of *low-cost* companies, which significantly increased competition in the sector, a fact that triggered a deep rupture and called into question the business model of the companies previously present in the market (Belobaba, 2011; Riwo-Abudho et al., 2013; Pathak, 2015; Singh, 2016). Since then, all companies in the market have had to adjust their offer, given the increased competition caused by the competitive offers of new *players* in the market. *Low-cost* airlines, by applying aggressive revenue management, largely based on lower prices, have threatened, and continue to threaten the economic viability of the traditional model, and have forced profound changes in the strategic management of traditional airlines (Michaels & Fletcher 2009; Agrawal, 2021). Kramer et al. (2018) showed that this fierce competition from *low-cost* carriers has forced traditional airlines to optimize their revenues.

On the other hand, Doganis (2009) indicates that the increase in liberalization and deregulation has led the sector to a situation of greater instability.

All this has resulted in a decrease in the operating and net margins of aviation companies and has caused the sector to be flagged as one of the most difficult to operate in the world (Saranga & Nagpal, 2016; Mahtani & Garg, 2018). Gossling (2020) severely criticised the situation that the sector was experiencing in the pre-pandemic context, pointing out that even then, it already demonstrated a high dependence on state aid, and this fact was even more evident during the crisis caused by the Covid-19 pandemic. Thus, the author suggests that in a post-pandemic scenario, companies in the aviation sector should adopt a new strategy in their business models, focusing essentially on increasing the profitability of revenues. Only in this way will it be possible to have aviation companies that are less indebted and have a greater capacity to face the crises that follow. This concern about corporate indebtedness is frequently mentioned in the literature (González, 2013; Ramelli & Wagner, 2020; Xiong et al., 2020; Heyden & Heyden, 2021; Agrawal, 2021; Ding et al., 2021; Kokény et al., 2022). The authors state that in a scenario of economic recession, the performance of companies with higher levels of indebtedness tends to be lower, since they are subject to a greater financial effort and, therefore, end up presenting a higher risk of bankruptcy compared to their competitors. Thus, the literature indicates that in a scenario of a strong expected slowdown in the sector, highly leveraged airlines are likely to have high losses.

EVIDENCE AT INTERNATIONAL LEVEL

Agrawal (2021) analysed the impact of the pandemic on the financial statements of Indian airlines. To this end, it used a comparative quantitative methodology from the year 2015 to the year 2020. The author analysed revenues, capital expenditures, fixed expenditures, cash and short-term investments, EBITDA, EBIT, EBITDA margin, EBIT margin, net margin, ROI, asset turnover, and coverage of interest and similar charges.

The results indicate that even before the pandemic, companies had a very weak economic and financial performance and only two of the eight analysed had a reduced risk of bankruptcy. The pandemic has drastically reduced turnover and caused a general reduction in companies' operating results. In this way, the author indicates that Indian companies will have a very difficult time reversing all the impact that the pandemic has caused. In addition, the author suggests that in a scenario where a strong decline in passenger traffic is expected, companies should be more agile to provide more air freight transport solutions, to minimize losses.

Silva and Silva (2022) indicate that the economic and financial crisis resulting from the Covid-19 pandemic negatively influenced many sectors of activity. Thus, the social isolation imposed by governments and the cancellation of air travel have put great pressure on the solvency capacity of companies in the aviation sector. It was in this context that the authors studied how the pandemic crisis influenced the financial statements of the 3 largest airlines in Brazil. The methodology used was a comparative quantitative analysis of the financial information for the years 2019 and 2020. The consolidated data of the balance sheet and the consolidated income statement were collected from the companies' reports and accounts. The authors concluded that the pandemic crisis had a significant impact on the economic and financial situation of companies, with sales falling by more than 50% in all of them. This shock has led companies to clearly reduce their investment and to have the need to raise capital from third parties to ensure their solvency.

Pereira and Mello (2021) evaluated the operational efficiency of Brazilian airlines during the period marked by the Covid-19 pandemic. The authors report that there was a major restriction of flights and an abrupt drop in demand. In addition, the analysis suggests that older companies with more diversified aircraft have shown greater resilience in the face of the challenge caused by the Covid-19 pandemic. One explanation for these facts is the low drop in air freight. Amankwah-Amoah et al. (2021) in their study show that companies that are wholly owned by states tend to systematically show losses. Deveci et al. (2022) analysed the impact of the pandemic on the financial statements of Turkey's aviation companies. The authors indicate that both *low-cost* and traditional companies have been strongly affected by the pandemic. The impacts were felt in the high decrease in sales, the reduction in the wage bill and the increase in losses and the level of indebtedness. The authors highlight the shift of Turkish companies' operations to freight flights to mitigate losses.

Fontanet-Pérez et al. (2022) analysed the impact of the Covid-19 pandemic on U.S. aviation companies. To this end, they analysed the performance of the top 10 passenger airlines operating in the country. The results presented indicate that all companies had large losses, however *low-cost* airlines were more successful in facing the crisis than traditional airlines. The data suggests that companies that had a higher business margin before the pandemic have been more resilient in the face of the large drop in demand and the consequent decrease in sales. The authors point out, however, that this difference between business models became clear only during the crisis. Already in the five years leading up to the pandemic, the growth in demand allowed all the airlines analysed to increase profits. Fontanet-Pérez et al. (2022) indicate that current business models do not adequately prepare aviation companies to face unexpected crises due to their low profit margins. Considering the vulnerabilities of the sector and the socio-economic externalities linked to it, the Covid-19 pandemic can be seen as an opportunity to reconsider the adequacy of current models, based on high sales volumes and low profit margins, as well as the desire to move towards a more sustainable economy.

EVIDENCE FOR PORTUGAL

Muchanga (2014) referred to TAP as being the largest Portuguese airline. According to the author, the various crises and the liberalization of the sector have posed many difficulties to traditional airlines. At the time, TAP was already in a situation of technical bankruptcy, as it had negative equity. Likewise, the author demonstrated that the prospects were not good for the company, since it did not seem to be able to adapt to the development and exponential expansion of *low-cost airlines* such as *Ryanair* and *easyJet*, in the national territory.

Cunha (2015) indicated that the TAP Group's main activity is the air transport of passengers and cargo, as well as a set of services provided to third parties in areas related to the Group's core businesses.

Thus, and taking into account that in November 2014, the Council of Ministers decided to relaunch the privatisation process of TAP, the author tried to assess what would be the fair value at which the company should be sold. The results presented by the analysis indicated that TAP would not be able to generate operating results in the future and, therefore, its fair value was negative, so it was expected that the Government should not register a financial income from the operation, ceding only to investors its position in the share capital and the respective obligations of the company.

The privatisation of TAP was eventually consummated in 2015. With this procedure, the participation of the state in relation to the future of TAP will be relieved of responsibility. However, this has always been a dossier that has always been undermined by much criticism, with special emphasis on the company's sale value, as well as its strategic importance. Critics of this action pointed out that this strategic importance would be at stake with private management (Pinto and Lucas, 2022). Later that year, a new government emerged, which decided to reverse the privatisation of TAP, ensuring that the State would hold 50% of the capital, even though it did not have great executive control over the management of the company. António Costa and his government had once again put taxpayers' money at risk, exposing it to a loss-making company with no capacity to control the management in which the State was left with the risk and the private sector with the management (Pinto and Lucas, 2022).

It was in this context that the Covid-19 pandemic emerged and with it a big hole in TAP's accounts. The company's management communicated to the government its pressing need for liquidity. In this way, and as can be seen in a government note2, a plan of 3,200 million euros was drawn up. In the same note, it is indicated that with this cash injection the company would not reduce the business and that it would be capitalized and able to continue operating and competing in a highly competitive market, to serve the Portuguese economy and Europe.

In Portugal, state support and the way in which the dossier was handled has been the subject of much criticism34, and at an early stage the European Commission5 cancelled the state support because it considered that it was not properly justified. The matter eventually resulted in the publication of a book on the subject.

In the book, Pinto, and Lucas (2022) are very critical of state support for TAP. The authors begin by saying that the reversal of privatisation was one of the most catastrophic decisions in Portuguese politics in the last 30 years. Since 2000, TAP has only had positive net results in only 2 financial years. Even before the pandemic, the carry-over results had already placed the flag carrier with negative equity, that is, TAP was already in a situation of technical bankruptcy before the impact of the pandemic. At the time, although it did not receive money directly from the State, the company was able to obtain financing with advantageous conditions because the financing had the explicit or implicit guarantee of the State. The authors indicate that in 2019, despite being marked by a strong growth in tourism, TAP still managed to have one of the largest losses in its history and, at the end of 2019, it already had the junk rating to issue debt. Therefore, the need for the injection of money from the State was already notorious and it would be unlikely that TAP would have been able to resist much longer without some public support, direct or indirect. Since this is prohibited by European law and observing other examples where the rejection of these injections led companies in the sector to bankruptcy, it would be natural that this would end up being TAP's fate, even without the pandemic. Ironically, the health crisis turned out to be TAP's salvation because the State Portuguese now had a "justification" to inject money into a company that would have needed it anyway.

The authors address all the points that have been defended at the level of political power for the injection of public money into the company. In summary, the authors argue that the best thing for the national interest would be for TAP to enter insolvency proceedings. With this procedure, according to what aviation history shows, it would be quite likely that another airline would emerge to replace TAP, taking advantage of its assets, as has happened in the past in Switzerland or Belgium. More examples have been given at European level which indicate that the disappearance of the flag carrier does not result in a fall in tourism or economic indicators, quite the contrary.

The authors indicate that in Portugal, TAP only has a decisive weight at Lisbon airport, which is precisely the airport where it would be easier to replace TAP flights, because currently there are several airlines that are interested in having more flights to Lisbon and only do not do so due to lack of slots. In addition, none of the main routes from Lisbon airport is exclusive to TAP.

In the book, another argument strongly referred to by the political power is discussed, which is the importance of the company for the balance of trade. In fact, TAP's weight in total Portuguese exports in 2019 amounted to 3,000 million (3% of the national total). However, if we consider direct imports, plus fuel purchases that have a high import content, TAP's contribution to the Trade Balance is between 1,000 and 1,500 million euros, less than half of the value of exports usually pointed out as its contribution to the Trade Balance.

In addition, exports are not valued for their absolute value, but for the added value they bring to the country. Exporting products or services at a loss, as was the case with TAP in most years, does not cause relevant positive effects for the economy. Purchases from national suppliers were also analysed, with the authors concluding that, except for the travel agency sector, which would continue to negotiate with airlines flying to Portugal, TAP does not have a significant weight in the sales of any sector in Portugal.

In terms of employment, Pinto, and Lucas (2022) indicate that in fact, TAP is a major employer, yet it has only a residual part of the country's total employment. Without the cash injection, jobs would end up being absorbed by the market, either by the aviation sector, when it regains its previous size, or by other sectors, given the level of qualifications of the workers.

The emigrant communities were also analysed by the authors, who concluded that, especially the most recent ones, they do not need TAP to have direct flights to Portugal. In the same way, the authors indicate that the connection to the PALOP countries is also already largely guaranteed by foreign airlines.

The tax matter was also addressed, with the authors being very critical of this argument, indicating that the company, because of its poor operational performance, does not pay IRC.

Pinto and Lucas (2022) also looked at the weight of public support for airlines in the public expenditure of the States in 2019. The results indicate that at the European level, TAP stands out with a total percentage of 4.1%, followed by Finnair with 1%. Luftahnsa accounted for just 0.4%. The authors conclude that no one can currently quantify how much it will cost TAP to the pockets of the Portuguese State and that support for TAP is not a loan, but a non-repayable transfer. In this way, the authors indicate that the use of public money should be more subject to an opportunity cost analysis. In this way, and in the current context, the authors see privatization as the best procedure to do to avoid that more state funds are placed in the company without it having a real structural transformation.

Having a critical position of reading the book, it is important to note that it was written by people with liberal positions and ideals that are public, so it may have a slightly biased view. The fact is that in 2020, the then Minister of Infrastructure Pedro Nuno Santos indicated in the presentation6 of the state support that the company, according to the economic model outlined, in 2025 would already be able to start repaying the money borrowed by the state Portuguese. However, the company's 2021 annual report already indicated that the €1.2 billion rescue loan had been converted into equity. And already in 2022, the company confirmed that it will not return the 3.2 billion euros that the State, with the restructuring plan, introduced in the airline.

METHODOLOGY

In this work, the collection and analysis of data on European companies will be carried out, as was done in the research by Kokény et al. (2022). The authors went to the *investing1 website* and collected the European companies listed on the Stock Exchange. In addition and taking into account that Portugal does not have any aviation company listed on the Stock Exchange, TAP was introduced in order to make a comparison between this Portuguese company and its European counterparts.

However, Kokény et al. (2022) did not consider the dates of the annual reporting of accounts or the currency in which each company presents its financial statements. Thus, and as recommended by Costa (2022), we removed from the sample companies that do not report their accounts in euros as well as companies that do not have December 31 as their reporting date. Table1 thus indicates the companies that have been selected, those that have been eliminated and the reason for their elimination.

As table 1 identifies, the final sample will consist of the following companies: TAP, Lufthansa, Air France-KLM, and Finnair.

On a methodological level, we will carry out a comparative quantitative analysis. This methodology was implemented in the investigations of Agrawal (2021), Florido-Benítez (2021), Silva and Silva (2022). Thus, we will analyze the companies' accounts in the years immediately before the pandemic (2018 and 2019) and compare them with the years that followed (2020 and 2021).

Table 1. Companies considered in the study

Company	Exclusion Reason	Accepted/Rejected
TAP	-	Accepted
Ryanair	Fiscal year starts in April and ends in March	Rejected
Lufthansa	-	Accepted
Norwegian Air Shuttle	Accounts are presented in Norwegian Krone (NOK)	Rejected
International Consolidated Airlines Group (IAG)	Accounts are presented in British Pound (GBP)	Rejected
SAS	Accounts are presented in Swedish Krona (SEK)	Rejected
Air France-KLM	-	Accepted
EasyJet	Accounts are presented in British Pound (GBP) Fiscal year starts in October and ends in September	Rejected
Wizz Air Holdings	Accounts are presented in British Pound (GBP)	Rejected
Finnair	-	Accepted
Esken	Accounts are presented in British Pound (GBP) Fiscal year starts in March and ends in February	Rejected

Source: Authors' production (2022)

ANALYSIS AND RESULTS

As already mentioned, we are going to look at TAP, Lufthansa, Air France-KLM, and Finnair. Considering the specificity of the study to be implemented, it is necessary to use several sources to constitute the sample. First of all, the figures relating to the financial statements of the companies listed on the stock exchange were collected from the website *of the world street newspaper*, the data from TAP's financial statements were collected from its annual accounts reports. Finally, the value of the State support provided to Lufthansa and Air France-KLM was taken from the study by Albers and Rundshagen (2020). The amount of State aid obtained by Finnair was obtained through the research of Pinto and Lucas (2022). Finally, the value of state support for TAP was obtained from the company's annual report. Table 2 indicates the amount of State aid each company received.

As already indicated in this work, the period of analysis will be between 2018 and 2021.

At the methodological level, initially a comparative quantitative analysis of the financial statements of the companies will be made. In addition, we will use some financial analysis indicators, such as the debt indicator, the EBITDA margin, and the net margin.

Fernandes et al. (2019) indicate that the debt ratio indicates the interdependence of the company on other people's capital and represents the proportion of liabilities in total financing sources. An excessive weight of other people's capital in the financing of the company may jeopardise its solvency. It is recommended that this indicator has a maximum value of 66%. Equation 1 indicates how this indicator is calculated.

Liabilities/Assets x 100   (1)

Another indicator that will be used is the *EBITDA* margin. This indicator does not consider interest and similar expenses incurred, interest and similar income earned, the amount of tax, the amount of depreciation and the value of amortization. It is a variable that clearly indicates the competitiveness and operational efficiency of each company (Costa et al., 2021). Equation 2 identifies how this variable is calculated.

EBITDA/Revenues x 100   (2)

The other profitability indicator to use is the net margin. Fernandes et al. (2019) indicate that this indicator evaluates the return in terms of net income from revenues realized. Thus, the higher the value of the indicator, the greater the propensity for the company to generate results. The authors add that it

Table 2. Amount of state aids each company received

Company	Amount in Million Euros (€)
Air France-KLM	7,000
Finnair	1,237
Lufthansa	9,000
TAP	3,188

Source: Authors' production (2022)

can be understood as the gain obtained in net terms, for each monetary unit sold. Equation 3 displays the way it is calculated.

Net Income/Recipes x 100 (3)

Next, an analysis will be made of the value of the state support considering the size of the company and the ability of the companies to repay their debt. The investigations by Costa (2022) and Ribeiro and Quesado (2017) indicate that *the value of total assets and the value of total revenues* can be used as a proxy for the size of companies.

Finally, Babel (2014) indicates that to analyse the repayment capacity of *companies, Net Debt to EBITDA is an indicator widely used by creditors, as it indicates the number of years necessary for companies to amortize their net financial debt, considering the value of their* EBITDA. Equation 4 indicates how *Net Debt to EBITDA is calculated*:

Financial Debt−Cash and Short-Term Investments/EBITDA (4)

With the results, the impact of the Covid-19 pandemic on the financial statements of companies is analysed, in a first phase. Subsequently, it will be assessed whether there were considerable differences in state support compared to the size of the companies. Finally, an analysis will be made of the level of indebtedness of companies in relation to what their capacity was before the pandemic, to understand whether they have a controlled level of indebtedness, or if, on the contrary, they have such a high level of indebtedness that the ability of companies to repay may be compromised. Thus, in this first phase, Tables 3, 4, 5 and 6 show the evolution of the profit and loss account and assets of Air France-KLM, Finnair, Lufthansa, and TAP, respectively.

After analysing the tables, it is possible to denote that in terms of size (measured through sales and assets), Lufthansa is the largest company in all the years analysed, followed by Air France-KLM. Before the pandemic, TAP and Finnair had very similar indicators, especially in terms of revenues.

Looking at the evolution of revenues before the pandemic, it is possible to see that all companies increased their revenues, with Finnair being the company that grew the most (9.24%) and Lufthansa being the one with the lowest growth rate (2.48%). This lower increase in Lufthansa's revenues can be explained by the size of the company, which makes it have fewer opportunities for growth (Costa, 2022). These data also confirm the studies by Agrawal (2021) and Dube et al. (2021) that 2019 was the best year ever for the aviation sector.

Also, before the pandemic, all companies, except for TAP, had positive *EBITDA* and net income figures. TAP had a positive *EBITDA* in 2018, however in that year the company's net result was negative. Thus, consequently, the company was the only one in the sample that in the pre-pandemic period had negative net margins.

The levels of corporate indebtedness in the pre-pandemic period were high compared to what are the reference values identified in the literature, which credits the study by Tretheway and Markhvida (2014) that signaled the sector with a high level of business risk. However, the company with the least debt in 2019 was Lufthansa, while TAP was the company with the highest level of debt.

Regarding business margins, the company with the highest *EBITDA* margin in 2019 was Air France-KLM, and Lufthansa was the one with the best net margin. In fact, even in 2018 it was also Lufthansa

Table 3. Evolution of Air France/KLM - Finnair

(In € million) Air France-KLM	2021	2020	2019	2018
Income Statement and Profitability Indicators:				
Sales	14,315	11,088	27,188	26,224
EBITDA	871	-1,897	4,018	4,291
Net Profit	-3,294	-7,105	276	397
EBITDA Margin	6.08%	-17.11%	14.78%	16.36%
Net Margin	-23.01%	-64.08%	1.02%	1.51%
Balance Sheet and Debt Indicators:				
Total Assets	30,683	30,181	30,735	29,637
Cash and ST Investments	7,129	7,017	4,498	3,896
Total Liabilities	37,650	35,523	28,839	28,242
Total Debt	18,053	16,597	9,827	9,687
Shareholders' Equity	-6,975	-5,351	1,881	1,383
Debt Ratio	122.71%	117.70%	93.83%	95.29%

Source: Authors' production (2022)

Table 4. Evolution of Finnair

(In € million) FIN	2021	2020	2019	2018
Income Statement and Profitability Indicators:				
Sales	838	829	3,098	2,836
EBITDA	-184	-287	432	439
Net Profit (Loss)	-464	-541	62	89
EBITDA Margin	-21.96%	-34.62%	13.94%	15.48%
Net Margin	-55.37%	-65.26%	2.00%	3.14%
Balance Sheet and Debt Indicators:				
Total Assets	4,047	3,647	3,878	3,944
Cash and Short-Term Investments	1,266	824	953	1,073
Total Liabilities	3,769	2,948	3,110	3,223
Total Debt	2,830	2,242	1,633	1,848
Shareholders' Equity	278	699	768	720
Debt Ratio	93.13%	80.83%	80.20%	81.72%

that had the best net margin (6.18%). This figure indicates that in 2018, the company made €6.18 in net profit for every €100.00 in sales.

The data is clear regarding the impact of the pandemic on companies' financial statements. Revenues fell significantly from 2019 to 2020. The company that showed the biggest drop in revenues was Finnair (-73.24%), while Air France-KLM was the company that showed the smallest drop in revenues, but still, the decrease in sales was (-59.22%).

Table 5. Evolution of Lufthansa

(In € million) LUF	2021	2020	2019	2018
Income Statement and Profitability Indicators:				
Sales	16,811	13,589	36,424	35,542
EBITDA	-732	-3,588	3,611	4,283
Net Profit (Loss)	-2,193	-6,766	1,245	2,196
EBITDA Margin	-4.35%	-26.40%	9.91%	12.05%
Net Margin	-13.05%	-49.79%	3.42%	6.18%
Balance Sheet and Debt Indicators:				
Total Assets	43,492	40,072	43,421	38,804
Cash and Short-Term Investments	7,666	5,460	3,385	3,235
Total Liabilities	39,002	38,685	33,165	29,231
Total Debt	16,281	14,928	9,559	6,625
Shareholders' Equity	4,450	1,347	10,147	9,463
Debt Ratio	89.68%	96.54%	76.38%	75.33%

Source: Authors' production (2022)

Table 6. Evolution of TAP

(In € million) TAP	2021	2020	2019	2018
Income Statement and Profitability Indicators:				
Sales	1,389	1,060	3,272	3,152
EBITDA	-999	-380	-64	41
Net Profit (Loss)	-1,599	-1,230	-134	-58
EBITDA Margin	-71.95%	-35.85%	-1.97%	1.31%
Net Margin	-115.16%	-116.04%	-4.10%	-1.84%
Balance Sheet and Debt Indicators:				
Total Assets	4,718	4,957	2,775	2,203
Cash and Short-Term Investments	813	519	426	224
Total Liabilities	5,186	6,111	2,770	2,098
Total Debt	2,119	2,590	1,358	776
Shareholders' Equity	-468	-1,154	5	105
Debt Ratio	109.92%	123.28%	99.82%	95.24%

Source: Authors' production (2022)

As of December 31, 2020, the value of cash and short-term investments of companies, except for Finnair, has increased dramatically when compared to the year 2019. This increase is documented in the studies by Almeida et al. (2004), Baum et al. (2008) and Bates et al. (2009) which indicate that in times of greater uncertainty, companies tend to seek to increase their liquidity levels and restrict their investment actions.

The exception of Finnair, on the other hand, can be explained by the fact that it is the company that least increased gross debt in percentage terms in 2020 (37.29%). In the same year, the company that increased the amount of gross debt the most was TAP (90.71%). However, and unsurprisingly, the company that increased debt the most in percentage terms in 2021 was Finnair, while TAP showed a decrease in the value of debt. This decrease is explained in the 2021 annual report and is reflected in the fact that the financing of the State Portuguese through the Restructuring Aid approved by the European Commission was converted into equity on 30 December 2021.

This work confirms Silva e Silva's (2022) study for the European reality, in the sense that the pandemic caused a decrease in sales, operating results and net results. On the other hand, this study confirms the increase in corporate liquidity as well as the increase in debt as a response to the strong pandemic impact.

The year 2021, despite being a year of recovery, with companies recording an increase in revenues, these are still far below the values recorded in the pre-pandemic period. These data indicate the hypothesis launched by Martins and Cró (2022) who pointed to a period of slow and prolonged recovery for the aviation sector.

Table 7 below shows the amount of State aid allocated to companies considering what the size was in the pre-pandemic period.

Analysing table 7, it is possible to denote that TAP received much more state support than its European counterparts, considering its size before the impact of the pandemic. This interpretation is valid based on revenues and assets. The support was more than double that given to Finnair, which was the next company in percentage terms. On the other hand, Lufthansa was in both metrics, the company that had the least state support. Thus, the results presented in this work validate the studies by Ding et al. (2021), Agrawal, (2021), Kokény et al. (2022) and Martins and Cró (2022) to the extent that larger, less indebted, and more profitable companies in the pre-crisis period showed a higher resilience to face the impact of the Covid-19 pandemic. Current news reports also seem to corroborate this theory. By November 2022, the German company had already returned all state aid.

Finally, and based on the studies by Babel (2014) and Pinto and Lucas (2022), the 2021 debt of companies will be analysed, considering their ability to settle it in the pre-pandemic period. According to the literature, this indicator serves as a proxy for the ability of companies to repay debt to their creditors, already in a normal scenario. Thus, table 8 shows the Net Debt to EBITDA of the companies, with the net debt, the amount recorded in the 2021 balance sheet and the EBITDA being the best among the period analyzed in a pre-pandemic scenario. It is important to note that EBITDA is a good indicator of the money that airlines make as a result of their operations, however this indicator does not take into account other expenses such as capex, interest and other similar expenses and the value of taxes. This form of analysis benefits TAP, as it was the only aviation company under analysis that presented a negative EBITDA in 2019.

Table 7. Proportion of state aid as a proportion of company size in 2019

Company	Proportion of State Aid to 2019 Revenue	Proportion of State Aid to 2019 Assets
Air France-KLM	25.75%	22.78%
Finnair	39.93%	31.90%
Lufthansa	24.71%	20.73%
TAP	97.42%	114.87%

Table 8. Debt repayment capacity of the companies

Company	Net Debt to EBITDA
Air France-KLM	2,55
Finnair	3,56
Lufthansa	2,01
TAP	31,58

Before analysing table 8, it is important to note that Babel (2014) identifies that companies with Net Debt to EBITDA values higher than 4 are highly indebted, and therefore run the serious risk of not being able to meet their debt service. In this sense, in table 8 it is possible to prove that it is almost considered absurd to compare TAP's indebtedness with that of other European airlines, since all the others have their debt under control. The results indicate that TAP needed 31 good years compared to its history to return all the debt contracted. In this way, and unlike the other airlines analysed, it is practically impossible for TAP to be able to meet its debt service without needing state aid again. It is important to emphasize that in this interpretation, no EBITDA value could be channeled to investment or other expenses that were previously mentioned that the indicator does not identify.

Another important aspect is that these data no longer consider part of the debt ceded by the State Portuguese, since these funds have already been channeled into the company's equity. To compare it to Lufthansa, the German company would be able to pay off all the debt with two good years' worth of EBITDA.

Thus, the results presented in this study are in line with the publication by Pinto and Lucas (2022) which indicates that there is no plausible scenario in which TAP's debt can be settled.

In fact, more recently, the company's CFO9 has already gone public stating that the State Portuguese will not recover the money injected into the company.

Pinto and Lucas (2022) indicate that in the current circumstances, the best that the government will Portuguese achieve is, at some point, to find another aviation company available to buy TAP. Private management will be able to manage it better and prevent it from needing more money in the future.

In fact, privatisation seems to be the government's current plan for the company, as the note 10 of October 2022 points out that "the integration of TAP into a large aviation group may even be the only way to ensure the viability of a strategic company for the country". The same note indicates that it has always been clear to the government that, in such a strongly globalised and competitive market, TAP would not be able to remain solvent in the medium term on its own. The integration of TAP into a group will create important synergies and bring the resilience to remain solvent in a sector that suffers from a lot of volatility.

CONCLUSION AND RECOMMENDATIONS

The aviation sector was one of those that suffered the most from the emergence of the Covid-19 pandemic. In this sense, the main objective of this study was to analyze the impact of the pandemic on the financial statements of companies at European level. To this end, a ranking was made so that the analysis was as homogeneous as possible. The final sample consisted of 4 companies, and the time horizon was between 2018 and 2021 and the methodology implemented was based on a method of comparative quantitative analysis.

The results indicate that the companies had a strong drop in revenues, and this was felt in the reduction of operating and net results. It was also possible to show that during the analyzed period, the companies favored liquidity, and thus clearly resorted to indebtedness.

The analysis also showed that State support differed when comparing its size with the size of companies. The analysis proved that the state support granted to TAP is undoubtedly much higher than that granted to all its counterparts.

The capacity of companies to cope with the current debt service was also analysed. Also in this indicator, TAP appears as an *outlier*, that is, unlike the other European companies analysed that have a framed level of liability, it is practically impossible for TAP to be able to meet the debt service without needing state aid again. In this sense, we agree with the current will of the government and with the publication of Pinto and Lucas (2022) who indicate that in the current situation, the best thing for the company and for Portuguese taxpayers would be to find another company in the aviation sector to acquire TAP, which would enhance it and thus free it from needing more money in the future.

It is confirmed that all companies received state support to respond to the impact of the pandemic, thus, this study tends to agree with the research of Fontanet-Pérez et al. (2022), as current business models do not adequately prepare aviation companies to face unexpected crises, essentially because of low profit margins.

Still, I corroborate with the studies by Ding et al. (2021), Agrawal, (2021), Kokény et al. (2022) and Martins and Cró (2022) and show that larger, more profitable, and less indebted companies proved to be more resilient in the face of the impact of the Covid-19 pandemic.

We also show that in 2021, despite an increase in revenues compared to 2020, this is still very insignificant, with the level of sales of companies at a much lower level compared to 2019.

REFERENCES

Abate, M., Christidis, P., & Purwanto, A. J. (2020). Government support to airlines in the aftermath of the COVID-19 pandemic. *Journal of Air Transport Management*, *89*, 101931. doi:10.1016/j.jairtraman.2020.101931 PMID:32952317

Agrawal, A. (2021). Sustainability of airlines in India with Covid-19: Challenges ahead and possible wayouts. *Journal of Revenue and Pricing Management*, *20*(4), 457–472. doi:10.1057/s41272-020-00257-z

Albers, S., & Rundshagen, V. (2020). European airlines' strategic responses to the COVID-19 pandemic (January-May, 2020). *Journal of Air Transport Management*, *87*, 101863. doi:10.1016/j.jairtraman.2020.101863 PMID:32834690

Alfaro, L., Chari, A., Greenland, A. N., & Schott, P. K. (2020). *Aggregate and firm-level stock returns during pandemics, in real time (No. w26950)*. National Bureau of Economic Research. doi:10.3386/w26950

Almeida, H., Campello, M., & Weisbach, M. S. (2004). The cash flow sensitivity of cash. *The Journal of Finance*, *59*(4), 1777–1804. doi:10.1111/j.1540-6261.2004.00679.x

Altig, D., Baker, S., Barrero, J. M., Bloom, N., Bunn, P., Chen, S., & Thwaites, G. (2020). Economic uncertainty before and during the COVID-19 pandemic. *Journal of Public Economics*, *191*, 104274. doi:10.1016/j.jpubeco.2020.104274 PMID:32921841

Amankwah-Amoah, J., Khan, Z., & Osabutey, E. L. (2021). COVID-19 and business renewal: Lessons and insights from the global airline industry. *International Business Review*, *30*(3), 101802. doi:10.1016/j.ibusrev.2021.101802 PMID:36568574

Bae, S. Y., & Chang, P. J. (2021). The effect of coronavirus disease-19 (COVID-19) risk perception on behavioural intention towards 'untact'tourism in South Korea during the first wave of the pandemic (March 2020). *Current Issues in Tourism*, *24*(7), 1017–1035. doi:10.1080/13683500.2020.1798895

Baker, S. R., Bloom, N., Davis, S. J., Kost, K., Sammon, M., & Viratyosin, T. (2020). The unprecedented stock market reaction to COVID-19. *Review of Asset Pricing Studies*, *10*(4), 742–758. doi:10.1093/rapstu/raaa008

Bates, T. W., Kahle, K. M., & Stulz, R. M. (2009). Why do US firms hold so much more cash than they used to? *The Journal of Finance*, *64*(5), 1985–2021. doi:10.1111/j.1540-6261.2009.01492.x

Baum, C. F., Caglayan, M., Stephan, A., & Talavera, O. (2008). Uncertainty determinants of corporate liquidity. *Economic Modelling*, *25*(5), 833–849. doi:10.1016/j.econmod.2007.11.006

Bebel, A. (2014). *Low Versus High Leverage*. LVH.

Belobaba, P. P. (2011). Did LCCs save airline revenue management? *Journal of Revenue and Pricing Management*, *10*(1), 19–22. doi:10.1057/rpm.2010.45

Chung, L. H. (2015). Impact of pandemic control over airport economics: Reconciling public health with airport business through a streamlined approach in pandemic control. *Journal of Air Transport Management*, *44*, 42–53. doi:10.1016/j.jairtraman.2015.02.003 PMID:32572319

Costa, L., Ribeiro, A., & Machado, C. (2021). Determinants of stock market price: Empirical evidence for the PSI 20. *Ge-Magazine*, (22), 41–53.

Costa, L. M. (2022). Determinants of Annual Abnormal Yields of Stocks belonging to the Euro stoxx 50 Index. *European Journal of Applied Business and Management*, *8*(2).

Cunha, J. M. V. (2015). *Evaluating the privatization of the portuguese national airline-tap* [Doctoral dissertation].

Deveci, M., Çiftçi, M. E., Akyurt, İ. Z., & Gonzalez, E. D. S. (2022). Impact of COVID-19 pandemic on the Turkish civil aviation industry. *Sustainable Operations and Computers*, *3*, 93–102. doi:10.1016/j.susoc.2021.11.002

Ding, W., Levine, R., Lin, C., & Xie, W. (2021). Corporate immunity to the COVID-19 pandemic. *Journal of Financial Economics*, *141*(2), 802–830. doi:10.1016/j.jfineco.2021.03.005 PMID:34580557

Doganis, R. (2009). *Flying off course: airline economics and marketing*. Routledge. doi:10.4324/9780203863992

Dube, K., & Nhamo, G. (2020). Major global aircraft manufacturers and emerging responses to the SDGs agenda. In *Scaling up SDGs Implementation* (pp. 99–113). Springer. doi:10.1007/978-3-030-33216-7_7

Dube, K., Nhamo, G., & Chikodzi, D. (2021). COVID-19 pandemic and prospects for recovery of the global aviation industry. *Journal of Air Transport Management, 92*, 102022. doi:10.1016/j.jairtraman.2021.102022 PMID:36567961

Fernandes, C., Peguinho, C., Vieira, E., & Neiva, J. (2019). *Financial Analysis: Theory and Practice – Application within the scope of the CNS*. Syllabus Editions.

Fetzer, T., Hensel, L., Hermle, J., & Roth, C. (2021). Coronavirus perceptions and economic anxiety. *The Review of Economics and Statistics, 103*(5), 968–978. doi:10.1162/rest_a_00946

Florido-Benítez, L. (2021). The effects of COVID-19 on Andalusian tourism and aviation sector. *Tourism Review, 76*(4), 829–857. doi:10.1108/TR-12-2020-0574

Fontanet-Pérez, P., Vázquez, X. H., & Carou, D. (2022). The impact of the COVID-19 crisis on the US airline market: Are current business models equipped for upcoming changes in the air transport sector? *Case Studies on Transport Policy, 10*(1), 647–656. doi:10.1016/j.cstp.2022.01.025 PMID:36157268

González, V. M. (2013). Leverage and corporate performance: International evidence. *International Review of Economics & Finance, 25*, 169–184. doi:10.1016/j.iref.2012.07.005

Gossling, S. (2020). Risks, resilience, and pathways to sustainable aviation: A COVID-19 perspective. *Journal of Air Transport Management, 89*, 101933. doi:10.1016/j.jairtraman.2020.101933 PMID:32952322

He, P., Sun, Y., Zhang, Y., & Li, T. (2020). COVID–19's impact on stock prices across different sectors—An event study based on the Chinese stock market. *Emerging Markets Finance & Trade, 56*(10), 2198–2212. doi:10.1080/1540496X.2020.1785865

Henkes, J. A. (2021). Civil aviation in times of pandemic and post-pandemic: A punctual analysis. *Brazilian Journal of Civil Aviation & Aeronautical Sciences, 1*(5), 1–3.

Heyden, K. J., & Heyden, T. (2021). Market reactions to the arrival and containment of COVID-19: An event study. *Finance Research Letters, 38*, 101745. doi:10.1016/j.frl.2020.101745 PMID:32895606

Kiraci, K., Tanriverdi, G., & Akan, E. (2022). Analysis of Factors Affecting the Sustainable Success of Airlines During the COVID-19 Pandemic. *Transportation Research Record: Journal of the Transportation Research Board*, 03611981221104462.

Kokény, L., Kenesei, Z., & Neszveda, G. (2022). Impact of COVID-19 on different business models of European airlines. *Current Issues in Tourism, 25*(3), 458–474. doi:10.1080/13683500.2021.1960284

Kramer, A., Friesen, M., & Shelton, T. (2018). Are airline passengers ready for personalized dynamic pricing? A study of German consumers. *Journal of Revenue and Pricing Management, 17*(2), 115–120. doi:10.1057/s41272-017-0122-0

Lee, J. (2019). Effects of operational performance on financial performance. *Management Science Letters, 9*(1), 25–32. doi:10.5267/j.msl.2018.11.003

Mahtani, U. S., & Garg, C. P. (2018). An analysis of key factors of financial distress in airline companies in India using fuzzy AHP framework. *Transportation Research Part A, Policy and Practice, 117,* 87–102. doi:10.1016/j.tra.2018.08.016

Maneenop, S., & Kotcharin, S. (2020). The impacts of COVID-19 on the global airline industry: An event study approach. *Journal of Air Transport Management, 89,* 101920. doi:10.1016/j.jairtraman.2020.101920 PMID:32874021

Martins, A. M., & Cró, S. (2022). Airline stock markets reaction to the COVID-19 outbreak and vaccines: An event study. *Journal of Air Transport Management, 105,* 102281. doi:10.1016/j.jairtraman.2022.102281 PMID:36034526

Merkert, R., & Swidan, H. (2019). Flying with (out) a safety net: Financial hedging in the airline industry. *Transportation Research Part E, Logistics and Transportation Review, 127,* 206–219. doi:10.1016/j.tre.2019.05.012

Michaels, L., & Fletcher, S. (2009). Competing in an LCC world. *Journal of Revenue and Pricing Management, 8*(5), 410–423. doi:10.1057/rpm.2009.7

Muchanga, A. P. (2014). *The impact of air transport liberalisation on the Portuguese market: low costs vs scheduled airlines: tap, easyjet and ryanair* [Doctoral dissertation].

O'Connell, J. F. (2018). The Routledge Companion to Air Transport Management. N. Halpern & A. Graham, (Eds.), The Routledge Companion to Air Transport Management. New York: Routledge.

Pagano, M., Wagner, C., & Zechner, J. (2020). *Disaster resilience and asset prices.* arXiv preprint arXiv:2005.08929.

Pereira, D., & de Mello, J. C. C. S. (2021). Efficiency evaluation of Brazilian airlines operations considering the Covid-19 outbreak. *Journal of Air Transport Management, 91,* 101976.

Ramelli, S., & Wagner, A. F. (2020). Feverish stock price reactions to COVID-19. *The Review of Corporate Finance Studies, 9*(3), 622–655. doi:10.1093/rcfs/cfaa012

Ribeiro, A., & Quesado, P. (2017). Explanatory Factors of Abnormal Annual Stock Returns. *European Journal of Applied Business and Management, 2017*(Special Issue), 109–126.

Riwo-Abudho, M., Njanja, L. W., & Ochieng, I. (2013). *Key success factors in airlines: Overcoming the challenges.*

Sadi, M. A., & Henderson, J. C. (2000). The Asian economic crisis and the aviation industry: Impacts and response strategies. *Transport Reviews, 20*(3), 347–367. doi:10.1080/014416400412841

Saranga, H., & Nagpal, R. (2016). Drivers of operational efficiency and its impact on market performance in the Indian Airline industry. *Journal of Air Transport Management, 53,* 165–176. doi:10.1016/j.jairtraman.2016.03.001

Silva, R. C., & da Silva, A. Q. (2022). Tourism, the aviation sector and the effects of Covid-19 A comparative study on airlines in Brazil: Azul, GOL and TAM. *Hermes Scientific Journal,* (31), 57–75. doi:10.21710/rch.v31i0.629

Singh, A. K. (2016). Competitive service quality benchmarking in airline industry using AHP. *Benchmarking*, *23*(4), 768–791. doi:10.1108/BIJ-05-2013-0061

Suau-Sanchez, P., Voltes-Dorta, A., & Cagueró-Escofet, N. (2020). An early assessment of the impact of COVID-19 on air transport: Just another crisis or the end of aviation as we know it? *Journal of Transport Geography*, *86*, 102749. doi:10.1016/j.jtrangeo.2020.102749 PMID:32834670

Tretheway, M. W., & Markhvida, K. (2014). The aviation value chain: Economic returns and policy issues. *Journal of Air Transport Management*, *41*, 3–16. doi:10.1016/j.jairtraman.2014.06.011

Xiong, H., Wu, Z., Hou, F., & Zhang, J. (2020). Which firm-specific characteristics affect the market reaction of Chinese listed companies to the COVID-19 pandemic? *Emerging Markets Finance & Trade*, *56*(10), 2231–2242. doi:10.1080/1540496X.2020.1787151

Yang, H. (2007). Airlines' futures. *Journal of Revenue and Pricing Management*, *6*(4), 309–311. doi:10.1057/palgrave.rpm.5160105

Chapter 5
COVID-19 Disruption on Tourism-Aviation in Madeira

Rui Castro Quadros
https://orcid.org/0000-0003-0685-259X
Instituto Superior de Educação e Ciências, Portugal

Ana Barqueira
Instituto Superior de Educação e Ciências, Portugal

Jorge Abrantes
https://orcid.org/0000-0003-4692-907X
Estoril Higher Institute for Tourism and Hotel Studies, Portugal & Universidade Aberta, Portugal

ABSTRACT

Madeira airport is the main gateway responsible for the entry of passengers into the Autonomous Region of Madeira (ARM). Is tourism in ARM heavily dependent on Air Transport? The specific objective is to establish, through Pearson's correlation analysis, the observed behavior of some indicators (in 2919 and 2020) on tourist activity and its relationship with air traffic. Several tourist indicators and their influence on tourism were studied, as well as the evidence that air transport is central to the tourist development of Madeira Island. The information collected and the correlations results shows a crucial importance of air transportation for the tourism activity in ARM. The existence of flights to the island means more capacity to generate traffic, more tourists, more occupation of hotels and greater economic development.

INTRODUCTION

The Autonomous Region of Madeira (ARM) is an archipelago of volcanic origin, located in the North Atlantic, in a region known as Macaronesia, about 450 kilometres north of the Canary Islands and 500 kilometres west of Morocco and about 1,000 kilometres from Mainland Portugal (Lisbon). The region includes two islands, Madeira, and Porto Santo, and two uninhabited groups, the Desertas and the Selvagens. Funchal, the regional capital, is located on Madeira Island (Visit Portugal, no date). The ARM

DOI: 10.4018/979-8-3693-0908-7.ch005

is made up of 11 municipalities and 54 parishes (10 municipalities and 53 parishes are located on the island of Madeira and the rest on the island of Porto Santo) (Madeira.best, 2021).

The resident population is 254.157 inhabitants in Madeira, representing 2.5% of the country's resident population. In terms of tourist accommodation Madeira has 1,194 units, a share of 20.5% of the total accommodation in the country. Regarding the number of guests, Madeira recorded 1,617,208 guests in 2019, (a weight of 6.8% from a total of 23,953,765 in mainland Portugal) (FFMS, 2019).

Madeira's Cristiano Ronaldo Airport, also known as Funchal or Santa Cruz Airport, opened on July 18th, 1964. It is one of the most important in Portugal and serves the island of Madeira but also operates domestic and international destinations, mainly within Europe. TAP Air Portugal is the airline that most serves Madeira airport with seven daily flights from Lisbon and two daily flights from Porto (Aeroportodamadeira.pt, 2022).

According to ANA – Aeroportos de Portugal, airport authority that manages all main airports in Mainland Portugal, Madeira and Azores, the effects of the COVID-19 pandemic in 2020, brought drastic reductions in the number of passengers in Madeira airport with a drop of 65.2% against Lisbon with a decrease of 70.3%. In the same period, the movement of aircraft at Madeira airport saw its capacity reduced by 52.3% and Lisbon by 60.1%. In the network of all ANA airports the number of passengers decreased by 69.6% and the number of movements in relation to 2019 fell by 57.5% (ANA, 2021, p. 12).

The COVID-19 pandemic has seriously affected the aviation industry, with air traffic falling by more than two thirds compared to 2019 levels. The prolonged drop in air traffic will undoubtedly have consequences for the years to come, threatening economic viability countries and companies, employment and working conditions (Delli, 2021). The number of air passengers carried dropped -60.2% in 2020 to 1,808 million (4,543million in 2019), with global revenue down -54.4%. Losses reached record values in 2020 (-137.7 billion of USD), after net profits in 2019 in the order of 26.4 billion. Regarding tourism, the behaviour was identical, with a -72.3% drop in international tourist arrivals (405 million in 2020 versus 1,466 in 2019), with revenues dropping by -63.2% in the same period (IATA, 2022; UNWTO, 2022).

Despite tourism having had a negative impact on a global level, Madeira Region was no exception. So the main question of investigation is to understand: Is tourism in ARM also heavily dependent on air transportation?

The general objective is to evaluate the effects that the reduction in traffic had on Madeira's tourism during the year of 2020. The specific objective is to establish, using Pearson's correlation analysis, the observed behaviour (2019/2020) of the following indicators of tourist activity in ARM: a) Air traffic; b) Total number of guests; c) Number of establishments in operation; d) Accommodation capacity; e) Net occupancy rate (bed); f) Average stay; g) Number of overnight stays; h) Personnel costs; i) Total revenue from tourist accommodation; j) Number of guests arriving; k) RevPAR (Revenue per Available Room).

The island regions, for being geographically more remote, very dependent on air and sea transport, are always good reasons to understand about their resilience, as it is the case of the ARM in the European space. Since it is a region with political independence (Autonomous Region), there is also the perception of understanding how the responses were caused and especially the impacts in the tourism sector. The contribution of the tourism sector to the regional GDP represents between 25% and 30% of RAM's GDP and accounts for about 12% to 15% of the jobs created in the region (ARDITI, 2015).

As of February 2020, a rapid spread of the virus appeared at European level, with a special incidence in France and Italy. Due to the growing number of positive cases in the world, on March 11, 2020, the World Health Organization (WHO) declared a pandemic alert for the first time since 2009 (WHO, 2020). In Portugal, the first case was registered on 2nd March 2020 with the first state of emergency decreed on

March, 18th, leading to mandatory confinement and restrictions on circulation on public roads, closing borders, restricting airspace, among other measures (DN, 2020).

The limitations imposed at borders and mainly in the transport sector, especially in commercial aviation, had severe consequences in tourism and transports. Globally, tourism activity in Portugal decreased significantly in terms of overnight stays (-74.9% than in 2019) as well as at airports (-69.9% compared to 2019). In the same period, Madeira recorded -66.2% in overnight stays and -65.2% in terms of passengers. The Azores and Madeira airports registered the smallest drops, due to their traffic profile, eminently domestic (a segment that presented a loss of operations less significant) (Abrantes & Quadros, 2022).

According to "Islands and COVID-19: Key messages from a global survey" (Sindico, Sajeva, Sharman, Berlouis, & Ellsmoor, 2020), overall islands performed very well, and their inhabitants were kept safe and away from the worst consequences of the pandemic. The pandemic has revealed the fragility of tourism, food security, health and digital infrastructure. United Nations (2021) estimated that COVID-19 caused a drop of 4.7% in GDP (Gross Domestic Product) of SIDS (Small Island Developing States) in 2020. In the same way, the European Parliament (2021), regarding the islands and ultra-peripheral territories in the European Union (belonging to 13 Member States, including Portugal) considered that the pandemic had a negative impact on island communities in terms of health crisis, job losses, food security, mobility, travel, and shipments.

Portugal has become one of the most competitive tourist destinations in the world and in 2019 registered a sustained growth in tourist activity (Santos and Moreira, 2021). The results on tourist accommodation reveal that after the first hit of the pandemic, there was a small recovery in some indicators of tourist activity, namely in the Algarve and Madeira, where tourism is fundamental, as already characterized above.

LITERATURE REVIEW

The Vital Link Between Air Transport and Tourism in Island Paradises

Air connectivity serves as a lifeline for the economic vitality of small island nations, offering them a crucial gateway to the global stage. For these remote and isolated communities, air travel isn't just a convenience; it's a lifeline for essential services and connections to the wider world (ATAG, 2020). In regions like the Caribbean, air transport has emerged as the primary mode for both domestic and international travel, with tourism serving as the cornerstone of the region's economy (CDB, 2018). The significance of air connectivity goes far beyond merely moving people; it is a driver of economic growth, enabling trade, tourism, investments, and various other economic activities (IATA, 2021a). As articulated by ATAG (2020, p. 21), "For small island states, the economic contributions from international tourists are immeasurable." In Small Island States, air transport sustains two million jobs, constituting 8.7% of total employment, and contributes a substantial $34.7 billion USD, equivalent to 10.6% of their GDP. Projections for 2038 are even more promising, with air transport and tourism expected to generate 2.6 million jobs (a 31% increase from 2018) and a staggering GDP contribution of $69 billion USD (a 100% increase) (ATAG, 2020).

The progressive liberalization of air transport services, a journey that began in 1978 with the Airline Deregulation Act in the United States, has revolutionized the movement of passengers and goods between countries. This evolution has made air travel more accessible and affordable, fostering competition among airlines, the emergence of low-cost carriers, route expansions, reduced airfares, and increased passenger volumes (CDB, 2018; OECD, 2018). Improved air connectivity results in more frequent, direct flights, ultimately reducing travel times and transportation costs (Crouch, 1994). As emphasized by IATA (2021a, p. 4), "Aviation is indispensable for tourism, a major engine of economic growth, particularly in many emerging economies," and for islands heavily reliant on tourism. According to the report, "the top 20 most connected countries in the world, weighted by GDP, are small states, almost all islands, and highly dependent on inbound tourism" (p. 46). The Azores provide a compelling example of how air transport is pivotal for tourism development and tourist flows, as seen when charter flights from Scandinavia to São Miguel began in 2000. In that year, the number of Swedish tourists visiting the Azores surged from 5,975 to 173,600, showcasing the profound impact of improved air connectivity (Abrantes, 2012).

Fageda, Suárez-Alemán, Serebrisky, and Fioravanti (2018) define connectivity as the ability of a network to transport passengers from one point to another with minimal connections and without an increase in fares. Ram, Reeves, and James (2018) argue that connectivity hinges on factors like the availability and cost of air travel, influenced by regulatory frameworks (where liberalization is essential), taxation (directly impacting costs), and the adequacy and utilization of infrastructure (inefficiency leading to higher airline overhead and fixed costs).

The International Civil Aviation Organization (ICAO, 2015) has outlined ten key criteria to gauge the connectivity index based on how effectively air carriers utilize connectivity opportunities. Similarly, the IATA Connectivity Index measures access between an airport, region, or country and the global economy (IATA, 2021). Many island territories exhibit significantly high aviation intensity, calculated as the volume of air passenger journeys adjusted for the country's population size. This is primarily due to the insular nature of these regions, where air transport often stands as the primary, if not the only, mode of transportation (CDB, 2018).

Fageda et al. (2018) have scrutinized air connectivity in remote areas, including islands, and have concluded that low demand alone may not incentivize airlines to operate flights to these locations. Hence, government policies become essential to ensure air connectivity, potentially including resident discounts and determining service levels, fares, and subsidies, although these measures can introduce competition distortions. Air transport has played an instrumental role in fostering tourism development and air connectivity in numerous island territories, with several examples illustrating the robust relationship between the two. Boopen, Raja Vinesh, Viraiyan, and Robin (2019) assessed the impact of air liberalization on tourism development in Mauritius between 1970 and 2015, finding a positive contribution, with factors like price sensitivity, infrastructure, and the island's development level also playing crucial roles in stimulating demand.

Ahyudanari (2021) evaluated connectivity in Indonesian airports to boost traffic to the islands. The decision to introduce scheduled flights to Rote Island, rather than charter flights, significantly boosted tourist numbers. Graham and Dennis (2010) examined the impacts of low-cost carrier operations in Malta, while Chung and Whang (2011) focused on Korean island tourism, and Papatheodorou & Lei (2006) on Great Britain. Similarly, Koo, Wu, and Dwyer (2009) assessed the impacts and enhancements of air travel in Australia, and Pearce (1999) conducted a study in New Zealand.

Concerning the Azores, Abrantes (2017), Vieira, Câmara, Silva, and Santos (2019), and Zsembera (2017) have all reached the same conclusion: liberalization and the introduction of low-cost operations have expanded choices for visitors and significantly increased tourist arrivals in the archipelago. These examples underscore the critical role of air transport in driving tourism development, especially in island territories. The greater the diversity of air transport alternatives, encompassing various business models, connectivity options, and infrastructure improvements, the more profound the impact on tourism development in these islands.

Profound Global Impact of COVID-19 on Tourism, Air Travel, and Airports: An Overview

The global tourism industry was flourishing until the unprecedented COVID-19 pandemic struck in the 21st century (Uğur & Akbıyık, 2020). Unlike previous outbreaks like SARS, COVID-19 spread rapidly and was declared a pandemic by the World Health Organization (WHO) in January 2020 (Salman, Kamerkar, Jaafar, & Mohamad, 2022).

In response to the crisis, the World Tourism Organization (UNWTO) reported that all global destinations had imposed restrictions by April 2020. These included border closures in 45% of places and the suspension of international flights in 30% (UNWTO, 2020). Europe and the Americas closed borders to international tourism at rates of 83% and 80%, respectively. Asia, the Middle East, and Africa also saw significant closures (UNWTO, 2020).

COVID-19's impact on tourism was profound, causing trip cancellations and a slow return of travel confidence even after the crisis (Uğur & Akbıyık, 2020). Research in 2020 focused on three main themes: challenges to the tourism industry, resilience, and global economic transformation (Sharma, Thomas, & Paul, 2021).

In 2020, international tourist arrivals dropped by 72.8% compared to 2019, worsening to 82.7% in Q1 2021 (UNWTO, 2021a). This resulted in just 398 million arrivals in 2020, down from 1,466 million in 2019, endangering 100 to 120 million tourism jobs (UNWTO, 2021b). Europe, the Americas, and Asia-Pacific witnessed significant declines (UNWTO, 2021a).

The commercial aviation sector mirrored tourism's downturn, with a 61.1% decrease in passengers in 2020 (IATA, 2021b). Airports also suffered, with a 45.7% drop in passenger traffic at the top 10 airports and a 64.6% decline globally (ACI, 2021a, ACI, 2021b).

In Europe, Eurocontrol reported a 55% decrease in traffic movements in 2020 compared to 2019. Passenger traffic globally decreased by 1.7 billion passengers, affecting low-cost and traditional carriers most (Eurocontrol, 2021).

In summary, COVID-19 had a far-reaching and mostly negative impact on global tourism, commercial aviation, and airports due to worldwide mobility restrictions. The economic repercussions were substantial, with the travel and tourism industry's contribution to global GDP dropping from 10.4% in 2019 to 5.5% in 2020. Moreover, 62 million jobs, particularly in SMEs, were lost. A swift recovery would require coordinated efforts, including clear protocols and rules to restore confidence and international travel (WTTC, 2021).

Impacts of COVID-19 on Island Territories: Tourism-Dependent Economies

The COVID-19 pandemic has had profound repercussions on island territories, especially Small Island Developing States (SIDS) within the United Nations framework, which rely heavily on tourism as a significant contributor to their GDP (United Nations, 2021). With the onset of COVID-19, tourism in these regions came to a standstill due to border closures and the cessation of tourism-related activities such as air travel and cruise ship visits, resulting in a substantial 4.7% decline in GDP in 2020 (United Nations, 2021).

Islands face distinctive challenges due to their geographical isolation, limited landmass, small populations, and limited economic opportunities (Briguglio, 1995). The impact of the pandemic on these islands extends beyond the usual focus on airport operations.

A notable report titled "Islands and Covid-19: A Global Survey" examined 83 islands from 52 countries, including regions like the Azores and the Autonomous Region of Madeira (RAM). Many islands implemented strict mobility measures, often preceding general lockdowns, and achieved relatively positive outcomes in pandemic control compared to mainland territories (Sindico et al., 2020).

The COVID-19 crisis has profoundly affected islands such as Vanuatu in the South Pacific and the Samoa archipelago, which heavily rely on tourism. These islands are now grappling with complex questions concerning the duration, self-sufficiency, diversification, sustainability, and the future of their tourism industries (Connell & Taulealo, 2021).

In Penang Island, Malaysia, renowned as a global tourist destination, the pandemic abruptly halted tourism. In 2019, Penang welcomed 2,920,160 tourists, of which 1,452,096 were international visitors. However, local lockdowns led to a cessation of tourist activities, affecting various sectors like air travel, tours, events, cruises, hotels, and restaurants (Salman et al., 2022).

The Maldives Islands, located in the Indian Ocean, also experienced a severe blow to their tourist industry (Gu et al., 2021). After witnessing a 14.4% increase in tourist arrivals in January 2020, tourist numbers plummeted, resulting in a 67.4% drop compared to 2019 and a staggering 98.7% decline in July 2020 compared to the previous year (Ministry of Tourism, 2021).

Similarly, Fernando de Noronha in Brazil saw its tourism revenues decrease by 35% in the first half of 2020, demonstrating a delayed response from the government in adopting mitigation measures (Paixão, Cordeiro, & Leite, 2021).

In Europe, the impact of COVID-19 on islands is consistent with the challenges faced by islands and ultra-peripheral territories in the European Union. These regions, including the Balearic Islands and the Canary Islands in Spain, faced significant economic losses due to their heavy reliance on tourism (European Parliament, 2021). Tourism accounted for 42.1% of the GDP in the Balearic Islands and 30.5% in the Canary Islands in 2017, making them particularly vulnerable (Newtral, 2020). The pandemic caused an 87.6% reduction in visitors to the Balearic Islands and a 71.5% decline in the Canary Islands in 2020 (Frontur, 2021).

Malta, which relies on tourism for over 27% of its economy, saw an 80% reduction in tourist inflows in 2020. To incentivize tourism and stimulate the economy, the Maltese government offered a 200 euro incentive for visitors staying on the islands for three or more days (Reuters, 2021).

Croatia, another prominent European tourist destination, witnessed a significant downturn in its tourism-dependent economy. The country's tourism sector, contributing nearly 40% of export earnings and 11% of GDP, suffered due to the pandemic, resulting in a substantial decline in GDP (Payne, Gil-Alana, & Mervar, 2021).

Greece, known for its tourism industry, also felt the impact of the pandemic, with losses estimated at 9-14% of GDP in 2020. The continued pressure on economic resources due to the pandemic's effect on tourism remains a significant concern (Papanikos, 2020).

These various examples highlight the dire consequences of COVID-19 on island territories and their heavy dependence on the tourism sector. The economic, social, and sustainability challenges faced by these islands underscore the need for tailored recovery strategies and diversification of their economies.

The Devastating Impact of COVID-19 on Tourism and Airports in Portugal

The COVID-19 outbreak hit Portugal hard, with its first reported case in March 2020. Even before that, the country had started implementing various restrictions, including suspending in-person education, limiting cruise travel, promoting teleworking, and halting air travel, particularly to and from Italy and Spain. A state of emergency was declared on March 18, 2020, which led to strict lockdowns and stringent public movement restrictions, with a total of 15 states of emergency declared and enforced for 173 consecutive days (Bizarro, 2021).

As in many other countries, COVID-19 had a devastating impact on Portugal's tourism industry, largely due to border closures and transportation restrictions, particularly in the commercial aviation sector. Data from Turismo de Portugal (2021) showed significant declines in key tourism indicators for 2020. The number of tourists dropped by 61.3%, falling from 16.6 million to 10.5 million, with the sharpest decline seen among foreign tourists, who plummeted by 75.7%. Overnight stays also saw a substantial decrease, especially in the international market, which dropped by 74.9%, from 36.7 million to 12.3 million. Overall, there was a 63% decrease in overnight stays. Preliminary figures for 2021 indicate some recovery, with 14.5 million guests and 37.5 million overnight stays, marking increases of 39.4% and 45.2% respectively compared to 2020. However, when compared to the same period in 2019, there were still significant declines of 46.4% in guests and 46.6% in overnight stays (INE, 2022).

The Azores Autonomous Region experienced the most substantial declines in the international market, with a decrease of 84.3% in guests and 83.7% in overnight stays, resulting in a loss of 1,496.6 thousand overnight stays. A similar situation unfolded in the Autonomous Region of Madeira (RAM), where overnight stays decreased by 66.2% compared to 2019. Although 2021 saw substantial growth in guests and overnight stays from foreign tourists (with increases of 166.4% and 154.8% respectively), these figures remained well below those recorded in 2019 (down by 41.8% and 41.5% in guests and overnight stays, respectively). In Madeira, the pattern was similar, with an 81.4% increase in overnight stays from foreign tourists in 2021, but still 47.3% below the 2019 levels (DREM, 2022; 2021; SREA, 2022a; 2021a, 2020a).

Portugal's airports, managed by ANA, also experienced a sharp decline in traffic, in line with the global trend seen at most European and worldwide airports. In 2020, nearly 18 million passengers passed through the ten ANA network airports, marking a staggering annual decrease of 69.6% compared to 2019, equivalent to 41.2 million fewer passengers. Passenger traffic at these airports dropped to levels last seen in 1998, and the number of movements recorded a 57.5% decline (246.4 thousand fewer movements compared to 2019). In 2021, Portuguese airports handled 24.8 million passengers, reflecting a 39% increase over 2020 but still remaining 58% lower than the 2019 figures (ANA, 2021; Expresso, 2022).

MATERIALS AND METHODS

The study aims to understand the impacts (variables dependents) suffered by COVID-19, through data collected from various sources (independent variables) in selected indicators of tourist activity in ARM, taking into consideration the contextualization, relevance and interconnection between air transport and tourism as mentioned before.

The approach of this study is exploratory, interpretative, and quantitative since the investigation performed and presented was obtained through observation and interpretation of statistical information.

The aggregation and interconnection and the establishment of correlations between the variables will help to better understand the relationships between air transport and tourism.

A quantitative methodology was applied due to its accuracy and greater stability in the results of an investigation (Caniato, Kalchschmidt, & Ronchi, 2011).

The data for this investigation about air transportation and tourism were obtained from the annual reports of ANA - Aeroportos de Portugal (ANA, 2021), the Portuguese National Institute of Statistics (INE, 2022), Pordata (2021) and from the Regional Directorate of Statistics of Madeira (DREM, 2021). The collected data were validated and imported into SPSS software (version 27) to perform statistical analysis. Descriptive Statistical methods were used to obtain the results presented, such as calculating frequencies, percentages, location measures, correlation analysis (Pearson's) and the creation of tables and graphs for the various variables under study. On the other hand, methods for estimating parameters such as hypothesis tests were also used. In particular, the Shapiro-Wilk test to verify the normality of the samples under study and the t-student test was used to compare the mean values of two independent samples, with the computation of the p-value being used as the decision criterion.

RESULTS

This section intends to analyse the data processed by SPSS and which should cover the research objectives.

Data Results

As Madeira has an Autonomous status, the regional government was able to make its own decisions regarding restriction of COVID-19. The regional governor of Madeira has made available PCR tests released to citizens who intend to travel or disembark at Madeira airports to stimulate tourism.

On the 13th of March, there was an abrupt drop in traffic in Portugal, according to Eurocontrol Daily Traffic Variation - States (Eurocontrol, 2020), which impacted also the Autonomous Region of Madeira and tourism infrastructures, mainly hotel sector.

RevPAR (Revenue per Available Room) is an extremely relevant key performance indicator (KPI) to hotels. It is used to assess a hotel's ability to fill its available rooms at an average rate. If RevPAR increases, it means that the average rate of the room or the occupancy rate is increasing (Guillot, 2018). In the same way, the average daily rate (ADR) is a metric used in the hospitality industry to report the average revenue earned by an occupied room on a given day.

According to Table 1, RevPAR reduced to 52% in the first hit of the pandemic. Between April and July, the reduction remained above 85%, except for the month of July (78.9%). In August, a typical month of the tourism and hotels high season, the RevPAR reduction was smaller, however, reaching almost 62%. The year of 2020 closes with a drop of 48% registered in December.

Regarding the traffic registered at Funchal airport (Figure 1) for the years 2019 and 2020, international passengers registered a decrease of almost 70% while domestic traffic reduced to 62%. Clearly, these drastic reductions in passengers justify the drop in average revenue from tourist accommodation.

Regarding the national network of airports and by type of traffic (Table 2), the total number of passengers in 2020 compared to 2019 decreased globally by 69% with Funchal recording a drop of 65% (Lisbon the main Portuguese airport had a break of around 70%). Regarding international traffic, the reduction was more severe in Funchal (-68%) than in Lisbon (-66%) or relative to the airport network

Table 1. Revenue per available room (RevPAR) in tourist accommodation

Month	RevPar 2019	RevPar 2020	Variation (2019/2020)
JAN	33.58		31.56 -6.0%
FEB	36.10		36.29 0.5%
MAR	42.84		20.50 -52.2%
APR	45.76		6.57 -85.6%
MAY	49.57		6.90 -86.1%
JUN	49.57		7.15 -85.6%
JUL	51.51		10.85 -78.9%
AUG	59.90		23.06 -61.5%
SEP	51.87		22.83 -56.0%
OCT	41.75		22.18 -46.9%
NOV	32.40		12.04 -62.8%
DEC	34.34		17.87 -48.0%
Accumulated JAN/DEC	**44.33**		**22.60 -49.0%**

Corresponds to all tourist accommodation establishments except local accommodation with a capacity of less than 10 beds.
Source: Regional Directorate of Statistics of Madeira

Figure 1. Funchal Airport commercial traffic, 2019 – 2020

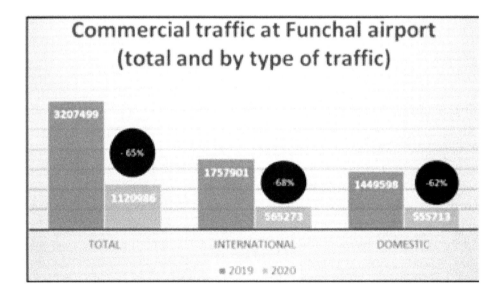

(-63%). In contrast, Funchal has a reduction of -62% in domestic traffic, compared with a sharper decline in Lisbon (-67%) and in the airport network (-65%). The restrictions of international mobility with several borders closed and the proximity of Madeira explained this behaviour.

Table 2. Commercial air traffic: Portugal´s airport and airfield network (2019-2020)

Passengers 2019	Passengers 2020	Variation (2019/2020)		
Total	Total Total			
Total Lisbon Funchal	Total Lisbon Funchal Total Lisbon Funchal			
60 114 157 31 184 594 3 207 499	18 392 550 9 267 968 1 120 986 -69% -70% -65%			
International		International International		
Total Lisbon Funchal	Total	Lisbon Funchal Total Lisbon Funchal		
49 533 820 27 578 655 1 757 901	14637 092	8 090 742 565 273 -70% -71% -68%		
Domestic		Domestic Domestic		
Total Lisbon Funchal	Total	Lisbon Funchal Total Lisbon Funchal		
10 580 337 3 605 939 1 449 598	3755 458	1 177 226 555 713 -65% -67% -62%		

Figure 2 considers the international and domestic passengers on scheduled flights, as analysed previously but also the non-scheduled flights, where the domestic sector achieved a reduction of -70% and the international traffic decreased by an expressive -83%. Concerning the behavior of traffic on regular domestic flights in 2020 compared with 2019, as it can be seen in the graph (left below) that it started to fall from early March to April, due to the closure of borders and airports, followed by a very slight recovery that lasted until June. The peak in August reflects the importance of tourism season in that month starting to go back down again after that month.

With respect to scheduled flights in international traffic (right below), they pattern is similar until the end of April, and from April to June, traffic was practically at a standstill. From the end of June, it started to grow timidly until October, due to the importance of Madeira for some markets during autumn and winter season.

The analysis of figure 3 shows that the impact of COVID-19 on the number of guests entering the Autonomous Region of Madeira (ARM) was negative since March 2020. However, it is possible to observe (top) that it existed an approximation to the number of Portuguese guests in 2019 during the months of August to October, the peak Portuguese tourism months. To compare the behaviour in average terms of the number of guests in the two years, we assessed the normality of the samples collected for this indicator and using the Shapiro-Wilk test, we concluded that the presumption of normality was verified (p-value equal to 0.708 for 2019, p-value equal to 0.352 for 2020). The t-student test allows to conclude that, on average, the number of guests entered in 2019 was significantly different from the number of guests entered in 2020 (p-value equal to 0).

Regarding the number of guests for international markets (below) the figure clearly shows the difficulties of these markets due to the pandemic moment. The application of the t-test concluded that there were significant differences in the averages of the two years both for the number of Portuguese guests (p-value equal to 0.006) and for the number of foreigners guests (p-value equal to 0).

The analysis of figure 4 allows us to observe that in the 2 indicators presented, the category of establishment most popular was the hotel industry (both in 2019 and in 2020).

It is possible to observe that the impact of COVID 19 on any of the categories presented was negative. However, the category that showed the smallest drop was local accommodation.

Figure 2. Passenger air traffic in Autonomous Region of Madeira – 2019/2020

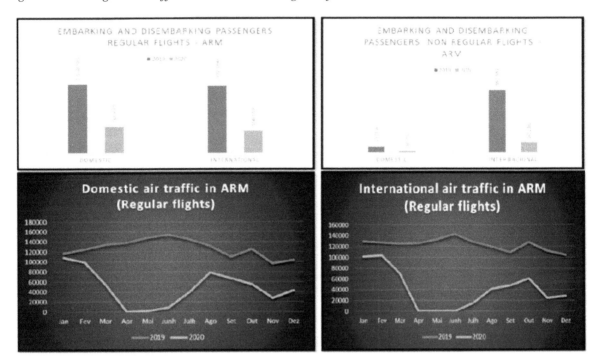

The analysis of figure 5 shows that the distribution of national and international guests in both years by category of stay was similar.

The only curious fact is that demand from Portuguese guests in rural tourism was greater in 2020 than in 2019. The same was not observed in guests from abroad. In the remaining categories of stay, there is a negative impact with COVID-19.

The analysis of figure 6 allows us to observe that the pandemic has changed the distribution of the number of guests by type of hotel establishment observed in 2019, with an increase in the number of guests in apartment hotels in 2020 compared to the value observed in 2019.

In the remaining categories of stay the impact was negative.

The observation of figure 7(a) allows us to conclude that the value of the average stay was lower in 2019 compared to 2020 (result confirmed with the t-student test with a p-value equal to 0.002), however, of all the indicators analyzed in this work, this was the one that suffered the least change in 2020 with the effects of COVID 19 (figure 7(b)). The median value for the average stay in 2019 was 5.17 and in 2020 it was 4.65.

The analysis of figure 8 to 10 allows us to observe that the value of RevPar that suffered the greatest negative impact with COVID19 was that of the hotel industry. In the other two categories, although the value was always lower in 2020 compared to 2019, the impact was less pronounced. This fact has to do with a greater demand from guests in the categories of local accommodation and tourism in rural areas and housing to the detriment of hotels in 2020.

Figure 3. Distribution of Portuguese guests (top) and foreigners (bottom) in autonomous Region of Madeira

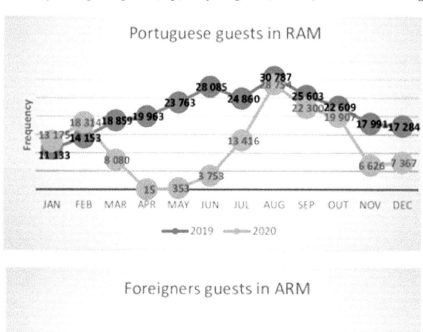

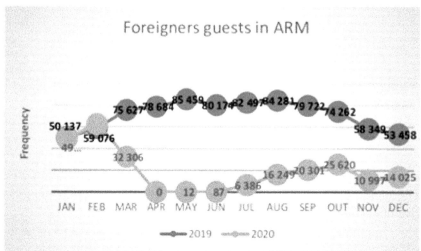

Correlation Analysis

Monthly data were also collected for the years 2019 and 2020 of some indicators of tourism activity in the Autonomous Region of Madeira, namely: a) Air traffic; b) Total number of guests; c) Number of establishments in operation; d) Accommodation capacity; e) Net occupancy rate (bed); f) Average stay; g) Number of overnight stays; h) Staff costs; i) Total income in tourism accommodation; j) Number of incoming guests; k) RevPAR. Based on this information, a correlation analysis was carried out between the various indicators, using Pearson's correlation coefficient (Table 3).

The correlation analysis of these tourist activity indicators considering the values observed in 2019 and 2020 presents some important (and at the same time some curious) results which are:

Figure 4. Number of Incoming Guests and Number of Overnight Stays by Category of Establishment in Autonomous Region of Madeira

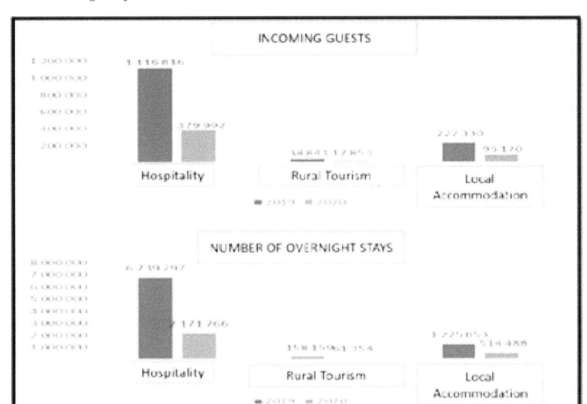

1. The indicators most strongly correlated (positively) with **Air traffic** in ARM are: Total number of guests (r = 0.919), Number of establishments in operation (r = 0.915), Accommodation capacity (r = 0.913); Net occupancy rate (bed) (r = 0.914).
2. The indicators most strongly correlated (positively) with the **Average stay** in ARM are: Number of overnight stays (r = 0.717); Net occupancy rate (bed) (r = 0.715); Staff costs (r = 0.709).
3. The indicators most strongly correlated (positively) with **the Accommodation Capacity** in ARM are: Total number of guests (r = 0.866); Number of establishments in operation (r = 0.997); Air traffic (r = 0.913); Staff Costs (r = 0.976).
4. The indicators most strongly correlated (positively) with the **Total Income from tourist accommodation** in ARM are: Number of overnight stays (r = 0.993); Net occupancy rate (bed) (r = 0.965); RevPAR (r = 0.993); Number of overnight stays (r = 0.993).
5. The indicators most strongly correlated (positively) with **Staff Costs** in ARM are: Number of incoming guests (r = 0.874); Number of establishments in operation (r = 0.98); Accommodation capacity (r = 0.976); Air traffic (r = 0.890).

Figure 5. Distribution of national and international guests by category of stay in Autonomous Region of Madeira

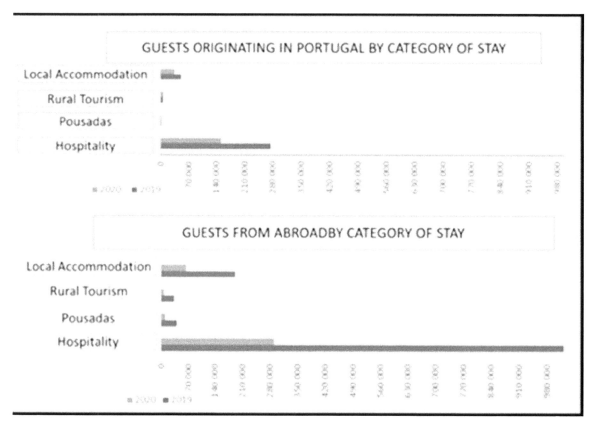

Figure 6. Number of guests by type of accommodation in Autonomous Region of Madeira

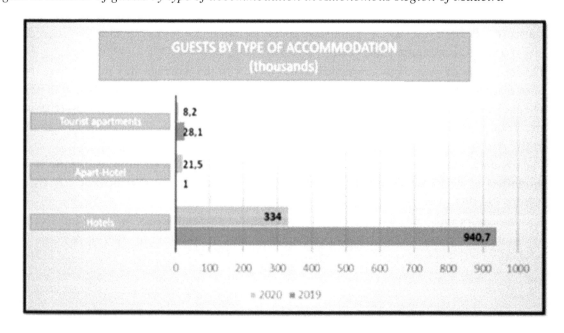

Figure 7. Average stay in Autonomous Region of Madeira

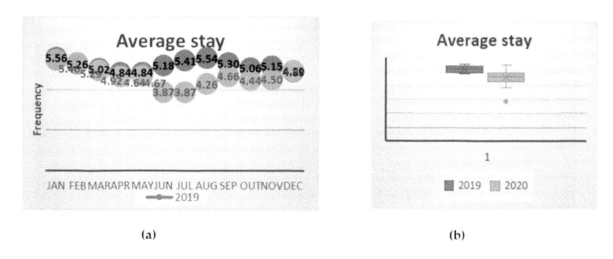

(a)   (b)

Figure 8. RevPAR in hotels in Autonomous Region of Madeira

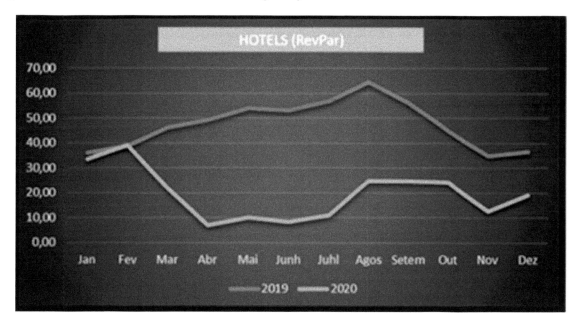

CONCLUSION

The information collected monthly in 2019 and 2020 served as the basis for an assessment of the impacts of COVID-19 on ARM. The main objective was to understand the degree of dependence of tourism on the ARM of the existence of Air Transports. A correlation analysis was performed between the various indicators mentioned previously, using Pearson's correlation coefficient. The results permitted to understand the strong correlation between air traffic and the number of guests and overnight stays and, consequently, with its contribution to the occupancy levels of hotels. Likewise,

Figure 9. RevPAR in housing and rural tourism in Autonomous Region of Madeira (the values of April, May, and June were not published by Regional Directorate of Statistics of Madeira)

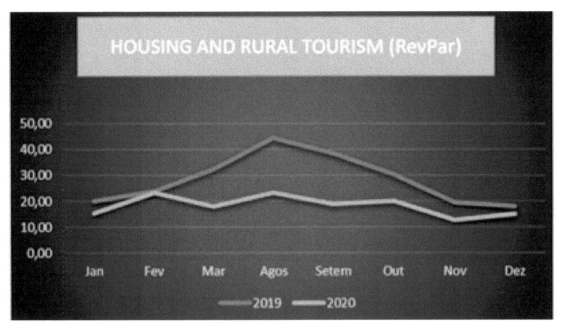

Figure 10. RevPAR in local accommodation in Autonomous Region of Madeira

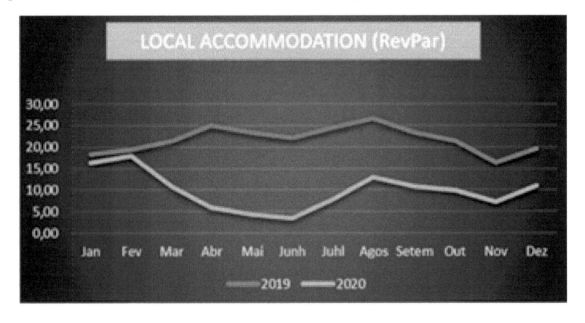

existing capacity levels are directly linked to demand, so the air traffic variable is once again inducing the ability to generate demand and business for the tourism sector. There is consistency between the results obtained in terms of Total Income from tourist accommodation and its strong relationship with overnight stays and occupancy, which in turn impact RevPAR. Finally, fixed staff costs are directly

Table 3. Matrix of Person´s correlation of 11 tourism indicators

	AT	TNG	NEO	AC	NOR(bed)	AS	NOS	SC	TITA	NIG	RevPAR
AT	1										
TNG	**0,919***	1									
NEO	**0,915***	0,858*	1								
AC	**0,913***	**0,866***	**0,997***	1							
NOR(bed)	**0,914***	0,876*	0,778*	0,782*	1						
AS	0,697*	0,681*	0,665*	0,676*	**0,715***	1					
NOS	0,809*	0,895*	0,845*	0,855*	0,880*	**0,717***	1				
SC	**0,890***	0,752*	**0,980***	**0,976***	0,782*	**0,709***	0,844*	1			
TITA	0,882*	0,890*	0,826*	0,839*	**0,965***	0,694*	**0,993***	0,826*	1		
NIG	0,808*	0,897*	0,841*	0,850*	0,872*	0,650*	0,888*	**0,874***	**0,985***	1	
RevPAR	0,870*	0,884*	0,793*	0,806*	0,874*	0,678*	0,885*	0,790*	**0,993***	0,885*	1

*significant correlation at 0.01 level

related to the increase in the number of guests, with the increase in the number of establishments in operation and with accommodation capacity, inducers to the ability to dilute fixed costs due to their greater productive use.

The absence of air transport and the absence of guests as it was visible during COVID-19 had a great impact in service activities. The results collected and the correlations shows that there is a clear indication that Air Transport and Funchal's Airport are very important, even imperative players in the region's tourism development. Some lines of investigation arising from this study. Explore how air traffic patterns for Madeira Island have evolved over the years and their correlation with tourist activity. Also analyse whether there are seasonal variations or trends that could show the future regarding tourism planning, infrastructure development and tourism offer. Another line would also be to study the resilience of the tourist industry in Madeira to disruptions in air transport, such as natural disasters, pandemics, or geopolitical events. Analyse strategies to mitigate risks and increase the resilience of both sectors together.

REFERENCES

Abrantes, J. (2017). Turismo e Transportes: Impactos na Acessibilidade aos Destinos Turísticos. In F. Silva, F. & J. Umbelino (Eds.), Planeamento e Desenvolvimento Turístico (pp. 135-147). Lidel.

Abrantes, J., & Quadros, R. (2022). Impacts caused by COVID-19 on airports and tourism in the main islands of the Autonomous Region of the Azores. In: *XIII International Tourism Congress. 27-29 October. Book of Proceedings*, Estoril Portugal.

ACI. (2021a). *The impact of COVID-19 on the airport business and the path to recovery*. ACI World. https://bit.ly/3rpRI6K

ACI. (2021b). *World data reveals COVID-19's impact on world's busiest airports*. ACI World. https://aci.aero/news/2021/04/22/aci-world-data-reveals-covid-19s-impact-on-worlds-busiest-airports/

Aeroportodamadeira.pt. (2022). Informação de Chegadas e Partidas. *Aeroporto da Madeira*. Available at: https://www.aeroportomadeira.pt/pt/fnc/voos-e-destinos/encontrar-voos/partidas-em-tempo-real

ANA. (2021). Relatório de Gestão e Contas 2020. *ANA - Aeroportos de Portugal*. ANA. https://www.ana.pt/pt/system/files/documents/ana_rgc_2020_pt_website_0.pdf

ARDITI. (2015). Madeira 2020: Estratégia Regional de Especialização Inteligente. *Agência Regional para o Desenvolvimento da Investigação, Tecnologia e Inovação*. ARDITI. https://ris3.arditi.pt/wp-content/uploads/2016/11/RIS3-RAM_2.2.2.1.pdf

Bizarro, T. (2021). Fim do Estado de Emergência em Portugal. *Euronews*. https://pt.euronews.com/2021/04/28/fim-do-estado-de-emergencia-em-portugal

Briguglio, L. (1995). Small island developing states and their economic vulnerabilities. *World Development*, *23*(9), 1615–1632. doi:10.1016/0305-750X(95)00065-K

Caniato, F., Kalchschmidt, M., & Ronchi, S. (2011). Integrating quantitative and qualitative forecasting approaches: Organizational learning in an action research case. *The Journal of the Operational Research Society*, *62*(3), 413–424. doi:10.1057/jors.2010.142

Connell, J., & Taulealo, T. (2021). Island tourism and COVID-19 in Vanuatu and Samoa: An unfolding crisis. *Small States & Territories*, *4*(1), 105–124.

Delli, K. (2021). Pergunta parlamentar | Impacto da crise da COVID-19 no setor da aviação | O-000033/2021. *Parlamento Europeu*. Europal. https://www.europarl.europa.eu/doceo/document/O-9-2021-000033_PT.html

DN. (2020, June 1st). Cronologia de uma pandemia em português. Os três meses que mudaram o país. *Diário de Notícias*. Available at: https://bit.ly/3sBZ4XJ.

DREM. (2021). *Estatísticas do Turismo da Região Autónoma da Madeira - Ano de 2020*. Direção Regional de Estatística da Madeira.

Duro, J. A. (2016). Seasonality of hotel demand in the main Spanish provinces: Measurements and decomposition exercises. *Tourism Management*, *52*, 52–63. doi:10.1016/j.tourman.2015.06.013

Duro, J. A., Perez-Laborda, A., Turrion-Prats, J., & Fernández-Fernández, M. (2021). Covid-19 and tourism vulnerability. *Tourism Management Perspectives*, *38*, 100819. doi:10.1016/j.tmp.2021.100819 PMID:34873568

Eurocontrol. (2020). *Daily Traffic Variation - States*. Eurocontrol. https://www.eurocontrol.int/Economics/2020-DailyTrafficVariation-States.html

Eurocontrol (2021). *Aviation Intelligence Unit* (Think Paper #8.). Eurocontrol. https://www.eurocontrol.int/sites/default/files/2021-02/eurocontrol-think-paper-8-impact-of-covid-19-on-european-aviation-in-2020-and-outlook-2021.pdf

European Parliament. (2021). *Le isole dell'unione europea: situazione attuale e sfide future*. Parlamento Europeo. https://bit.ly/3JngAEK

Europeu Parliment. (2021). *Le isole dell'unione europea: situazione attuale e sfide future*. Parlamento Europeu. https://www.europarl.europa.eu/RegData/etudes/STUD/2021/652239/IPOL_STU(2021)652239(SUM01)_IT.pdf

FFMS. (2019). Retrato da Madeira PORDATA. Edição 2019. *Fundação Francisco Manuel dos Santos*. Por Data. https://www.pordata.pt/ebooks/MA2019v20190712/mobile/index.html

Frontur (2021). *Movimientos turísticos en fronteras (FRONTUR)*. Secretaria de Estado de Turismo. https://www.dataestur.es/general/frontur/

Gratton, C., & Jones, I. (2010). *Research methods for sports studies* (Vol. 2). Routledge. doi:10.4324/9780203879382

Gu, Y., Onggo, B. S., Kunc, M. H., & Bayer, S. (2021). Small Island Developing States (SIDS) COVID-19 post-pandemic tourism recovery: A system dynamics approach. *Current Issues in Tourism*, (pp. 1–28). Taylor & Francis. doi:10.1080/13683500.2021.1924636

Guillot, A. (2018). What Is RevPar? How to Calculate & Improve RevPAR at Your Hotel? *Amadeus Hospitality*. https://bit.ly/3w9uIg6

IATA. (2021). *Outlook for the global airline industry - April 2021 update*. IATA. https://www.iata.org/en/iata-repository/publications/economic-reports/airline-industry-economic-performance---april-2021---report/

IATA. (2022). *Airline Industry Economic Performance – June 2022*. International Air Transport Association. https://bit.ly/3QLM7TL.

INE. (2021). Estatísticas do turismo. *Instituto Nacional de Turismo*. https://bit.ly/3K5PFyb.

Madeira.best (2021). Cidades e Municípios da Ilha da Madeira, Cidades e Municípios da Ilha da Madeira. *Madeira Best*. https://bit.ly/3C6Hek7.

McCabe, S., & Qiao, G. (2020). A review of research into social tourism: Launching the Annals of Tourism Research Curated Collection on Social Tourism. *Annals of Tourism Research*, *85*, 103103. doi:10.1016/j.annals.2020.103103

Ministry of Tourism. (2021). *Monthly Statistics - December 2020*. Ministry of Tourism - Republic of Maldives. https://www.tourism.gov.mv/statistics/publications/year-2020

Newtral (2020). *Baleares y Canarias, las comunidades más expuestas a la caída del turismo*. Newtral.es. https://www.newtral.es/baleares-canarias-ccaa-expuestas-caida-turismo/20200623/

Oriental, A. (2021, July 7). Empresários apreensivos com lenta retoma do turismo. *Ano CLXXXVI, 21225*, 6.

OTA. (2021). *O impacto da COVID-19 nas empresas turísticas. Observatório do Turismo nos Açores*. OTA. https://otacores.com/inquerito/o-impacto-da-covid-19-nas-empresas-turisticas/

Paixão, W., Cordeiro, I., & Leite, N. (2021). Efeitos da pandemia do COVID-19 sobre o turismo em Fernando de Noronha ao longo do primeiro semestre de 2020. *Revista Brasileira de Pesquisa em Turismo, 15*(1), 2128, 1-20. doi:10.7784/rbtur.v15i1.2128

Papanikos, G. T. (2020). The impact of the Covid-19 pandemic on Greek tourism. *Athens Journal of Tourism, 7*(2), 87–100. doi:10.30958/ajt.7-2-2

Payne, J. E., Gil-Alana, L. A., & Mervar, A. (2021). Persistence in Croatian tourism: The impact of COVID-19. *Tourism Economics, 1354816621999969*. doi:10.1177/1354816621999969

Pordata (2021). Alojamentos Turísticos. *Pordata*. https://bit.ly/3AqMuOp

Reuters (2021). *COVID-battered Malta to pay tourists who visit this summer*. Reuters. https://www.reuters.com/world/europe/covid-battered-malta-pay-tourists-who-visit-this-summer-2021-04-09/

Salman, A., Kamerkar, U., Jaafar, M., & Mohamad, D. (2021). Empirical analysis of COVID-19 induced socio cognitive factors and its impact on residents of Penang Island. *International Journal of Tourism Cities*. doi:10.1108/IJTC-05-2020-0091

Santos, N., & Moreira, C. O. (2021). Uncertainty and expectations in Portugal's tourism activities. Impacts of COVID-19. *Research in Globalization, 3*, 100071. doi:10.1016/j.resglo.2021.100071

Scerri, M., & Grech, V. (2020). The Spanish flu, COVID-19 and Malta's reactions: Contrasts and similarities. *Early Human Development, 105252*, 105252. doi:10.1016/j.earlhumdev.2020.105252 PMID:33223126

Serrano, F., & Kazda, A. (2020). The future of airports post COVID-19. *Journal of Air Transport Management, 89*, 101900. doi:10.1016/j.jairtraman.2020.101900 PMID:32834696

Sharma, G. D., Thomas, A., & Paul, J. (2021). Reviving tourism industry post-COVID-19: A resilience-based framework. *Tourism Management Perspectives, 37*, 100786. doi:10.1016/j.tmp.2020.100786 PMID:33391988

Sindico, F., Sajeva, G., Sharman, N., Berlouis, P., & Ellsmoor, J. (2020). Islands and COVID-19: A Global Survey. Report. University of Strathclyde Publishing., Available at https://strathprints.strath.ac.uk/75109/, Retrieved July 20, 2022, from.

Škare, M., Soriano, D. R., & Porada-Rochoń, M. (2021). Impact of COVID-19 on the travel and tourism industry. *Technological Forecasting and Social Change, 163*, 120469. doi:10.1016/j.techfore.2020.120469 PMID:35721368

SREA. (2019a). *Estatísticas do Turismo: janeiro a dezembro 2018*. Serviço Regional de Estatísticas dos Açores. https://srea.azores.gov.pt/Conteudos/Relatorios/lista_relatorios.aspx?idc=392&idsc=6454&lang_id=1

SREA. (2019b). *Estatísticas dos Transportes - 2018*. Serviço Regional de Estatísticas dos Açores. https://srea.azores.gov.pt/Conteudos/Relatorios/lista_relatorios.aspx?idc=392&idsc=971&lang_id=1

SREA. (2020a). *Estatísticas do Turismo: janeiro a dezembro 2019*. Serviço Regional de Estatísticas dos Açores. https://srea.azores.gov.pt/Conteudos/Relatorios/lista_relatorios.aspx?idc=392&idsc=6454&lang_id=1

SREA. (2020b). *Estatísticas dos Transportes - 2019*. Serviço Regional de Estatísticas dos Açores. https://srea.azores.gov.pt/Conteudos/Relatorios/lista_relatorios.aspx?idc=392&idsc=971&lang_id=1

SREA. (2021a). *Estatísticas do Turismo: janeiro a dezembro 2020*. Serviço Regional de Estatísticas dos Açores. https://srea.azores.gov.pt/Conteudos/Relatorios/lista_relatorios.aspx?idc=392&idsc=6454&lang_id=1

SREA. (2021b). *Estatísticas dos Transportes - 2020*. Serviço Regional de Estatísticas dos Açores. https://srea.azores.gov.pt/Conteudos/Relatorios/lista_relatorios.aspx?idc=392&idsc=971&lang_id=1

SREA. (2021c). *Hóspedes, Dormidas e Estada Média por Ilha*. SREA. https://srea.azores.gov.pt/Reportserver/Pages/ReportViewer.aspx?%2fTurismo%2fHospedes+Dormidas+e+Estada+Media+por+Ilha&ilhas=Ilha+Terceira

SREA. (2021d). *Hóspedes, Dormidas e Estada Média por Ilha - Ilha de São Miguel*. SREA. https://srea.azores.gov.pt/Reportserver/Pages/ReportViewer.aspx?%2fTurismo%2fHospedes+Dormidas+e+Estada+Media+por+Ilha&ilhas=Ilha+de+S%C3%A3o+Miguel

SREA. (2021e). *Passageiros Embarcados, Desembarcados, em Transito, por Ilha, Tipo de Voo, Ano e Mês - Ilha da Terceira*. Serviço Regional de Estatísticas dos Açores. https://srea.azores.gov.pt/ReportServer/Pages/ReportViewer.aspx?%2fRelatoriosVarios%2fTransportes-A%C3%A9reos&Ilha=Terceira

SREA. (2021f). *Passageiros Embarcados, Desembarcados, em Transito, por Ilha, Tipo de Voo, Ano e Mês - Ilha de São Miguel*. Serviço Regional de Estatísticas dos Açores. https://srea.azores.gov.pt/ReportServer/Pages/ReportViewer.aspx?%2fRelatoriosVarios%2fTransportes-A%C3%A9reos&Ilha=S%C3%A3o%20Miguel

SREA. (s.d.). *Estimativas da População Média*. Serviço Regional de Estatística dos Açores. https://srea.azores.gov.pt/ReportServer/Pages/ReportViewer.aspx?%2FDemografia%2FEstimativas+da+Popula%C3%A7%C3%A3o+M%C3%A9dia&rs:Command=Render

Turismo de Portugal. (2021). *Turismo em números - dezembro 2020*. Travel BI by Turismo de Portugal. https://travelbi.turismodeportugal.pt/pt-pt/Documents/Turismo%20em%20Portugal/turismo-em-numeros-dez-2020.pdf

Uğur, N. G., & Akbıyık, A. (2020). Impacts of COVID-19 on global tourism industry: A cross-regional comparison. *Tourism Management Perspectives*, *36*, 100744. doi:10.1016/j.tmp.2020.100744 PMID:32923356

United Nations. (2021). *COVID-19 in SIDS | Office of the High Representative for the Least Developed Countries, Landlocked Developing Countries and Small Island Developing States*. United Nations. https://www.un.org/ohrlls/content/covid-19-sids

UNWTO. (2020). *100% of Global Destinations now have Covid-19 Travel Restrictions, UNWTO reports*. UNWTO. https://www.unwto.org/news/covid-19-travel-restrictions

UNWTO. (2021a). *World Tourism Barometer, 19*(3). UN.

UNWTO. (2021b). *2020: Worst Year in Tourism History with 1 Billion Fewer International Arrivals.* UNWTO. https://www.unwto.org/news/2020-worst-year-in-tourism-history-with-1-billion-fewer-international-arrivals

UNWTO. (2022). Word Tourism Barometer – May 2022: Vol. 20. *Issue 3*. World Tourism Organization.

Visit Azores (s.d.). *Férias nos Açores — Descubra os Açores durante umas férias em Portugal.* Visit Azores. https://www.visitazores.com/pt/the-azores/the-9-islands/geography

VisitPortugal.com. (n.d.). *Madeira and Porto Santo Guide.* Visit Portugal. https://bit.ly/3SV6eRC.

WHO. (2020). *WHO Director-General's opening remarks at the media briefing on COVID-19.* WHO. https://bit.ly/3QLj3fh

WTTC. (2021). *Travel & Tourism Economic Impact 2021: Global Economic Impact & Trends 2021 - June 2021.* World Travel & Tourism Council. https://wttc.org/Portals/0/Documents/Reports/2021/Global%20Economic%20Impact%20and%20Trends%202021.pdf?ver=2021-07-01-114957-177

Zsembera, J. (2017). *O turismo nos Açores e a liberalização do espaço aéreo. Análise das perceções das partes interessadas na ilha de São Miguel.* [Dissertação de Mestrado, Universidade Aberta]. Repositório Comum. https://repositorioaberto.uab.pt/bitstream/10400.2/7287/1/TMG/MBA_JanineZsembera.pdf

Chapter 6
Green Finance in the Airline Industry

António Rodrigues
https://orcid.org/0000-0001-5550-5581
ISG - Business & Economics School, Lisboa, Portugal

Jorge Abrantes
https://orcid.org/0000-0003-4692-907X
Estoril Higher Institute for Tourism and Hotel Studies, Portugal & Universidade Aberta, Portugal

Rui Quadros
Estoril Higher Institute for Tourism and Hotel, Portugal & Instituto Superior de Educação e Ciências, Portugal

Salim Kurnaz
https://orcid.org/0000-0002-8060-5151
Istanbul Aydın University, Turkey

ABSTRACT

The objective of this chapter is to analyze the main sustainability and green financing challenges for the airline sector. Qualitative research, based on a literature review and mainly on official sustainability and green financing documents, was used. The methodology is suitable for collecting information within the scope of the study of subjective phenomena, which, in the opinion of Yin, favors a more critical position on the part of the researcher. The conclusion reached is that regulatory changes and society's greater focus on environmental issues lead to changes in the aviation industry, although they cannot be immediately applied to all flights and by all airlines. It is not enough to modernize planes and operations. Aviation support activities must also be part of the sustainability equation. Without adequate financing, it is not possible to reinvent the business. Financing through mixed financing agreements with public and private resources is one of the alternatives discussed in academia and the financial market. Capital needs to find good projects.

DOI: 10.4018/979-8-3693-0908-7.ch006

INTRODUCTION

The origins of sustainable finance can be traced back almost over 30 years, with The Equator Principles, a risk management framework for determining, assessing and managing environmental and social risk, formally established in 2003. The issue of sustainability in aviation is related to the fact that emissions per kilometer are among the highest and, mainly, the total number of kilometers compared to other means of transport has enormous significance.

Aviation currently represents 2% of global CO_2 emissions and 3.8% of emissions in the European Union. However, predicted growth in air traffic will triple global emissions by 2050. In October 2020, the European Union's European Aviation Safety Agency (EASA) launched its Sustainable Aviation Program in accordance with environmental protection regulations (Article 87 of Regulation (EU) 2018/1139 of The European Parliament and of the Council of 4 July 2018) and in accordance with the European Green Deal.

The program is implemented through an environmental strategy comprising the following areas: Robust certification & Green Standards, Operational Efficiency & Sustainable Aviation Fuels, Air transport decarbonization, electric & hydrogen powered aircraft solutions, Environmental impact of Drones & Air Taxis and Research towards zero emissions aviation

A 2020 survey by EASA of European passengers revealed that the majority of respondents overestimated the percentage of aviation emissions. This fact supports the need for consumers to obtain credible and reliable environmental information on the environmental impacts of aviation. The main conclusions from the responses of around 9500 participants from 18 European countries provided the following indications:

Within the scope of this article, the main conclusions from the responses of around 9500 participants from 18 European countries provided the following indications:

- only 5% are aware of the amount of CO_2 they use when traveling by air
- 80% would like to obtain environmental information about the flights they board
- three out of four would welcome an environmental label

EASA has been looking at incentives for the use of sustainable aviation fuels (SAF), hybrid electric and hydrogen aviation, and an environmental label for aviation. In its Sustainable Aviation Program it defines the following as fundamental priorities:

- support and promote new, greener technologies through certification and environmental standards;
- facilitate the decarbonization of the aviation system through various incentive initiatives;
- promote gains in operational efficiency in areas such as maintenance, training and air traffic management, with a proven positive impact on aviation's environmental performance.

The 2022 EASA environmental report highlighted the following aspects:

-Support for the achievement of European environmental objectives
-Integration of effective environmental measures into the European Air Traffic Management system
-Increase the supply and use of SAF

-Promote research and identify solutions to address environmental and climate impacts, as well as acquire resilience to climate change

-Encourage technological innovation through continued international cooperation on regulatory standards

-Foster green airport operations and infrastructure

-Promote investments and market-based measures to improve aviation sustainability

In the context of a global commitment to drastically reduce the impact on the environment, the European Union (EU) has set ambitious goals (such as climate neutrality by 2050), which have been adopted in aviation, forced to quickly and widely adopt a new generation of aircraft with decisive improvements in performance. This is a complicated challenge, affecting the entire aircraft manufacturing value chain, both in the development of lighter structures, with new designs and materials, and more sustainable propulsion systems. Added to this is the strong inertia of a sector in introducing changes to its certification processes, which take many years of development and are therefore very expensive. R+D projects such as Caelestis - EU-funded research project into using virtual prototyping to innovate tomorrow's zero carbon aircraft by 2050 - contribute to introducing such changes, based on new design concepts for lightweight components and new ways of manufacturing, from a digital perspective.

Aviation faces challenges in demonstrating the sustainability of its activities, which explains the initial reluctance of investors to mobilize green capital towards this sector. A clear vision of aeronautical activities that could be considered ecologically sustainable with a balanced approach to monitoring, whilst avoiding the risk of greenwashing. Clear technical criteria will likely be the main driver of pre-issuance necessary to bring about significant change in this area.

The financial sector will have to face the challenge of measuring the risks of companies and their physical assets in the face of climate change and developing and monitoring key performance indicators in areas related to decarbonization and the sustainability of investments and the companies that finance with these instruments.

FINANCING SUSTAINABLE GROWTH

In 2018, the European Commission created the Action Plan: Financing Sustainable Growth, whose objectives are:

1) reorient capital flows towards sustainable investments to ensure sustainable and inclusive growth,

2) manage financial risks arising from climate change, resource depletion, environmental degradation and social issues,

3) promote transparency and a long-term vision in economic and financial activities.

Specifically,

a) Reorienting capital flows towards sustainable investments Among investors it is still not clear what a sustainable investment actually is, which becomes harmful, resulting in a colossal deficit in terms of investment in transport and energy infrastructure and resource management. This constitutes an obstacle to investment in infrastructure to respond to social issues of inequality and inclusion (European Commission, 2018). The EU is committed to the transition to a greener economy, as a way of reducing the planet's environmental footprint and eradicating inequalities, committing to allocate 20% of the budget to climate-related measures.

b) Manage financial risks arising from climate change, resource depletion, environmental degradation and social issues Including environmental and social objectives in the financial decision-making process aims to mitigate the financial impacts resulting from social and environmental risks. For banks this becomes essential, as they will be more exposed to possible losses resulting from the lower profitability of client companies. This happens because the more companies are exposed to the risks of climate change or the more they depend on scarce natural resources, the lower their profitability will be. According to this report, around half of the risk exposure of banks located in the euro area is, either directly or indirectly, linked to risks arising from climate change. Factors of a social nature, such as precarious working conditions, can also impact financial institutions, particularly in terms of legal risks, as companies' failure to comply with these conditions negatively affects their reputation and may lead to financial losses.

c) Promote transparency and a long-term vision in economic and financial activities to manage risks and adequately assess the creation of long-term value, there must be transparency in companies with regard to sustainability issues, which will allow ensure information for market participants and help companies pursue a more sustainable and long-term trajectory. From this perspective, sustainability and long-term vision are inseparable since investment with social and environmental objectives requires a long-term orientation. Taking these objectives into account, the action plan consists of ten actions to achieve them:

1. Establish an EU classification system for sustainable activities the establishment of a common classification system, or a taxonomy, common to the entire EU will make it possible to understand more clearly which activities are considered sustainable. This is the priority action. In this sense, the European Commission will present detailed information about suitable sectors and activities, allowing greater information to be provided to investors who intend to invest in these sectors.

2. Creation of standards and labels for "green" financial products the standards and labels created for sustainable financial products will be based on the EU Taxonomy and aim to protect the integrity and foster confidence in sustainable financial markets. This action becomes especially useful for small investors, as they increasingly seek to ensure that their investments take climate, environmental and social issues into account. The demand for green financial products such as Green Bonds, Social Bonds, Sustainable Bonds, Green Loans, Sustainable Investment Funds, Green Mortgages and Blended Finance is becoming increasingly common in the European market, with a tendency to increase.

3. Promote investment in sustainable projects The transition to a more sustainable economy involves mobilizing private capital for more sustainable projects, mainly infrastructure, which represents a large part of GHG emissions, so that these can be associated with public funds.

4. Incorporate sustainability into the provision of financial advice Investment and insurance mediation companies are obliged to provide products suited to the needs of their clients, assessing investment objectives and their risk tolerance. However, sustainability issues are, in most cases, not preferred by either investors or beneficiaries, neglecting their importance when providing advice.

5. Develop sustainability benchmarks that play a central role in shaping the prices of financial instruments and other relevant assets, which allow investors to track and measure different

performances and affect their assets accordingly." Suppliers of these indices have been developing ESG benchmarks to encompass sustainability objectives, however, it is still necessary to develop more solid and transparent methodologies in order to reduce the risks of misleading marketing under the pretext of using green factors.

6. Better integrate sustainability into ratings and market studies In recent years, there has been an increase in concern about the integration of ESG factors in the assessment of performance, by companies, market research providers and research agencies. credit risk rating, contributing to an improvement in the flow of information and a more sustainable allocation of capital. Still, it is necessary to understand the extent to which credit rating agencies are integrating sustainability factors.

7. Clarify the duties of institutional investors and asset managers institutional investors and asset managers often still do not consider sustainability factors and risks when making investments. Consequently, they also do not disclose to their clients how they consider these factors, who, therefore, do not receive all the necessary information in terms of sustainability to make decisions.

8. Incorporate sustainability into prudential requirements. Banks, insurance companies and pension funds are the main source of external financing for the European economy and constitute an important channel for savings for investment. Even so, they may be exposed to risks linked to sustainable economic development, which leads to greater consideration of risks associated with climate change and other environmental factors. Furthermore, it is necessary to consider the negative impact that bank loans, investment activities and other sustainable financing activities have in Europe.

9. Strengthen sustainability disclosures and accounting rules In order to allow investors and interested parties to assess the long-term value creation and risk exposure of companies, companies communicate information regarding sustainability issues. Regarding the financial sector, it is important to reinforce the transparency of asset managers and institutional investors with regard to disclosure regarding the way in which sustainability risks and their exposure to risks arising from climate change are considered. Furthermore, it is essential to ensure that current accounting standards do not directly or indirectly discourage investments in sustainable, long-term sectors.

10. Promote sustainable corporate governance and mitigate short-termism in capital markets. Promoting corporate governance that is more conducive to sustainable investments allows companies to adopt necessary measures to develop new technologies, reinforce their business models and, therefore, improve their performance and their risk management and competitiveness practices. Company managers may be excessively focused on short-term performance, neglecting environmental and social sustainability issues, which could encourage unnecessary exposure to long-term sustainability risks.

TASK FORCE ON CLIMATE-RELATED FINANCIAL DISCLOSURES: TCFD

The environmental issue has been gaining prominence in the financial sector, environmental sustainability can only be achieved through the commitment of the financial sector and financial stability can only be achieved in a context of environmentally sustainable growth.

To achieve carbon neutrality and a green economy, it is essential that banks align capital flows with this objective, thus practicing sustainable financing. This will allow the pursuit of economic, social inclusion and environmental regeneration objectives, filling the existing gap in financing sustainable development and protecting the financial system from the impacts of climate change.

Financial markets need clear, comprehensive, and high-quality information about the impacts of climate change, so that companies can be prepared and adopt procedures to mitigate them. Investors need to know how the company is anticipating and adapting to climate change.

Banks need to understand their exposure to climate risk and how they can minimize it. Therefore, in order to help financial and non-financial companies adequately assess climate-related risks and opportunities and price them, the Financial Stability Board (FSB) created the Task Force on Climate-Related Financial Disclosures (TCFD). For financial institutions, it is crucial to understand the financial risks resulting from climate change in order to minimize them.

Therefore, the TCFD divides these risks into two categories: physical risks and transition risks. Physical risks translate into risks that result from events related to climate change and which can be event-oriented (acute), such as droughts, floods or hurricanes, or long-term changes (chronic), such as a sustained increase in temperatures, which can lead to rising sea levels and changes in weather patterns. These can have major financial implications, such as direct damage to assets and indirect impacts by disrupting the organizations' supply chain. In addition, they can also lead to changes in the availability, supply and quality of water, safe food and extreme changes in temperature that will affect facilities, operations, the value chain, transportation, and safety needs of employees and, in turn the overall performance of organizations (TCFD, 2017).

Transition risks constitute the financial risks that result from the process of adjusting the economy towards becoming a low-carbon economy. Political-legal, technological and market changes to respond to climate adaptation and mitigation requirements can lead to a reassessment of the value of a variety of assets as change costs and opportunities become evident. Political actions around climate action continue to increase towards adapting to or mitigating climate change, for example carbon pricing mechanisms to reduce GHG emissions by using lower emission energy sources.

METHODOLOGY

For this article, a descriptive research with a qualitative approach was carried out, supported through a bibliography review process with the aim of discussing the continued importance of sustainability for aviation will accelerate the need for capital to develop new technologies, infrastructure and fuels. The use of green finance can help industry obtain this capital.

The methodology is suitable for collecting information within the scope of the study of subjective phenomena, which, in the opinion of Yin (2016), favors a more critical positioning on the part of the researcher.

GREEN FINANCE IN THE AVIATION SECTOR

Flight Net Zero, an alliance of airlines that requires all carbon dioxide (CO2) emissions to be offset by 2050, is a very ambitious goal, so much so that airlines are not sure how to achieve it. The biggest challenge for the aviation sector is financing: on the one hand, a path has been drawn up to use some fuels, but the problem is that these fuels do not exist or are very expensive (IATA, 2023).

This is a very ambitious goal, so much so that airlines are not sure how to achieve it. The biggest challenge facing the aviation sector is financing: on the one hand, a path has been drawn up to use some fuels, but the problem is that these fuels do not exist or are very expensive (IATA, 2023).

Based on the Green Bond Principles, the Loan Market Association (LMA) launched the Green Loan Principles in March 2018. This has been followed by the Sustainability Linked Loan Principles in March 2019, which in turn has been followed by the Sustainability-Linked Bond Principles in June 2020. The Green Loan Principles aim to promote consistency in the methodology used across the green loan market. They comprise voluntary recommended guidelines clarifying the instances in which a loan might be categorized as "green," essentially on a 'use of proceeds' model, based on the underlying characteristics of the transaction. A non-exhaustive list of eligible "green projects" include energy efficiency, pollution prevention and control, clean transportation, climate change adaption and renewable energy. The Principles require that the funds are ring-fenced for "green projects" and their use tracked, something relatively easily satisfied by the purchase of an asset using funds drawn down once for that purpose, provided that the relevant asset can be categorized as a "green project." The updated Guidance published by the LMA in May 2020 clarifies that the Green Loan Principles can be satisfied by a green project identified as such at the outset or by the establishment of a framework under which green projects are identified as eligible during the life of the loan (for example under a revolving credit facility).

The Guidance published by the LMA in May 2020 regarding Green Lending Principles (GLP) considers that projects that significantly improve the efficiency of fossil fuel use are potentially eligible, provided the relevant project is aligned with the four main components of the Liquefied Petroleum Gas (LPG), and the borrower commits to an ambitious path of decarbonization reasonably considered to be in line with the Paris Agreement. The Guidance states that observed market practice is that these projects can be labeled as "light green" or "transition".

However, the EU Taxonomy Regulation, which introduces a classification system (or taxonomy) to determine which products can be marketed to investors as environmentally sustainable, does not include aviation. Nevertheless, the EU Technical Expert Group (TEG) on Sustainable Finance recommended that aviation "should be addressed by the Taxonomy Regulation in the future, given the importance of the sector's emissions". However, it would be expected that any inclusion of aviation would impose strict criteria, in addition to the reorientation towards more efficient aircraft, but still with traditional propulsion.

In addition to traditional asset financing structures, there is a set of projects that airlines intend to undertake for which the Green Lending Principles and the Sustainability-Linked Lending Principles could be available, although transactions that comply with both are rare in practice. Several airlines have announced investments in alternative fuels. In August 2019, British Airways announced a partnership with renewable fuels company, Velocys, to build a facility that converts household and commercial waste into sustainable renewable aviation fuel for its fleet, committing further funding to the project in May 2019. In February 2020, Delta Air Lines pledged to invest US$1 billion to become "carbon neutral" with the ambition to achieve this goal by 2030, investing in the advancement of clean air travel technologies, accelerating reductions in waste and emissions, and establishing new offsetting and natural carbon sequestration projects.

Airbus, Air France, Total and Paris Airports (ADP) in 2021 regarding the joint initiative implemented through the first Paris - Montreal intercontinental flight in which fuel with a mixture of 16% oil was used for frying, constitutes the ambition to decarbonize air transport and develop the production of sustainable aviation fuels in France, a condition for use in the country's airports. According to Air France's calculations, the use of this frying oil mixture represents an additional cost per passenger of around four euros for the route between the French capital and the Canadian city. To avoid loss of competitiveness, the objective is to generalize the use of these biofuels for all airlines. For example, French regulations stipulate that from 2022, 1% of biofuels must be used on all flights departing the country, a percentage that will have to increase to 2% in 2025 and 5% in 2030. On the other hand, while it may not be easy to justify using a green loan to purchase aircraft, airlines could use them to refinance other assets that comply with the Green Loan Principles, such as energy-efficient office buildings.

The International Civil Aviation Organization's (ICAO) new global carbon offsetting scheme, Carbon Offsetting and Reduction Scheme for International Aviation (CORSIA), can also act as a driver for airline-funded green projects. CORSIA requires airlines to purchase and deliver offset credits known as "emissions units" on a three-year compliance cycle relative to the number of emissions attributed to routes flown between participating states during that period. Until 2026, only flights between voluntary participating states are covered, but from 2027, emissions units must be purchased for all international flights. Several airlines, including IAG, EasyJet and Air France-KLM, have also committed to voluntarily offsetting all domestic emissions. Although emissions units can be purchased from carbon trading companies, it is likely that large airlines will seek to establish their own offset schemes and may use green and sustainable financing to achieve this.

Many current rating systems have traditionally required funded projects to be aligned with the Paris Agreement, which is complicated by aviation's unclear decarbonization trajectory. As a result, the majority of green finance issuance in aviation has been done by airports, using current debt issuance regulations to finance cleaner buildings, electric vehicles and climate change adaptation.

In 2019, Swedish airport operator Swedavia AB issued a US$118 million green bond with a 5.25-year maturity to finance projects that address climate change and sustainability. This operation aligned with the Green Bond Principles (GBP) was followed by other issues by the Royal Schiphol Group, specifically to finance clean transport and sustainable buildings in Amsterdam and other airports it operates in the Netherlands.

This framework has also been used in subsequent issuances, most recently for the issuance of a $910 million green bond by the Royal Schiphol Group, specifically to finance clean transport and sustainable buildings in Amsterdam and other airports it operates in the Netherlands. However, although the GBP defines categories of eligible green projects ranging from green buildings to clean transport and renewable energy, it does not cover aviation assets and is therefore only useful for a limited number of opportunities.

There are several airlines that access various types of green loans and green products. Although access to these financing and products has been lower in the United States than in Europe and Asia, JetBlue Airways, in February 2020, was the first airline to obtain green financing with interest indexed to meeting ESG goals. In December 2019, Etihad Airways was the first airline to finance a project with a €100 million Sustainable Development Goals (SDG)-based commercial loan to finance several projects, including the expansion of an eco-home and apartments for the cabin crew. In this financing, similar to the previous example, the interest rate is indexed to a portfolio of eligible projects falling within several SDGs, including Green Buildings, Investment in Biofuels, Carbon Footprint Reduction, Waste Management and Recycling, Humanitarian Efforts and Protection of Wild life.

Despite this, aviation has seen very little use of green finance. This is a supply problem, with considerable latent demand from sustainable investors keen to diversify their portfolios. However, many of the current classification systems have traditionally required the projects funded by the capital to align with the Paris Agreement, which is complicated by the unclear decarbonization trajectory for aviation. As a result, most green finance issuances in aviation have been by airports, using existing frameworks to issue debt to fund cleaner buildings, electric vehicles, and climate change adaption.

Swedavia AB, a major airport operator in Sweden, issued a $118 million green bond with a 5.25-year maturity in 2019 to fund projects addressing climate change and sustainability. This used a framework developed by SEB and Swedbank, which aligns with the 2018 Green Bond Principles (GBP) defined by the International Capital Market Association. This framework has also been used by subsequent issuances, most recently for the issuance of a $910 million green bond by the Royal Schiphol Group, specifically to finance clean transportation and sustainable buildings at Amsterdam and other airports it operates around the Netherlands. However, while the 2018 GBP defines eligible green project categories ranging from green buildings to clean transportation and renewable energy, it does not cover aviation assets and is therefore only useful for a limited number of opportunities.

DISCUSSION AND CONCLUSION

Airlines have promised to achieve carbon neutrality by 2050, but the question is how. The batteries have weight and discharge time limitations to be used in large commercial aircraft, while hydrogen or green ammonia are still far away. The alternative at hand, which is already being used, is the so-called sustainable aviation fuels (SAF), but they also have a problem: the limitation of supply.

In 2022, according to the International Air Transport Association (IATA), 300 million liters were produced, three times more than in 2021, but far from the needs of the industry. In 2023, it is estimated that SAF will represent only 0.1% of the airline industry's fuel consumption. To advance on its path to decarbonization, aviation will need a supply of 8 billion liters annually by 2025, 23 billion by 2030, and 449 billion by 2050.

The short-term reality presents a pressing dilemma: the aviation sector currently lacks viable means to counter its growing greenhouse gas emissions. Current technological progress, fuel and operational efficiency are not capable of maintaining, let alone reducing, levels of emissions from aviation. The readily available tool to address emissions is offsetting, which the sector takes advantage of through CORSIA and voluntary carbon markets.

Since the early 2000s, airlines have been introducing voluntary carbon offset (VCO) programs for customers, a trend now embraced by even prominent low-cost carriers who were previously hesitant. However, compensation does not solve all problems, is complex and has limitations. Its own limitations highlight the broader sustainability dilemmas facing the aviation sector.

Moderating the growth of aviation is an illusion, the International Air Transport Association (IATA) estimates that the number of passengers will reach four billion in 2024, thus exceeding pre-COVID levels, corresponding to 103% of what was the reality in 2019. In this scenario, airlines resort to compensation mainly for its reputational benefits. Regulators remain reticent, often opting for flight taxes as a seemingly simpler solution. This presentation explores these pressing questions, examining the implications for the future of aviation.

Beyond ongoing efforts to improve fuel efficiency and reduce emissions through fleet upgrades, improved operations and infrastructure, other initiatives are gaining momentum. Ground equipment is being electrified, sustainable aviation fuels are moving from testing to commercial production, and electric propulsion is becoming a practical reality.

Accelerating these efforts to achieve the goals that airlines and airports are committing to will require significant capital. The Energy Transitions Commission (ETC) estimates the abatement cost for aviation to be approximately $170 per metric ton of CO2. When applied to the sector's 2019 emissions, this suggests an industry cost of more than $155 billion, equivalent to more than 7 years of total industry profits.

The doubt of several authors regarding green aviation fuel is characterized by being too expensive and too scarce. The introduction of hydrogen into aviation will begin with smaller and shorter-range aircraft and will take some years, but is not a solution that can be applied to everyone and not immediately. It is necessary that these aircraft be conceived, marketed and produced at affordable prices, therefore, as real and possible solutions that we can incorporate in order to advance the decarbonization of the sector without the use of Aviation fuels sustain the efficiency of operations.

Another point of view is the need to modernize the global air traffic system, time is lost in breaks that do not directly harm the environment. It is not enough to modernize aircraft and operations, we must also think about why the aircraft will not disappear in the activities that surround aviation and that contribute to a less sustainable business.

The growing appetite for more sustainable financing of economic activities has prompted financial markets to create relevant tools and products. Green emission labeling debt has today become an important part of the sustainable market, mobilizing more than 754 billion dollars in green assets and projects accumulated at the end of 2019. These initiatives were carried out by the financial markets initially, then approved by several governments and multilateral organizations around the world.

Environmental labeling initiatives adhere to the sector's desire to have a uniform understanding and approach to green financing. Currently operating characteristics or needs of the issuer, a green debt issue can be carried out through various systems or standards, such as the Bond Standards Climate Bond Standards, the Principles Applicable to Green Bonds

Green finance includes internalizing environmental externalities and adjusting risk perceptions to boost environmentally sustainable investments and reduce those that harm the environment. This covers a wide range of financial institutions and asset classes, both public and private, and involves the effective management of environmental risks across the entire financial system. Green bonds are debt instruments that finance projects with environmental benefits. Issuers can be companies, governments or agencies that commit to using the proceeds exclusively for financing climate- or environment-related projects, assets or activities. This commitment is what sets green bonds apart from traditional bonds.

The financial characteristics of green bonds such as structure, risk and returns are similar to those of traditional bonds. Their credit quality ranges from investment grade to non-investment grade, although most corporate green bonds are investment grade. The credit profile of a green bond is the same as that of a traditional bond from the same issuer, and in terms of pricing there is no significant difference between a green and non-green bond. The liquidity of green bond issuers varies across sectors and regions given the rapidly growing global market. So, in regions where liquidity options are more limited, investors' ability to sell may be impacted. Green bond holders have the same recourse to the issuer. Essentially, they are standard bonds with an additional green element. Green bonds come in short- or long-dated maturities and have various types of coupons and yields.

Despite this, aviation makes little use of green finance. This is a supply problem, with considerable latent demand from sustainable investors eager to diversify their portfolios. However, many of the current classification systems have traditionally required equity-funded projects to align with the Paris Agreement, which is complicated by aviation's unclear decarbonization trajectory. As a result, the majority of green finance issuances in aviation have been carried out by airports, using existing frameworks to issue debt to finance cleaner buildings, electric vehicles and climate change adaptation.

Financing and sustainable investment are necessary to achieve the objective of sustainable aviation. The use of sustainable fuel is essential, but investment is necessary to increase production and reduce costs. The involvement of interested parties in the financing of ESG factors and sustainability issues is fundamental, with the registration, awareness and incentives necessary to promote sustainable finance and ESG practices in the aviation sector. Green financing can support the reduction of emissions and promote sustainable development in aviation, but more investments and collaboration are necessary.

The main challenges of green finance are two-level, issuers and investors. In relation to the first, the additional bureaucracy associated with issuance, verification costs, reporting and transparency requirements and too many strict definitions can limit the selection of assets eligible for inclusion under green bond agreements. For investors, the coupons that can be lower stand out and very few industries issue green bonds although the supply gradually increases, the choice of investors is limited.

In conclusion, the main contributions of this article are:

It summarizes the current state of the debate on green finance in the airline sector and proposes paths for future reflection and debate.

Provides an understanding of green financing practices for airlines through the sector's leading international organizations.

It contributes to clarifying the concerns of industry actors and main international organizations associated with the difficulties of achieving short-term decarbonization targets, the involvement of banks, their requirements and their role in financing sustainable projects

FUTURE STUDIES

As future studies, the following are suggested:

1) new legislative regulations on green finance for the aeronautical industry
2) support from the financial sector for the aeronautical industry in the transition to sustainability
3) transition costs to sustainability
4) comparison between the cost of green credits and the cost of traditional credits
5) the importance of greenwashing in evaluating airlines for green financing
6) study of external perception of the impact of green financing on the image of airlines
7) evaluation of the premises and impacts in the development of taxonomies that allow a green transition for the different sectors of the aeronautical industry
8) comparative studies of the maturity of green finance between airlines

REFERENCES

Carbon Offsetting and Reduction Scheme for International Aviation (CORSIA). (n.d.). *Home*. ICAO. https://www.icao.int/environmental-protection/CORSIA/Pages/default.aspx

EASA - The European Authority for aviation safety. (n.d.). *Home*. EASA. https://www.easa.europa.eu/en/light

Energy Transitions Commission (ETC). (n.d.). *Home*. Etc. https://www.energy-transitions.org/

EU taxonomy for sustainable activities. (n.d.). Europa. https://finance.ec.europa.eu/sustainable-finance/tools-and-standards/eu-taxonomy-sustainable-activities_en

Eur-Lex. (2018). Regulation (EU) 2018/1139 of the European Parliament and of the Council of 4 July 2018. *Official Journal of the European Union*. https://eur-lex.europa.eu/legal-content/EN/TXT/?uri=celex%3A32018R1139

European green bond standard. (n.d.). Europa. https://finance.ec.europa.eu/sustainable-finance/tools-and-standards/european-green-bond-standard_en

European Green Deal. https://commission.europa.eu/strategy-and-policy/priorities-2019-2024/european-green-deal_en

European Union Aviation Safety Agency (EASA). (n.d.). *Home*. EASA. https://www.easa.europa.eu/en/light

FSB Task Force on Climate-related Financial Disclosures. (n.d.). FSB Taskforce. https://www.fsb-tcfd.org/

Green Loan Principles. (n.d.). LSTA. https://www.lsta.org/content/green-loan-principles/

Hooda, S. K., & Yadav, S. (2023). Green Finance for Sustainable Aviation: Stakeholder Perspectives and Systematic Review. *International Journal of Professional Business Review*, 8(5), e02085. doi:10.26668/businessreview/2023.v8i5.2085

International Capital Market Association. (2022). *Green Bonds Principles*. ICMA. https://www.icmagroup.org/assets/documents/Sustainable-finance/2022-updates/Green-Bond-Principles-June-2022-060623.pdf

International Civil Aviation Organization (ICAO). (n.d.). *Home*. ICAO. https://www.icao.int/Pages/default.aspx

Karaman, A. S., Kilic, M., & Uyar, A. (2018). Sustainability reporting in the aviation industry: World-wide evidence. Sustainability Accounting. *Management and Policy Journal*, 9(4), 362–391. doi:10.1108/SAMPJ-12-2017-0150

La Oportunidad de las Finanzas Verdes en el Sector de la Aviación. (n.d.). A21. https://a21.com.mx/rumbo-altura-y-velocidad/2021/02/14/la-oportunidad-de-las-finanzas-verdes-en-el-sector-de-la

Plan, A. Financing Sustainable Growth. Retrieved October 16, 2023, from https://eur-lex.europa.eu/legal-content/EN/TXT/?uri=CELEX%3A52018DC0097

Sustainability in aviation. (n.d.). EASA. https://www.easa.europa.eu/en/light/topics/sustainability

TCFD. (n.d.). *Recommendations of the Task Force on Climate-related Financial Disclosures*. TCFD. https://www.fsb-tcfd.org/recommendations/

Technical expert group on sustainable finance (TEG). https://finance.ec.europa.eu/publications/technical-expert-group-sustainable-finance-teg_en

Watson F. & Williams. (2022). *Get into the Green Scene: Sustainability linked finance in aircraft finance.* Watson Farley & Williams. https://www.wfw.com/articles/get-into-the-green-scene-sustainability-linked-finance-inaircraft-finance/

Yin, R. K. (2016). *Qualitative Research from Start to Finish* (2nd ed.). Guilford Publications.

Zakaria, I. H., Mohammad, N., Abashah, A., Alshuaibi, M. S. I., Othman, A., Ahmad, N., Yaziz, M. F. A., & Akanmu, M. D. (2023). Preparation of Aviation Industry Transition on COVID-19 From Pandemic to Endemic Phase: A Review. *International Journal of Professional Business Review*, 8(4), e0824. doi:10.26668/businessreview/2023.v8i4.824

Chapter 7
The Fastest-Growing Aviation/ Aerospace Cluster in Portugal and What We Can Learn From It

Miguel Centeno Moreira
ⓘ https://orcid.org/0000-0001-8140-4514
Atlântica Instituto Universitário, Portugal

ABSTRACT

This investigation reports on the recent evolution of a regional aviation/aerospace cluster in Portugal, located in Ponte de Sor, a small city in the region of Alentejo. Recognized as one of the driving forces of the cluster´s significant growth, the municipal aerodrome anchors the local and regional development in the last decade in this sector. In this chapter, recent and future investment cycles and their socioeconomic impacts are analyzed, the growing diversity and complementarity of activities are presented, and the municipal strategy is discussed going forward. The investigation, based on a Porter´s diamond model analysis, leads us to the conclusion that the Ponte de Sor cluster is set to become one of Portugal´s major aviation/aerospace keystones in future years.

INTRODUCTION

In the last two years, the aviation industry has faced an enormous challenge, after airlines and their supply chains were globally brought to the ground by the COVID 19 pandemic, with countries worldwide experiencing severe economic downfall. As a direct consequence of this unprecedented crisis, global air transport has seen a dramatic loss in capacity of up to 80% due to systematic and widespread flight cancellations (Sobieralski, 2020). In 2020, airlines hemorrhaged USD 168 billion in economic losses, followed by airports losing USD 31.6 billion (Bower et al., 2022). While governments came into the rescue of airlines and international airports with significant financial aid packages, not all segments of the aviation industry received immediate relief, or any relief at all (Rust et al., 2021). In Portugal, for example, only one (TAP Air Portugal, the flag carrier) out of seven Portuguese scheduled airlines ben-

DOI: 10.4018/979-8-3693-0908-7.ch007

efited from a direct government aid, while ANA Aeroportos (the entity managing all major international airports) was able to avoid resourcing to the lay-off of its workers.

Both international and smaller airports, or regional aerodromes, are often the backbone supporting and enabling a set of businesses that constitute an aviation or aerospace cluster (Hassen, 2009; Benzler & Wink, 2010). Several examples are known of regions within countries that developed strong aviation/aerospace cluster environments: from large international airports such as Montréal, Hamburg, or Toulouse, to smaller-sized airports such as Friedrichshafen, to even smaller regional aerodromes like Donauwörth in Germany (which has a demographic dimension comparable to the subject aerodrome in the present study), to name a few. The aeronautical and aerospace industries are known to be levers for territory development, as they have significant impact on territorial elements (Klein et al., 2003; Hassen et al., 2012; Paone & Sasanelli, 2016).

In this chapter, a regional aviation/aerospace cluster (located in Ponte de Sor, Portugal) is presented and analyzed from its inception to its present-day complex of activities. Following the pioneering work by Neves & Marques (2017), this constitutes the very first in-depth analysis of the cluster, its evolution and impacts in the period 2017-2023. Brief descriptions of the cluster´s origin and evolution open the present chapter, and the author then proceeds with the methodological approach used. The contribution to the Portuguese aerospace ecosystem is then analyzed and discussed, and a section on conclusions drawn and prospects closes the document.

BIRTH AND EARLY EVOLUTION OF PONTE DE SOR´S AERODROME INFRASTRUCTURE (2006 – 2017)

Ponte de Sor is a small city (home to about 17,000 inhabitants), located 120 km NE of Lisbon, Portugal, served by a municipal aerodrome located 8 km south of the urban area. Historically, aeronautical activities date back to 1919 when an aviation field was inaugurated, located in what is now the city center (Revista Aeronáutica, 1921). Aeronautical activities in Ponte de Sor flourished until the eve of WWII, after which they came to a complete halt for many decades. The re-emergence of such activities took place in the early 2000s, when two small light aircraft manufacturing companies were installed in Ponte de Sor, attracted by the incentive measures created at the time with the expansion of the industrial zone near the city center. The presence of these companies then led the City Council to start the construction of a small airfield. In 2006, however, the Portuguese State launched a national tender for the constitution of the national headquarters of civil protection air resources. Ponte de Sor won the tender, but the specifications required the construction of a much longer runway and a state-of-the-art new hangar. Consequently, a series of investments were needed to accommodate the main base of the Portuguese forest firefighting fleet and operations. The direct investment for this first phase (new 1800 m runway, new taxiways, apron expansion and maneuvering areas, and the new hangar) amounted to EUR 12.86 M (Neves & Marques, 2017), which represented a very significant effort for a municipality with a typical annual budget of around EUR 21 M.

After this first investment phase, the aerodrome was certified by the Portuguese Civil Aviation Authority for public use as a Class II, code 3C, rescue and firefighting Category 2 infrastructure, owned and operated by the Ponte de Sor Municipality. Its approved traffic type is VFR (Visual Flight Rules), exclusively, and as an approved service provider, the Municipality has obtained the privilege to provide the following services: (i) air traffic services (AFIS – Aerodrome Flight Information Service), and (ii) communication, navigation, or surveillance (or CNS) services. As a direct result, the aerodrome became the only regional aerodrome in Portugal duly certified, under EASA – European Union Aviation Safety Agency regulations, to be able to receive medium-haul commercial airplanes such as the Airbus A320 and Boeing B737. It is also the only regional aerodrome equipped with an ILS – Instrument Landing System, that allows aircraft to conduct runway precision approaches based on two radio beams which together provide pilots with both vertical and horizontal guidance during an approach to land. The infrastructure is centrally located in the national territory, with an airspace free of obstacles and without operating restrictions, which constitutes an added value, enhancing its use as a training center for flight personnel and as a destination for the fixation of aviation/aerospace companies.

However, being seasonal in nature, firefighting activities alone could not generate any real income for the municipality. Consequently, and prioritizing the monetization of the first investment done, a second phase of investment followed immediately, resulting in additional hangar capacity at the aerodrome. Three new hangars were inaugurated in 2013, and that same year the largest airline pilot training school in Portugal, Escola de Aviação Aerocondor (founded in 1979 and based in Cascais aerodrome near Lisbon), started operating in Ponte de Sor, thus expanding its training operations into a less occupied airspace, as the training efficiency near the Lisbon international airport was already extremely limited. This second phase of investment amounted to a total of EUR 2.8 M (Neves & Marques, 2017).

At this stage, the aerodrome infrastructure allowed for several companies to develop their activities in Ponte de Sor:

- Escola de Aviação Aerocondor (EAA): airline pilot training School, an EASA approved training organization offering Airline Transport Pilot License (ATPL) courses for both fixed-wing and rotary-wing aircraft, with a fleet of 35 airplanes and 6 helicopters. In 2015, EAA also became an EASA approved maintenance organization. This capability made it possible to ensure the maintenance of its own fleet (engines, components, and structures) and to provide maintenance services to third parties.
- Heliavionics Lab: operates a business of maintenance and repair, specializing on Kamov helicopters. It maintains an EASA part 145 certificate and holds widespread further qualifications. It also offers the inspection of helicopters and their engines, parts, and components, including sales of parts and accessories.
- Flytech: offers parts and services for ultralight and light aircraft. Founded in 2005 by two aeronautical enthusiasts and professionals with more than thirty years' experience in aeronautical maintenance, Flytech has significant know-how in services and products for the general aviation segment.
- National Civil Protection Authority (ANPC): maintains a base for their Kamov and Ecureil helicopters, also providing maintenance and repair for the whole fleet.
- Aeroclube de Portugal (glider division): founded in 1909, with headquarters in Cascais and Évora, it is the oldest aeronautical institution in Portugal and one of the oldest in the world.
- Aerodrome firefighters rescue and firefighting Service: a fire brigade ensures qualified first intervention and executes the necessary tasks to operate in aviation emergencies.

The excellent operating conditions of the runway, the existing infrastructure, as well as the availability of additional land for future constructions, boosted the continuity of investments. Recognizing the ability of the newly established flight school to attract significant numbers of international pilot students, as the school was successfully managing theoretical training bases in several countries (Italy, Angola, and the UAE), the Municipality created at the aerodrome a new campus with an accommodation capability of up to 226 students (113 double rooms), equipped with several classrooms, student lounges, and a restaurant. This investment of EUR 4.6 M (Neves & Marques, 2017) was aimed at creating an academic environment for student pilots, but also for university levels students from partner higher education institutions, as the qualification of professionals for the aviation industry was recognized as a strategic goal. The campus was inaugurated in June 2016.

On the other hand, the commitment of the Municipality and a focused strategic vision allowed the continued development of the aerodrome by the creation of a multipurpose support Infrastructure to anchor additional activities. In this context, the construction of the Aeronautical Industry Business Center aimed at creating logistical conditions to respond to the demand from investors and players in the aeronautics and aerospace sectors, that is, creating a regional infrastructure for business reception, with real capacity to ensure a favorable environment for the development of companies in the Aeronautical Industry in the Municipality. Located at the Municipal Aerodrome, the Business Center has a built area of around 3,500 m^2, encompassing meeting rooms, cafeterias, and common administrative areas, in addition to the areas to be made available to companies. Following the municipal investment of additional EUR 1.4 M (Neves & Marques, 2017) on the Aeronautical Industry Business Center, the TEKEVER consortium started in April 2017 the production in Ponte de Sor of all the drones for maritime surveillance in the European Union, under a EUR 70 M contract won with EMSA – European Maritime Surveillance Agency. Tekever, which stimulates an economic group currently composed of 7 companies, is organized in two main areas: Information and Aerospace Technologies, Defense and Security. The company is active in Brazil, the United States, England, the Netherlands, China, and the United Arab Emirates through subsidiary companies.

An Emerging Aviation/Aerospace Cluster in Ponte de Sor (2018-2023)

As the notoriety of the aerodrome grew within the sector, the attraction of new businesses to Ponte de Sor reached interesting new levels. Ulmer Aeronautique (rebranded as AS Breathing), a French company from Seine-Saint-Denis, producer of oxygen masks for supersonic military aircraft and high-altitude helicopters and transport aircraft, intended to expand its business in the European market and in Portuguese-speaking countries. As such, Ulmer opened a new factory at the municipal aerodrome, occupying an existing small infrastructure.

The emergence of an aviation/aerospace cluster in Ponte de Sor was not limited to the aerodrome facilities. In 2018 the French consortium Rexiaa Group acquired an industrial installation in the industrial zone of Ponte de Sor near the city center. Created in 1986 and based in Issoire near Clermont-Ferrand (France), the Rexiaa consortium of 8 companies can design, develop, and produce, completely in-house, components, assemblies and sub-assemblies in composite, metal, and hybrid materials. Rexiaa is a supplier of major global industry players such as AIRBUS Helicopters, DASSAULT Aviation, and Safran.

Also in 2018, the EAA flight school was bought by an US technological giant, L3 Electronic Systems, a manufacturer of full flight simulators that had recently launched an airline pilot training division, the L3 Flight Academy, upon acquisition of CTC Aviation, a leading pilot academy based in the UK. With training bases in the US and the UK, L3 sought to develop its activity so that Ponte de Sor was to become its leading training base across continental Europe, due to the excellent operational and weather conditions.

The year of 2018 also marked the beginning of a systematic effort by the municipality to promote the cluster in an international context. Since then, the Ponte de Sor cluster (branded as Aerospace Hot Spot Ponte de Sor) is regularly present in international fairs such as the Paris Airshow (France), Farnborough International Airshow (UK), Aero Friedrichshafen and ILA Berlin (Germany), Dubai Airshow, the Arab Aviation Summit, and the Global Investment in Aviation Summit (UAE). As part of its international strategy, Ponde de Sor launched the annual event "Portugal Air Summit" aimed at bringing the national and international sectors together, while also seeking to attract the young generations into Aviation and Aerospace careers. The innovative aspect of such an event was that, unlike most aeronautical events in Europe, it focuses on a three-day conference program, although also including an air show and large exhibitor spaces. Since its first edition back in 2017, Portugal Air Summit has become the largest aeronautical and aerospace summit in the Iberian Peninsula and has had a significant impact on the Ponte de Sor region, but also at a national and international level. The 2022 edition had more than 12,000 visitors on site and more than 100 companies as exhibitors, reached an online audience in more than 60 countries, generated a turnover of Euro 10M, and marked important milestones as Cirrus and Diamond aircraft manufacturers successfully sold units at the event, and a SATA Azores airline AIRBUS A320 aircraft landed in Ponte de Sor making it the first ever heavy commercial aircraft landing in the history of the municipal aerodrome.

Finally, three additional hangars and a new control tower building were inaugurated in the last two years at the municipal aerodrome, stemming from the last cycle of infrastructure investments made by the Municipality which totaled Euro 9.3 M. This allowed for additional businesses to be attracted to Ponte de Sor, diversifying the types of activities offered: LD Helmets (a Swiss-owned company originally based in Italy that manufactures helmets for high-altitude helicopters and supersonic military aircraft), Avionicel (specialized in aircraft electronic systems and avionics equipment), the SEVENAIR Group that includes the SEVENAIR Academy providing training for both airline pilots and aircraft maintenance technicians, and Aeromec, an EASA Part 145 and NATO certified company, owned by the OMNI Aviation Group, specialized in commercial and military aircraft maintenance. The new control tower facility includes several meeting rooms, an auditorium with capacity for 75 people, two classrooms, and a small hangar, providing excellent opportunities for education and training activities to be held at the aerodrome in cooperation with several leading Portuguese higher education institutions with which the Municipality of Ponte de Sor has established partnerships.

Comprehensive View of the Portuguese Aeronautical, Space and Defense Cluster

The Portuguese Aeronautics, Space and Defense Cluster (AED Cluster Portugal) was created in Lisbon as a private not-for-profit association and formalized before the Portuguese public Institute IAPMEI in August 2016. IAPMEI is the public agency for competitiveness and innovation, supporting small and medium companies and Innovation. In the scope of the Portuguese Ministry of Economy and Maritime Affairs and covering all fields of industry, except tourism, IAPMEI´s mission is to promote competitiveness and business growth through the management of instruments and programs aimed at strengthening SME innovation, entrepreneurship, and business investment. In 2017, the AED cluster was considered by the Portuguese Government as a "Strategic National Competitiveness Cluster" for Aeronautics, Space and Defense.

The AED Cluster was the result of the joint efforts and merger of three previous sector associations (PEMAS - National Association of the Aeronautical Industry, PROESPAÇO - Portuguese Space Industries Association and DANOTEC - Association of Defense, Armament and New Technology Companies, respectively), aiming at hosting common initiatives and actions to more easily capture European structural and investment funds, capitalize on experiences of the aeronautical and automotive industry and integrate, in a dedicated structure, the main capabilities and businesses of the sector. In early 2017, the AED cluster was composed of more than 70 companies from different fields of activity, involved around 18,500 workers, and had been gaining weight in the national economic activity (Gabinete Oliveira das Neves [GON], 2017). Today, with 125+ full members and with a turnover of EUR 1.72 B (of which 53% for industry, 36% for ITC, and 11% for universities and R&D centers), a volume of exports of 87% and a weight in GDP of about 1.5%, the sector is expected to double its contribution to the Portuguese GDP in the next two or three years (AED Cluster Portugal, 2023a).

Composition

Table 1 below lists the different types of organizations that make up the AED cluster as of 2022. Out of a total of 112 full members in 2022, the aeronautics division has the largest participation (94 members), followed by the defense (80 members) and space (67 members).

Most of the 13 institutions indicated in Table 1 are higher education institutions (universities and polytechnical institutes) but included are also two municipalities of which Ponte de Sor was the first to become a full member of the AED cluster in late 2017. Focusing specifically on the field of aviation and supporting activities, the distribution of the AED cluster competencies is shown in Table 2:

For reference, a complete matrix of capabilities of the AED cluster members is given in AED Cluster Portugal (2023b). A list of the cluster network with an individual brief description of each one of its members is available in AED Cluster Portugal (2023c).

The consideration of an aerospace cluster in Portugal must allow for the specificity of a sector of the economy that is divided between the civil and military branches, and is based on aircraft manufacturing companies, commercial aviation companies and the Air Force, comprising a vast network (supply-chain) of product and service providers. It is worth that the AED Portugal Cluster gained a leading global aircraft manufacturer, as AIRBUS joined formally the cluster in 2023. In fact, AIRBUS opened in 2022 a new Global Business Services Center in Lisbon, after AIRBUS Atlantic (fully owned by AIRBUS) inaugurated a production unit in the north of the country (Santo Tirso). In 2023, their Lisbon Global

Table 1. Types of AED cluster members

Type of organization	Number
Research	33
Design & Engineering	50
Manufacturing	56
MRO – Maintenance, Repair & Overhaul	14
Consulting & Services	46
Institutions	13

Source: AED Cluster Portugal.

Table 2. AED cluster areas of competence in aviation

Competency	Number
Aircraft Structures	34
Engines	21
Cabin Interior and furnishing	20
Equipment and aircraft electronics	34
Airport and Air traffic management	16
Unmanned Aerial Systems	25
Production, Equipment, Tools, and Tooling	37
Testing, Certification and Quality Assurance	27
Packaging, Handling, Storage and Transportation	11
Training Schools, Systems and Other Support	36

Source: AED Cluster Portugal.

Business Services Center opened a subsidiary facility in Coimbra. As a result, Portugal is now the fifth European country where AIRBUS is present by number of employees.

Territorial Distribution

The small size of the country and the levels of accessibility between the different existing centers give the AED Cluster a national characteristic, with evident centralities in Lisbon and Porto. According to AED Cluster Portugal (2023b), in regional terms, the North Region stands out with 34.7% of entities and the Lisbon Region with 38.9% (distribution by number of NUTS - *Nomenclature of Territorial Units for Statistics* II entities); This distribution highlights an asymmetrical territorial positioning of the Cluster (74.6% of entities located in two regions), but the strengthening of the sector in the Central Region and the development of the Alentejo regional hubs of Évora and Ponte de Sor, allow us to envisage a more comprehensive territorial development. Alentejo currently hosts 9.7% of the total AED Cluster members, but as discussed in the remainder of this chapter, this number is expected to increase.

METHODOLOGICAL APPROACH

Literature on the development of the Ponte de Sor aerodrome and businesses based therein is virtually non-existent or extremely limited. Moreira (2015) first reported on a new airline pilot training center that started its flying activities in 2013. Neves & Marques (2017) conducted the first and so far, the only published study on the investments made in the municipal aerodrome in the period 2005-2017. They analyzed their results and impacts by focusing on the following main aspects: (i) to characterize the investments made and the companies and business activities present at the aerodrome, (ii) to identify the type of activities offered by the Portuguese Aeronautics, Space and Defense Cluster (AED Cluster Portugal), (iii) to briefly describe the sociodemographic, economic, and territorial environment under which the complex of aeronautical activities in Ponte de Sor has been developing, (iv) to characterize the different dimensions of return on investment, identifying both direct and indirect effects, and (v) to identify investment and employment opportunities related to the activities being developed at the aerodrome.

This investigation builds on the previous study by Neves & Marques (2017) by analyzing the Ponte de Sor Aerospace Cluster considering the methodology used by Paone & Sasanelli (2016), which is based on Michael Porter´s Diamond Model. Porter (1990) gave a conceptual definition of a Business Cluster, defined as a "*geographically proximate group of interconnected companies and associated institutions in a particular field, linked by commonalities and complementarities*". But also developed a framework to assess the overall business environment of clusters, describing the different interactions that arise between its factors during the processes of innovation and competition. The Diamond Model includes four components that are interdependent (factor conditions, demand conditions, related and supporting industries, and context for strategy and rivalry) and two external variables (chance and government). These determine the level of the interactions between the cluster´s components. Below is a brief description of each of these elements:

- Factor conditions are deeply rooted in a cluster's socioeconomic, political, and geographic context, influencing its competitiveness and innovation. These conditions include human capital, infrastructures, knowledge, financing sources, and expertise. Some are unique to the cluster and cannot be replicated (the location, for example), while others are a result of long-standing development processes and require long-term strategic commitment to replicate. These factors are crucial for a cluster's success.
- Demand conditions refer to specific customers in specialized segments, influencing firms' innovation and competitive advantage. Different natures, origins, and consistency of demand necessitate tailored adaptation strategies. Attracting and satisfying large shares of demand is crucial for a cluster's competitiveness and innovation (Alberti & Pizzurno, 2015; Steiner et al., 2010).
- A network of interconnected supporting industries is crucial for innovation, providing cost-effective specialized inputs and participating in the process. The level of interconnection with related and supporting industries determines the cluster's ability to generate system-level innovation and widespread socioeconomic development.
- Strategy and rivalry: Success in the competitive market is influenced by the way companies are set up, managed, and targeted. Strategic rival interaction is a key factor in driving innovation. Strategic collaboration among companies can leverage local innovation potential by sharing resources and expertise. The cluster effect is a micro-foundation of this effect, with the outcome being larger than its components. Proper structures and policies are essential for optimal conditions for rivalry and cooperation.
- Chance refers to uncontrollable events that create discontinuities, allowing some actors to gain competitiveness and others to lose positions.
- Government: The government's actions, including economic intervention, legislation, and regulation, can significantly influence individual components at local, regional, national, or international levels.

Since learning processes are an essential part of innovation, appropriate pathways for the transfer of knowledge are needed. The Triple Helix Model, first presented by Etzkowitz & Leyesdorff (1995) and revised by Farinha & Ferreira (2013), can be used to understand the processes by which knowledge is conveyed, shared, and developed to generate innovation. The model demonstrates the interaction patterns between academia, industry, and government in an economy, highlighting their nonlinear interactions and overlapping regions of intervention. This results in hybrid phenomena and trilateral networks, promoting information spread throughout the system.

We thus used the Triple Helix Model to characterize the emerging aviation/aerospace cluster in Ponte de Sor, by analyzing the various factors that support or undermine its competitive advantage. This made it possible to derive some broad conclusions about the ensuing components, such as:

a) Factor Conditions
  ◦ Location and Infrastructures
  ◦ Colleges and research institutes
  ◦ Capacity for talent development and retention
  ◦ Favorable ecosystem for innovation and entrepreneurship
  ◦ Financing mechanisms available
  ◦ Proximity and concentration
  ◦ Know-how and expertise, and low cost of labor
b) Context for Strategy and Rivalry
  ◦ Foreign Direct Investment and national strategy
  ◦ Active collaboration between Institutions
  ◦ Level of Public Intervention
  ◦ Incentives to start-ups and R&D
  ◦ Presence and diversification of anchor firms
  ◦ Network of specialized SMEs
  ◦ Involvement in international programs
c) Related & Supporting industries
  ◦ Interconnections with other aerospace clusters, and with other sectors
  ◦ Participation in larger networks
  ◦ Specialization
  ◦ Support from research sector
  ◦ Internationalization
d) Demand Conditions
  ◦ High demand for innovation
  ◦ Capacity to draw in global demand
  ◦ Emerging players (threats)
  ◦ Domestic civil and defense demand
  ◦ Exports

Following Paone & Sasanelli (2016), we classify each of these elements according to their impact (positive, limited, or negative) on the cluster competitiveness.

Diagnosis of Investments Done

According to Neves & Marques (2017), investment in the municipal aerodrome was a milestone in the development of the Municipality, being one of the axes adopted for the implementation of one of the main guidelines of the Ponte de Sor Strategic Charter elaborated in 1996. The Strategic Charter pointed to the need of qualification of the local economic base and the reinforcement of the regional integration of Ponte de Sor, and these guidelines were included in the approved version of the Municipal Master Plan through the reservation of soils to be considered for the location of an aerodrome. To attract aeronautical industry segments requires a new dimension of territory qualification, considering its high strategic interest, demanding technology, business qualifications, manpower, infrastructure, and strong R&D investment, promoting interaction between industry and scientific and technological systems. Furthermore, the aeronautical industry's dynamics often lead to changes in local productivity due to outsourcing new skills and technologies, which can be applied to other sectors.

The currently existing infrastructure resulted from several investment cycles that totaled 42 million euros (until 2022), of which around 29 million euros came from support from different programs. This public investment initiative corresponds to the traditional cycle of launch and gradual consolidation of projects of a structuring nature that have evolved (in terms of existing capabilities and installed dynamics) into logistics supporting the "clusterization" of activities: economic, knowledge and innovation, and skills training.

Since 2017, the municipal aerodrome economic and business activities have evolved towards providing additional pilot training capacity and aircraft maintenance and repair services. This growing market offers opportunities for specialization with public and private players, enhancing education and training modalities and emerging services in the cluster's value chain. At the same time, in the former facilities of the extinct company Delphi, the Ponte de Sor Business and Technological Center was created in an area of more than 10,000 m², which has several business reception areas made up of industrial pavilions (to install companies, with dimensions adjustable to the intentions of investors who continue to seek out the municipality) and spaces for training, laboratories and R&D activities, study and meeting rooms, auditorium and common areas for exhibitions/business events and other social aspects. This Business and Technological Center will also house a training center for professionals in the aeronautical industry capable of promoting training activities in the areas of aircraft maintenance, composite production, automation/robotics, industrial maintenance, and renewable energy (a municipal project in partnership with IEFP, the Institute of Employment and Professional Training, inaugurated in July 2023).

The various investments mentioned above are linked to segments that reveal diversification of the AED Cluster's chain of activities and value creation (manufacture of drones and development of control software, manufacture of oxygen masks for supersonic aircraft, manufacturing of aeronautical components in composite materials, maintenance of large aircraft and mobility and transport - MCG Transportation group, supplier of train and bus manufacturers and new areas of training technicians for cluster activities, public and private initiatives). At the scale of Ponte de Sor, these activities have a high impact on employment, estimated at the end of 2022 at around 300 direct jobs, to which approximately 400 more should be added in established companies that will be fully operational between 2023 and 2024.

In this approach to investment cycles, it is worth mentioning the approval and ongoing execution of three Mobilizing Agendas of the Recovery and Resilience Plan (PRR) in which the Municipality of Ponte de Sor participates as a partner entity, alongside companies located in Ponte de Sor:

- Aero.Next Portugal - aims to develop complete aeronautical programs in Portugal offering 3 products: light regional manned aircraft with capacity for 19 passengers, 2000 kg of cargo and range of 2000 km; unmanned aircraft capable of operating maritime surveillance; and advanced air mobility service. The action plan will allow the generation of 72 new products, services, and patents by 2027 with a turnover of €109M.

- Neuraspace - aims to help solve problems related to space debris, with a radar being created in Ponte de Sor to respond to this need. The project is estimated at around €20M and 20 to 30 direct jobs created.
- Newspace - related to the production of microsatellites, the agenda comprises around €60M and will create more than a hundred jobs in the coming years.

Access to EU incentives has over time constituted a factor of high consideration for companies that decided to set up their businesses in Ponte de Sor, which benefits from integration into a European Convergence Region (Alentejo) for the purpose of accessing the European Structural Funds and investment.

The results of municipal investment demonstrate a capacity for municipal initiative focused on the strategic commitment of providing Ponte de Sor with a set of instruments for attracting exogenous investment, in response to problems that affect most of the territories of low density, namely, economic decline, unemployment, lack of alternative occupations and living conditions for young people and other residents (Moreira, 2020; Lappas & Kourousis, 2016). The approach adopted by the Municipality of Ponte de Sor was based on two operational aspects, phased in time:

- Creation of basic infrastructural conditions that would enhance locational factors (geographical location, climate and airspace characteristics, accessibility), comprising the various investments in the aerodrome. This investment made it possible to attract a set of activities that involve air movement (civil protection, aircraft maintenance and repair, flights, pilot training).
- Investments aimed at hosting business activities that correspond to the "attracting companies and investments" aspect. These interventions, which explore new locative factors enhanced by the proximity of the agglomeration of resources in the context of the cluster, have return dimensions that appear associated with economic and business dynamics, including market orientation (internationalization).

In summary, the recent evolution of additional investments done is consistent with the arguments put forward by Neves & Marques (2017) that recommended a more demanding standard of intervention aimed at attracting investments and more robust companies, namely competing for foreign direct investment, with emphasis on companies focused on manufacturing components in order to strengthen the relationship links with the value chain of the AED Cluster, around branches of activity with potential employers supported by local skills training responses for standard jobs in the chain, generating local recruitment opportunities.

The Aviation/Aerospace Industry as a Lever for the Development of Territories

The aviation/aeronautical industry is consensually considered as an industry of high strategic interest, mainly due to the socio-economic development associated with it. Therefore, it is not surprising that the State and/or Municipalities are diligent in their efforts to attract first-rate manufacturers, suppliers, and users to their Industrial Parks, because it is expected that the co-location of these companies will translate into employment growth, better wages, and the concomitant leap in local economic prosperity.

The last decade has seen an adaptation of the European aeronautical industry at different levels (efficiency gains, risk sharing, pressure on suppliers, etc.): employment (highly qualified: 38% of the active population have university education), has known between 2009 and 2014 a growth of 2.2%, while turnover in 2014 was 199.4 billion euros (Aerospace and Defense Industries, 2015; GON, 2017), which shows that this is a sector of great economic importance for the development of any territory, largely represented by SMEs (70% in 2003). In addition, it is expected that in the next 20 years the demand for air travel will double, aerospace manufacturing will exceed 5.6 trillion dollars (GON, 2017), more than enough reason to bet politically on attracting and even promoting the clustering of activities of the Aeronautical and Aerospace Industry.

Not being a sector of easy and fast development, because it requires long periods of R&D activities and long receipt cycles, from the initial investment in production support to the financial return of the manufactured products, the Aeronautical and Aerospace Industry has the capacity to be able to respond to two markets with different dynamics, the civilian and the military that share the turnover (51.3% of the civilian market and 48.7% of the military).

This is the macroeconomic and investment context that underlines the main question posed to the development of Ponte de Sor´s aerospace cluster. The question is whether investing in aeronautical activities at a municipal airfield in Portugal, like Ponte de Sor, is a socioeconomically sustainable and territorially cohesive option. To this point, Hassen (2012) examined recent studies on aeronautics' relationship with local and global territories, revealing the sector's impact on these two territorial dimensions at various levels such as urban, agglomeration economies, private initiative and public policies, and markets and competition models. We give below a brief overview of such dimensions and related main references identified by Hassen (2012):

a) Urban and metropolitan dimension:
    ◦   Aeronautics has strong local roots and remains very integrated at the metropolitan level (Klein et al., 2003), making considerable impact on the urban centers where it is concentrated (Leriche, 2004).
    ◦   Aeronautics remains very geographically concentrated. A small number of places managed to quickly develop benefits that proved insurmountable to competitors, hence the concentration (Terral, 2003).
    ◦   The identity of some cities, such as Toulouse, is linked to aeronautical activities, and the interconnection between company strategies and local development policies is a very present fact. Airbus organized its production according to a network company model, based on a division of labour between several cities, each of them housing a complex of activities (Zuliani & Jalabert, 2005; Jalabert & Zuliani, 2009).
    ◦   This industry is often concentrated in large cities: it is a "metropolitan industry" (Beckouche, 1996).
    ◦   The territorial base of aeronautics in large urban centers is explained by the availability of resources necessary for the development of this sector, such as knowledge and qualified (Scott & Mattingly, 1989).
b) Agglomeration economies:
    ◦   The spatial concentration of the sector is explained by agglomeration economies that constitute a force of attraction for companies and accentuate this concentration (Scott, 1993).
    ◦   Companies located close to other companies in the same sector have rapid growth (Beaudry & Swann, 2009).
    ◦   Changes in the location logic of large European companies (market and product strategies) reinforce the importance of proximity (Benzler & Wink, 2010; Wink, 2010).

- Relational proximity plays an important role in terms of innovation in the aeronautical sector in Montreal (Tremblay et al., 2012).
- Proximity in institutional, organizational, and geographic versions articulates coordination between the company and subcontractors (Kechidi & Talbot, 2006).
- Community involvement in aeronautics is partially explained by the presence of large "anchor companies", such as Bombardier in Montreal and Airbus in Toulouse (Niosi & Zhegu, 2005, 2010).
- The birth of aviation in Montreal was mainly influenced by the presence of an important shipbuilding and railway industry. These industries played the role of founding industries for aeronautics (Zhegu, 2007).

c) Private initiative and public policies:

- Private initiative was predominantly behind the creation of the aeronautical industry in Montreal. Government policies regarding the location of activities must be coherent with market solutions to create local innovation systems (Niosi & Zhegu, 2005).
- The aeronautical industry has grown from an arsenal logic, where locations are imposed by the State, to a market logic, where locations are imposed by costs. The sector's location logic is influenced by two forces: international relocations and integration into local networks to benefit from proximity to other actors (Bélis-Bergouignan et a., 2001).

d) Markets and competition model:

- Aeronautics integrates more international information and knowledge networks than other high technology sectors (Niosi & Zhegu, 2005).
- Aeronautics markets are global. The outsourcing of production encourages the transfer of technologies and knowledge to emerging countries and threatens the competitiveness of industry in Western countries (MacPherson & Pritchard, 2003).
- The geographic location of subcontractors is no longer a determining factor. Aeronautics subcontractors must adopt world-class management practices.
- Regardless of the type of activity, the competition to which companies are subject is international (Kraft & Ravix, 2000).
- Aeronautics hubs are globally interconnected. The structure of relationships and exchanges perfectly illustrates the idea of Pierre Veltz's "archipelago economy" (Frigant et al., 2006).

ANALYSIS AND DISCUSSION

Since the inception of Embraer´s production activities in Évora (Alentejo) in 2012, the Portuguese aeronautical ecosystem has seen significant development. Embraer invested €177 M in two factories devoted to strategic areas (metallic structures and composite-made components) to "simultaneously develop Embraer's global presence and work on local skills and capabilities." (Lusa, 2012). The project was focused on the production of parts for the Legacy 450 and 500 business aviation aircraft and the military aircraft KC-390. According to Embraer Portugal´s CEO, the decision to invest in Portugal was determined by two fundamental aspects: the stability of institutions in Europe and the Portuguese Government' s policy of developing an aeronautical cluster (Lusa, 2012). Together with OGMA, a maintenance, production and engineering company partly owned by Embraer and based in Lisbon, this allowed for the development and growth of a national network with companies, universities and R&D institutions directly involved in the production and the entire life cycle of the KC-390 aircraft. The experience gained in such a project demonstrated the Portuguese aeronautical know-how which then led to increased participation in international aeronautical projects.

But Portugal also benefits from significant opportunities in the space sector. The Portuguese Space Agency (Portugal Space, also known as PT Space) is an organization created by the Portuguese Government to implement the National Strategy for Space 2030. The founding members of the Agency are the Foundation for Science and Technology (FCT), the National Innovation Agency (ANI), the Ministry of Defense, the Regional Government of the Azores, and the Autonomous Region of Madeira which joined as an observer in December 2019, with a view to also becoming a full member of the Agency. The Agency's main objective is to promote and strengthen the ecosystem and value chain of the space sector in Portugal, for the benefit of society and the national and international economy, acting as a business and development unit for universities, research institutes and companies. It coordinates the Portuguese participation in the European Space Agency (ESA) and is also Portugal´s national representative at the European Commission for matters related to Space, namely the European Space Program (Copernicus, Galileo, GOVSATCOM, SSA) and Horizon Europe.

Portugal has quickly adapted to and integrated itself into space programs after joining the European Space Agency fifteen years ago, leading to an economic return of more than 120% in the last ten years. Between 2006 and 2015, the Portuguese space industry ecosystem—which employed more than 1400 people—generated a €890 million turnover (Portugal Space, 2020). The development of expertise in several fields, such as augmented reality, cyber systems, telecommunications, Earth observation, navigation, and space exploration, is credited with this progress in scientific institutions and businesses. The OECD analysis indicates Portugal's ESA return on investment has a multiplier effect of 4 to 5 for public R&D funding. An FCT economic impact study shows that for each euro invested in ESA space programs, over two euros were generated for the national economy (Portugal Space, 2020). Portugal and ESA have launched a joint incubation program for companies, resulting in 30 companies and 240 highly qualified jobs in the period 2018-2020, with over half of the European Union's Horizon 2020 investment coming from the business community.

The term "New Space" refers to the new wave of private funding-attracting international space players and business models that make up the "New Space Industries" sector. Mega-constellations of micro- and nanosatellites are needed for communication and information systems. Portugal and other small- and medium-sized nations have new prospects in data production, data generation, and infrastructure development thanks to this sector. The goal is to create mega-constellations and micro- and nanosatellites, which will presumably make low-altitude and sun-synchronous orbits more accessible to a wider range of people. Portugal's advantageous location in the Atlantic opens new global prospects, especially for the establishment of infrastructure for measurement and observation. The Atlantic Interactions agenda and the Atlantic worldwide Research Centre (AIR Center) support worldwide R&D cooperation to strengthen knowledge on space-Ocean-climate interaction through North-South / South-North cooperation, as this gives a comparative advantage.

Within this context, a Porter´s Diamond cluster analysis was carried out to provide a detailed understanding of the Ponte de Sor distinctive features and conditions under which the aviation/aerospace cluster has been implemented and evolving. Figure 1 below briefly summarizes the features of the Factor Conditions, the Context for Strategy and Rivalry, Demand Conditions, and the Related and Supporting Industries. In this figure, the same notation used by Paone & Sasanelli (2016) was adopted.

Figure 1. Porter´s diamond analysis of the Ponte de Sor aerospace cluster

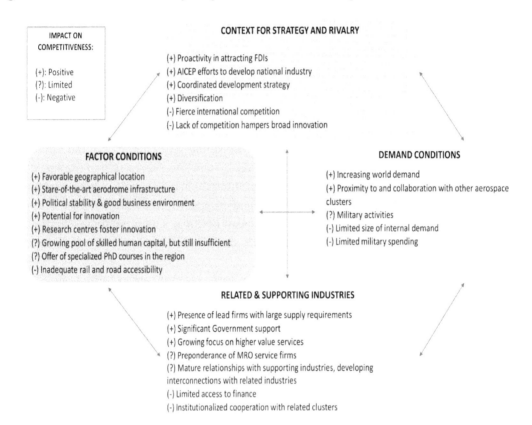

Factor Conditions

In its favor, the Ponte de Sor cluster benefits from some relevant geographical features: located in a very sunny, obstacle-free, and flat region that is ideal for the development and growth of both a leading academy for airline pilot training activities and the operation of drones in experimental and mission-specific flights, and also the proximity with other relevant locations such as the Évora aerodrome (where the Embraer factories are based, now owned by the Spanish Group AERNNOVA), and the Beja airport, where HiFly´s main MRO facilities are located (HiFly is one of the largest charter airlines in the world, operating heavy commercial aircraft exclusively). Ponte de Sor also offers unrivalled infrastructure, with the longest runway among regional aerodromes in Portugal, as well as state-of-the-art hangars, including one of the largest available hangars for MRO activities in the country.

Portugal is renowned for Its political stability and good business environment, as in recent years the country has attracted world leading events such as the Web Summit and global players such as AIRBUS have invested very significantly in the country. In this regard, the Ponte de Sor cluster initiative has gained important recognition from the Portuguese Government as a best practice case for focused strategies to develop the interior regions of Portugal which face severe demographic and economic challenges. Ponte de Sor has also gained recognition from the International Civil Aviation Organization (ICAO) as an example of an *Aviation for Good* initiative, fostering the social and economic development of small communities.

In terms of innovation, the Global Innovation Index (GII) 2023 ranks Portugal among the world's 30 most innovative economies. Portugal has gone up two spots in the GII, to 30th place among the 132 global economies (World Intellectual Property Organization, 2023). According to the report, the Portuguese economy's strengths are the national industry's diversity, the percentage of the domestic product invested in software, and the scientific or technical papers published in the country. Among the European economies, Portugal performed higher than average in the following categories: Creative Outputs, Human Capital, Research, and Institutions. In these areas, Portugal ranked respectively 19th, 23rd e 35th in the global ranking.

Regarding R&D, the national aerospace ecosystem has a significant network of universities and research institutions led by the most prominent higher education institutions in Portugal, which are indirectly present in Ponte de Sor through their participation in the three mobilizing agendas mentioned above (Aero.Next, Neuraspace, and Newspace). However, in the Alentejo region where Ponte de Sor is situated only the University of Évora offers PhD programs (three) related to the field: these are Earth and Space Sciences, Engineering and Mechatronics, and Computer Science. Although the R&D activities do contribute very significantly to the innovation in the Portuguese aerospace sector, a stronger presence in Ponte de Sor is needed to provide a growing pool of skilled human capital in the region. This will allow recruiting highly qualified professionals locally, keeping the cost of labor at competitive levels.

An element of concern is a lack of adequate road and railroad accessibility to the Ponte de Sor cluster. Road accessibility is decisive for economic activity and key to making the region more competitive, more attractive, more connected, and more resilient. It is essential to conclude some structural projects for Alentejo, so that it is possible to take advantage of a geographical position that is an added value in the national and Iberian context. The conclusion of the IC13 road (of which only a short segment has been built so far) is crucial to efficiently connect Ponte de Sor with both the Lisbon international airport and the logistics platform in Elvas (located at the border with Spain) towards Madrid. On the other hand, The Alentejo railway network can play a fundamental role in consolidating the national network, especially regarding to the transport of goods, and contributing to a more competitive and attractive territory for investment and the installation of companies. In this regard, the requalification of the railway network through Ponte de Sor is a much-needed step.

Strategy and Rivalry

Ponte de Sor has been capable of attracting relevant FDI at an early stage in its inception, with a focus on the French market (the Rexiaa Group and AS Breathing), followed by the Swiss and Italian markets (LD-Helmets). The opportunity with Rexiaa Group was born from an active role of the Government Foreign Affairs Ministry, together with AICEP Portugal Global Trade & Investment Agency, a government body focused on the development of a competitive business environment that contributes to the globalization of the Portuguese economy. As a reputable business-oriented agency, with specialized professionals in Portugal and a global network in over 50 countries, AICEP's mission is to increase Portugal's competitiveness and reputation, by fostering structural investment and promoting the internationalization of Portuguese companies.

The recent strategic goal by AIRBUS of establishing production units and offices in Portugal is yet another example of a favorable and coordinated national development strategy, implemented with active collaboration between institutions. Such anchor firms are instrumental in the consolidation of the Portuguese aerospace sector, and their diversification is a positive factor for the sustainability of the whole ecosystem in the country, as small and medium suppliers from various segments of the supply chain are attracted.

In this context, the Ponte de Sor emerging cluster faces fierce international competition which requires a well-defined strategy for growth. Pilot training activities in Ponte de Sor have been so far dominated by a single pilot academy, which hampers innovation in pilot training. Most pilot academies in Portugal are based in Cascais (greater Lisbon), but it appears that the Portuguese Government intends to centralize in Cascais all the business aviation jet operations (thus creating vacancies at the Lisbon international airport for additional large commercial aircraft). This will imply that all Cascais-based flight academies must then relocate, which should constitute an opportunity for Ponte de Sor to attract other flight training companies, thus fostering rivalry in one of its core activities. The small number of participating firms in Ponte de Sor and their distribution over the whole supply chain is detrimental to local rivalry and international competition, but it is expected that the inception of the three mobilizing agendas will change the competition landscape.

Supporting Industries

The presence in Portugal of leading firms with large supply requirements such as AIRBUS, EMBRAER, THALES, FedEx, and LAUAK (a Tier 1 supplier to OEMs – Original Equipment Manufacturers and Tier 2 to renowned aerospace companies, with two facilities in Alentejo), is of fundamental importance to leverage the competitiveness of the Portuguese aerospace sector. The sector has gained considerable attention and support from the Portuguese Government as the cluster was recognized as a "Strategic National Competitiveness Cluster". With a focus on value-added solutions and increased levels of innovation, the Portuguese sector seeks to maximize its integration in the European and global supply chains.

At a regional level, the Ponte de Sor cluster is developing additional capabilities, of which the presence of a first MRO firm at the municipal aerodrome is a recent example. Mature relationships with supporting industries and developing interconnections with related industries is yet to be achieved, but the three mobilizing agendas under implementation in Ponte de Sor will fundamentally change the landscape in this regard.

Access to capital and financial support is a concern, as typically Portuguese SMEs have limited capability to invest in infrastructure and in the participation in large and complex European projects. This undermines opportunities for growth and innovation, limits their ability to enter new markets and to compete effectively with larger, better funded, and established companies.

Cooperation with related clusters is of the utmost importance. As an example, Ponte de Sor can benefit from the relative proximity to the Coimbra-Badajoz axis. NOVExport is a European innovative acceleration program project designed to increase the competitiveness of small and medium-sized businesses in the space and digital technologies sector in the South-West of Europe, and to support their internationalization toward Latin America's markets. Six hubs are opened in Montpellier (FR), Bayonne (FR), Bilbao (SP), Madrid (SP), Badajoz (SP) and Coimbra (PT). The Ponte de Sor aerospace cluster has yet to consolidate this type of relationship.

Demand Conditions

World markets in aviation and aerospace are growing and recovering from a halt due to the COVID pandemic. The worldwide network of suppliers, manufacturers, distributors, and service providers that makes up the aerospace and military sector is extensive and intricate. A Deloitte analysis states that the industry brought in $763 billion in sales in 2019 and is expected to increase at a compound annual growth rate of 3.3% between 2022 and 2025. Environmental and sustainability issues also affect the aerospace sector. Two percent of the world's carbon dioxide emissions are attributed to the aviation sector, according to the International Air Transport Association (IATA). Manufacturers are therefore under pressure to implement sustainable practices across their supply chains and lessen their carbon footprint.

In 2024, automation and digitalization are anticipated to have a big impact on the aircraft supply chain. The global aerospace and defense digital twin market is anticipated to develop at a compound annual growth rate (CAGR) of 12.3% from $3.6 billion in 2020 to $6.4 billion in 2025, according to a report published by Market & Markets. Through automation and digitalization, businesses may save waste, increase productivity, enhance inventory management, and obtain real-time supply chain information. For instance, Airbus has developed a digital supply chain platform called Skywise that optimizes maintenance, decreases downtime, and boosts operational efficiency using big data analytics and machine learning. Airbus hopes to have 30,000 airplanes linked to Skywise by 2024.

Portugal, like many European countries, has faced economic challenges in the preceding years, and military expenditures had remained relatively constant. According to idD Portugal Defense (2023), the weight of Defense in Portuguese Exports was 1.8% in 2010, (Euro 992 M of a total of Euro 54 732 M), and in 2021 it increased to 2.5% (Euro 2224 M of a total of Euro 90 607 M). However, in recent years, there was a growing awareness of the need to modernize and invest in defense capabilities to meet the evolving security landscape in Europe. This included investments in areas such as cybersecurity, maritime surveillance, and participation in international peacekeeping missions. Portugal only absorbs about 13% of the national production by the Portuguese aerospace ecosystem, as most of the production (87%) is exported. However, the growing number (363) of companies and of R&D and Education/ Training Entities (61) that are active in Defense in Portugal has led to increased employment by 5.8%, despite the crisis in 2020.

As the Portuguese aerospace sector becomes more and more exposed to an environment marked by intense and growing rivalry from emerging players, collaboration between the Portuguese aerospace sector and other aerospace clusters presents challenges regarding international competition as well as promising market opportunities. To succeed, a very aggressive international commercial strategy is needed and in this regard the Ponte de Sor Aerospace cluster has been extremely active in the last 5 years.

CONCLUSION AND FUTURE PROSPECTS

The Ponte de Sor emerging cluster was presented, and its recent evolution was characterized. The different cycles of investment and impacts were analysed. The growing diversity and complementarity of activities were presented, and a Porter´s Diamond Model analysis was discussed.

The project in question is the outcome of a territorial strategy designed to support employment, social cohesion, sustainable development, competitiveness, and land use planning. Ponte de Sor has demonstrated a methodical and continuous effort in the aviation and aerospace sector over the past

10 years with the realization of significant direct investments. The consolidation of the Ponte de Sor Municipal Aerodrome as a key infrastructure of Portugal's aerospace cluster is particularly beneficial to the region's economy, as Alentejo is a region with strong socio-economic asymmetries classified as a European Convergence Region.

Going forward, with the timely implementation of the three mobilizing agendas financed by the Portuguese Recover and Resilience Plan It is expected that the Ponte de Sor regional cluster will hold a prominent position in the forefront of Portuguese knowledge in the medium term thanks to the strengthening of strategic and operational partnerships with aeronautical and aerospace firms and training institutions, and the creation of a niche for applied research and scientific dissemination. These goals are achievable and, if attained, will establish Ponte de Sor as a sustained center for excellence in aerospace business activities.

REFERENCES

Aerospace and Defense Industries. (2015). *Facts & Figures*. ASD. https://nag.aero/wp-content/uploads/2022/01/ASD-Key-facts-figures-2015.pdf

Alberti, F. G., & Pizzurno, E. (2015). Knowledge exchanges in innovation networks: Evidence from an Italian aerospace cluster. *Competitiveness Review*, 25(3), 258–287. doi:10.1108/CR-01-2015-0004

Beaudry, C., & Swann, G. M. P. (2009). Firm Growth in Industrial Clusters of the United Kingdom. *Small Business Economics*, 32(4), 409–424. https://www.jstor.org/stable/40344561. doi:10.1007/s11187-007-9083-9

Beckouche, P. (1996). La France en villes (Félix Damette). Flux, (23), 50-51.

Bélis-Bergouignan, M.-C., Frigant, V., & Talbot, D. (2001). *L'Articulation Global/Local des Modèles Industriels Pharmaceutique, Automobile et Aéronautique*. Institut fédératif de recherches sur les dynamiques économiques. https://www.academia.edu/en/23599595/Global_local_articulation_in_industrial_models_for_phamaceuticals_automobile_and_aeronautics_In_French_

Benzler, G., & Wink, R. (2010). From agglomerations to technology-and knowledge driven clusters: Aeronautics cluster policies in Europe. *International Journal of Technology Management*, 50(3/4), 318–336. doi:10.1504/IJTM.2010.032679

Bouwer, J., Krishnan, V., Saxon, S., & Tufft, C. (2022, March 31). *Taking stock of the pandemic's impact on global aviation*. McKinsey & Company. https://www.mckinsey.com/industries/travel-logistics-and-infrastructure/our-insights/taking-stock-of-the-pandemics-impact-on-global-aviation

AED Cluster Portugal. (2023a, September 2). *About us*. AED Cluster Portugal. https://www.aedportugal.pt/en/about/

AED Cluster Portugal. (2023b, September 2). *Capabilities Matrix*. AED Cluster Portugal. https://www.aedportugal.pt/wp-content/uploads/2023/05/AED-Capabilities-Matrix-1.pdf

AED Cluster Portugal. (2023c, September 2). *Cluster Network Members*. AED Cluster Portugal. https://www.aedportugal.pt/wp-content/uploads/2023/04/Catalogue-AED-Cluster-Portugal-long-version-2023-06.pdf

Etzkowitz, H., & Leyesdorff, L. (1995). The Triple Helix—University-Industry-Government Relations: A Laboratory for Knowledge-Based Economic Development. *EASST Review*, *14*, 14–19.

Farinha, L., & Ferreira, J. J. (2013). *Triangulation of the triple helix: a conceptual framework*. (Working Paper 1). Triple Helix Association.

Frigant, V., Kechidi, M., & Talbot, D. (2006). *Les territoires de l'aéronautique: EADS, entre mondialisation et ancrage*. France: Editions L' Harmattan.

Gabinete Oliveira das Neves. (2017). *Avaliação de resultados e impacto do investimento realizado no aeródromo municipal de Ponte de Sor*.

Hassen, T. B. (2009). Toulouse, l'avion et la ville, de Guy Jalabert et Jean-Marc Zuliani, Toulouse. *Canadian Journal of Regional Science*, *32*(3), 511+. https://link.gale.com/apps/doc/A245543046/AONE?u=anon~f6482c3e&sid=googleScholar&xid=1fd072f9

Hassen, T. B. (2012). Le Système Régional D' ['*Aéronautique à Montréal Entre Dynamiques Territoriales et Sectorielles*.]. *Innovations: Technology, Governance, Globalization*, L.

Hassen, T. B., Klein, J.-L., & Tremblay, D.-G. (2012). Interorganizational Relations, Proximity, and Innovation: The Case of the Aeronautics Sector in Montreal. *Canadian Journal of Urban Research*, *21*(1), 52–78. https://www.jstor.org/stable/26193883

idD Portugal Defense. (2023, September 25). *Factsheet Defence Economy in Portugal*. IDDPortugal. https://www.iddportugal.pt/wp-content/uploads/2022/10/Factsheet-Economia-de-Defesa-em-Portugal-2022-EN.pdf

Jalabert, G., & Zuliani, J.-M. (2009). *Toulouse, l'avion et la ville. Privat, coll*. Aviation.

Kechidi, M., & Talbot, D. (2006). *L'industrie aéronautique et spatiale: d'une logique d'arsenal à une logique commerciale*. HAL. https://EconPapers.repec.org/RePEc:hal:journl:hal-02376465

Kechidi, M., & Talbot, D. (2010). Institutions and coordination: What is the contribution of a proximity-based analysis? The case of Airbus and its relations with the subcontracting network. *International Journal of Technology Management*, *50*(3/4), 285–299. doi:10.1504/IJTM.2010.032677

Klein, J., Tremblay, D., & Fontan, J. (2003). Local systems and productive networks in the economic conversion: the case of Montreal. *Géographie Économie Société, 5*.

Krafft, J., & Ravix, J.-L. (2000). *Competition and industrial coordination*. Krafft J. (ed.), post-print halshs-00464275. HAL. https://ideas.repec.org/p/hal/journl/halshs-00464275.html

Lappas, I., & Kourousis, K. I. (2016). Anticipating the Need for New Skills for the Future Aerospace and Aviation Professionals. *Journal of Aerospace Technology and Management*, *8*(2), 232–241. doi:10.5028/jatm.v8i2.616

Leriche, F. (2004). Metropolization et Grands Equipements Structurants. In C. Siino, F. Laumière, & F. Leriche (Eds.), *Presses Universitaires du Mirail*.

Lusa (2012, September 19). *Embraer investiu 177 ME nas duas fábricas de Évora que já têm quase 100 trabalhadores*. RTP Notícias. https://www.rtp.pt/noticias/economia/embraer-investiu-177-me-nas-duas-fabricas-de-evora-que-ja-tem-quase-100-trabalhadores_n588412

MacPherson, A., & Pritchard, D. (2003). The international decentralisation of US commercial aircraft production: Implications for US employment and trade. *Futures*, *35*(3), 221–238. doi:10.1016/S0016-3287(02)00055-1

Moreira, M. C. (2015). A New Training Center in Portugal: A Unique Project to Boost the Next Generation of Aviation Professionals. *ICAO Training Report*, *5*(1), 28–30.

Moreira, M. C. (2020). Local governments as enablers of the aviation workforce: A case in Portugal. In *Engaging the Next Generation of Aviation Professionals* (pp. 7–10). Routledge.

Neves, A. O., & Marques, R. J. (2017). O Aeródromo Municipal de Ponte de Sor como Motor de Desenvolvimento Local/ Regional. In *XI Congresso da Geografia Portuguesa, As dimensões e a Responsabilidade Social da Geografia*, Porto, Faculdade de Letras da Universidade do Porto, Associação Portuguesa de Geógrafos. 78-989-54030-2-8.

Niosi, J., & Zhegu, M. (2005). Aerospace Clusters: Local or Global Knowledge Spillovers? *Industry and Innovation*, *12*(1), 1, 5–29. doi:10.1080/1366271042000339049

Niosi, J., & Zhegu, M. (2010). Anchor tenants and regional innovation systems: The aircraft industry. *International Journal of Technology Management*, *50*(3/4), 263–284. doi:10.1504/IJTM.2010.032676

Paone, M., & Sasanelli, N. (2016). *Aerospace Clusters: World's Best Practices and Future Prospects*. Academia. https://www.academia.edu/33388664/AEROSPACE_CLUSTERS_Worlds_Best_Practice_and_Future_Perspectives

Porter, M. E. (1990). *The Competitive Advantage of Nations*. Free Press. doi:10.1007/978-1-349-11336-1

Portugal Space. (2020). *Portugal Space 2030 - A Research, Innovation and Growth Strategy for Portugal*. PT Space. https://ptspace.pt/wp-content/uploads/2020/08/PortugalSpace2030_EN_web.pdf

Revista Aeronáutica. (1921). *Aero-Club de Portugal, VIII* (3).

Rust, D. L., Stewart, R. D., & Werner, T. J. (2021). The Duluth International Airport Aviation Business Cluster: The Impact of COVID-19 and the CARES Act. *Research in Transportation Economics*, *89*, 101–135. doi:10.1016/j.retrec.2021.101135

Scott, A. J. (1993). *Technopolis: high-technology industry and regional development in Southern California*. Univ of California Press.

Scott, A. J., & Mattingly, D. J. (1989). The Aircraft and Parts Industry in Southern California: Continuity and Change from the Inter-War Years to the 1990s. *Economic Geography*, *65*(1), 48–71. doi:10.2307/143478

Sobieralski, J. B. (2020). COVID-19 and airline employment: Insights from historical uncertainty shocks to the industry. *Transportation Research Interdisciplinary Perspectives*, *5*(100123), 1–9. doi:10.1016/j. trip.2020.100123 PMID:34173453

Steiner, M., Gil, J. A., Ehret, O., Ploder, M., & Wink, R. (2010). European medium-technology innovation networks: A multi-methodological multi-regional approach. *International Journal of Technology Management*, *50*(3/4), 229–262. doi:10.1504/IJTM.2010.032675

Terral, L. (2003). *Les Industries Aérospatiales en Amérique du Nord: Entre Permanences et Recompositions Territoriales*. [Doctoral dissertation, Université de Montréal]. Papyrus database.

Tremblay, D., Klein, J., Hassen, B., Tarek, & Dossou-Yovo, A (2012). Les acteurs intermédiaires dans le développement de l'innovation: une comparaison intersectorielle dans la région de Montréal. *Revue d'Économie Régionale & Urbaine*, 431-454. doi:10.3917/reru.123.0431

Wink, R. (2010). Structural changes in international aeronautics markets–regional, organizational, and technological dimensions. *Gestion Technologique*, *50*(3/4), 225.

World Intellectual Property Organization. (2023). *Global Innovation Index 2023 – Innovation in the face of uncertainty*. WIPO. https://www.wipo.int/edocs/pubdocs/en/wipo-pub-2000-2023-en-main-report-global-innovation-index-2023-16th-edition.pdf

Zhegu, M. (2007). *La coévolution des industries et des systèmes d'innovation: l'industrie aéronautique*. UQAM.

Zuliani, J., & Jalabert, G. (2005). L'industrie aéronautique européenne: Organisation industrielle et fonctionnement en réseaux. *L'Espace Geographique*, *34*(2), 117–144. doi:10.3917/eg.342.0117

Chapter 8

Global Commercial Aviation Zero Emissions Target:
Analysis of Scenarios of Evolution of CO2 Emissions in Commercial Aviation in Relation to Carbon

Carolina Correia Vieira
Instituto Superior de Educação e Ciências, Portugal

Rui Castro e Quadros
iD https://orcid.org/0000-0003-0685-259X
Instituto Superior de Educação e Ciências, Portugal & Escola Superior de Hotelaria e Turismo do Estoril, Portugal

ABSTRACT

These perspectives are primarily reflected on a global scale for 2050 with individual perspectives of the continuation of current technology, advancement in technology and operations, aggressive development of sustainable fuels and a technologically aggressive perspective. Where is considered the average annual percentage of air traffic growth, technology development, improvements in operations and infrastructure, sustainable fuels (SAF – sustainable aviation fuel), and use of offsetting. These scenarios will allow an analysis of the developments studied, with reference to the relationship between CO2 emissions from air transport and the volume of passengers transported, use of new more sustainable models for short and long-distance routes, discrepancies in the development of countries and consequently in achieving the targets. It also enables an overview of the aeronautical industry in the face of various barriers at political, social, economic, and technological level.

INTRODUCTION

Air transport is one of the polluting sectors, through the emission of various greenhouse gases, with carbon dioxide emissions standing out because they constitute the greatest negative impact. This study

DOI: 10.4018/979-8-3693-0908-7.ch008

arises from the need to understand which factors where investments should be made, so that it is possible to achieve carbon neutrality in commercial aviation.

It is necessary to understand and develop methods to ensure an evolution that guarantees the sustainability of the sector and future generations. It is essential to achieve a balanced relationship between the environment and air transport.

Given the need to understand the various players until neutrality is achieved are studied the carbon emissions, the increase in air passenger transport, the zero emissions goal and the contribution of innovations to achieve this goal. Having said this, it is possible to apply investments on specific factors, in order to establish the various scenarios of possible evolution of emissions.

The main objective of this analysis is to study the evolution scenarios of CO_2 emissions in the aeronautical sector until 2050. It intends to analyse how the reduction of carbon emissions from air transportation will be and if it will be possible to achieve the zero emissions goal.

The specific objectives are to observe the values of emissions from aviation, analyse the growth of air traffic, verify the optimization of emissions with the entry of innovations and study the evolution of emissions due to differences in the various contributing factors. Through this, the evolution of emissions related to the growth of air traffic is studied, and how it will be possible to counterbalance these values, with the goal of achieving zero emissions through the contribution of innovations in the sector.

That said, the purpose of this study is to be an essential source of information for all entities directly related to commercial aviation, in order to understand what the essential investment factors are to lead aviation through the best scenario, taking into consideration the differences and inequalities of evolution between countries.

LITERATURE REVIEW

Carbon emissions are one of several greenhouse gases released by aircraft operations, due to combustion by the engines. They stand out more prominently from the other gases emitted because they have a greater impact on the environment. This is due to the fact that these gases trap heat in the earth's atmosphere, and when released at high altitudes they directly affect the greenhouse gas layer (increase in global warming) and simultaneously remain in the atmosphere for a long number of years (Betiolo, Rocha, & Machado, 2015).

It is possible to observe an increase in global temperature over the last few years, according to the increase in carbon emissions released into the atmosphere, this growth being justified by the fast economic and industrial development.

In the face of this growth, it is essential to understand that the increase in emissions presents several discrepancies due to the different rates of development of the countries. These asymmetries in the evolution of emissions between countries are also felt in the outlook for the future (Gates, 2021).

Starting in 2020 and carrying out the analysis until 2040, the advanced economies manage to significantly reduce their values. On the other hand, middle and low-income countries show a large increase in their emissions of pollutant gases. Countries like China, it is predicted that until 2030 will continue to increase their values and then show a slow reduction until 2040 (Gates, 2021).

Thus, the urgent need arises to control the increase in global warming caused by emissions from air transport.

Currently air transport contributes with approximately 2% of carbon dioxide emissions (Betiolo, Rocha, & Machado, 2015), which may reach 3% in 2050, this being justified by the sharp growth in global air traffic, encouraged by population growth and trivialization of air transport (Gates, 2021).

However, this growth may be threatened in case no viable solutions are found for the environmental impact of aircraft operations, with special focus on greenhouse gas emissions (Rodrigues & Henkes, 2021).

According to EASA (2019), forecasts show an increase in the number of flights by 42% between 2017 and 2040.

EUROCONTROL (2022) states that flights in Europe have expanded rapidly due to market expansion through the development of low-cost airlines and economic expansion.

It is therefore essential to raise the questions of how and when the impact of emissions will be minimized and simultaneously achieve the zero emissions goal throughout the aviation system. The contribution of electrification, use of sustainable fuels (SAF) with emission reduction factors and the use of hydrogen for air transport need to be considered as answers. The development of these factors is essential to achieve the target, however regional development, economic and policy implications need to be considered. In theory, net zero CO_2 in aviation can be achieved by 2050, but this will require continued intergovernmental collaboration on long-term targets and further development of global carbon.

The idea is to achieve neutrality, in other words, that there is a balance. This balance corresponds to the fact that the planet, through the plants, is able to absorb practically the same amount of emitted carbon dioxide.

Gates (2021) refers that there is a need for innovation to enter the sector to reduce the emission values, since without innovation we will never be able to reach carbon neutrality. It is understood that technological advancement consists in the solution for sustainable growth, which will allow ensuring adequate conditions for future generations.

The goal now is to achieve neutrality, through various factors, with the essential inclusion of innovation and targets, by 2050 (ATAG, Waypoint 2050, 2021).

Thus, it is verified in the countries under the influence of EASA, the existence of 4 pillars for the reduction of emissions:

- Develop improvements in technology, including the implementation of low emission fuels;
- More efficient aircraft operations;
- Infrastructure improvements, including modern air traffic management systems;
- A single comprehensive measure in the market to fill the gaps.

Likewise, ICAO provides the necessary bases and means for international aviation to move towards carbon neutrality.

It is understood that commercial aviation faces major challenges in terms of environmental impacts, it is essential that aviation is able to evolve in a balanced manner with economic, social and environmental objectives, and simultaneously achieve ecological balance, thus avoiding the depletion of natural resources and continued climate aggravation (ATAG & Climate Action Takes Flight, 2017).

The industry has demonstrated several positive advances in improvements in operational efficiency (ATAG, 2021), however this progress is not proving sufficient to strike a balance on environmental issues.

The high level of scientific understanding of the long-term climate effect of aviation emissions makes the target clear and important for mitigation efforts. It is necessary for countries considered rich to achieve carbon neutrality by 2050, followed by middle income countries soon after, and finally the rest of the world is expected to follow suit.

The urgency of achieving neutrality as soon as possible is understandable, noting that the outlook for 2050 shows many similarities to today and many differences at the same time.

METHODOLOGY

This study has as methodology the explanatory, descriptive and direct investigation of scientific articles and reports of certified entities, with the application of review of the existing literature.

The methodology used is related to the analysis of the progress of the reduction of CO_2 emissions from air transport until 2050 and whether it will be possible to achieve the goal.

Thus, there is the need to study the various contributing factors, focusing on the entry of innovations in the sector and consequent adaptation of the value of CO_2 emissions.

In this way, the evaluation of various development scenarios of the various factors in question in commercial aviation is possible.

CIRCUMSTANTIAL FACTORS OF CO2 EVOLUTION IN COMMERCIAL AVIATION

CO_2 Emissions

The main pollutant gases emitted from the operation of current aircraft engines are carbon dioxide (CO2), water vapour, nitrogen oxides (NOx), sulphur oxides (SOx), unburned hydrocarbons (HC), carbon monoxide (CO) and other particulates (EASA, 2019).

In the face of rapidly growing carbon emissions, it is essential to implement measures to counter this advance. Progress towards sustainable development is key to reducing global emissions.

According to EUROCONTROL (2022), carbon neutrality can be achieved by eliminating 279 million tonnes of CO_2 in Europe through:

- Increased efficiency in conventional aircraft (17%);
- More efficient, hydrogen-powered aircraft (2%);
- Improvements in ATM (Air Traffic Management) and operations (8%);
- Sustainable fuels (41%);
- Other measures (32%).

Sustainable fuels are found to have the highest contribution for 2050 (41%), followed by market-based/ other measures (32%), these being key to correcting the emissions that remain after aviation applies all minimization methods.

Despite the high contribution of these factors, challenges are observed (EUROCONTROL, 2022):

- Long-haul flights as a source of CO_2 emissions;
- Carbon neutrality by 2050 is achievable but challenging;
- Essential and immediate focus on ATM efficiency;

Figure 1. Emissions from a twin engine aircraft operating a one hour flight with 150 passengers
Source: (EASA, 2019)

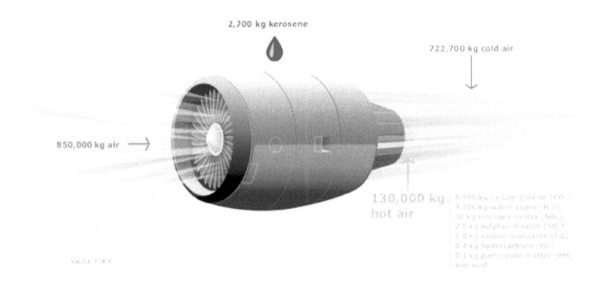

- Optimisation of the use of SAF.

Worldwide, according to Waypoint 2050 (2021), the measures implemented throughout the sustainable development process have managed to avoid the emission of 11GT of CO_2 since 1990. Figure 2 shows the progress from 1990 to 2050, with the implementation of emission reduction measures to achieve the 2050 targets.

Analysis:

The 11 GT of CO_2 avoided is due to the implementation of effective measures for minimizing environmental impact, and it is possible to observe the high impact of the current performance if the technologies established in 1990 were used.

Figure 2. Efficiency improvements: Evolution of emissions
Source: (ATAG, Waypoint 2050, 2021)

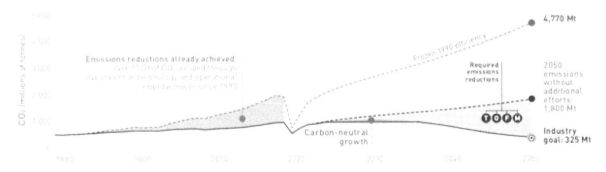

The effect of the COVID-19 pandemic in 2020 is verified, with an abrupt decrease in emissions. Subsequently, the beginning of the sector's recovery appears.

Currently a recovery phase is present. It is understood that the advances achieved so far were quite significant, however they are still not enough, being necessary a continuous investment in the Development and Research of air transport.

During the next decades, a number of decisions will determine the evolution of CO_2 emissions, including:

- How investment in sustainable fuel (SAF) and new technologies will be prioritized;
- Can energy provide for increased production of SAF and hydrogen simultaneously;
- Will governments, financial institutions and passengers play their part in accelerating the energy transition.

The solution lies in the union of these various factors, in this way it will be possible to reduce a large percentage of emissions by 2050 and achieve neutrality in the following years (2060/65), with several parts of the world reaching the goal before this date. Efficiency needs to continue to be improved and modern air transport will continue as the key to connectivity.

Increased Air Traffic

Improvements in efficiency are not sufficient to counterbalance the increase in CO_2 from growth in flight numbers, aircraft size and route distances.

It is necessary to consider that developed countries have higher traffic growth percentages than other countries. Although developing countries show high growth figures in the aviation sector (EASA, 2019).

The forecasts made by ATAG (2021) show more than 10 billion passengers by 2050. Thus, through improvements in technology, operations and fuels, air passenger transport will account for 1800 mega-tonnes of CO_2.

In 2016 air traffic counted 35.8 million flights, carrying 3.8 million passengers. The number of passengers carried is expected to grow by 6.9 billion by 2035.

This increase in passenger numbers for the future shows that carbon emissions from air transport will continue to rise. So, it is necessary to counterbalance this increase in pollutants by bringing innovations into the sector (ATAG & Climate Action Takes Flight, 2017).

Zero Emissions Objective

IAG (2020) sets short, medium and long-term goals, through the Flightpath Net Zero programme, in order to reduce CO_2 emissions.

The short-term objective is based on reducing CO_2 emissions per passenger/kilometer by 10% by 2025. This can be achieved through investments in new aircraft and improvements in fuel consumption efficiency, the goal is to reach 3.17 litres per 100 passenger/kilometers, compared to 3.79 litres (2015 figure).

The medium-term objective is to reduce carbon emissions by 20% by 2030, avoiding 22 000 tonnes of CO_2, so by 2030 it will be possible to quantify 160 000 tonnes of carbon emissions from aviation.

In order to achieve this goal, it is necessary to improve all sources of emissions in the sector.

Figure 3. Grams of CO$_2$ per passenger/kilometre (2025 target)
Source: (IAG, 2020)

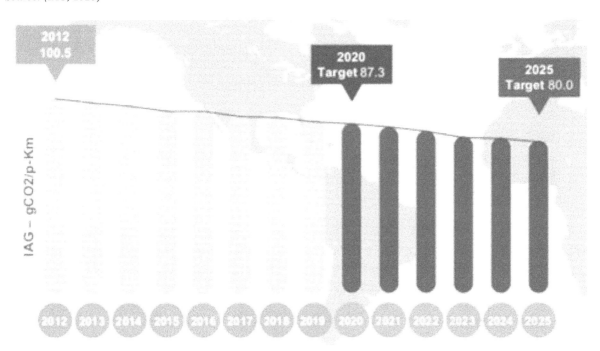

The long-term objective focuses on the goal of achieving carbon neutrality by 2050, it is essential to continue to develop to reach the 2030 target and then continue to invest in evolution through investments in sustainable fuels, low emission aircraft and carbon capture technologies.

Industry partners need to do their part in addressing emissions reduction innovations and government policies and incentives for decarbonization are essential. This 2050 target represents the united nations' goal of limiting global warming to 1.5 degrees.

CONTRIBUTION OF INNOVATIONS TO REDUCING CO$_2$ EMISSIONS

Technology

It is possible the identification of improvements in airframe and propulsion systems, energy storage and advanced concepts as mechanisms to reduce emissions through technological improvements.

Technological improvements include:

- Accelerating research into airframe designs, and electric and hydrogen propulsion;
- Forming partnerships with non-aeronautical technology providers;
- Providing opportunities for new green technologies;
- Preparation for electric and hydrogen power requirements for aircraft;
- Development of an energy strategy, with the development of SAFs, including hydrogen and low emission electricity requirements;

Figure 4. Technological improvements in aircraft to reduce CO$_2$ emissions
Source: (Yoshimura, 2022)

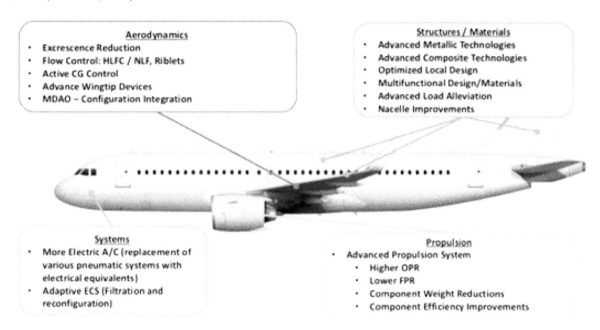

- Focus on procurement of new efficient aircraft and explore sustainable financial opportunities;
- Collaborate on synergies in order to develop pathways to integrate the battery technologies sector and hydrogen into aviation.

At the aircraft level itself, the technologies contributing to fuel efficiency improvements and emissions reductions are mainly:

- Fuselage (aerodynamics, lightweight materials and structures, equipment and systems, new configurations, power management and electrification);
- Propulsion systems (engine architecture, propulsion efficiency, combustion technologies, advanced materials and electrification).

Today, there are aircraft with improved aerodynamics and lighter weight (use of composite materials) compared to older aircraft. Each new generation of aircraft reduces fuel use by 15-20% compared to the model they will replace. Through the development of new technologies, a passenger, on average, produces 54.3% less CO$_2$ than the same flight in 1990.

The evolution of technology will continue to be developed, thus bringing about 20% improvement in fuel efficiency for each generation of aircraft.

Over the next 30 years, the industry is expected to undergo radical changes and by 2050 hydrogen and electric propulsion is expected to serve regionally and on short-haul flights.

On long-haul flights liquid fuel will continue to be required, with a transition to 100% sustainable fuels and low emission energy sources (ATAG, 2021).

Operations and Infrastructure

According to ATAG (2021), several measures can be implemented by airlines, airports and air traffic management to reduce CO_2 emissions from operations.

These improvements in operations and infrastructure include:

- Partnerships to rebuild air traffic volumes based on an optimised flight profile;
- Full implementation of fixed ground power sources, efficient base weight measures, continuity in approaches and take-offs, collaborative airport decision making, aerodynamic efficiency opportunities and assisted taxiing opportunities;
- Collaboration in order to accelerate research through certification and testing of new efficiency measures;
- Encouraging efficiency actions in systems;
- Research into new approach technologies and procedures at all applicable airports;
- Investigation of opportunities to increase the use of intermodality, including airport connectivity and access.
- Focus on improvements in operational procedures for the aviation system;
- Partnerships between the energy industry and airports so that there is a low carbon energy supply;
- Fund infrastructure improvements and system efficiency developments;
- Lobbying the community and aviation for new procedures and techniques for air traffic management.

It is understood that improvements in air traffic management (ATM) efficiency and aircraft operations demonstrate the greatest percentage contribution to the goal.

Energy Sources

The various energy sources for commercial aviation are SAF, electro-fuels and electric and hydrogen aircraft.

SAF

Sustainable fuels are essential to provide a clean source of energy for all fleets globally, thereby enabling the environmental impact of the millions of passengers carried each year to be lowered.

The term "Sustainable fuels" includes biofuel and all other fuels produced from other alternative sources, including non-biological sources. Production consists of blending paraffin with renewable hydrocarbons (JetA1).

Thus, this alternative can be used in aircraft without requiring technical modifications to the aircraft and airport infrastructure, also allowing air transport over long distances, which is one of the limitations of other sustainable energy sources (ATAG & Climate Action Takes Flight, Beginner's Guide to Sustainable Aviation Fuel, 2017).

It is understood that the faster the production and use of this energy source, the faster aviation will achieve its environmental goal (EUROCONTROL, 2022).

Based on the Waypoint 2050 (2021), efficient measures can be identified to overcome the barriers and achieve an accelerated evolution:

- All airlines should investigate opportunities for the use of SAF;
- Diffusion of the use of SAF should be done with support from governments, including financial support;
- Attract passengers on board with funding for SAF;
- Prioritise aviation in the use of alternative fuels;
- Explore the potential for SAF development at national and regional levels;
- Support, by governments, the development of the SAF industry;
- Implement SAF research programmes in the way of technology, raw materials and emission reduction improvements factors, production efficiency improvements;
- Need for the energy industry to demonstrate commitment to the production and diffusion of sustainable fuels.

In terms of cost, most carbon-free solutions have higher prices (green taxes) than fossil fuels. This is partly because fossil fuel prices do not reflect the environmental damage they cause, this provides the false impression that they are cheaper compared to alternatives.

After analysis of the various development factors, forecasts suggest that by 2050 aviation will require around 450 - 500 million tonnes of SAF per year. The revised figures show that this is achievable, with strict sustainability criteria (ATAG, 2021).

Figure 5. Evolution of the use of SAF
Source: (ATAG, Waypoint 2050, 2021)

	2020	2025	2030	2035	2040	2045	2050
Commuter » 9-50 seats » < 60 minute flights » <1% of industry CO₂	SAF	Electric and/or SAF	Electric and/or SAF	Electric and/or SAF	Electric and/or SAF	Electric and/or SAF	Electric and/or SAF
Regional » 50-100 seats » 30-90 minute flights » ~3% of industry CO₂	SAF	SAF	Electric or Hydrogen fuel cell and/or SAF	Electric or Hydrogen fuel cell and/or SAF	Electric or Hydrogen fuel cell and/or SAF	Electric or Hydrogen fuel cell and/or SAF	Electric or Hydrogen fuel cell and/or SAF
Short haul » 100-150 seats » 45-120 minute flights » ~24% of industry CO₂	SAF	SAF	SAF	SAF	Electric or Hydrogen combustion and/or SAF	Electric or Hydrogen combustion and/or SAF	Electric or Hydrogen combustion and/or SAF
Medium haul » 100-250 seats » 60-150 minute flights » ~43% of industry CO₂	SAF	SAF	SAF	SAF	SAF	SAF	SAF potentially some Hydrogen
Long haul » 250+ seats » 150 minute + flights » ~30% of industry CO₂	SAF	SAF	SAF	SAF	SAF	SAF	SAF

The diffusion of SAF will be progressive, together with electrification and hydrogen, until the goal is reached by commercial aviation.

Electrofuels

Electrofuels use clean electricity to join the hydrogen from water with the carbon from carbon dioxide, resulting in hydrocarbon fuel. Because of the need to use electricity, these types of fuels are referred to as electrofuels. The barrier to these more environmentally sustainable alternatives is that there are high costs associated with this adaptation. Thus, a significant effort is needed in the development of more affordable biofuels and electrofuels.

Electric and Hydrogen

Electric and hydrogen powered systems have the potential for zero emissions but have limitations in terms of flight distances.

Even with these limitations, they are an evolutionary factor in the reduction of CO2 emissions on the planet, so it is necessary to continue investing in the development of aircraft that use this clean energy source (EUROCONTROL, 2022).

Conclusion of Energy Sources

Due to the high weight of an aircraft, SAF are proving to be the most sustainable option for long distance flights. Other alternative energy sources, such as electric or hydrogen powered aircraft are viable for short distance flights.

Thus, aviation should focus on the adaptation and diffusion of SAF while continuing the development of other solutions with low environmental impact (ATAG & Climate Action Takes Flight, 2017).

Medidas com Base no Mercado

As medidas estabelecidas com base no mercado, incentivam a redução das emissões da aviação, de forma direta e indireta. São utilizadas de forma complementar, de modo a preencher a lacuna que permanece após serem aplicadas as medidas relacionadas aos fatores principais para a neutralidade. Estas medidas exigem que as companhias aéreas contrabalancem as suas emissões de carbono, através do pagamento pelas emissões emitidas (EUROCONTROL, 2022).

Conclusion of the Subject

There is a need for aviation to invest in new efficient technologies, with this need being reflected in the fact that technologies (including electric and hydrogen-powered aircraft) are a viable option for short-haul flights.

Following analysis of the various energy sources, it is understood from Eurocontrol (2022) that the main factors for aviation to achieve neutrality are:

- Evolutionary improvements in aircraft and engines, making them more efficient;

- Revolutionary technologies in aircraft, as well as the development of electric and hydrogen powered aircraft, together with the necessary infrastructure;
- More efficient flights, from operational improvements;
- Gradual increase in the use of sustainable fuels.

To achieve the long-term sustainability goal, decides to invest in three factors:

- Operations, which includes air and ground operations;
- Technology, in terms of alternative energy sources, more efficient airframe design, improved propellants and other advanced concepts.
- Fuels, which includes the fuels themselves (biofuels, cryogenic fuels and electricity) and the energy sources (wind, solar, nuclear, solid and liquid waste, biomass, fossil resources and industrial waste gases).

RESULTS

Perspective One

Perspective 1 reflects 4 scenarios of CO_2 emissions evolution for 2050 at global level, taking into account technological advances, operations and infrastructure, SAF and Offsetting, based on an 3.0% annual air traffic growth.

1.1. Scenario 0 - Continuation of Current Technology

Scenario 0 (zero) is the continuation of current efficiency without any acceleration of improvements.

It is characterised by technological development at current performance, mid-range improvements and improvements in airlines capacity in operations and infrastructure, continuation of current investments in SAF and mandatory use of offsetting to achieve the target.

Analysis: At the technological level there is a 13% contribution to the reduction of CO_2 emissions by 2050. Operations and infrastructures the reduction is 11%. As regards fuels, if the evolution of SAF is slow, there is a reduction of 4%; in the situation of a fast evolution the contribution is 26%.

In this scenario, offset represents the most significant factor. This plan will have a direct relationship with SAF, because if the evolution of SAF is slow, the offset will contribute with a 72% reduction; if SAF progresses in a large scale, the offset will contribute with only 50% of CO_2 emissions reduction.

Scenario One: Advances in Technology and Operations

Technology improvements are prioritised, with ambitious expectations for unconventional airframe aircraft and the transition to a fleet of electric/hybrid models from 2035/2040.

With significant investments in improvements in operations and infrastructure, substantial results in improvements and CO_2 reduction are achieved. The CO_2 emissions gap, after the improvements in operations and infrastructure, is closed with the use of sustainable fuels (SAF). In view of this situation large quantities of SAF with a high level of emission reduction are required. In this scenario, offset is not considered as a major influencing factor in 2050, however its applicability will be necessary between 2035 and 2050 to serve as a transition mechanism.

Figure 6. Scenario zero, perspective one
Source: (ATAG, Waypoint 2050, 2021)

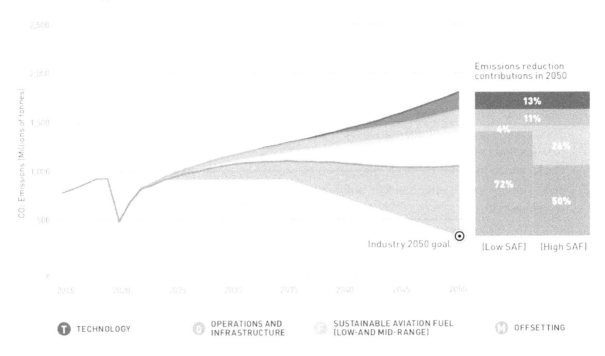

Factors: technological development to prioritise the development of electric and hybrid aircraft for short-haul flights, long-range and cargo capacity improvements for airlines, use of SAF for the reduction of 900 megatonnes of CO_2, with 290 to 390 megatonnes of SAF, and use of offsetting to correct the emissions gap remaining until 2050.

Analysis: In this scenario, the SAF represent the most relevant contribution for the reduction of carbon emissions, with 61%; this percentage is constituted using this alternative together with the offset, in this case used to correct the emissions gap that remains.

In second place in contribution to CO_2 reduction is technology with 27%. Operations and structures contribute with 12% in the reduction of emissions.

Cenário Two: Desenvolvimento Agressivo dos Combustíveis Sustentáveis

Based on improvements in technology, with new configurations in aircraft, including the body of the wing, but whereas it is based on current structures and technologies, i.e. there is no shift to electric or hybrid power sources, with the industry prioritising investments in sustainable fuels. Investments in operations and infrastructure that result in CO_2 reduction. The remaining gap is closed with the use of sustainable fuels (large amounts of SAF required). In this case, offset is not expected to play a key role in achieving the target in 2050 but could be used as a transition mechanism between 2035 and 2050.

Factors: technological development with new fuselage configurations with improvements in aerodynamic performance and wing body, mid-range improvements and improvements in airline cargo capacity against operations and infrastructure are considered, use of 350 to 450 megatonnes of SAF reducing 1100 megatonnes of CO_2 and use of offsetting if needed to correct the gap.

Figure 7. Scenario one, perspective one
Source: (ATAG, Waypoint 2050, 2021)

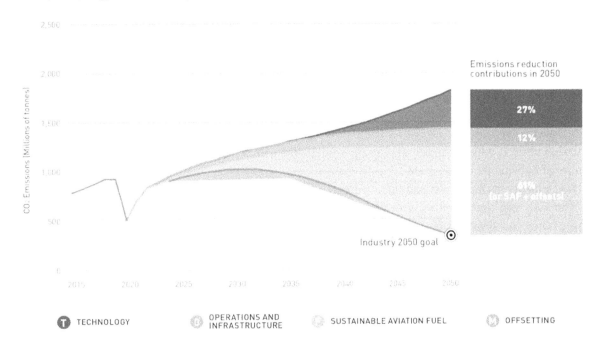

Figure 8. Scenario two, perspective one
Source: (ATAG, Waypoint 2050, 2021)

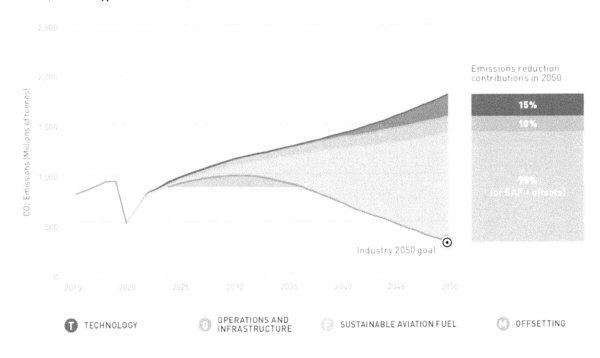

Analysis:

With the highest representation are SAF together with offset (in case of the need to correct the remaining emissions gap) with 75% contribution to reduce CO_2 emissions in 2050.

Technologies with a contribution of 15% and then the operations and infrastructure factor with 10% contribution.

Scenario Three: Aggressive Technological Outlook

It focuses on very ambitious technological developments with electric aircraft of up to 100 seats, zero-emission aircraft with hydrogen as a power source and with a capacity of 100 to 200 seats, and unconventional hybrid/electric aircraft.

Investments in operations and infrastructure result in reduced emissions.

The CO_2 gap that remains after technological and operations and infrastructure improvements is closed using sustainable fuels (SAF), thus requiring large quantities of it. Again, offsetting will not play a key role in 2050, but will serve as transition mechanisms.

Factors: technological development with a very aggressive acceleration of introduction of electric, hybrid and zero-emission aircraft between 2035-2040, mid-range improvements and improvements in airline cargo capacity in operations and infrastructure, investments in 20 to 144 megatonnes of SAF, and use of offsetting as a key factor towards the goal.

Analysis: presents as the greatest contribution to reducing emissions in 2050 the use of SAF, together with offset, with 50%. Technology shows 42% contribution to the goal. These are the two factors with the greatest impact in this scenario. Operations and infrastructure show a contribution of 8%.

Figure 9. Scenario three, perspective one
Source: (ATAG, Waypoint 2050, 2021)

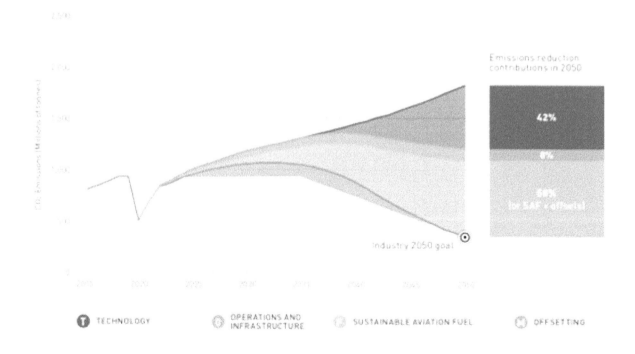

Perspective One Analysis

In 2050 the aviation sector will be an industry where in many ways it is similar to today's industry, but also very different.

At this point (2050) aviation will be responsible for 325 million tonnes of CO_2 (a third of the emissions produced by the sector in 2019), with around 10 billion passengers per year (more than double compared to 2019), supporting 180 million jobs and being a major factor in the global economy.

Some parts of the world the aviation sector will have already achieved neutrality and the rest of the global industry will be on track to achieve the same goal.

In terms of short-haul routes they have the possibility to use new energy sources that will power the energy needs of the flights, with 0% CO_2 emissions (electric and hydrogen). Electric and hybrid aircraft will operate to cover secondary cities and small communities with large hubs to connect different routes.

Long-haul flights will be performed by next-generation aircraft, which will operate almost entirely on SAF derived from various energy sources (including fuels produced by combining low-carbon electricity with CO_2 from the atmosphere).

At airport level, these will be hubs for renewable energy production and distribution. The whole industry will have adopted a zero-waste strategy and the rest of the economy is also struggling to reduce emissions and evolve new ways of doing business.

Perspective Two

In perspective 2 are developed 3 European paradigms which consider how aviation will meet sustainability related challenges through aircraft and engine improvements, with changes in aircraft design and propulsion. Considering the inclusion of SAF on a large scale.

These factors change according to the scenarios under study, with the established paths affecting the price of air passenger transport and its evolution. The course of the elements enables estimates of CO_2 emissions from aviation to be defined.

Paradigm One

This is the most ambitious, it features a high increase in air traffic from the sustained growth of the economy.

It is characterised by 19.6 million flights in 2050 (+76% than me 2019), an average annual growth rate of 1.8% (rate of 2% between 2019 and 2034 and 1.7% between 2035 and 2050, deceleration due to the maturity of markets, aircraft models with greater capacity and airport capacity constraints) and by intense technological investments to support the diffusion of SAF, with a noticeable reduction in their prices afterwards.

With the use of SAF, a rapid adoption of new aircraft models is expected. Between 2030 and 2035 new fleet designs (electric, hydrogen / electric and hydrogen aircraft) will be implemented.

The study verifies 2050 with twice as many flights as in 2005 and simultaneously a 65% reduction in CO_2 emissions. A significant increase in air traffic is understood, with the minimisation of its impact through the various contributing factors.

Figure 10. Paradigm one, perspective two
Source: (EUROCONTROL, 2022)

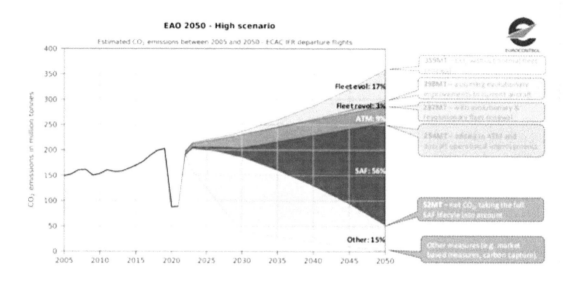

Paradigm Two

It is the most realistic, characterised by moderate economic growth, forecast annual air traffic growth of 1.2% with 16 million flights in Europe in 2050. SAF availability is forecast to increase and airports are shown to be a problematic factor in the future in airport congestion issues.

There is a 40% (2005/2050) reduction in CO_2 emissions through the use of sustainable fuels (SAF) and new aircraft models (electric aircraft for short flights and hydrogen propulsion for slightly longer distances). Bearing in mind that these new models are still new and will not constitute the dominant part of the fleet in 2050.

Europe will remain a hub for routes crossing the world, considering inequalities in growth. Air transport in Europe and the rest of the world will continue to be driven by tourism and business, while maintaining major concerns related to sustainability.

Paradigm Three

Characterised by a low economic growth paradigm, with higher prices on fuel, SAF and carbon, making the price of travel higher, a contributing factor to slower economic development.

As a result, airlines become more vulnerable, leading to the industry being less likely to invest in fleet renewal. Investments in new technologies will be more limited, or at least will happen later compared to the other scenarios in this outlook. Air traffic will have to adapt to an environment with potential restrictions, since variables are considered where the price of energy will be particularly high and where the economy may fall after a period of 30 years.

Thus, 13.2 million flights are expected in 2050, 19% more than in 2019 (0.6% annual growth) and 46% reduction in CO_2 emissions (2005/2010).

Figure 11. Paradigm two, perspective two
Source: (EUROCONTROL, 2022)

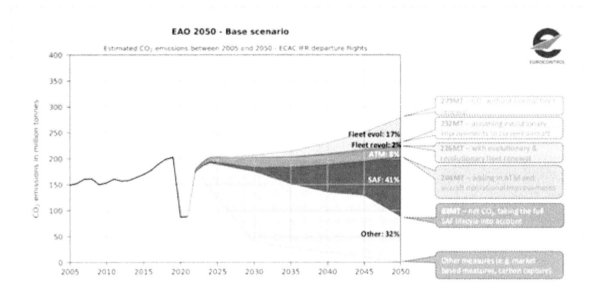

In graphical terms, paradigm 3 is identical to paradigm 2, despite the differences registered in the variables.

Analysis Perspective Two

The various paradigms outline different growth patterns and there is a need to counterbalance the emissions caused by the increase in traffic.

Long-haul flights will remain the main source of CO_2 emissions and at the same time the number of flights longer than 4000km will increase in all paradigms, accounting for approximately half of the emissions by 2050. To counterbalance this, SAF and improved aircraft efficiency are observed as a solution.

In the case of shorter distance flights, there are viable substitutes.

Figure 12. Air traffic growth 2050
Source: (EUROCONTROL, 2022)

ECAC	IFR Flights						
	2019		2050			2050/2019	
	Total (million)	Avg. daily (thousands)	Total (million)	Avg. daily (thousands)	Extra flights/day (thousands)	Total growth	AAGR
High scenario			19.6	53.6	23.2	+76%	+1.8%
Base scenario	11.1	30.4	16.0	43.7	13.4	+44%	+1.2%
Low scenario			13.2	36.2	5.8	+19%	+0.6%

Renewal to a proactive fleet is an essential factor to achieve a significant reduction of CO_2 emissions. It is thus understood that in the various paradigms the focus is on new aircraft types, adaptation to sustainable fuels, improvements in fuel consumption efficiency, and improvements in air traffic management and operations.

Analysed the various factors, the SAF reveal themselves with the highest percentage in the progress towards the objective, but the optimal solution lies in the balance and progress as synergy of the various elements.

Impact of Pandemic COVID-19

The COVID-19 pandemic had a very significant impact on aviation, with an almost total shutdown of the aviation system, grounding 64% of the world fleet.

This factor caused many orders for new aircraft to be cancelled, other situations, aircraft were produced and remained on hold to be delivered. From the moment restrictions are lifted, factors arise that positively and negatively affect the sustainable development of aviation:

- Strong acceleration of the retirement of older (less efficient) aircraft;
- Entry of a large number of new (more efficient) aircraft into the fleet;
- Short-term reduction in the delivery of modern aircraft;
- Medium-term reduction in the purchase of new aircraft.

Currently a significant recovery of the sector is observed.

It is possible to establish a comparison of traffic evolution in three different scenarios, with pre-pandemic and post-pandemic analysis (including impacts).

It is understood that there is a 16% reduction in air traffic evolution in the pre and post-pandemic comparison, referring to the baseline scenario. Following the analysis of the impacts caused by the pandemic situation starting in 2020, the aviation industry has committed to maintain long-term efficiency in the emissions reduction strategy.

Figure 13. Percentages of contribution of the factors to the objective.
Source: (EUROCONTROL, 2022)

Net zero CO_2 can be achieved by 2050 via the following:	Low Scenario	Base Scenario	High Scenario
Required CO_2 reduction for Net zero	194MT	279MT	359MT
Fleet evolution: More efficient conventional aircraft	17%	17%	17%
Fleet revolution: Electric & hydrogen powered aircraft	2%	2%	3%
ATM: Better air traffic management and airline operations	6%	8%	9%
Sustainable Aviation Fuels	34%	41%	56%

Figure 14. Comparison of pre-covid and post-covid air traffic evolution
Source: (EUROCONTROL, 2022)

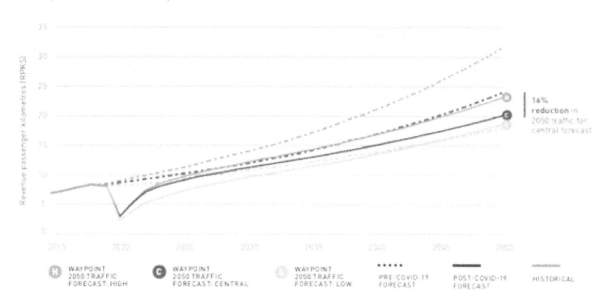

Impact of the Invasion of Ukraine

Russia's invasion of Ukraine has economic effects on aviation. In the short to medium term, the influence on the energy transition process is observed and in the long term is visible the negative impact on the growth of European aviation.

Beyond 2050

In theory aviation neutrality could be achieved by 2050, but this requires continued intergovernmental collaboration, with long-term targets and future global carbon market developments.

Some parts of the world may be in a position to advance air transport neutrality quickly. On the other hand, other countries may take longer to reach the goal. Thus, the target is most likely to be reached between 2060 and 2065, with the use of the offset to close the gap that remains after all other CO_2 mitigation factors have been developed. Looking at the contributing factors, new aircraft models (hybrid, electric and hydrogen) are observed as a key element, SAF will be 100% in use by 2060, along with offsetting to close the gap. Offsetting may remain an essential gap-filling factor even after 2050.

It is possible to analyse the evolution of CO_2 emissions after 2050, based on scenario 1 and scenario 3 of perspective 1.

In both scenarios it is possible to achieve global aviation carbon neutrality by 2060. It should be considered that in these two possible analyses the entry of innovations and developments in technology after 2050 is not included. The SAF, together with the offset, can be observed to fill the gaps, with a large contribution to the goal, followed in terms of contribution by technology and then operations and infrastructure.

Figure 15. Evolution after 2050 (Scenario one and scenario three)
Source: (EUROCONTROL, 2022)

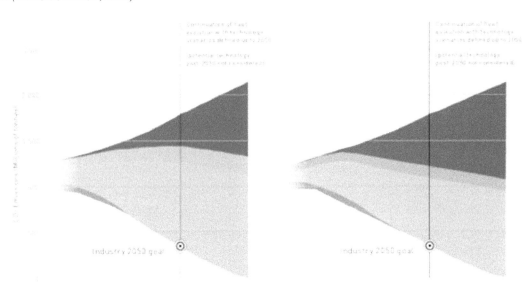

CONCLUSION

As a result of the negative impact on the environment caused by aviation CO_2 emissions and the rapid growth of air traffic derived from its trivialisation together with globalisation, it is essential to establish methods for the carbon neutrality of the sector.

In this way, it was possible to establish two perspectives, which include different scenarios/paradigms of evolution in the face of the introduction of the different factors, taking into consideration different patterns of technological and economic advances, and factors external to aviation (COVID-19 and the invasion of Ukraine).

They allow understanding that it will be possible to achieve the goal in 2050, however, countries show irregularities in their development. For this reason, it is expected that developed countries achieve neutrality by the established target, that developing countries achieve the same in the following years and finally it is expected that less developed countries, in a delayed way, achieve the same results.

The use of SAF, for long distance flights, together with electric and hydrogen models, for short distances, improvements in technology and operations and infrastructure, fleet evolution and revolution and the use of offset to fill the remaining gap, make the goal seem realistic in commercial aviation.

Through this there is a clear understanding of where investments, support and strengths should be applied to ensure the sustainability of the aviation sector, being applicable and of essential use by airlines, airports, Research and Development, competent entities and authorities, investors and Governments.

REFERENCES

ATAG. (2017). *Climate Action Takes Flight*. Beginner's Guide to Sustainable Aviation Fuel.

ATAG. (2021). *Waypoint 2050*. ATARG. www.atarg.org

Betiolo, C. R., Rocha, G. C., & Machado, P. (2015). *Iniciativas da Aviação para Redução das Emissões de CO2*. DABR. http://dcabr.org.br/download/publicacoes-tecnicas/Iniciativas_da_Aviacao_para_Reducao_das_Emissoes_de_CO2.pdf

EASA. (2019). European Aviation. *Environment Reporter*, 2019.

EUROCONTROL. (2022). *EUROCONTROL Aviation Outlook, 2050*, 24.

Gates, B. (2021). *How To Avoid a Climate Disaster: The Solutions We Have and the Breakthrough We Need.* Random House Publishing.

IAG. (2020). *IAG Flightpath net zero*. IAG.

Yoshimura, H. (2022). *ICAO CAEP Report that Explores the Feasibility of a Long-term Aspirational Goal for International Civil Aviation CO2 Emission Reductions*. LTAG.

Chapter 9

Determination of Ideal Aircraft Utilizing Analytical Decision-Making Tools:
A Case Study for Turkish Airlines

Beyzanur Cayir Ervural

Department of Aviation Management, Necmettin Erbakan University, Turkey

ABSTRACT

The critical and strategic position of the aviation industry has increased the interest in research studies on aviation topics. Particularly, determining the ideal preferences for aircraft is a complete decision problem because it contains many complex and qualitative/quantitative elements. The purpose of this study is to highlight the missing points by presenting a more comprehensive analysis for airline companies to choose the ideal aircraft model by using analytical models from a holistic perspective. Some technical, economic, and environmental criteria should be considered to identify the most proper aircraft. The selection of the most suitable aircraft in line with the characteristics determined as a result of the opinions received from aviation experts and extensive literature research is evaluated with recently developed multi-criteria decision-making (MCDM) methods such as complex proportional assessment (COPRAS), emergency descent arrest systems (EDAS), and weighted aggregated sum product assessment (WASPAS), then sensitivity analysis is applied to demonstrate the reliability of the methods after comparing the results obtained with each other.

INTRODUCTION

The aviation industry has always maintained its top priority, thanks to the numerous advantages it offers to countries and investors (Heracleous and Wirtz, 2009). Due to the developments in the aviation sector and its dynamic structure, it has been the focus of attention of all researchers with different important issues such as aircraft selection, airport selection, determination of the most suitable flight route, and planning of the most ideal crew team (Su et al., 2021).

DOI: 10.4018/979-8-3693-0908-7.ch009

Improvement studies, efficiency-enhancing activities, and cost-reducing actions contribute significantly to this issue (Gössling and Humpe, 2020). The sector's strategic position has enabled it to carry out important investment studies in the domestic and foreign markets and to work with systems integrated with the latest technological developments (Aviation Benefits, 2020). In order to gain dominance in the market, companies need to develop effective strategies evaluating market conditions, airline factors, and aircraft and hardware infrastructures (Zachariah et al., 2023). Therefore, choosing the ideal aircraft is a critical issue to ensure success in the operational management of the airline fleet, taking into account all the company's multidimensional business models (Operations Management, 2023).

Aviation management consists of many factors, such as complex processes, interactive and multi-stage system flow, and a constantly dynamic structure in the system. Due to the multi-structured and complex nature of the aviation management decision process, it requires the application of Multi-Criteria Decision-Making (MCDM) methodologies on problematic issues. This problem-solving method is generally preferred as an analytical thinking method because it is more practical, easy to apply, and objective. In the literature reviews, there are many MCDM methods such as Analytic Hierarchy Process (AHP), VlseKriterijumska Optimizacija I Kompromisno Resenje (VIKOR), Technique for Order Preference by Similarity to Ideal Solution (TOPSIS), ELimination and Choice Translating REality (ELECTRE), Preference Ranking Organization METHod for Enrichment of Evaluations (PROMETHEE), Multi Attribute Utility Theory (MAUT), Analytic Network Process (ANP), Measuring Attractiveness by a Categorical Based Evaluation Technique (MACBETH), etc. implemented in different fields to solve real-life applications.

The COmplex PROportional ASsessment (COPRAS) method was presented by Zavadskas et al. (1994) evaluating the higher and lower index values, and the effect of total indexes of attributes on the assessment of the result. COPRAS method is favored by most scholars due to the powerful ranking advantages and which applied in various fields such as supplier performance assessment, machine tool selection, project selection, material selection, and risk evaluation problems (Popovic et al., 2012; Xia et al., 2015; Valipour et al., 2017; Alinezhad and Khalili, 2019; Krishankumar et al., 2021).

The Evaluation based on Distance from Average Solution (EDAS) technique is one of the MCDM methods which was introduced by Ghorabaee et al. (2015) and the method based on distance from average solution. EDAS method is adapted to diverse areas such as supply chain management, inventory classification, logistics problems, green project selection problems, and robot selection problems (Ghorabaee et al., 2017; Ecer, 2018; Kundakcı, 2019; Rashid et al., 2021; Torkayesh et al., 2023), because of the simplicity and consistency of the method.

The Weighted Aggregated Sum Product ASsessment (WASPAS) method is a relatively new and efficient MCDM technique developed by Zavadskas et al. (2012). The method integrated both the weighted sum model (WSM) and the weighted product model (WPM), considering the relative importance of each criterion to provide a powerful and consistent result. WASPAS method is employed in various areas such as supplier selection, determination of helicopters, and manufacturing decision problems (de Assis et al., 2023). As can be seen from the studies, these methods have been recently developed and applied in different fields, but a very limited number of applications have been encountered in the aircraft selection problem. According to literature research, these three techniques have not been used together in an airplane preference problem. In this study, we aim to propose various decision-making (DM) methods to identify the most appropriate aircraft model for airline companies from a broader perspective considering numerous factors. (Quantitative and qualitative points).

In this context, a focus group meeting was organized to get the opinions of experts and managers from different airlines in Turkey (IGA, Ankara, and Konya) on the characteristics of the most preferred aircraft alternatives in the civil aviation sector. Once the most important factors have been identified, recently developed MCDM approaches such as COPRAS, EDAS, and WASPAS are employed to aggregate the opinions of decision-makers using different operators, showing their changes and advantages over each other. The obtained results are compared to each other, and the sensitivity analyzes demonstrate the performance of each decision model. The utilized criteria were identified according to literature reviews and expert opinions from airline management units. Under three main criteria such as technical, economic, and environmental factors, and nine sub-criteria are evaluated as maximum take-off mass, maximum cargo capacity, maximum range, speed, seat capacity, purchasing cost, fuel consumption, carbon emission, and noise (Bruno et al., 2015; Ozdemir and Basligil, 2016; Dožić et al., 2018; Kiracı and Akan, 2020) and seven alternative aircraft models (Yeh and Chang, 2009; Kiracı and Akan, 2020; Deveci et al., 2022) identified. This study aims to provide a more comprehensive analysis to select ideal aircraft models for airline companies utilizing analytical models with holistic viewpoints to emphasize missing points.

The study contributed to the literature from different sides as follows:

- The data set with the handled cases are real-life applications and unique data sets implemented in the model. The data set can be adapted to other problematic issues of the sector to get efficient results.
- Different DM tools provide more reliable and robust results to analyze the issue from wider angles. -And limited studies have been conducted on this subject although discussed the importance of the subject. The integrated models have not been implemented previously in the Turkish Airline company using COPRAS, EDAS, and WASPAS methods.

The rest of this paper is structured as follows. In the next section of this study, a brief background information on the subject of aircraft selection in the literature is given in Section 2. Then, in the third section, there is a description of the decision-making tools SWARA, COPRAS and WASPAS approaches. The application of the proposed model is presented in the fourth section. The results obtained and the sensitivity analysis, comparative analyzes and findings are given in the fifth section, sixth section and seventh section respectively. In the last part, the results and future directions are discussed in the eighth part.

STRATEGIC MANAGEMENT AND POLICY IN THE GLOBAL AVIATION INDUSTRY

The aviation industry is a symbol of superiority that plays an important role in the world. In order for countries to implement sustainable policies in the global market, they need to master aviation management policies and achieve success in the sector.

Therefore, strategic decisions in aviation play a critical role. Properly managed strategic decisions can lead to the right crew, fleet planning and scheduling, and investment decisions.

Strategic management includes decision-making and evaluation methods, analyzing and obtaining meaningful results, and high-level management techniques. By investigating the ideal conditions of the issue, the most appropriate decision is easily made with advanced strategic thinking/analytical methods and then the necessary actions are taken to solve the problems effectively.

Investment strategies can be shaped in line with the right strategic plans. Any decision step in the aviation industry has a major impact on the system because large cost and profit margins make up a significant share of the equilibrium system on a large scale. Therefore, the aviation sector makes a significant contribution to the financial economy. Since there are large losses and large profits, it creates both an advantageous and disadvantageous situation for the sector.

In this context, strategic policy management in the global aviation sector is an important issue due to its direct or indirect impact on all sectors.

Every development and improvement activity in the aviation sector ensures a strong position in the global market, and thus, states with a strong aviation side have a say in decision-making mechanisms all over the world. Effective decision-making methods are important in the aviation sector where strategic decisions are at the highest level. While approaches such as SWOT analysis and PEST analysis used in strategic policy decisions are mostly used in qualitative research, it can be said that multi-criteria decision-making methods are more successful and acceptable because they provide objective and rational results and have a high power of persuasion with their numerical results.

For airlines, decisions such as determining a new destination or adding a new route, organizing aircraft fleets and aircraft scheduling are non-operational decisions and need to be planned correctly in the long term. Since the cost of each action to be taken in such decisions is critical, it requires multidimensional evaluation and effective decision-making ability.

In the light of all these explanations, strategic management decisions play an indispensable and effective role in the aviation sector. From this perspective, the importance and contribution of the issue directly concerns the global aviation industry and will help managers and decision makers who will work and invest in the aviation industry.

LITERATURE REVIEWS

Airlines are highly strategic arenas all over the world to provide competitiveness and a smooth flow of passenger and freight/cargo movement. According to the literature reviews, there are numerous studies that have been conducted to investigate aircraft types for different purposes. Most of the studies analyze the determination of the ideal aircraft utilizing DM methods. The identification of optimal aircraft decisions is a complicated and multi-dimensional issue, and for this reason, it necessitates the implication of analytical thinking approaches to assign better options among a set of various alternatives.

It is hard to assess the most suitable choice with considering each aspect of the specifications of aircraft such as speed, weight, capacity, cost, number of seats, etc. Kiracı and Akan (2020) evaluated commercial aircraft selection problems utilizing a hybrid AHP and TOPSIS methods in interval fuzzy sets type 2 concepts under technical, economic, and environmental performance. Deveci et al. (2022) applied interval type 2 hesitant fuzzy entropy-based WASPAS technique for preferring the most appropriate aircraft type. Dozic et al. (2018) proposed fuzzy AHP to select the most suitable aircraft while considering passenger expectations. And differently, a logarithmic fuzzy preference programming approach has been implemented using three criteria and ten subcriteria. Gao et al. (2023) applied a fuzzy best-worst methodology by integrating grounded theory to evaluate the priority of used aircraft acquisition. Ozdemir and Basligil (2016) combined fuzzy ANP and Choquet integral approach for assessment and preference of the purchasing of the optimal aircraft for an airline company. The obtained results are compared with the fuzzy AHP method. Bruno et al. (2015) proposed two methods that integrate AHP and Fuzzy Set Theory to eliminate the deficiencies of the previous studies to assess aircraft. Yeh and Chang (2009) suggested a fuzzy Multi-Attribute Value Theory (MAVT)-based MCDM method to evaluate aircraft selection issues.

As can be seen in the literature reviews, although the subject is very important, there is a limited number of studies which are given in Table 1. TOPSIS, AHP, and best-worst methods are extensively

Table 1. A brief literature reviews

Authors	Methodology	Criteria	The Obtained Results
Gao et al. (2023)	Fuzzy best-worst methodology	Four main aspects: Economy, market, industry, technical and forty sub-criteria	C39 (Physical situation of the aircraft), C3 (Global CPI), and C14 (Price of aircraft) are the most desired three criteria
Deveci et al. (2022)	interval type 2 hesitant fuzzy Entropy based WASPAS	Revenue, capacity, customer expectation, cost, competition	Airbus 32C is the best alternative, while Airbus 320 is the worst alternative.
Tanrıverdi and Lezki (2021)	FTOPSIS based on FAHP	Sector Density, The growth rate of the Sector, Fixed Costs, Competitors' Product Diversity, Obstacles to Exit, Economies of Scale, Product Diversity of Potential Competitor, Investment (Capital) Requirements, Supplier Density, Cost of Transition to Substitute Products etc.	The best strategy for the Turkish air cargo industry: cost-focused strategy, cost leadership strategy, differentiation-focused strategy, differentiation strategy
Kiracı and Akan (2020)	Hybrid AHP and TOPSIS in interval fuzzy sets type 2	Seat capacity, fuel consumption, MTOW, price, fuel per seat	Airbus A321neo is the most proper aircraft alternative
Sánchez-Lozano and Rodríguez (2020)	Fuzzy Reference Ideal Method, AHP	Combat ceiling, endurance, thrust, weight at take-off, operational speed, take-off race, rational speed, range, tactical capability, maneuverability, ergonomics, compatibility	Trainer aircraft ranking: Alenia Aermacchi M-346 Master, KAI-T-50 Golden Eagle, Yakovlev YAK-130, Northrop F-5 Freedom Fighter
Dozic et al. (2018)	Fuzzy AHP	Seat capacity, MTOM, aircraft range, maintenance cost, purchasing cost, cost per available seat miles, delivery time, payment cond., fleet commonality, comfort	The rank of aircrafts respectively obtained as CRJ 700, ATR 72–600, ATR 72–500, Q400 NG, CRJ 900, CRJ 1000E, and ERJ190
Ozdemir and Basligil (2016)	Fuzzy ANP and Choquet integral approach	Purchasing cost, operation and spare cost, maintenance cost and salvage cost, security, dimension, reliability and suitability for service quality, delivery time, and useful life	middle-of-the-range standard body, and single corridor aircraft ranking: B, C, A
Sánchez-Lozano et al. (2015)	AHP, TOPSIS, Fuzzy set	Service ceiling, cruising speed, stalling speed, endurance, take-off distance, load factor, human factors, security systems, tactical capability	The best alternative Pilatus PC-21, the second-best alternative is Beechcraft T-6C, third is CASA C.101 Aviojet.
Bruno et al. (2015)	AHP and Fuzzy Set Theory	Operation cost, price, speed, autonomy, comfort, cabin luggage size, noise, environmental pollution	The best aircraft alternatives: Sukhoi SSJ100, Bombardier CRJ1000, Embraer ERJ190
Yeh and Chang (2009)	Fuzzy MAVT-based MCDM method	Maintenance requirement, pilot adaptability, aircraft reliability, maximum range, passenger preference, noise level, operational productivity, economy of scale, purchasing price, consistency with corp. strategy, direct operating cost	Ranking of five aircraft types: B757-200, MD-82, B767-200, A310-300, A-321
Wang and Chang (2007)	Fuzzy TOPSIS	Fuel cap., power plant, service ceiling, distance for landing, distance for take-off, etc.	Training aircraft ranking: KT1, PC-9, T-6A, PC-7-MK2, T27, T-34, PC-7.

used in the literature, either individually or in combination, and as can be seen, they are also evaluated in a fuzzy environment. However, it is concluded that the MCDM methods (COPRAS, EDAS, WASPAS) in the study are not frequently applied, and it is expected to contribute to the literature in this respect.

Various decision-making tools offer more consistent and robust concerns to investigate the issue from broader viewpoints. It seems that a similar problem has been addressed by different researchers, but they differ in terms of methodological application. Although the significance of the issue is assessed, the limited number of studies have been implemented on this topic. Combined models utilizing COPRAS, EDAS and WASPAS methods have not been applied on Turkish airline company before.

When the previous studies in the literature were analyzed, it was seen that there was no study of this similarity and no evaluation was made with these mixed decision-making approaches in this application area. It is thought that the study will enrich the scientific literature in terms of analytical evaluation with more than one quantitative approach and is expected to guide researchers working on this subject.

Methods

In this section, the methods applied to the data structure are presented, namely COPRAS, EDAS, and WASPAS, respectively:

COmplex PRoportional ASsessment (COPRAS)

COPRAS was first proposed by Zavadskas et al. (1994) as a DM tool and the procedure of the COPRAS method consists of stages are presented as follows:

1. Construction of the DM matrix $K = \left[X_{ij} \right]_{m*n}$ shown as follows:

$$K = X_{ij} = \begin{bmatrix} x_{11} & x_{12} & . & x_{1n} \\ x_{21} & x_{22} & . & x_{2n} \\ . & . & . & . \\ x_{m1} & x_{n2} & . & x_{mn} \end{bmatrix} \tag{1}$$

2. The normalization of the DM matrix.

$$x_{ij}{}^* = \frac{x_{ij}}{\sum_{i=1}^{m} x_{ij}} \tag{2}$$

($i=1,...,m$ and $j=1,...,n$)

where x_{ij} is the evaluation indicator of the ith option with respect to the jth criterion, and $x_{ij}{}^*$ is the normalized value, m and n are the number of options.

3. The weighted normalize decision matrix.

$$\left[d_{ij}\right]_{m*n} = x_{ij}^{*} w_{j} \tag{3}$$

where w_j denotes the significance weight of criterion $C_{j.}$

4.   The maximizing and minimizing indexes.

$$S_{+i} = \sum_{j=1}^{n} d_{+ij} \tag{4}$$

$$S_{-i} = \sum_{j=1}^{n} d_{-ij} \tag{5}$$

where d_{+ij} and d_{-ij} are the weighted normalized values for benefit-based and cost-based criteria. The higher the value of S_{+i}, the better is the option, and the lower the value of S_{-i}, the better is the option.

5.   The relative significance values are calculated as follows:

$$Q_i = S_{+i} + \frac{S_{-min}\sum_{i=1}^{m} S_{-i}}{S_{-i}\sum_{i=1}^{m}(S_{-min}/S_{-i})} = S_{+i} + \frac{\sum_{i=1}^{m} S_{-i}}{S_{-i}\sum_{i=1}^{m}(1/S_{-i})} \tag{6}$$

$(i=1, 2,...,m)$

where S_{-min} is the lowest value of S_{-i}. The higher value of Q_i is the significance of the alternative.

6.   The quantitative utility (U_i) for each alternative is measured. The grade of an option's utility which provides to position of alternatives, is identified by comparing the importance of all choices with the most effective one.

$$U_i = \left[\frac{Q_i}{Q_{max}}\right] * 100\% \tag{7}$$

where Q_{max} is the maximum relative importance value. The ranking of candidates is sorted in ascending order depending on utility scores.

Evaluation Based on Distance from Average Solution (EDAS)

The EDAS approach was offered by Ghorabaee et.al. (2015) and the process specifies distances from the average solution, which calculate the positive distance from the average (PDA) and the negative distance from the average (NDA) and so the obtained measurements demonstrate change between each solution-alternative and average solution. The assessment of the alternative points is implemented according to greater values of PDA and worse values of NDA. The greater values of PDA and lower values of NDA show the ideal alternative is better than the average result. The mathematical background for the EDAS method for a multi-dimensional DM problem with n criteria and m options can be analyzed following the steps:

1. Build the DM matrix $X = \left[X_{ij} \right]_{m*n}$ shown as follows:

$$X_{ij} = \begin{bmatrix} x_{11} & x_{12} & . & x_{1n} \\ x_{21} & x_{22} & . & x_{2n} \\ . & . & . & . \\ x_{m1} & x_{n2} & . & x_{mn} \end{bmatrix} \tag{8}$$

where x_{ij} shows the performance indicator of ith alternative on j^{th} criterion. $i = 1,2, …, m$ and $j = 1,2, …, n$.

2. Identification of the average answer according to all criteria. $AV = \left[AV_j \right]_{1*n}$

$$AV_j = \frac{\sum_{i=1}^{m} x_{ij}}{m} \tag{9}$$

3. Measurement of the PDA and the NDA depending on benefit or cost-related criteria.

$$PDA = \left[PDA_{ij} \right]_{m*n} \tag{10}$$

$$NDA = \left[NDA_{ij} \right]_{m*n} \tag{11}$$

If the jth criterion is a benefit-based criterion,

$$PDA_{ij} = \frac{\max\left((0,\left(x_{ij} - AV_j\right)\right)}{AV_j} \qquad (12)$$

If the jth criterion is the cost-based criterion,

$$NDA_{ij} = \frac{\max\left(0,\left(AV_j - x_{ij}\right)\right)}{AV_j} \qquad (13)$$

where PDA_{ij} and NDA_{ij} symbolize the positive and negative distance of the ith option from the average result in terms of the jth criterion, respectively.

4.   Identify the weighted sum of PDA and NDA for all alternatives, given as follows:

$$SP_i = \sum_{j=1}^{n} w_j PDA_{ij} \qquad (14)$$

$$SN_i = \sum_{j=1}^{n} w_j NDA_{ij} \qquad (15)$$

where w_j is the weight of jth criterion.

5.   Normalize the scores of SP and SN for all options, displayed as follows:

$$NSP_i = \frac{SP_i}{max_i\left(SP_i\right)}, \qquad (16)$$

$$NSN_i = 1 - \frac{SN_i}{max_i\left(SN_i\right)} \qquad (17)$$

6.   Evaluate the appraisal score (AS) for all options as given follows:

$$AS_i = \frac{1}{2}\left(NSP_i + NSN_i\right) \qquad (18)$$

where $0 \le AS_i \le 1$.

7.   The options are sorted according to the declining values of appraisal value AS_i. The highest AS_i score is the best option among the options.

The Weighted Aggregated Sum Product Assessment (WASPAS)

The WASPAS approach was proposed by Zavadskas et al. (2012) and the method is based on determining the relative importance of each attribute, and then evaluating and prioritizing alternatives. WASPAS is a kind of DM approach that considers the WSM and the WPM together. The procedure of the WASPAS process is given as follows:

1.   The decision matrix is created firstly, $X = \begin{bmatrix} X_{ij} \end{bmatrix}_{m*n}$ as follows:

$$X_{ij} = \begin{bmatrix} x_{11} & x_{12} & . & x_{1n} \\ x_{21} & x_{22} & . & x_{2n} \\ . & . & . & . \\ x_{m1} & x_{n2} & . & x_{mn} \end{bmatrix} \tag{19}$$

where x_{ij} shows the performance indicator of the ith option on the jth criterion. $i = 1,2, ..., m$ and $j = 1,2, ..., n$.

2.   To evaluate all elements in the decision matrix with comparable levels (due to unit and size differences), the normalization process should be applied according to cost or benefit criterion type using the following two formulas:

$$\overline{x}_{ij} = \frac{x_{ij}}{\max_i x_{ij}} \tag{20}$$

is utilized for beneficial criteria and

$$\overline{x}_{ij} = \frac{\min_i x_{ij}}{x_{ij}} \tag{21}$$

is used for cost criteria. $\overline{x}_{ij}$ shows the normalized value of the x_{ij}.

3. After the normalization procedure, in the WASPAS technique a joint criterion of optimality is searched depending on the optimality principle. The initial criterion of optimality is the WSM and the second one is the WPM.

$$Q_1^{(1)} = \sum_{j=1}^{n} \overline{x}_{ij} w_j \tag{22}$$

where w_j is the weight of the jth criterion.

$$Q_1^{(2)} = \prod_{j=1}^{n} \left(\overline{x}_{ij} \right)^{w_j} \tag{23}$$

4. To get a more accurate and reliable DM process, the generalized final equation for the total relative importance of the ith alternative is determined as follows:

$$Q_1 = \lambda Q_1^{(1)} + \left(1 - \lambda\right) Q_1^{(2)} = \lambda \sum_{j=1}^{n} \overline{x}_{ij} w_j + \left(1 - \lambda\right) \prod_{j=1}^{n} \left(\overline{x}_{ij} \right)^{w_j}, \lambda = 0, 0.1, 0.2, \ldots, 1 \tag{24}$$

As can be seen, the Q values are obtained depending on the variation of weight values. Ideal alternatives are ordered according to their Q scores; The best option has the highest Q score.

APPLICATION OF THE PROPOSED MODELS TO THE AVIATION SECTOR: A CASE STUDY FOR TURKISH AIRLINES

In this study, the ideal aircraft model to be added to the aircraft fleet to manage the airline passenger transportation system rationally and properly is proposed from a holistic perspective within the framework of different DM methods. The considered model based on COPRAS, EDAS, and WASPAS methods and specifications of the aircraft to be selected are specified in Table 2. Evaluation criteria are determined based on literature reviews and expert opinions of airline professionals with 10-20 years of experience in their fields of study. Commonly accepted aircraft criteria are grouped under three main headings: technical, economic, and environmental, and seven alternative aircraft models are identified. The hierarchy diagram of the decision problem is given in Figure 1. And nine sub-criteria are defined as maximum take-off mass, maximum cargo capacity, maximum range, speed, seat capacity, purchasing cost, fuel consumption, carbon emission, and noise, and described below in detail:

Technical Criteria

Maximum take-off mass (C1): It is the maximum weight at which the pilot is allowed to take-off due to structural or other limitations. Maximum Take-Off Weight (MTOW) is the highest level of weight limitation at which the aircraft can be ensured to meet all possible airworthiness requirements. An aircraft's MTOW does not vary depending on various factors, such as altitude, air temperature, and the length of the runway to be used for take-off or landing.

Maximum cargo capacity (C2): It is the maximum volume of cargo that can be carried or held in the limited space of the aircraft cargo area. The payload capacity of each aircraft may vary depending on size and capacity factors.

Maximum Range (C3): It is the furthest distance an aircraft can fly between takeoff and landing operations.

Maximum Speed (C4): It indicates the highest speed achieved by the aircraft in flight and varies depending on the aircraft model due to some speed tests and aircraft technical designs.

Seat Capacity (C5): The amount of private space available to accommodate the number of passengers on the flight. It indicates the carrying capacity and depends on different factors.

Economic Criteria

Purchasing Cost (C6): The total cost of having an aircraft includes shipping, taxes, and handling fees, and these factors change depending on the size of the airplane.

Fuel consumption (C7): The fuel burn data needed to provide flight operation and depends on various factors such as take-off weight and cruising altitude etc. Since it is an indicator of economic efficiency, it is an important contributing factor in choosing the most suitable aircraft option.

Figure 1. The hierarchy scheme of the decision problem alternatives

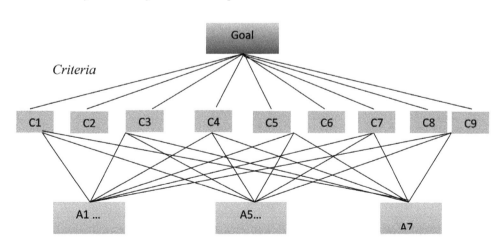

Environmental Criteria

Carbon emission (C8): Airplanes use fossil fuel which releases CO_2 and Greenhouse gas emissions are the combustion outputs. In order to make the climate safe, carbon emission reduction policies have been implemented and some carbon footprint measurements applied strictly to airline companies.

Noise (C9): The sound of an airplane and high airplane noise annoying and have negative side effects on health (damage hearing, distract concentration, etc.). The noise level depends on aircraft engines, and it affects the lower or higher noise level.

* In the study, the priorities of all criteria were assumed to have equal weight.

Application of the COPRAS Method

In the COPRAS method, the decision matrix is first constructed as given in Table 2. The related criteria sets are categorized according to the benefit-based or cost-based attribute and the aim is to maximize benefit criteria while minimize cost criteria. After creating a decision matrix which is normalized utilizing Eq.2 and shown in Table 3.

Secondly, the weighted normalized decision matrix is obtained utilizing Eq. 3 as given in Table 4.

The sum of the weighted normalized values for the beneficial criteria ($S+$) and for non-beneficial criteria ($S-$) are calculated using Eq. 4 and Eq. 5 as shown in Table 5.

Finally, the relative significance value and the quantitative utility score for each alternative are calculated utilizing Eq. 6 as given in Table 6.

According to the obtained results, the order of ideal aircraft emerged as A1>A3>A7>A6>A2>A5>A4 and A1 is the most appropriate choice among other aircraft options.

Table 2. Decision matrix (Alternatives and criteria)

Alternatives	Max. take-off mass (Tones) B	Criteria							
		Technical				Economical		Environmental	
		Maximum Cargo Capacity (m³) B	Max Range (NM) B	Speed (km/h) B	Seat Capacity B	Purchasing Cost ($ M) C	Fuel consumption (L) C	Carbon emission (%) C	Noise (DB) C
A1	617,3	162	8,1	956	321	308,1	2,39	3,8	94
A2	529,1	105,3	6,35	880	280	256,40	3,11	4,1	96
A3	529,1	94,96	7,25	880	406	231,50	3,3	2,1	95
A4	174,2	11,25	3,115	938	162	106,10	2,45	11,3	93
A5	187,7	11,74	3,265	823	187	112,60	2,38	2,3	84
A6	560	105,78	7,635	954	290	292,50	2,37	5,5	90
A7	775	142,7	7,37	920	396	375,50	2,91	10,7	75
Average	481,771	90,532	6,155	907,285	291,714	240,385	2,701	5,685	89,571
*B: Benefit-based criteria, C: Cost-based criteria									

Table 3. Normalized decision matrix

0,183	0,256	0,188	0,151	0,157	0,183	0,126	0,095	0,150
0,157	0,166	0,147	0,139	0,137	0,152	0,164	0,103	0,153
0,157	0,150	0,168	0,139	0,199	0,138	0,175	0,053	0,152
0,052	0,018	0,072	0,148	0,079	0,063	0,130	0,284	0,148
0,056	0,019	0,076	0,130	0,092	0,067	0,126	0,058	0,134
0,166	0,167	0,177	0,150	0,142	0,174	0,125	0,138	0,144
0,230	0,225	0,171	0,145	0,194	0,223	0,154	0,269	0,120

Table 4. Weighted normalized matrix

0,020	0,028	0,021	0,017	0,017	0,020	0,014	0,011	0,017
0,017	0,018	0,016	0,015	0,015	0,017	0,018	0,011	0,017
0,017	0,017	0,019	0,015	0,022	0,015	0,019	0,006	0,017
0,006	0,002	0,008	0,016	0,009	0,007	0,014	0,032	0,016
0,006	0,002	0,008	0,014	0,010	0,007	0,014	0,006	0,015
0,018	0,019	0,020	0,017	0,016	0,019	0,014	0,015	0,016
0,026	0,025	0,019	0,016	0,022	0,025	0,017	0,030	0,013

Table 5. Beneficial and non-beneficial factors

	A1	0,104			0,06
	A2	0,083			0,06
	A3	0,090			0,06
S+	A4	0,041	**S-**		0,07
	A5	0,041			0,04
	A6	0,089			0,06
	A7	0,107			0,09

Table 6. Relative significance value, utility index, and ranks

Q	U	RANK	
0,171	100	1	A1
0,148	86,533	5	A2
0,163	95,011	2	A3
0,101	58,866	7	A4
0,138	80,848	6	A5
0,154	89,668	4	A6
0,155	91,154	3	A7

Application of the EDAS Method

The defined criteria are set desperately according to beneficial or cost-based characteristics and then we try to reach higher values for beneficial-based criteria and to reach lower values for cost-based criteria. The calculated average solution for all evaluation criteria is given in Table 2.

Then the PDA and the NDA matrixes according to the benefit or cost-based criteria as shown in Table 7 and Table 8.

Then the weighted sum of *PDA* and *NDA* (SP_i and SN_i) for each alternative obtained using Eq. 10-Eq. 15 is shown in Table 9.

Then the *SP* and *SN* values are normalized using Eq. 16-Eq. 17, and NSP_i and NSN_i are obtained which are all given in Table 10. And the calculated appraisal score (AS_i) using Eq. 18 for each alternative is given in Table 10.

The ranking of the alternatives according to their appraisal scores in descending order is given in Table 11 below.

Application of the WASPAS Method

Firstly, the decision matrix is normalized using Eq. 20-Eq. 21 as given in Table 12, then the WSM is utilized to identify the first total relative significance value (Q1) using Eq. 22 and secondly the WPM is applied to specify the second total relative significance value (Q2) using Eq 23 as given in Table 13.

Table 7. Positive distance matrix

0,281	0,789	0,316	0,053	0,100	0	0,115	0,331	0
0,098	0,163	0,031	0	0	0	0	0,278	0
0,098	0,048	0,177	0	0,391	0,036	0	0,630	0
0	0	0	0,033	0	0,55	0,093	0	0
0	0	0	0	0	0,531	0,118	0,595	0,062
0,162	0,168	0,240	0,051	0	0	0,122	0,032	0
0,608	0,576	0,197	0,014	0,357	0	0	0	0,162

Table 8. Negative distance matrix

0	0	0	0	0	0,281	0	0	0,049
0	0	0	0,0301	0,040	0,066	0,151	0	0,071
0	0	0	0,0301	0	0	0,221	0	0,060
0,638	0,875	0,493	0	0,444	0	0	0,987	0,038
0,610	0,870	0,469	0,092	0,358	0	0	0	0
0	0	0	0	0,005	0,216	0	0	0,004
0	0	0	0	0	0,562	0,077	0,881	0

Table 9. Weighted sum of PDA and NDA

SP_i		SN_i	
	0,220		0,036
	0,063		0,039
	0,153		0,034
	0,076		0,386
	0,145		0,266
	0,086		0,025
	0,212		0,169

Table 10. Normalized values of SP and ND and the obtained appraisal scores

NSP_i		NSN_i		AS_i	
	1		0,095		0,952
	0,287		0,103		0,592
	0,696		0,089		0,803
	0,344		1		0,172
	0,658		0,690		0,483
	0,391		0,065		0,663
	0,964		0,437		0,763

Table 11. Alternative ranks

	RANK
A1	0,952
A3	0,803
A7	0,763
A6	0,663
A2	0,592
A5	0,48
A4	0,172

The overall total relative significance value (Q_i) is evaluated by Eq. 24 where the WASPAS aggregation factor λ value is accepted as 0.5 to ensure the robustness of the output according to literature reviews.

And finally, all data provided, and calculation phases the final ranking of the alternative aircraft shown in Table 14.

Comparison of the Obtained Results

According to the obtained results from COPRAS, EDAS, and WASPAS methods, the same ranks have been provided for the ideal aircraft selection problem. Airbus A350-900 is the most suitable type of

Table 12. The normalized decision matrix

0,797	1,000	1,000	1,000	0,791	0,344	0,992	0,553	0,798
0,683	0,650	0,784	0,921	0,690	0,414	0,762	0,512	0,781
0,683	0,586	0,895	0,921	1,000	0,458	0,718	1,000	0,789
0,225	0,069	0,385	0,981	0,399	1,000	0,967	0,186	0,806
0,242	0,072	0,403	0,861	0,461	0,942	0,996	0,913	0,893
0,723	0,653	0,943	0,998	0,714	0,363	1,000	0,382	0,833
1,000	0,881	0,910	0,962	0,975	0,283	0,814	0,196	1,000

Table 13. WSM and WSM results for the WASPAS method

Q1	0,808	Q2	0,769
	0,688		0,671
	0,783		0,761
	0,557		0,411
	0,642		0,505
	0,734		0,692
	0,780		0,686

Table 14. Final aircraft ranking using the WASPAS method

	Q_1	Q_2	Q_{ort}	Rank
A1	0,808	0,769	0,788	1
A2	0,688	0,671	0,680	5
A3	0,783	0,761	0,772	2
A4	0,557	0,411	0,484	7
A5	0,642	0,505	0,573	6
A6	0,734	0,692	0,713	4
A7	0,780	0,686	0,733	3

aircraft, secondly Airbus A330-200 and thirdly Boeing 777-300 ER models have been obtained among aircraft options. As seen from Table 15, Boeing 787-9 Dreamliner, Airbus A330-300, Boeing 737-900 ER, and Boeing 737-800 aircraft models are obtained respectively. The obtained analysis results show that the most appropriate aircraft model is Airbus A350-900 whereas the least suitable model emerged as Boeing 737-800.

Although the working principles of the methods used are different from each other, they give the same results according to the determined criteria. The obtained results provide a clear preference for the most appropriate alternative and reliably provide the least preferred aircraft model thanks to consistent results from the methods.

Table 15. Comparison of the results

Aircraft types	COPRAS	EDAS	WASPAS	Rank
Airbus A350-900	A1	A1	A1	1
Airbus A330-200	A3	A3	A3	2
Boeing 777-300 ER	A7	A7	A7	3
Boeing 787-9 Dreamliner	A6	A6	A6	4
Airbus A330-300	A2	A2	A2	5
Boeing 737-900 ER	A5	A5	A5	6
Boeing 737-800	A4	A4	A4	7

FINDINGS

Within the framework of managerial implications, this paper guides both airline managers and policy makers in making long-term investment decisions in airports.

In this study, analytical decision-making methods are used to determine the most appropriate aircraft type for airline companies, and the problem is evaluated under technical, economic, and environmental factors. Three different decision-making methods were applied to the aircraft selection problem and obtained similar rankings. According to the results, the Airbus A350-900 is the most appropriate type of aircraft, followed by the Airbus A330-200 and the Airbus Boeing 777–300 ER models. Then, Boeing 787–9 Dreamliner fourth rank, Airbus A330-300 fifth rank, sixth rank, Boeing 737–900 ER, and Boeing 737–800 aircraft model obtained seventh rank.

Despite the highest purchase cost of the Airbus A350-900, it has emerged as the most desirable alternative due to its other superior features. The Boeing 737–800 aircraft model is the least desirable option because its characteristics are inferior to the others in comparison.

When these evaluations are examined, it is seen that this ranking is at the top of the reports and statistics of most airline companies, and aircraft purchasing decisions are made accordingly.

The multidimensional evaluation of the study was also revealed by scenario analysis. The research problem has already been addressed with three different methods, and the findings have been presented.

In this study, the evaluation was made only for seven aircraft models. Of course, better models will be produced and launched with technological developments. Accordingly, the latest models can be re-evaluated by adding them to the content of the study and updating appropriate alternatives.

Sensitivity Analysis

In order to investigate the power of impact (i.e. sensitivity) of the criteria weights on the ranking of options, we conducted a sensitivity analysis trial. Using changing grades of criteria weights, we measured the alterations of the consequence. Particularly, six cases were analyzed using a sensitivity analysis context, but the results (i.e. the ranking of alternative strategies) remain mostly the same. The zero case is the reference point while the others are the consequences of the sensitivity analysis.

Table 16 presents different criteria weights. According to the results revealed in Table17-Table 19 where the new cases are compared against the baseline depending on each method (COPRAS, EDAS, WASPAS). Minor variations obtained depend on different case studies and the obtained results provided in the following tables. The different rankings depend on the working principle of the methods, but for the most part, the ranking is similar in the selection of the ideal aircraft model. In all cases a1 is the best alternative, while a4 is the worst alternative in the study.

According to EDAS results, cases 5 and 6 provide the same ranking, while the remaining cases 1-2-3-4 provide similar ranking results as given in Table 17.

According to the COPRAS results, cases 5 and 6 provide the same ranking, while the remaining cases 2-3-4 provide similar ranking results, the first rank in case 1 is obtained as a7 and the rest of the ranking is in the same order as given in Table 18.

Table 16. Weights of criteria according to different cases

	C1	C2	C3	C4	C5	C6	C7	C8	C9
Case 0	0,111	0,111	0,111	0,111	0,111	0,111	0,111	0,111	0,111
Case 1	0,3	0,2	0,071	0,071	0,071	0,071	0,071	0,071	0,071
Case 2	0,2	0,3	0,071	0,071	0,071	0,071	0,071	0,071	0,071
Case 3	0,071	0,071	0,300	0,200	0,071	0,071	0,071	0,071	0,071
Case 4	0,071	0,071	0,200	0,300	0,071	0,071	0,071	0,071	0,071
Case 5	0,071	0,071	0,071	0,071	0,071	0,071	0,071	0,300	0,200
Case 6	0,071	0,071	0,071	0,071	0,071	0,071	0,071	0,200	0,300

Table 17. EDAS results of the sensitivity analysis

CASE 0	CASE 1	CASE 2	CASE 3	CASE 4	CASE 5	CASE 6
a1	a1	a1	a1	a1	a3	a1
a3	a7	a7	a7	a7	a1	a3
a7	a3	a6	a6	a6	a5	a5
a6	a6	a3	a3	a3	a2	a7
a2	a2	a2	a2	a2	a6	a2
a5	a5	a5	a5	a5	a7	a6
a4	a4	a4	a4	a4	a4	a4

Table 18. COPRAS results of the sensitivity analysis

CASE 0	CASE 1	CASE 2	CASE 3	CASE 4	CASE 5	CASE 6
a1	a7	a1	a1	a1	a3	a5
a3	a1	a7	a7	a7	a5	a3
a7	a6	a6	a3	a3	a1	a1
a6	a3	a3	a6	a6	a2	a2
a2	a2	a2	a2	a2	a6	a6
a5	a5	a5	a5	a5	a7	a7
a4	a4	a4	a4	a4	a4	a4

According to the WASPAS results, cases 3 and 4, and the remaining cases 1-2 provide the same ranking result and then the remaining cases 5-6 present mostly the same ranking as given in Table 19. As a conclusion, the obtained results support each other. Methodological differences and different priority weights of criteria lead to variations in the ranking order of alternatives and as is well known, result in minor modifications.

CONCLUSION AND FUTURE RESEARCH

The most appropriate flight plan for air transportation can be met primarily by determining the best aircraft model. Many important factors such as fuel consumption, price, performance, carbon emission, and number of passengers are evaluated for the ideal aircraft option, and an optimal decision is made by the airline company. In competitive conditions, especially in the aviation industry, resources need to be used efficiently and rationally. Aircraft are the most important cost portion of airline operations and require a large investment. Therefore, the performance of aircraft should be evaluated under the most appropriate set of criteria for making the right aircraft purchasing and selection investment decisions.

In this study, each criterion is evaluated with equal importance weights and then COPRAS, EDAS, and WASPAS methods are applied subsequently. The obtained results demonstrated that Airbus A350-900 is the highest priority, Airbus A330-200 came as the second highest priority, Boeing 777-300 ER is the third highest priority rank, Boeing 787-9 Dreamliner is the fourth highest priority, Airbus A330-300 is the fifth highest priority, and six important alternatives Boeing 737–900 ER. The Boeing 737–800 choice has the lowest priority rank among all options. The same ranking results were obtained using three different methods, which show the reliability and accuracy of the study. Sensitivity analysis was then applied with different criterion weights to demonstrate the reliability of the methods. The results show that the rankings obtained from the methods are largely similar, with minor differences.

In this study, the current ranking order is obtained when each criterion is of equal importance. However, rankings may change when the relative importance of technical, economic, and environmental criteria are weighted separately. If environmental factors are more important, the ranking may change as the weighting increases accordingly. The Airbus A330-200 and Boeing 737–900 ER models are expected to take the first two places. If technical factors are more significant than other criteria, the ranking may

Table 19. WASPAS results of the sensitivity analysis

CASE 0	CASE 1	CASE 2	CASE 3	CASE 4	CASE 5	CASE 6
a1	a1	a1	a1	a1	a3	a3
a3	a7	a7	a3	a3	a1	a1
a7	a3	a3	a7	a7	a5	a7
a6	a6	a6	a6	a6	a2	a6
a2	a2	a2	a2	a2	a6	a2
a5	a5	a5	a5	a5	a7	a5
a4	a4	a4	a4	a4	a4	a4

alter as the weighting increases accordingly. The Airbus A350-900 and Boeing 787–9 Dreamliner models are expected to take the first two places.

Future research requires a more comprehensive evaluation of various other aircraft model options, supplemented by other classical and fuzzy MCDM tools. More diverse criteria may also be considered for a broader assessment of the problematic issue. The obtained results can be compared in terms of advantages and disadvantages.

For future studies, the evaluated problem context can be extended and more criteria, parameters, and constraints can be included using a decision support system to control users' expectations and the management of municipal objectives. In particular, for decision-making problems under uncertainty, fuzzy approaches offer successful results. Thus, a decision model integrated with a fuzzy approach and a decision support system that offers the opportunity to analyze different scenarios can achieve more comprehensive successful results.

With new aircraft models joining the fleet every day, a pool system where all options are evaluated with different criteria for airline operators and/or investors to determine the most suitable aircraft type may be beneficial in the long run. Because this problem will always exist as long as the aviation industry exists, appropriate solution methods will help researchers and decision makers interested in this issue.

REFERENCES

Alinezhad, A., & Khalili, J. (2019). COPRAS Method. *International Series in Operations Research and Management Science, 277*, 87–91. doi:10.1007/978-3-030-15009-9_12

Aviationbenefits. (2020). *Aviation: Benefits Beyond Borders*. Aviationbenefits. https://aviationbenefits.org/

Bruno, G., Esposito, E., & Genovese, A. (2015). A model for aircraft evaluation to support strategic decisions. *Expert Systems with Applications, 42*(13), 5580–5590. doi:10.1016/j.eswa.2015.02.054

de Assis, G. S., dos Santos, M., and Basilio, M. P. (2023). Use of the WASPAS Method to Select Suitable Helicopters for Aerial Activity Carried Out by the Military Police of the State of Rio de Janeiro. *Axioms, 12*(1), 77. doi:10.3390/axioms12010077

Deveci, M., Öner, S. C., Ciftci, M. E., Özcan, E., & Pamucar, D. (2022). Interval type-2 hesitant fuzzy Entropy-based WASPAS approach for aircraft type selection. *Applied Soft Computing, 114*, 108076. doi:10.1016/j.asoc.2021.108076

Dožić, S., Lutovac, T., & Kalić, M. (2018). Fuzzy AHP approach to passenger aircraft type selection. *Journal of Air Transport Management, 68*, 165–175. doi:10.1016/j.jairtraman.2017.08.003

Ecer, F. (2018). Third-party logistics (3Pls) provider selection via Fuzzy AHP and EDAS integrated model. *Technological and Economic Development of Economy, 24*(2), 615–634–615–634. doi:10.3846/20294913.2016.1213207

Gao, F., Wang, W., Bi, C., Bi, W., & Zhang, A. (2023). Prioritization of used aircraft acquisition criteria: A fuzzy best–worst method (BWM)-based approach. *Journal of Air Transport Management, 107*, 102359. doi:10.1016/j.jairtraman.2023.102359

Ghorabaee, M. K., Amiri, M., Zavadskas, E. K., & Turskis, Z. (2017). Multi-criteria group decision-making using an extended EDAS method with interval type-2 fuzzy sets. *E+M. Ekonomie a Management*, *20*(1), 48–68. doi:10.15240/tul/001/2017-1-004

Ghorabaee, M. K., Zavadskas, E. K., Olfat, L., & Turskis, Z. (2015). Multi-Criteria Inventory Classification Using a New Method of Evaluation Based on Distance from Average Solution (EDAS). *Informatica (Vilnius)*, *26*(3), 435–451. doi:10.15388/Informatica.2015.57

Gössling, S., & Humpe, A. (2020). The global scale, distribution and growth of aviation: Implications for climate change. *Global Environmental Change*, *65*, 102194. doi:10.1016/j.gloenvcha.2020.102194 PMID:36777089

Heracleous, L., & Wirtz, J. (2009). Strategy and organization at Singapore Airlines: Achieving sustainable advantage through dual strategy. *Journal of Air Transport Management*, *15*(6), 274–279. doi:10.1016/j.jairtraman.2008.11.011

Kiracı, K., & Akan, E. (2020). Aircraft selection by applying AHP and TOPSIS in interval type-2 fuzzy sets. *Journal of Air Transport Management*, *89*, 101924. doi:10.1016/j.jairtraman.2020.101924 PMID:32989347

Krishankumar, R., Garg, H., Arun, K., Saha, A., Ravichandran, K. S., & Kar, S. (2021). An integrated decision-making COPRAS approach to probabilistic hesitant fuzzy set information. *Complex & Intelligent Systems*, *7*(5), 2281–2298. doi:10.1007/s40747-021-00387-w

Kundakcı, N. (2019). An integrated method using MACBETH and EDAS methods for evaluating steam boiler alternatives. *Journal of Multi-Criteria Decision Analysis*, *26*(1–2), 27–34. doi:10.1002/mcda.1656

Operations management. (2023). *The Vital Role of Efficient Operations Management for Startup Airlines*. NY Air Ops. https://myairops.com/blog/2023/09/operations-management-startup-airlines/

Ozdemir, Y., & Basligil, H. (2016). Aircraft selection using fuzzy ANP and the generalized choquet integral method: The Turkish airlines case. *Journal of Intelligent & Fuzzy Systems*, *31*(1), 589–600. doi:10.3233/IFS-162172

Popovic, G., Stanujkic, D., & Stojanovic, S. (2012). Investment Project Selection by Applying COPRAS Method and Imprecise Data. *Serbian Journal of Management*, *7*(2), 257–269. doi:10.5937/sjm7-2268

Rashid, T., Ali, A., & Chu, Y. M. (2021). Hybrid BW-EDAS MCDM methodology for optimal industrial robot selection. *PLoS One*, *16*(2), e0246738. doi:10.1371/journal.pone.0246738 PMID:33561144

Sánchez-Lozano, J. M., & Rodríguez, O. N. (2020). Application of Fuzzy Reference Ideal Method (FRIM) to the military advanced training aircraft selection. *Applied Soft Computing*, *88*, 106061. doi:10.1016/j.asoc.2020.106061

Sánchez-Lozano, J. M., Serna, J., & Dolón-Payán, A. (2015). Evaluating military training aircrafts through the combination of multi-criteria decision making processes with fuzzy logic. A case study in the Spanish Air Force Academy. *Aerospace Science and Technology*, *42*, 58–65. doi:10.1016/j.ast.2014.12.028

Su, Y., Xie, K., Wang, H., Liang, Z., Art Chaovalitwongse, W., & Pardalos, P. M. (2021). Airline Disruption Management: A Review of Models and Solution Methods. *Engineering (Beijing)*, *7*(4), 435–447. doi:10.1016/j.eng.2020.08.021

Tanrıverdi, G., & Lezki, Ş. (2021). Istanbul Airport (IGA) and quest of best competitive strategy for air cargo carriers in new competition environment: A fuzzy multi-criteria approach. *Journal of Air Transport Management*, *95*, 102088. doi:10.1016/j.jairtraman.2021.102088

Torkayesh, A. E., Deveci, M., Karagoz, S., & Antucheviciene, J. (2023). A state-of-the-art survey of evaluation based on distance from average solution (EDAS): Developments and applications. *Expert Systems with Applications*, *221*, 119724. doi:10.1016/j.eswa.2023.119724

Valipour, A., Yahaya, N., Md Noor, N., Antuchevičienė, J., & Tamošaitienė, J. (2017). Hybrid SWARA-COPRAS method for risk assessment in deep foundation excavation project: An Iranian case study. *Journal of Civil Engineering and Management*, *23*(4), 524–532. doi:10.3846/13923730.2017.1281842

Wang, T. C., & Chang, T. H. (2007). Application of TOPSIS in evaluating initial training aircraft under a fuzzy environment. *Expert Systems with Applications*, *33*(4), 870–880. doi:10.1016/j.eswa.2006.07.003

Xia, F., Wei, H., & Yang, L. W. (2015). Improved COPRAS Method and Application in Material Selection Problem. *Applied Mechanics and Materials*, *707*, 505–508. . doi:10.4028/www.scientific.net/AMM.707.505

Yeh, C. H., & Chang, Y. H. (2009). Modeling subjective evaluation for fuzzy group multicriteria decision making. *European Journal of Operational Research*, *194*(2), 464–473. doi:10.1016/j.ejor.2007.12.029

Zachariah, R. A., Sharma, S., & Kumar, V. (2023). Systematic review of passenger demand forecasting in aviation industry. *Multimedia Tools and Applications*, *2023*(30), 1–37. doi:10.1007/s11042-023-15552-1 PMID:37362707

Zavadskas, E. K., Turskis, Z., Antucheviciene, J., & Zakarevicius, A. (2012). Optimization of Weighted Aggregated Sum Product Assessment. *Elektronika ir Elektrotechnika*, *122*(6), 3–6. doi:10.5755/j01.eee.122.6.1810

Chapter 10
Personalization Strategies and Passenger Satisfaction Analysis in Full-Service Airlines:
A Study of Lisbon Airport's Leading Carriers

Marcelo Martins
Instituto Superior de Educação e Ciências, Portugal

Rui C. Castro e Quadros
🆔 https://orcid.org/0000-0003-0685-259X
Instituto Superior de Educação e Ciências, Portugal & Escola Superior de Hotelaria e Turismo do Estoril, Portugal

Ana Barqueiro
Instituto Superior de Educação e Ciências, Portugal

ABSTRACT

The personalization of services is a crucial element in full-service airlines, as they seek to meet the needs of their passengers. This work aimed to analyze the personalization strategies adopted by the main airlines with the largest number of passengers at Lisbon Airport and to evaluate the level of passenger satisfaction in relation to these strategies. The research was carried out through a questionnaire survey applied to passengers, so that it was possible to assess the level of customer satisfaction in relation to the strategies adopted by the full-service airlines under study. Data were analysed quantitatively. The results revealed that the personalization strategies adopted by the studied airlines are similar, contrary to the initial hypothesis that there would be significant differences between them. In addition, the level of passenger satisfaction regarding these strategies was also similar, indicating that airlines are responding equally satisfactorily to the individual needs and preferences of passengers.

DOI: 10.4018/979-8-3693-0908-7.ch010

INTRODUCTION

In the ever-evolving landscape of the aviation industry, customer satisfaction emerges as a linchpin for success, steering business profitability and sustainability. The significance of content customers is particularly pronounced in full-service airlines, where comprehensive amenities and inclusive services define their competitive edge. Among the myriad strategies to enhance customer satisfaction, service personalization takes center stage. This chapter embarks on a journey to unravel the intricacies of service personalization strategies adopted by major airlines operating at Lisbon Airport, probing into the depths of their approaches during reservation, customer service, and the integration of technology. Guided by the overarching question—"What are the service personalization strategies adopted by the airlines with the highest Number of Passengers at Lisbon Airport, and what is the Satisfaction Level of passengers regarding these strategies?"—this chapter undertakes a systematic exploration of the multi-faceted dimensions of service personalization. Through an extensive examination of collected data and a comprehensive review of existing literature, the chapter aims to decipher the underlying trends and differentiating strategies employed by TAP Portugal and other major airlines.

The main goal of this chapter is to identify, analyze, and compare the service personalization strategies implemented by the major full-service airlines operating at Lisbon Airport. Specifically, the focus will be on TAP Portugal, SATA Internacional, IBERIA, Lufthansa, and British Airways. The chapter aims to uncover the unique approaches employed by these airlines and evaluate the satisfaction levels of passengers regarding the personalized services they offer.

BACKGROUND

Contextualization

This chapter provides a comprehensive review of relevant literature on service personalization in full-service airlines. Service personalization is crucial for full-service airlines as it can enhance customer satisfaction, loyalty, and retention. The review aims to establish a solid theoretical and empirical foundation for the project by delving into the current state of knowledge on the subject. It will explore aspects related to the definition of service personalization, its significance for full-service airlines, and other pertinent topics. The review will be organized in a clear and structured manner, offering a critical and systematic analysis of the consulted sources.

Airline Business Models

For Oliveira and Huse (2009), airlines can be classified in various ways, with the primary differentiation being between full-service and low-cost carriers.

According to Doganis (2006), full-service airlines are characterized by their comprehensive service offerings to passengers and operate based on the traditional airline business model. On the other hand, low-cost carriers are known for their low prices and reduced cost structure. These companies aim to maximize efficiency by minimizing production costs, offering only essential services to passengers.

Doganis (2006) emphasizes that compared to full-service airlines, low-cost carriers have a leaner cost structure due to their simplified business model, allowing passengers to save money. However, for passengers seeking a variety of services, this may be a disadvantage.

In contrast, Hunter (2006) argues that low-cost carriers have a competitive advantage over full-service carriers as they can offer lower prices to passengers without compromising service quality. Additionally, low-cost carriers have a simpler organizational structure, making them more flexible and responsive to market changes.

In Table 1, titled "Key Differences between FSC and LCC", the main differences between the business models are outlined.

Service Personalization: Concepts and Applications

Service personalization is widely recognized as a crucial mechanism for enhancing customer satisfaction and fostering customer loyalty to the company (Paraskevas and Nudurupati, 2015). According to Grönroos (2008), personalization is an approach that seeks to meet individual customer needs by offering products or services tailored to their preferences and requirements. Additionally, Zeithaml, Bitner, and Gremler (2008) argue that personalization is fundamental for creating value for the customer, as it enables companies to provide customized solutions that address each customer's specific needs.

This strategy is increasingly employed by businesses across various sectors, including the travel and tourism industry. Service personalization involves adapting the services offered to customers based on their needs and preferences. Some examples of service personalization in the airline industry, as noted by Hunter (2006), include:

- Offering personalized seat and onboard meal options based on customer preferences.

Table 1. Key differences between FSC and LCC

Characteristics	FSC	LCC
Generic Strategy	• *Differentiation*	• *Cost Minimization*
Operational Model	• *Hub and spoke/Multiple hubs and spokes, connecting to feeder routes;* • *Mix of short/medium and long-distance routes;* • *Various types of aircraft;* • *Moderate capacity utilization.*	• *Point-to-point, without interlining; short sector length (400-600 nautical miles);* • *Primarily short distance;* • *Uniform aircraft type:* • *High capacity utilization, rapid turnaround between sectors, low margins.*
Market	• *Typically in competition with other FSCs, leading to differentiation through service class (quality) with a high service image;* • *Frequent scheduling and flight flexibility;* • *Extensive onboard services;* • *Comprehensive ground services;* • *Use of major airports.*	• *Budget travel sector of the market, segmented by booking time and flight choice;* • *Basic service quality;* • *Limited flexibility for flight changes (use it or lose it!);* • *No catering or charged meals;* • *Typically use secondary airports.*
Inventory Management	• *Pre-booked tickets and seats;* • *Complex reservation system due to feeder routes;* • *Use of travel agents.*	• *Simplified inventory management;* • *Online reservations, ticketless, no use of travel agents.*

Source: (Hunter 2006)

- Providing customized travel packages including flights, hotels, and activities tailored to customer preferences.
- Using customer behavior data to offer personalized promotions and discounts.
- Providing check-in options, such as early check-in, based on customer needs.

According to Gustafsson, Kristensson, and Witell (2005), service customization is an effective way to enhance customer satisfaction, increase loyalty, and boost sales. Additionally, Kotler and Armstrong (2010) emphasize that service customization serves as a competitive differentiator, enabling companies to stand out from the competition.

Importance and Challenges of Service Customization in Airlines

The aeronautical industry is evolving, driven by technology and a demand for personalized travel experiences (McIvor et al., 2003). Gures et al. (2014) stress that meeting elevated customer expectations in travel requires service customization.

Service customization positively correlates with customer satisfaction and loyalty (Hendrawati et al., 2019; Parise & Sheng, 2021). Krasnova et al. (2020) show its effectiveness in increasing satisfaction and retention, suggesting its value for the aeronautical industry.

Zhang and Hu's (2018) study notes the aviation industry's growing trend toward service customization. Gustafsson et al. (2005) highlight positive outcomes for companies investing in customization.

Despite its importance, challenges arise in real-time data collection, balancing customization, and privacy, and navigating regulatory restrictions (Heung & Tsang, 2016; Y.-H. Chen & Huang, 2017; S. Sundar & Sukor, 2020).

In aviation, customization faces unique challenges due to security, regulatory compliance, and space limitations (S. Sundar & Sukor, 2020). Organizational culture and change management pose additional hurdles (S. Sundar & Sukor, 2020).

To succeed, airlines must address these challenges, emphasizing transparency, innovation, and collaboration (Manca et al., 2018). Service customization remains a crucial strategy for full-service airlines, aiming to meet rising customer expectations for a unique travel experience.

Technology and Service Customization

As mentioned, several times, according to Krasnova et al. (2020), service customization is a growing trend in many sectors, and airlines are no exception. With the help of technology, companies can provide more personalized and relevant services to their customers, leading to increased customer satisfaction and loyalty (Gustafsson, Johnson, and Roos 2005). In the following subchapters, we will analyze the various technologies that assist in customization.

Big Data

Big Data is quite complex, requiring advanced technological tools and algorithms capable of adapting to innovations. It can be defined through the 3Vs: volume, velocity, and variety (Furht and Villanustre 2016). Large volumes of data are continuously generated from millions of devices and applications. For a better understanding, a study conducted by Statista (2022) was analyzed, showing the evolution of Big

Data volume. In 2010, there were 2 zettabytes of data/information created, captured, copied, and consumed worldwide, whereas today there are 97 zettabytes. It is estimated that by 2025, there will be about 181 zettabytes in this "big" database. For perspective, 1 zettabyte equals 1,000,000,000,000 gigabytes.

Velocity is another characteristic of Big Data, as this data is automatically generated from the moment a user accepts simple cookies. Four significant examples of this speed include online video viewing platforms and supermarket chains, which automatically create algorithms from the moment a simple click is made. Variety in Big Data is a crucial feature because this data can be generated in any computer format. In addition to these 3Vs, there are two others that are typically seen as secondary but applicable: value and veracity of data. Value refers to the benefit/value derived from using Big Data, while veracity refers to the reliability of the data (Sharma and Mangat 2015). There are more Vs such as verification, validation, among others, which are more specific and cannot be applied to all issues (Gandomi and Haider 2015).

One characteristic of Industry 4.0 is the need to provide services increasingly tailored to the specific peculiarities of each consumer (Rüßmann et al. 2015).

In the aviation industry, data analysis and Big Data can be used for various purposes, including service customization. These technologies can help airlines better understand their customers by analyzing information about their preferences, travel history, purchasing behavior, among other factors (Bieger et al. 2012).

Through this technology, airlines can offer personalized services, such as exclusive offers based on customer preferences or cabin upgrades based on travel history (Dolnicar and Grün 2014). It can also be used to predict customer needs, offering a personalized menu according to their dietary preferences, for example, Y Chen and Zhang (2014).

However, Big Data also presents challenges in the industry, such as collecting and processing large volumes of data and concerns about customer privacy. Therefore, it is essential for airlines to follow data protection regulations and ensure the security of the collected information (Bieger et al. 2012; Dolnicar and Grün 2014).

Recommendation Systems

Recommendation systems are software tools that use machine learning algorithms to suggest relevant and personalized items to users based on their browsing histories, ratings, and purchasing behaviors (Su and Khoshgoftaar 2009). These technologies are widely used across various sectors, including e-commerce, media, entertainment, and tourism (Lekakos, Giaglis, and Vrechopoulos 2008).

In the tourism sector, service personalization is one of the primary areas where recommendation systems can be applied. Airlines, for instance, can employ these technologies to recommend personalized flights and complementary services to their customers based on their preferences, travel histories, and other relevant data (Y Chen and Zhang 2014).

Service personalization is considered a growing trend in the tourism sector, and many authors emphasize the importance of recommendation systems in this process. For example, Huang, Benyoucef, and Poon (2018) state that service personalization enhances user experience, while Mishra and Mishra (2018) highlight personalization as one of the key trends in the tourism industry.

Recommendation systems are frequently cited as essential tools for service personalization in the tourism sector. Gretzel et al. (2015) assert that recommendation systems play a fundamental role in this process, and Yubo Chen, Xiang, and Li (2019) point out that personalized recommendations are a key factor in customer satisfaction. Additionally, Pan, Xie, and Huang (2017) state that recommendation systems can be used to enhance the efficiency and effectiveness of tourism services.

Service personalization can bring various benefits to tourism businesses. According to Yubo Chen, Xiang, and Li (2019), personalization can increase customer satisfaction, reduce customer acquisition costs, and improve customer loyalty. Furthermore, personalization can be used to boost sales and revenue, as indicated by Huang, Benyoucef, and Poon (2018). However, the implementation of recommendation systems in the tourism industry also poses challenges, such as collecting and processing large volumes of data, ensuring customer privacy, and ensuring the accuracy of recommendations (Y Chen and Zhang 2014).

In terms of specific research on recommendation systems in the aviation industry, some authors have explored the application of these technologies in different contexts, such as recommending cabin upgrades for frequent flyers (Moghavvemi, Sharabati, and Ismail 2016) and personalizing in-flight menus (Y Chen and Zhang 2014).

In summary, service personalization in airlines is an area where recommendation systems can be successfully applied. However, it is essential to consider the challenges related to implementing these technologies and ensure customer information privacy and security.

Chatbots and Virtual Assistants

The use of chatbots and virtual assistants has been one of the major trends in the aviation industry (Sarol, Mohammad, and Rahman 2023). According to Berthon et al. (2012), chatbot technology can provide personalized and interactive service to customers, enhancing their experience and satisfaction. Moreover, Li et al. (2019) and Sarol, Mohammad, and Rahman (2023) state that service personalization through chatbots can increase customer loyalty and reduce customer service costs.

One of the main advantages of chatbots is the ability to personalize customer service. By collecting customer data such as purchase history, preferences, and behaviors, it is possible to offer more efficient and personalized service. According to S. S. Sundar et al. (2017), data-driven personalization can enhance the effectiveness and efficiency of chatbots, providing customers with more relevant and accurate recommendations.

Another form of service personalization gaining prominence is the use of chatbots with human-like voices. According to van der Aa et al. (2018), the use of chatbots with human-like voices can instill greater trust and empathy from the customer, enhancing brand loyalty. This approach can be used to provide more human and personalized service, with more natural and spontaneous responses.

However, it is essential to highlight that service personalization through chatbots can raise ethical challenges, such as customer data privacy. As pointed out by van der Aa et al. (2018), it is crucial for companies to establish clear data privacy and security policies to ensure customer trust.

Examples of Service Personalization in Full-Service Airlines

As seen earlier, service personalization is a crucial strategy for full-service airlines as it can enhance customer satisfaction and loyalty. There are several forms of service personalization that can be employed by airlines to meet individual customer needs and enhance their travel experience.

Loyalty Programs and Rewards

In full-service airlines, an example of service personalization is the loyalty and rewards programs, which offer exclusive benefits to their frequent customers, such as discounts on tickets, cabin upgrades, lounge access, and the accumulation of air miles (Waemustafa 2014).

According to Waemustafa (2014), loyalty and rewards programs are one of the main mechanisms used by airlines to personalize services and thus retain their customers. In addition to providing exclusive benefits, these programs also allow airlines to better understand their customers' preferences and tailor their services according to their needs. For Whyte (2004), loyalty programs can increase customer retention and airline revenue, as well as enhance the customer experience by offering personalized benefits.

A study conducted by Tripathi (2017) on the influence of loyalty programs on customers' behavioral intentions towards airlines found that loyalty programs have a positive impact on the intention to repurchase. In other words, customers participating in these programs are more likely to continue using the airline's services and recommend it to others.

However, it is important to note that loyalty programs are not a foolproof strategy. According to Yubo Chen and Xie (2008), the effectiveness of these programs can be affected by various factors such as service quality, competition, changes in customer preferences, and the management of the loyalty program itself. Therefore, it is essential for airlines to develop effective loyalty and rewards programs that align with the needs of their customers.

Seat Selection

Seat selection is a widely used personalization service by full-service airlines. According to Meyer-Waarden (2013), seat selection allows customers to choose their preferred seat on the plane based on their personal preferences, such as window or aisle, proximity to the restroom, among others. This customization option is often offered for free to business class customers, members of loyalty programs, or for an additional fee to other passengers.

Seat selection can be an effective strategy to increase customer satisfaction and the revenue of airlines. According to Meyer-Waarden (2013), seat selection can positively influence customers' intention to repurchase and loyalty. Furthermore, offering such services can be a way to differentiate from competitors and attract customers who value personalization and a unique experience.

However, it is important to note that the implementation of additional personalized services can pose challenges for airlines. According to Meyer-Waarden (2013), seat selection can increase operational complexity and costs for the airline. Additionally, offering additional personalized services can raise customers' expectations, and dissatisfaction may arise if these expectations are not met.

Offer of Personalized Menus and Dietary Preferences

According to a study conducted by Prentice et al. (2023), taking customers' dietary preferences into account can significantly improve customer satisfaction. Furthermore, offering personalized meal options can be a way to differentiate from competitors and meet their specific needs.

Another relevant study is by Waemustafa (2014), which highlights the importance of offering personalized menus to differentiate airlines from their competitors and enhance the customer experience. Waemustafa (2014) also points out that technology can be used to facilitate the offering of personalized menus and accommodate customers' dietary preferences. For example, the introduction of apps that allow passengers to select their dietary preferences before the flight can simplify the selection process and meal preparation.

However, according to Waemustafa (2014), offering personalized menus might not be enough to ensure customer satisfaction. He argues that the quality of the meals offered is a determining factor for passenger satisfaction, regardless of menu customization. Therefore, it is important for airlines to consider both customers' dietary preferences and the quality of the meals offered.

Offering Personalized In-Flight Entertainment

The provision of personalized in-flight entertainment is a strategy employed by various airlines to offer a unique and differentiated flight experience to their customers. According to Jin and Kim (2022), personalized in-flight entertainment can positively influence customer satisfaction, loyalty, and enhance the airlines' competitiveness against their competitors.

To offer personalized in-flight entertainment, airlines can employ different technologies such as in-flight entertainment systems and Wi-Fi connectivity systems (Jin and Kim 2022). These technologies allow customers to choose from a variety of entertainment options, including movies, TV shows, games, and music, tailored to their personal preferences (Alamdari 1999). Additionally, personalized entertainment offerings can be complemented with additional services such as onboard product sales and exclusive experiences like live sports events.

However, Jin and Kim (2022) note that providing personalized in-flight entertainment can pose operational and logistical challenges, such as the need to keep technology up-to-date and ensure service quality throughout the flight. Moreover, offering personalized entertainment can increase the operational costs for airlines, requiring investments in technology and high-quality content.

Despite these challenges, providing personalized in-flight entertainment can be an effective strategy to enhance the customer experience and increase their loyalty to the airline. According to Alamdari (1999) and Jin and Kim (2022), personalized in-flight entertainment can be a decisive factor in customers' choice of an airline, positively influencing their intention to repurchase and recommend the airline to others.

Benefits of Service Personalization in Full-Service Airlines

Service personalization is an increasingly utilized strategy by full-service airlines to enhance customer experience and increase customer loyalty, revenue, and operational efficiency (H.-M. Chen et al. 2017). The literature has highlighted various benefits of service personalization in airlines, which will be discussed in these subchapters.

Increased Customer Satisfaction

Service personalization in airlines can significantly increase customer satisfaction (Jin and Kim 2022). The availability of personalized in-flight entertainment and Wi-Fi offerings are valued by passengers and are positively related to overall satisfaction, willingness to return, and the likelihood of recommendation, as concluded by Jin and Kim (2022). They also emphasized that in-flight entertainment is a crucial aspect of airlines' competitiveness, and personalization is a way to differentiate from competitors. Moreover, offering personalized services based on customer preferences, such as special meals or exclusive amenities, can enhance customer satisfaction and their perceived value (Jin and Kim 2022).

Increased Customer Loyalty

Service personalization can also enhance customer loyalty. According to Wang, So, and Sparks (2014), offering personalized services can increase customer loyalty and decrease the likelihood of switching to other airlines. Similarly, the results of a study by Kusumawardani and Aruan (2019) suggest that providing personalized services can lead to greater brand commitment and the intention to recommend the company to others.

Increased Revenue Through Additional Sales and Upselling

Service personalization can be an opportunity for full-service airlines to increase their revenues. For example, offering premium services, such as in-flight product sales or the option to choose a seat with more legroom, can lead to additional sales and upselling (Kusumawardani and Aruan 2019). Moreover, providing personalized services can help airlines differentiate themselves from other companies and consequently charge higher prices for these services (Areiqat et al. 2019).

Improved Operational Efficiency and Cost Reduction

Service personalization can assist full-service airlines in enhancing operational efficiency and reducing costs. For instance, by offering personalized services, airlines can optimize the use of onboard resources, such as reducing food waste or decreasing the need for additional meal preparation (Kusumawardani and Aruan 2019). Additionally, service personalization can help full-service airlines provide faster and more efficient service, minimizing delays and issues (Kusumawardani and Aruan 2019).

DATA

Identification of Airlines

The identification of the selected airlines for this study is a crucial aspect to ensure the representativeness and relevance of the obtained results.

The selection of airlines was made considering the number of passengers transported, and the data source will be the latest quarterly statistical bulletin from ANAC.

Each selected airline will be subject to detailed analysis, allowing a comprehensive understanding of their service personalization strategies, operational processes, and approaches to meeting passengers' demands and expectations.

In Table 2, extracted from ANAC's quarterly statistical bulletin, we can see that the top five full-service airlines with the largest market share and number of passengers are: TAP Portugal (TAP), Deutsche Lufthansa (DLH), Iberia (IBE), SATA Internacional (RZO), and British Airways (BAW).

It's worth noting that these airlines were chosen based on criteria from the full-service airline business models mentioned in the literature review.

Table 2. The ten largest airlines at Lisbon Airport.

Top 10 Airlines	Market Share / Number of Passengers
TAP Portugal (TAP)	47%
Ryanair (RYR)	13%
EasyJet Europe Airlines (EJU)	8%
Vueling Airlines (VLG)	3%
Deutsche Lufthansa (DLH)	2%
Iberia (IBE)	2%
Transavia France (TVF)	2%
SATA Internacional (RZO)	2%
Easyjet Airline Company (EZY)	2%
British Airways (BAW)	2%

Source: (ANAC 2022)

Case Study to Identify Adopted Strategies

The identification of service customization strategies is a fundamental aspect of this study, as it allows understanding how full-service airlines approach service customization and meet the individual needs of their customers. The case study will involve the previously selected full-service airlines, and these companies will be subject to in-depth analysis to identify and describe the service customization strategies adopted by each of them.

The analysis of service customization strategies will take into account different aspects that will be based on criteria studied in the literature review. By identifying the service customization strategies used by full-service airlines, these will be substantiated based on the literature review.

Case Study: Tap Portugal

TAP Portugal is the leading Portuguese airline and one of the major airlines in Europe (Castilho Rafael 2020). With a fleet of over 100 aircraft, TAP flies to more than 90 destinations worldwide and has a reputation for excellence in terms of services and quality (Castilho Rafael 2020). The company has invested in innovative technologies and loyalty programs to enhance the travel experience of its customers and make its brand even more appealing (Publituris 2022).

TAP Portugal offers a wide range of personalized services, such as seat selection, special meals, and loyalty programs (TAP Air Portugal n.d.). The airline has also invested in technologies to enhance its customers' travel experience (Publituris 2022).

One of the main personalized services offered by TAP Portugal is its loyalty program, TAP Miles&Go (TAP Air Portugal n.d.). This program allows customers to accumulate miles and enjoy various benefits, such as cabin upgrades, lounge access, among others. TAP Portugal has been expanding its program with the introduction of new partnerships and exclusive offers, such as hotel discounts, car rentals, and other perks (TAP Air Portugal n.d.).

TAP's customer service team is available to assist passengers with special requests throughout the travel journey, from booking to disembarkation. Customers can contact them by phone, email, or through social media for personalized assistance and to clarify doubts ("Contact Form – Send Requests, Suggestions, or Complaints I TAP Air Portugal" n.d.).

The airline has launched its app, allowing customers to book flights, select seats and meals, view real-time flight information, and more. The application also offers personalized services, such as flight alerts, check-in notifications, and suggestions for activities and restaurants at travel destinations (TAP Air Portugal n.d.).

Case Study: Sata Internacional

SATA International is a Portuguese airline that stands out in the regional and international aviation scene. With a fleet of modern aircraft, the company offers personalized services to meet the needs and preferences of passengers.

One of the key areas where SATA International excels is its loyalty program, SATA IMAGINE (SATA Air Açores n.d.). The program allows passengers to accumulate miles and enjoy a variety of exclusive benefits, such as cabin upgrades, lounge access, and discounts with the company's partners (SATA Air Açores n.d.).

Additionally, SATA International offers passengers the option to select seats during the booking process. This allows passengers to choose seats according to their individual preferences, such as seats with extra legroom or ones close to windows. This flexibility in seat selection contributes to a personalized and comfortable travel experience (SATA Azores Airlines n.d.).

SATA International's customer service team is trained to provide attentive and personalized service. Passengers can rely on the team's support in case of issues, flight changes, or other needs during the journey ("Contact Us I Azores Airlines" n.d.).

The airline also invests in innovative technologies to enhance passengers' travel experience. SATA International has launched its mobile application, which offers a range of personalized features, including flight booking, seat and meal selection, access to real-time flight information, and much more (SATA Azores Airlines n.d.). This technological integration allows passengers to customize their journey according to their individual preferences.

Case Study: Iberia

IBERIA is one of Spain's leading airlines and a reference in the international aviation sector (IBERIA n.d.). In this case study, we will examine the strategies adopted by IBERIA regarding service personalization, considering different aspects, from offering personalized services to the technologies used and passenger perception.

IBERIA stands out by offering a wide range of personalized services to its passengers. The airline provides passengers with the option to select seats of their preference during the booking process (IBERIA n.d.). This personalization allows passengers to choose seats with extra legroom, seats close to windows, or any other individual preference. This flexibility contributes to a more comfortable travel experience tailored to each passenger's needs.

Additionally, IBERIA invests in loyalty programs to reward passenger loyalty. IBERIA's loyalty program, called Iberia Plus, allows passengers to accumulate points/miles that can be exchanged for exclusive benefits, such as cabin upgrades, lounge access, discounts with partners, and much more

(IBERIA n.d.). This approach aims to strengthen the relationship with passengers and offer personalized services that go beyond the flight itself.

The airline also utilizes innovative technologies to enhance passengers' travel experience. IBERIA provides a mobile application that allows passengers to make reservations, check in online, access real-time flight information, among other personalized features (IBERIA n.d.). This technological integration facilitates passengers' interaction with the airline and allows them to customize their journey according to their individual preferences.

IBERIA is known for its customer service, offering personalized support to passengers. The team is ready to assist with issues related to reservations, flight changes, additional services, and any other customer demands ("Customer Service - Iberia Portugal" n.d.).

In summary, IBERIA adopts a comprehensive approach to service personalization. Through the offering of personalized services, loyalty programs, and the use of innovative technologies, the airline aims to provide a unique travel experience tailored to each passenger's individual needs. IBERIA demonstrates a continuous commitment to providing high-quality personalized services.

Case Study: Lufthansa

Lufthansa is a German airline and the largest airline group in Europe in terms of revenue (Lusa 2021). In this case study, we will examine the strategies adopted by Lufthansa regarding service personalization, considering different aspects, from offering personalized services to the technologies used, passenger perception, and the loyalty program.

Lufthansa offers a personalized travel experience through its loyalty program, known as Miles & More (Lufthansa n.d.). Program members can accumulate miles on Lufthansa flights and partner airlines, enjoying a variety of exclusive benefits. These benefits include cabin upgrades, lounge access, priority boarding, additional baggage allowance, and other advantages, allowing passengers to customize their travel experience based on their individual preferences and needs.

In addition to the loyalty program, Lufthansa offers personalized services in various areas. One of them is seat selection, where passengers have the option to choose preferred seats during the booking process, considering their individual preferences, such as location in the cabin, windows, or aisles (Lufthansa n.d.). The airline also offers a wide selection of special meals, catering to specific dietary requirements and passenger food preferences (Lufthansa n.d.).

Lufthansa values customer service and provides a dedicated team to ensure a personalized experience. Passengers can reach out for assistance on various aspects, from reservations to baggage-related issues and special services ("Help & Contact | Lufthansa" n.d.)

Lufthansa invests in innovative technologies to enhance service personalization. Through its mobile application, passengers have access to personalized features, such as flight notifications, real-time itinerary information, booking management, and upgrade options (Lufthansa n.d.). The airline uses data and analytics to offer personalized recommendations to passengers, such as flight offers based on previously searched destinations or travel preferences.

Case Study: British Airways

Lastly, British Airways is one of the leading airlines in the United Kingdom and one of the largest in the world (British Airways n.d.). In this case study, we will examine the strategies adopted by British

Airways regarding service personalization, considering different aspects, from offering personalized services to the technologies used, passenger perception, and the loyalty program.

British Airways offers a wide range of personalized services to its passengers, aiming to meet individual needs and preferences. One key area of service personalization is the airline's loyalty program, known as the Executive Club (British Airways n.d.). Executive Club members have access to exclusive benefits such as mileage accrual, cabin upgrades, lounge access, priority boarding, and other advantages (British Airways n.d.). The program allows passengers to customize their travel experience based on their membership level and individual preferences.

In addition to the loyalty program, British Airways offers personalized services related to seat selection, dining, and in-flight entertainment. Passengers have the option to choose preferred seats during the booking process, considering factors such as cabin location, windows, or aisles, and individual travel preferences (British Airways n.d.). The airline also offers a variety of special meal options, catering to dietary restrictions and specific passenger preferences (British Airways n.d.). Furthermore, British Airways provides an extensive in-flight entertainment program, allowing passengers to personalize their entertainment experience during the flight (British Airways n.d.).

British Airways stands out for its high-quality customer service. The team is available to assist passengers at every stage of the journey, providing personalized support, resolving issues, and ensuring a satisfactory experience ("Customer Support Plan | Information | British Airways" n.d.).

British Airways utilizes innovative technologies to enhance service personalization. The airline's mobile application offers personalized features such as flight alerts, itinerary information, and access to exclusive offers for Executive Club members (British Airways n.d.). Through these technologies, British Airways enhances the travel experience, allowing passengers to customize their journey according to their preferences and needs.

Identification of Strategies

Throughout these sub-chapters, the variables chosen based on the above-written case studies will be presented. These variables are grounded with examples from each airline.

Loyalty Program

A loyalty program is an essential strategy to reward and encourage customer loyalty (Waemustafa 2014). Each analyzed airline offers its own loyalty program, providing exclusive benefits for its members. Below are examples from each airline:

- TAP Portugal: The TAP Miles&Go program allows members to accumulate miles from flights and partners for redemption purposes, including upgrades and exclusive benefits.
- SATA Internacional: The SATA IMAGINE program offers members the opportunity to accumulate points that can be exchanged for free flights, class upgrades, and additional benefits.
- Iberia: The Iberia Plus program rewards members with points that can be used for discounts on flights, class upgrades, and lounge access.
- Lufthansa: The Miles & More program enables members to accumulate miles and enjoy advantages such as class upgrades, lounge access, and preferential reservations.

- British Airways: The Executive Club program offers benefits such as Avios (points) accumulation, upgrades, lounge access, and flexible booking options.

Customization Options During Booking

Airlines provide customization options during the booking process to cater to passengers' individual preferences (Kusumawardani and Aruan 2019). Here are the examples from each airline:

- TAP Portugal: During booking, passengers have the option to choose preferred seats, add extra baggage, and request special meals.
- SATA Internacional: Passengers can select their seat preferences, add additional services such as ground transportation, and request special assistance if needed.
- Iberia: During booking, passengers can customize their experience by choosing seats, adding extra services such as in-flight Wi-Fi, and selecting their meal preferences.
- Lufthansa: During the booking process, passengers have the option to choose seats, special meals, and add extra services.
- British Airways: During booking, passengers can personalize their trip by selecting seats, adding extra services such as car rentals and travel insurance, and choosing their meal preferences.

Customized Customer Service

Personalized customer service is essential to create a unique experience for passengers (Sarol, Mohammad, and Rahman 2023). Here are the examples from each airline:

- TAP Portugal: TAP's customer service team is available to assist passengers with special requests throughout their journey, from the moment of booking to disembarkation. Customers can contact them via phone, email, or social media for personalized assistance and to clarify any doubts.
- SATA Internacional: SATA Internacional's customer service team is trained to provide attentive and personalized service. Passengers can rely on the team's support in case of issues, flight changes, or other needs during the trip.
- Iberia: Iberia stands out for its high-quality customer service, offering personalized support to passengers. The team is ready to assist with issues related to bookings, flight changes, additional services, and any other customer demands.
- Lufthansa: Lufthansa values customer service and provides a dedicated team to ensure a personalized experience. Passengers can contact them for assistance in various aspects, from reservations to baggage-related issues and special services.
- British Airways: British Airways is known for its high-quality customer service. The team is available to assist passengers at every stage of the journey, providing personalized support, resolving issues, and ensuring a satisfactory experience.

Offer of Personalized Additional Services

Full-service airlines provide personalized additional services to better meet passengers' needs (Meyer-Waarden 2013). Here are the examples from each airline:

- TAP Portugal: Offers personalized additional services such as the option to purchase class upgrades, access to lounges, and reservation of special seats.
- SATA Internacional: Provides personalized additional services such as the possibility to request ground transportation service, reservation of preferred seats, and purchase of extra onboard amenities.
- Iberia: Iberia offers personalized additional services such as the option to purchase spacious seats, access to exclusive lounges, reservation of special meals, and the purchase of onboard entertainment services.
- Lufthansa: Provides personalized additional services such as the option to purchase class upgrades, access to lounges, reservation of special menus, and purchase of onboard entertainment services.
- British Airways: Offers personalized additional services such as the option to purchase class upgrades, access to exclusive lounges, reservation of special meals, and purchase of onboard entertainment services.

Use of Technologies for Personalization

Full-service airlines utilize advanced technologies to enhance service personalization (Krasnova et al. 2020). Here are the examples from each airline:

- TAP Portugal: TAP utilizes technologies such as its mobile application to personalize offers and recommendations to customers.
- SATA Internacional: SATA Internacional also uses its mobile application to personalize offers and recommendations to customers.
- Iberia: Iberia uses mobile applications and digital platforms to provide personalized customer service.
- Lufthansa: Lufthansa uses mobile applications to provide a personalized experience to passengers.
- British Airways: British Airways offers an application that allows customers to customize their travel preferences.

PRESENTATION OF RESULTS AND DISCUSSION

Introduction

In this chapter, a statistical analysis will be conducted to understand if the level of passenger satisfaction with service customization differs among the major full-service airlines at Lisbon Airport. Accompanied by statistical calculations, the results will be discussed to provide a comprehensive understanding of the outcomes.

Data Processing

The analysis of Figure 1 reveals that concerning the first question of the questionnaire, aiming to ascertain if the respondents have flown with full-service airlines, 73.6% of the respondents answered affirmatively.

To validate the previous question, the following query was posed: "Which of these airlines is your most frequent choice for flying?" As observed in Table 3, some respondents indicated low-cost airlines.

With the analysis of Table 3, it is easy to see that respondents mentioned low-cost airlines, specifically "Ryanair" and "EasyJet". Since this project focuses on full-service airlines, it was decided not to consider these questionnaires. Consequently, the study has a final sample of 94 respondents.

Figure 1. Preference analysis: Respondents who flew with the studied full-service airlines
Source: *Own Elaboration*

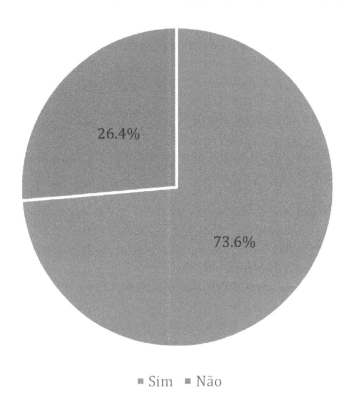

Table 3. Main airline choices

Airlines	Number of respondents
TAP Portugal	*69*
SATA Internacional	*11*
Lufthansa	*6*
Bitish Airways	*6*
IBERIA	*2*
easyJet	*8*
Ryanair	*8*

Source: Own Elaboration

The analysis of Table 3 also shows that the vast majority of respondents travel with TAP Portugal, which is an expected result considering that, according to the information from Table 2, previously analyzed, TAP Portugal has the largest market share.

Since the number of responses obtained for SATA Internacional, Lufthansa, British Airways, and IBERIA was very low, it was decided to group these four airlines into an "others" category and conduct a comparative study between TAP Portugal and this group. Therefore, a statistical analysis will be conducted between TAP Portugal and "others", which includes these four airlines.

DISTRIBUTION OF RESPONSES OBTAINED FOR EACH STRATEGY

Loyalty Program

The loyalty program strategy employed by many airlines aims to retain customers. However, what our data allowed us to observe (Figure 2) is that few respondents enroll in loyalty programs, both among those who travel with TAP and those who travel with other airlines.

Figure 2 Responses given to the question "Are you a member of any Loyalty Program?"

Customization During Reservation

Analyzing this customization strategy, we can see from Figure 3 that there were an equal number of responses '3' and '4' in satisfaction level for TAP Portugal. However, in the 'other' airlines, there were a higher number of '3' responses.

Figure 2. Responses given to the question "Are you a member of any loyalty program?"
Source: *Own Elaboration*

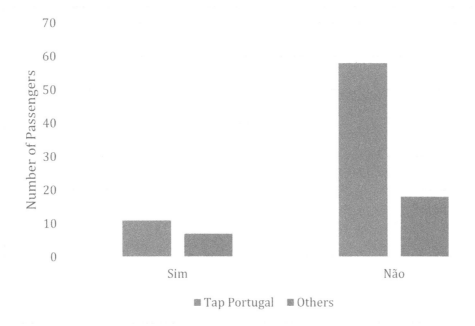

Figure 3. Number of responses given per level regarding the 'customization during reservation' strategy
Source: *Own Elaboration*

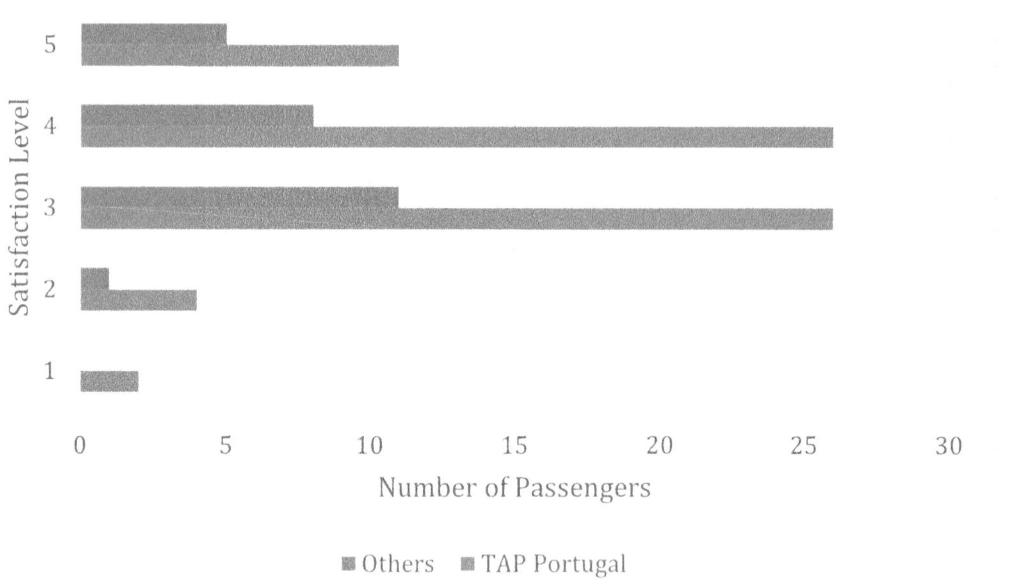

In Table Ap 1 in the Appendix, it is possible to see that the average satisfaction score obtained for TAP was 3.58, and for the 'other companies' group, it was 3.68.

Customized Customer Service

Analyzing this customization strategy, we can see in Figure 4 that the most indicated Satisfaction Level both for TAP Portugal and the "Others companies" group was 4.

In Appendix Table Ap 1, it is possible to see that the average Satisfaction Level value for the strategy under study for TAP Portugal is 3.51, and for the "Others companies" group, it is 3.76.

Customized Additional Services

In this personalization strategy, we can see in Figure 5 that the most indicated Satisfaction Level both in TAP Portugal and in the "Other Companies" group was 3. The average satisfaction level was 3.38 for TAP Portugal and 3.64 for the "Other Companies" group (see Table Ap 1).

Use of Technologies

Analyzing this personalization strategy, we can see in Figure 6 that regarding the use of technologies, the most indicated Satisfaction Level in TAP Portugal was 3, while in the "Others companies" group, it was 4.

In Table Ap 1 in the Appendix, it is possible to see that the average Satisfaction Level for the strategy under study for TAP Portugal is 3,38, and for the "Others companies" group, it is 3,64.

Figure 4. Number of responses given by level regarding the "customized customer service" strategy
Source: *Own Elaboration*

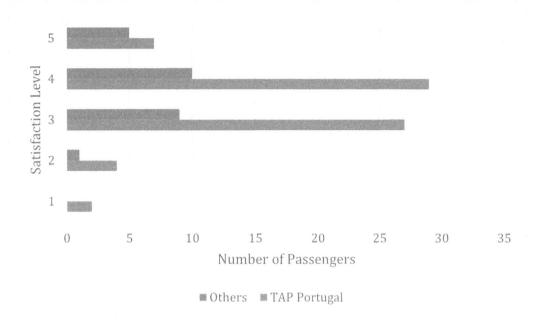

Figure 5. Number of responses given by level for the "customized additional services" strategy
Source: *Own Elaboration*

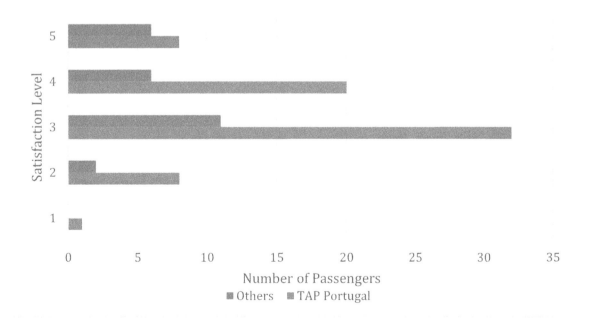

Figure 6. Number of responses given by level regarding the "additional personalized services" strategy
Source: *Own Elaboration*

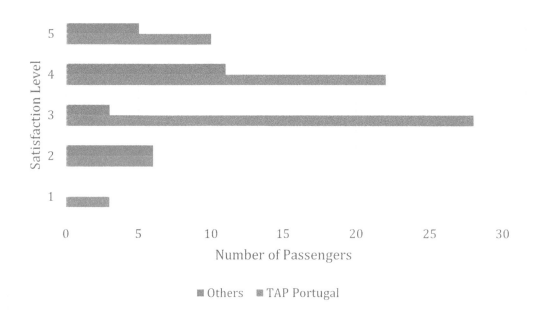

Comparative Study of the Satisfaction Level of the Strategies Under Study Among Various Companies

In this chapter, a statistical study will be conducted to analyze if there are significant differences in the Satisfaction Level of passengers for the various strategies under study, excluding the 'Frequent Flyer Program' due to the limited number of affirmative responses, which made it impossible to apply methodologies that would identify significant differences in the adherence to loyalty programs between TAP and other companies.

Firstly, the Normality test was performed to verify whether there is normality in the samples under study.

In Table 4, analyzing the p-value obtained (indicated by 'Sig.' in the table) with the application of the Shapiro-Wilk test, we observe that for all samples under study, its value is less than 0.05. Therefore, we conclude that the samples of responses obtained for various strategies in the two groups under study do not have a normal distribution.

Following this step and based on the conclusion drawn, we move on to the study of identifying differences between the airlines under study. Using the two categories in the 'airlines' variable, the Mann-Whitney test will be applied.

The analysis of Table 5 allows us to conclude that there are no significant differences in the Satisfaction Level between TAP Portugal and the "Others" group in the various strategies under study, as the p-value obtained for all strategies is always greater than 0.05. Therefore, we can conclude that passengers traveling with TAP Portugal and in the "Others" group do not show significant differences in their Satisfaction Level regarding the four measured strategies.

Table 4. Normality test

	Airline Companies	Kolmogorov-Smirnova[a]			Shapiro-Wilk		
		Statistics	gl	Sig.	Statistics	gl	Sig.
Customization During Reservation	Others	,267	25	<,001	,847	25	,002
	TAP Portugal	,211	69	<,001	,879	69	<,001
Personalized Customer Service	Others	,220	25	,003	,864	25	,003
	TAP Portugal	,237	69	<,001	,865	69	<,001
Additional Personalized Services	Others	,269	25	<,001	,853	25	,002
	TAP Portugal	,258	69	<,001	,883	69	<,001
Utilization of Technologies	Others	,284	25	<,001	,836	25	<,001
	TAP Portugal	,206	69	<,001	,891	69	<,001
a. Significance Correlation of Lilliefors							

Source: Own Elaboration with SPSS Data

Table 5. Hypothesis test summary

	Null Hypothesis	**Test**	**Sig.[a,b]**	**Decision**
1	The distribution of 'Personalization During Reservation' is equal across the categories of 'airlines'.	Independent Samples Mann-Whitney U Test	,799	Retain the null hypothesis.
2	The distribution of 'Personalized Customer Service' is equal across the categories of 'airlines'.	Independent Samples Mann-Whitney U Test	,273	Retain the null hypothesis.
3	The distribution of 'Customized Additional Services' is equal across the categories of 'airlines'..	Independent Samples Mann-Whitney U Test	,279	Retain the null hypothesis.
4	The distribution of 'Technology Utilization' is equal across the categories of 'airlines'.	Independent Samples Mann-Whitney U Test	,418	Retain the null hypothesis.
a. The significance level is 0.050.				
b. Asymptotic significance is displayed.				

Source: Own Elaboration with SPSS Data

CONCLUSION

Throughout this project, the aim was to examine the personalization strategies adopted by the major full-service airlines operating at Lisbon Airport, including personalization during reservation, personalized customer service, additional personalized services, and the use of technologies. Through careful analysis of the collected data and interpretation of the results, trends in the strategies adopted by TAP Portugal were identified and compared with the Others airlines.

In this chapter, the conclusions drawn from the analysis of the work carried out and the results obtained will be presented. The main findings, limitations, and suggestions for future research will be discussed.

Main Results

Throughout this project, it was possible to delve into the proposed topic in a manner that allows answering the research question. Revisiting the research question, which was, "What are the service customization strategies adopted by the airlines with the highest Number of Passengers at Lisbon Airport, and what is the Satisfaction Level of passengers regarding these strategies?" To answer this question, detailed analyses of the data collected through questionnaires were conducted, exploring the customization strategies implemented by the airlines under study.

The major full-service airlines with the highest Number of Passengers at Lisbon Airport were identified, and through a case study conducted for each one, their strategies for service customization were identified. These strategies were supported by the literature review. It was concluded that the adopted strategies are the same across different studied airlines, thereby refuting Hypothesis 1, which stated that "Airlines with the highest Number of Passengers at Lisbon Airport adopt different service customization strategies to meet the individual needs and preferences of their customers."

The satisfaction level of services for each studied strategy was also examined. Through statistical methods, it was observed that there were no significant differences in Satisfaction Level. In other words, passengers' Satisfaction Level with the studied service customization strategies is similar. This conclusion also refutes Hypothesis 2, which stated that "Passengers' Satisfaction Level with service customization differs among full-service airlines with the highest passenger flow at Lisbon Airport."

Suggestions For Future Research

For future research, we recommend gathering a larger number of responses and addressing all service customization strategies to obtain a more comprehensive and accurate understanding of passengers' Satisfaction Level regarding different airlines. These suggestions can contribute to enhancing the quality and relevance of future research in this area.

As a conclusive note, it is essential to highlight two relevant suggestions for future studies in this field.

Firstly, we suggest the development of a service customization satisfaction index. This index could be constructed based on a multidimensional approach, considering various service customization variables. With such an index, it would be possible to assess passengers' Satisfaction Level more comprehensively and systematically concerning the service customization strategies adopted by airlines.

Additionally, it is advisable to conduct a study evaluating the economic impact of service customization strategies in airlines. This study could analyze relevant financial indicators and investigate how the implementation of customization strategies affects these indicators.

These suggestions for future studies can significantly contribute to deepening the knowledge about service customization in the aviation sector.

REFERENCES

Alamdari, F. (1999). Airline In-Flight Entertainment: The Passengers' Perspective. *Journal of Air Transport Management*, *5*(4), 203–209. doi:10.1016/S0969-6997(99)00014-9

ANAC. (2022). *Boletim Estatístico Trimestral N.º 56*. ANAC.

Berthon, P., Pitt, L., Plangger, K., & Shapiro, D. (2012). Marketing Meets Web 2.0, Social Media, and Creative Consumers: Implications for International Marketing Strategy. *Business Horizons*, *55*(3), 261–271. doi:10.1016/j.bushor.2012.01.007

Bieger, T., Laesser, C., Wittmer, A., & Wittmer, D. (2012). Big Data in the Aviation Industry: Introduction and Preliminary Results. *Journal of Air Transport Management*, *25*, 1–2.

British Airways. (n.d.) *About the Club: Executive Club*. British Airways. https://www.britishairways.com/pt-pt/executive-club/about-the-club?source=MNVEXC1about_the_executive_club

Chen, Y., Xiang, Z., & Li, X. (2019). The Dynamics of Customer Satisfaction with Personalized Recommendations in the Tourism Industry. *Journal of Travel Research*, *58*(8), 1421–1437. doi:10.1177/0047287518786887

Chen, Y., & Zhang, H. (2014). Big Data Analytics for Personalized and Context-Aware Travel Services. *Journal of Hospitality Marketing & Management*, *23*(5), 524–542.

Chen, Y.-H., & Huang, S.-L. (2017). Analysis of Airline Service Personalization and Passengers' Intention. *Journal of Air Transport Management*, *58*, 42–49.

Dettmer, B., Socorro, C., & Katon, H. T. (2002). Marketing de Servicios-Análise Da Percepçâo Da Qualidade de Serviços Através Da Ferramenta Servqual Em Uma Instituiçâo de Ensino Superior de Santa Catarina. *Ciencias Da Administraçao, 4*(8), 5. https://dialnet.unirioja.es/servlet/articulo?codigo=4014179&info=resumen&idioma=ENG

Doganis, R. (2006). *The Airline Business* (2nd ed.). Routledge.

Dolnicar, S., & Grün, B. (2014). The Effect of Innovations Relevant to Hotel Performance on Key Customer Outcomes: A Data Mining Approach. *Journal of Business Research*, *67*(9), 1967–1976.

Formulário de Contacto – Envie Pedidos, Sugestões Ou Reclamações. (n.d.). TAP Air Portugal. https://www.flytap.com/pt-pt/suporte/fale-connosco

Furht, B., & Villanustre, F. (2016). Introduction to Big Data. In *Big Data Technologies and Applications* (pp. 3–11). Springer International Publishing. doi:10.1007/978-3-319-44550-2_1

Gandomi, A., & Haider, M. (2015). Beyond the Hype: Big Data Concepts, Methods, and Analytics. *International Journal of Information Management*, *35*(2), 137–144. doi:10.1016/j.ijinfomgt.2014.10.007

Gretzel, U., Sigala, M., Xiang, Z., & Koo, C. (2015). *Recommender Systems in Tourism*. Springer.

Grönroos, C. (2008). *Service Management and Marketing: Customer Management in Service Competition*. John Wiley & Sons.

Gures, N., Arslan, S., & Tun, S. Y. (2014). Customer Expectation, Satisfaction and Loyalty Relationship in Turkish Airline Industry. *International Journal of Marketing Studies*, *6*(April). doi:10.5539/ijms.v6n1p66

Gustafsson, A., Johnson, M. D., & Roos, I. (2005). The Effects of Customer Satisfaction, Relationship Commitment Dimensions, and Triggers on Customer Retention. *Journal of Marketing*, *69*(4), 210–218. doi:10.1509/jmkg.2005.69.4.210

Gustafsson, A., Kristensson, P., & Witell, L. (2005). Customer Co-Creation in Service Innovation. *Journal of Service Research*, *7*(2), 111–124. doi:10.1177/1094670520908929

Hendrawati, Erna, I Gede Juanamasta, Ni Made, Nopita Wati, Wiwin Wahyuni, Mira Pramudianti, Nugrahini Wisnujati, et al. (2019). The Role of Customer Service through Customer Relationship Management (CRM) to Increase Customer Loyalty and Good Image the Role of Customer Service through Customer Relationship Management (CRM) to Increase Customer Loyalty and Good Image. *International Journal of Scientific & Technology Research*, *49*, 310.

Heung, V. & Nga-Ching, T. (2016). Personalization of Airport Services: The Role of Passenger Data and Technology. *Journal of Travel Research, 56*(8).

Huang, Z., Benyoucef, M., & Poon, S. K. (2018). Service Personalization: A Comprehensive Review and Future Research Directions. *Computers in Human Behavior*, *83*, 500–519.

Hunter, L. (2006). Low Cost Airlines. Business Model and Employment Relations. *European Management Journal*, *24*(5), 315–321. doi:10.1016/j.emj.2006.08.001

IBERIA. (n.d.) *Iberia No Seu Telemóvel - Iberia Portugal*. IBERIA. https://www.iberia.com/pt/pt/iberia-app/

Jin, M. J., & Kim, J. K. (2022). Customer Adoption Factors for In-Flight Entertainment and Connectivity. *Research in Transportation Business & Management*, *43*(June), 100759. doi:10.1016/j.rtbm.2021.100759

Kotler, P., & Armstrong, G. (2010). *Principles of Marketing*. Pearson Education.

Krasnova, H., Eling, N., Schneider, O., Wenninger, H., & Widjaja, T. (2020). Personalization of Online Services and Its Effect on Customer Satisfaction and Loyalty: The Mediating Role of Trustworthiness. *Journal of Management Information Systems*, *37*(2), 547–585.

Kusumawardani, A. M., & Daniel Tumpal, H. A. (2019). Comparing the Effects of Service Quality and Value-for-Money on Customer Satisfaction, Airline Image and Behavioural Intention between Full-Service and Low-Cost Airlines: Evidence from Indonesia. *International Journal of Tourism Policy*, *9*(1), 27–49. doi:10.1504/IJTP.2019.100078

Lekakos, G. (2008). Recommender Systems for Large-Scale e-Commerce Applications. *Decision Support Systems*, *45*(4), 892–903.

Leotti, V. B., Coster, R., & Riboldi, J. (2012). *Normalidade de Variáveis : Métodos de Verificação e Comparação de Alguns Testes Não-Paramétricos Por Simulação*. UFRGS. https://lume.ufrgs.br/handle/10183/158102

Li, X., Zhao, H., Liu, D., & Ma, Y. (2019). Customized Recommendations for Tourism Products Based on LDA Topic Modeling. *Journal of Ambient Intelligence and Humanized Computing*, *10*(1), 173–182. doi:10.1007/s12652-017-0632-6

Lufthansa. (n.d.). *Miles & More - o Nosso Programa Para Passageiros Frequentes*. Lufthansa. https://www.lufthansa.com/ao/pt/miles-and-more

Manca, C., Grijalvo, M., Palacios, M., & Kaulio, M. (2018). Collaborative Workplaces for Innovation in Service Companies: Barriers and Enablers for Supporting New Ways of Working. *Service Business*, *12*(3), 525–550. doi:10.1007/s11628-017-0359-0

McIvor, R., O'Reilly, D., & Ponsonby, S. (2003). The Impact of Internet Technologies on the Airline Industry: Current Strategies and Future Developments. *Strategic Change*, *12*(1), 31–47. doi:10.1002/jsc.618

McKight. P. E. (2010). Kruskal-Wallis Test. The Corsini Encyclopedia of Psychology. Wiley. doi:10.1002/9780470479216.corpsy0491

Meyer-Waarden, L. (2013). The Impact of Reward Personalisation on Frequent Flyer Programmes' Perceived Value and Loyalty. *Journal of Services Marketing*, *27*(3), 183–194. doi:10.1108/08876041311330681

Mishra, A. K., & Mishra, D. (2018). Service Personalization in Tourism: A Systematic Literature Review. *Journal of Hospitality and Tourism Management*, *35*, 81–91.

Moghavvemi, S., Sharabati, M., & Wan, K. W. I. (2016). Airline Frequent Flyer Program: Predicting Customers' Satisfaction Using Logistic Regression and Neural Network Models. *Journal of Air Transport Management*, *52*(July), 117–124.

Oliveira, A. V. M., & Huse, C. (2009). Localized Competitive Advantage and Price Reactions to Entry: Full-Service vs. Low-Cost Airlines in Recently Liberalized Emerging Markets. *Transportation Research Part E, Logistics and Transportation Review*, *45*(2), 307–320. doi:10.1016/j.tre.2008.09.003

Pan, B., Xie, K.-L., & Huang, Z. (2017). An Empirical Study of Online Reviews and Customer Ratings on Booking Likelihood. *International Journal of Hospitality Management*, *60*, 58–69. doi:10.1016/j.ijhm.2016.09.003

Paraskevas, A., & Nudurupati, S. S. (2015). Customer Customization in Services: A Review and Future Research Directions. *International Journal of Operations & Production Management*, *35*(5), 489–516.

Parise, S., & Sheng, M. L. (2021). Customizing Services to Build Stronger Relationships. *MIT Sloan Management Review*, *62*(3), 39–47.

Plano de Apoio Ao Cliente. (n.d.). British Airways. https://www.britishairways.com/pt-pt/information/legal/local-requirements/south-korea/customer-service-plan

Prentice, C., Hsiao, A., Wang, X., & Sandra, M. C. L. (2023). Mind, Service Quality, Relationship with Airlines. *Journal of Strategic Marketing*, *31*(1), 212–234. doi:10.1080/0965254X.2021.1894216

Publituris. (2022). *Programa de Fidelização Da TAP é o Melhor Da Europa e África Para Os Freddie Awards*. Publituris. https://www.publituris.pt/2022/04/28/programa-de-fidelizacao-da-tap-e-o-melhor-da-europa-e-africa-para-os-freddie-awards

Rafael, C. (2020). TAP: Tudo Sobre a Principal Companhia Aérea de Portugal. *Melhores Destinos*. https://www.melhoresdestinos.com.br/tap-portugal.html

Rüßmann, M., (2015). *Industry 4.0: The Future of Productivity and Growth in Manufacturing Industries*.

Sarol, S. D. (2023). Mobile Technology Application in Aviation: Chatbot for Airline Customer Experience. In Technology Application in Aviation, Tourism and Hospitality, 59–72. Singapore: Springer Nature Singapore. doi:10.1007/978-981-19-6619-4_5

Sharma, S., & Mangat, V. (2015). Technology and Trends to Handle Big Data: Survey. In *International Conference on Advanced Computing and Communication Technologies, ACCT*. Institute of Electrical and Electronics Engineers Inc. 10.1109/ACCT.2015.121

Statista. (2022). *Total Data Volume Worldwide 2010-2025*. Statista. https://www.statista.com/statistics/871513/worldwide-data-created/

Su, X., & Khoshgoftaar, T. M. (2009). A Survey of Collaborative Filtering Techniques. *Advances in Artificial Intelligence*, *2009*, 1–19. doi:10.1155/2009/421425

Sundar, S., & Sukor, M. (2020). Personalized Services in the Aviation Industry: Challenges and Opportunities. *Journal of Air Transport Management*, *87*, 101856.

Sundar, S. S., Bellur, S., Oh, J., Xu, Q., Jia, H., & Meduri, S. (2017). User Customization vs. Defaults: The Effect of Defaults and User Expectation Congruence on Perceived Trust in Recommender Agents. *International Journal of Human-Computer Studies*, *98*, 52–65.

Tripathi, G. (2017). Customer Satisfaction and Word of Mouth Intentions: Testing the Mediating Effect of Customer Loyalty. *Journal of Services Research*, *17*(2), 1–16.

van der Aa, H., Buil, L., Kabadayi, S., & van der Heijden, H. (2018). The Effects of Chatbot's Conversational Human Voice and Mode of Conversational Voice on Customers' Loyalty. *Computers in Human Behavior*, *89*, 347–356.

Waemustafa, W. (2014). *Customer Satisfaction and Loyalty in the Airline Industry: A Case Study of Malaysia Airlines (MAS) and Air Asia*.

Wang, Y., Kevin, K. F. S., & Sparks, B. A. (2014). *What Technology-Enabled Services Do Air Travelers Value? Investigating the Role of Technology Readiness*. Sage. doi:10.1177/1096348014538050

Whyte, R. (2004). Frequent Flyer Programmes: Is It a Relationship, or Do the Schemes Create Spurious Loyalty? *Journal of Targeting, Measurement and Analysis for Marketing, 12*(3), 269–80. . doi:10.1057/palgrave.jt.5740114

Zeithaml, V. (2008). *Services Marketing : Integrating Customer Focus across the Firm*. 7th ed. Mcgraw-Hill Education.

Zhang, X., & Hu, Y. (2018). Big Data Analytics in the Airline Industry: A Review and Future Research Directions. *Journal of Air Transport Management*, *68*, 1–10.

APPENDIX: DESCRIPTIVE STATISTICS

Table 6. Descriptive statistics

		Airline		Statistics	Standard Test Statistics
Personalization During Booking	Other (SATA Internacional, Lufthansa, British Airways, IBERIA)	Mean		3,6800	,17049
		95% Confidence Interval for Mean	Lower Limit	3,3281	
			Upper Limit	4,0319	
		5% Trimmed Mean		3,6889	
		Median		4,0000	
		Variance		,727	
		Standard Error		,85245	
		Minimum		2,00	
		Maximum		5,00	
		Range		3,00	
		Interquartile Range		1,00	
		Skewness		,260	,464
		Kurtosis		-,822	,902
	TAP Portugal	Mean		3,5797	,11196
		95% Confidence Interval for Mean	Lower Limit	3,3563	
			Upper Limit	3,8031	
		5% Trimmed Mean		3,6208	
		Median		4,0000	
		Variance		,865	
		Standard Error		,92999	
		Minimum		1,00	
		Maximum		5,00	
		Range		4,00	
		Interquartile Range		1,00	
		Skewness		-,409	,289
		Kurtosis		,342	,570

continued on following page

Table 6. Continued

		Airline		Statistics	Standard Test Statistics
Personalized Customer Service	Other (SATA Internacional, Lufthansa, British Airways, IBERIA)	Mean		3,7600	,16613
		95% Confidence Interval for Mean	Lower Limit	3,4171	
			Upper Limit	4,1029	
		5% Trimmed Mean		3,7778	
		Median		4,0000	
		Variance		,690	
		Standard Error		,83066	
		Minimum		2,00	
		Maximum		5,00	
		Range		3,00	
		Interquartile Range		1,00	
		Skewness		,021	,464
		Kurtosis		-,666	,902
	TAP Portugal	Mean		3,5072	,10451
		95% Confidence Interval for Mean	Lower Limit	3,2987	
			Upper Limit	3,7158	
		5% Trimmed Mean		3,5403	
		Median		4,0000	
		Variance		,754	
		Standard Error		,86811	
		Minimum		1,00	
		Maximum		5,00	
		Range		4,00	
		Interquartile Range		1,00	
		Skewness		-,509	,289
		Kurtosis		,764	,570

continued on following page

Table 6. Continued

	Airline		Statistics	Standard Test Statistics
Personalized Additional Services	Other (SATA Internacional, Lufthansa, British Airways, IBERIA)	Mean	3,6400	,19044
		95% Confidence Interval for Mean — Lower Limit	3,2470	
		95% Confidence Interval for Mean — Upper Limit	4,0330	
		5% Trimmed Mean	3,6556	
		Median	3,0000	
		Variance	,907	
		Standard Error	,95219	
		Minimum	2,00	
		Miximum	5,00	
		Range	3,00	
		Interquartile Range	1,50	
		Skewness	,192	,464
		Kurtosis	-1,010	,902
	TAP Portugal	Mean	3,3768	,10748
		95% Confidence Interval for Mean — Lower Limit	3,1623	
		95% Confidence Interval for Mean — Upper Limit	3,5913	
		5% Trimmed Mean	3,3792	
		Median	3,0000	
		Variance	,797	
		Standard Error	,89281	
		Minimum	1,00	
		Miximum	5,00	
		Range	4,00	
		Interquartile Range	1,00	
		Skewness	,065	,289
		Kurtosis	-,107	,570

continued on following page

Table 6. Continued

	Airline			Statistics	Standard Test Statistics
Utilization of Technologies	Other (SATA Internacional, Lufthansa, British Airways, IBERIA)	Mean		3,6000	,21602
		95% Confidence Interval for Mean	Lower Limit	3,1541	
			Upper Limit	4,0459	
		5% Trimmed Mean		3,6111	
		Median		4,0000	
		Variance		1,167	
		Standard Error		1,08012	
		Minimum		2,00	
		Miximum		5,00	
		Range		3,00	
		Interquartile Range		1,50	
		Skewness		-,388	,464
		Kurtosis		-1,087	,902
	TAP Portugal	Mean		3,4348	,11946
		95% Confidence Interval for Mean	Lower Limit	3,1964	
			Upper Limit	3,6732	
		5% Trimmed Mean		3,4758	
		Median		3,0000	
		Variance		,985	
		Standard Error		,99230	
		Minimum		1,00	
		Maximum		5,00	
		Range		4,00	
		Interquartile Range		1,00	
		Skewness		-,326	,289
		Kurtosis		,079	,570

Source: Own Elaboration with SPSS Data

Chapter 11
Beyond the Horizon:
Exploring AI's Role in Enhancing Aviation Safety and Efficiency – An Airline Perspective

Kübra Nur Cingöz
Gaziantep University, Turkey

Vildan Durmaz
Eskisehir Technical University, Turkey

ABSTRACT

The aviation industry is evolving, driven by advanced techology like autonomous systems, machine learning, and data analytics. Artificial intelligence (AI) applications, including predictive maintenance, flight planning, and air traffic management, are transforming operations and safety. However, integrating these technologies poses challenges and ethical dilemmas explored in this chapter. The authors analyze AI's impact on safety, efficiency, customer service, and cost-effectiveness in the airline industry. Through a systematic examination, the authors seek to offer insights into the pivotal question of whether the preference should lean towards a fully automated AI-driven system, human operation, or a harmonious AI-human partnership within the airline industry. By weighing the pros and cons of each approach, the authors aim to shed light on the path that holds the greatest promise for the future of aviation, ultimately ensuring the industry's continued excellence and sustainability.

INTRODUCTION

Like numerous other industries, the aerospace sector has undergone a remarkable transformation through automation and digitalization as part of the Industry 4.0 revolution (Andrei et al., 2022). As we enter the era of Industry 4.0, the ground-based maintenance, support, and IVHM/PHM systems are evolving into a comprehensive digital platform. This transformation involves the seamless integration of artificial intelligence (AI), cloud computing, big data analytics, additive manufacturing, augmented

DOI: 10.4018/979-8-3693-0908-7.ch011

reality, sophisticated software, and precise data prediction tools, autonomous systems, machine learning algorithms, data analytics (Chang et al., 2019; Vincent et al, 2021) and it's challenging to identify any sphere of human activity where digital technologies are not employed (Molchanova et al., 2020). Digital technologies are heralding a new era in aviation, widespread use of digital channels and platforms, the use of multiple devices, growing social media popularity, and differentiation of travel decision-making processes (Büyüközkan et al., 2020) and AI (Artificial Intelligence)-powered applications are poised to revolutionize the way airlines operate and make crucial decisions. Among the myriad applications, predictive maintenance, flight planning optimization, and air traffic management emerge as vanguards, promising heightened operational efficiency and safety.

It is obvious the importance of digitalization, AI, and innovation in organization setup (Silling, 2019). Many airlines, airports, and stakeholders of the aviation industry have been adopting new technology and AI in their business model for both economic and social benefits like operation efficiency, customer service efficiency, (Vincent et al., 2021) effective usage of the sources, and high profitability. AI has also proven to have huge potential benefits for autonomous drone systems, allowing them to optimize and enhance drone control, especially in unstable and aggressive environments, or to learn from experience (Konert and Balcerzack, 2021). Although AI usage such effective, profitable, and reasonable to use, it also brings some concerns such as security issues, lack of education and human error, data privacy and security, regulatory challenges, personal reduction and skill, ethical implications, the brilliance of human life is not given, avoidance of collateral damage, respecting privacy rights, dependency and reliability, lack of human reasoning, prejudice and discrimination, integration and interoperability, unemployment and heightened disparities in wealth (Makridakis, 2017; Stahl and Wright, 2018)

On the other hand, strategic management and policy are crucial components for the success of airlines, airports, and related businesses. When considering the integration of artificial intelligence (AI) in the aviation industry, these two areas become even more interconnected.

AI technology offers numerous benefits in terms of enhancing business value, encompassing higher revenue generation, decreased expenses, and enhanced operational efficiency. In a survey involving over 2,500 executives spanning various industries, over 90% of respondents concurred that AI presents a significant business opportunity and is regarded as essential for their company's success (Alsheiabni et al., 2020). In their study, Rane et al. (2019) emphasized that companies striving for success should harness advanced technologies like AI and big data analytics to both generate and seize value.

On the other hand, after evaluating the possible applications of AI tools in the air transport industry, particularly within managerial departments, certain applications stand out as being especially valuable for the strategic decision-making process. Examples of these applications include the use of Neural Network models for tasks such as market analysis, cost estimation, and negotiation in hedging (Pérez-Campuzano et al, 2021). Furthermore, Artificial Intelligence (AI) plays a vital role in assisting airlines and aviation-related businesses in effectively positioning themselves within the market. This encompasses tasks such as selecting optimal flight routes, refining pricing strategies, making informed judgments, and distinguishing their services from competitors.

In that scope, considering the efficiency, AI plays a crucial role. It is not only important for positioning in the market but also allocating resources efficiently, such as aircraft, personnel, and capital, market expansion and risk management, and for airline disruption management (Ogunsina and DeLaurentis, 2022)

In addition, the integration of AI in the aviation industry requires careful strategic planning and adherence to policies and regulations.

Airlines and other aviation-related businesses need to consider factors such as data privacy, safety, and ethical AI use (Rana et al, 2022). Moreover, policies must evolve to accommodate the changing landscape of AI in aviation, addressing issues related to data sharing, liability, and cybersecurity. Contrary to the benefits of AI, it also has some drawbacks (Amariles and Baquero, 2023). One prominent drawback is the potential for overreliance on automation. As AI systems become more sophisticated, there is a risk that pilots and air traffic controllers may become complacent, relying too heavily on technology to handle critical tasks. This can lead to a degradation of manual flying skills, making human operators less capable in emergencies where AI systems might fail or encounter unforeseen challenges. Additionally, the complexity of AI algorithms and the data they rely on make them susceptible to vulnerabilities and cyberattacks, posing a substantial security risk to the aviation industry (Gruetzemacher et al, 2020; Makridakis, 2017, Tao et al, 2019; Piotrowski, 2023; Stahl and Wright, 2018; Norori et al., 2021; Wach et al, 2023; Amariles and Baquero, 2023; Rana et al, 2022)

From a strategic management view, the decisional situations that need human judgment and analysis regularly relate to issues where problems are far from being well-structured (Keding, 2021)

In the scope of this chapter, our main objective is to conduct a thorough analysis of the pros and cons related to the implementation of Artificial Intelligence (AI) in the aviation sector. We will meticulously assess how AI affects various facets of this dynamic industry, such as safety, efficiency, customer service, and cost-effectiveness. Through a systematic investigation, our goal is to provide insights into the central question of whether the preference should shift towards a fully automated AI-driven system, human operation, or a harmonious AI-human partnership in the airline industry. By carefully weighing the advantages and disadvantages of each approach, we aim to illuminate the path that holds the most potential for the future of aviation, ultimately ensuring the industry's ongoing excellence and sustainability.

In the chapter, the author employed the Analytical Hierarchy Process (AHP) Technique for the Order of Preference by Similarity to the Ideal Solution (TOPSIS) method, which is one of one of the multi-criteria decision analysis methods (de Farias Aires, and Ferreira, 2019), created by Hwang and Yoon in 1981, later applied by Zeleny in 1982, and further developed by Lai and Liu in 1993 (Özgüner and Özgüner, 2020).

BACKGROUND

Definition and Importance of Artificial Intelligence in Aviation

Artificial intelligence is a field of computer science that aims to facilitate the design and development of computers that can perform activities that are the domain of people, in particular, requiring intelligence. (Legal and ethical aspects of rules for the operation of autonomous unmanned aircraft with artificial intelligence). The concept of artificial intelligence is also defined as "digital technology and/or applications with the ability to mimic human behavior, interact, learn, adapt, and apply their experiences to expand possibilities. (Tamer and Övgün, 2020). According to Chang et al. (2019), AI is characterized as the field of science and technology that focuses on creating intelligent machines, particularly intelligent computer programs. It shares similarities with the task of employing computers to comprehend human intelligence, although AI is not restricted to methods that can be observed in biological systems. EASA defined AI as 'any technology that appears to emulate the performance of a human' (Roadmap,2020).

The term "artificial intelligence" was first used by McCarthy and his colleagues in a summer research project in 1955. This project was based on the assumption that any form of learning or intelligence, in principle, could be replicated by a machine (İşler and Kılıç, 2021). Between 1952 and 1969, IBM developed the first program capable of playing chess. In 1965, Joseph Weizenbaum developed Eliza, an intriguing program that engaged in English dialogues on various topics (Sucu, 2019). İşler and Kılıç have classified the stages of artificial intelligence development as follows (İşler and Kılıç, 2021).

As seen in Figure 1, from the first usage of the concept of artificial intelligence in 1955 to 2017, many innovations were made, and finally, in 2017, memory was added to artificial intelligence.

The concept of artificial intelligence has evolved into various subfields depending on the nature of the problem to be solved, from that time to the present day. These include Artificial Neural Networks (ANN), Fuzzy Logic, Simulated Annealing, Expert Systems, Computer Vision, Genetic Algorithms, Speech Recognition, Chaotic Modeling, and Robotics (Sircar et al., 2021; İşler and Kılıç, 2021). An Artificial Neural Network (ANN), which is a computational model influenced by the information processing mechanisms observed in biological nervous systems, including the human brain (Zupan, 1994), comprehends and adapts to data, Fuzzy Logic, often applied in the optimization of good placement, has been shown to expedite the good placement process when employed in conjunction with the Neuro-Fuzzy approach (Sircar, 2021) and other subfields of Artificial intelligence (AI) which is considered to be one of the pacemaker technologies of the 4th industrial revolution (Schulze-Horn et al., 2020) are of significant importance in the aviation industry.

Figure 1. The stages of artificial intelligence development
Reference: *İşler and Kılıç, 2021*

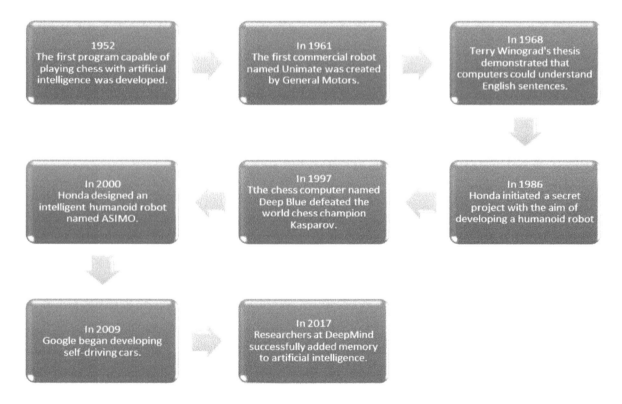

The integration of Artificial Intelligence-based neural networks in civil aviation is significantly reshaping the contemporary air transportation sector. Prominent airlines worldwide are embracing this technology to enhance the efficiency of their customer service operations, thereby elevating the overall experience of their passengers(Vincent et al, 2021)

Predictive maintenance leverages data-driven insights to preemptively identify and address potential faults in aircraft systems, mitigating the risk of unexpected failures and reducing downtime significantly. Such a proactive approach ensures aircraft remain in optimal condition, bolstering both operational efficiency and passenger safety, Decision-making, and route optimization (Soori et al, 2023). The AI employed pioneering technology to enhance the efficiency of developing aviation systems at every stage of their life cycle, thereby augmenting the security of aviation systems and its unique capability to learn, enhance, and anticipate challenging scenarios (Shmelova et al., 2020). It has a great impact not only on efficiency but also on flight planning optimization. It leverages AI algorithms and Machine Learning to streamline route planning and fuel efficiency. By harnessing vast amounts of data, including weather patterns, airspace restrictions, and aircraft performance metrics, airlines can make data-informed decisions, optimizing flight paths to minimize fuel consumption and emissions while ensuring on-time arrivals. Furthermore, the increasing demand for flights is driving the need for innovative solutions in aviation, where AI plays a significant role in balancing safety and efficiency, predictive maintenance, and process optimization (Soori et al, 2023; Baumann and Klingauf, 2020). AI-powered air traffic management systems analyze real-time data from various sources, providing controllers with enhanced situational awareness and the ability to manage traffic flow dynamically. By predicting potential conflicts and identifying optimal routing options, these systems reduce the risk of collisions, improve airspace capacity, and facilitate more seamless travel experiences for passengers (Degas et al, 2022; Soori et al, 2023; Baumann and Klingauf, 2020). In addition, Artificial Intelligence (AI) has become an indispensable facet within airlines, revolutionizing the industry and enhancing the passenger experience. Advanced AI algorithms are employed to optimize flight scheduling, route planning, and resource allocation, resulting in increased efficiency and reduced operational costs (Soori et al, 2023; Baumann and Klingauf, 2020). Passengers now enjoy a seamless travel experience with AI-powered self-check-in kiosks, automated baggage handling systems, and real-time updates on flight status through mobile apps. Moreover, AI-driven predictive maintenance ensures higher aircraft reliability, improving safety standards and minimizing delays (Vincent et al, 2022). As airlines continue to harness the potential of technology and AI, the future of air travel holds the promise of even greater connectivity, personalization, and sustainability.

The primary goal of artificial intelligence systems is to enhance the safety and well-being of individuals. Nevertheless, numerous instances have arisen in which AI-based systems have been found to replicate pre-existing biases, such as racial biases in facial recognition and court sentencing determinations. Several conceptual frameworks exist to address these and other challenges, but practical methodologies for their implementation remain scarce (Hallows et al., 2022). Alongside the promising prospects of AI, there exists a looming shadow (Ertel,2009). It comes with its set of challenges such as privacy, data security, and potential job displacement, and ethical considerations such as data collection and the potential for AI to perpetuate biases or make critical decisions without human intervention. Ensuring the robustness and reliability of AI algorithms is paramount, as any erroneous decisions can have significant repercussions on flight safety. Additionally, the issue of data privacy and security must be addressed to safeguard sensitive information shared between airlines and AI systems. Moreover, the human-AI collaboration raises questions about liability and accountability in the event of incidents involving AI-controlled systems (Gruetzemacher et al, 2020; Makridakis, 2017, Tao et al, 2019; Piotrowski, 2023; Stahl and Wright,

2018; Norori et al., 2021; Wach et al, 2023; Amariles and Baquero, 2023; Rana et al, 2022). Striking a balance between harnessing the benefits of technology and maintaining ethical standards remains a paramount challenge for airlines as they navigate the ever-evolving landscape of AI and its applications.

LITERATURE REVIEW

Digital technology has an enormous impact on both business and society. Over time, digital transformation has come to be recognized as the "fourth industrial revolution," marked by the fusion of technologies that erode the distinctions between the physical, digital, and biological realms. This convergence includes innovations such as artificial intelligence, robotics, and autonomous vehicles. Artificial Intelligence (AI) technologies are garnering significant attention due to their swift responsiveness and robust ability for generalization, leading to a surge in research and heightened emphasis on AI in various fields (Sircar et al., 2021)

In their study, Moudani and Mora-Camino (2000) addressed the challenges related to the allocation of aircraft to flights and the scheduling of fleet maintenance operations. While recent methodologies employ artificial intelligence techniques on mainframe computers to tackle combinatorial optimization problems in routine operations, their approach takes into account dynamic conditions encountered during online operations. Their proposed solution combined a Dynamic Programming approach to handle the fleet assignment problem and a heuristic technique to address the embedded maintenance scheduling problem. They applied this approach to a medium-sized charter airline, and their findings demonstrated that it exhibited acceptable characteristics for operational circumstances, delivering efficient and effective solutions.

Moudani and Mora-Camino (2000) addressed the challenges related to the allocation of aircraft to flights and the scheduling of fleet maintenance operations. While recent methodologies employ artificial intelligence techniques on mainframe computers to tackle combinatorial optimization problems in routine operations, their approach takes into account dynamic conditions encountered during online operations. Their proposed solution combined a Dynamic Programming approach to handle the fleet assignment problem and a heuristic technique to address the embedded maintenance scheduling problem. They applied this approach to a medium-sized charter airline, and their findings demonstrated that it exhibited acceptable characteristics for operational circumstances, delivering efficient and effective solutions.

Within their research, Takeichi et al. (2017) explored the potential of using artificial neural networks to forecast flight delays based on pre-departure information, such as weather forecasts and projected flight paths. Their research revealed that the artificial neural network accurately predicts the average delay but faces challenges in forecasting the sudden fluctuations in delays, particularly during congested periods.

Stahl and Wright (2018) examined 809 papers concerning ethics in AI and Big Data, discovering that 177 of them specifically delved into the topic of privacy and data protection. This highlighted privacy as the most prominent concern among the papers analyzed

Pillai and Devrakhyani (2020) examined the role of Artificial Intelligence (AI) and the Internet of Things (IoT) in the context of Customer Relationship Management (CRM) within the airline industry. Their primary objective was to enhance CRM practices through the judicious utilization of AI and IoT technologies, with a particular emphasis on engaging airports in the implementation of intelligent CRM strategies. The ultimate goal was to ensure long-term profitability and the continued generation of revenue in the airline sector.

Pérez-Campuzano et al (2021) aimed to investigate the possibilities of utilizing Artificial Intelligence (AI) applications for enhancing strategic decision-making in the airline industry during the COVID-19 pandemic. The objective was to outline a roadmap that could inspire collaboration between scholars and industry practitioners in implementing these AI tools effectively within airline corporations. Their research revealed that specific pathways hold notable significance for the strategic decision-making processes within airlines. Many of these pathways rely on Machine Learning (ML) algorithms and training methods that are presently underutilized or overlooked in certain business domains. Examples include the use of Neural Network models for unsupervised market analysis and supervised cost estimation, which have the potential to offer substantial benefits.

Chakraborty et al. (2021) analyzed to assess the effects of airlines' adoption of modern technology in the context of post-COVID-19 safety measures for passengers, along with its impact on passenger confidence, satisfaction, and positive Word of Mouth (WOM). Their study suggests that by incorporating Internet of Things (IoT) and artificial intelligence (AI)-driven sustainable practices, airlines can significantly bolster passengers' confidence when traveling. Furthermore, the research proposes that AI and IoT-enabled systems can transform traditional airport and in-flight processes into modern service capabilities. This transformation, in turn, results in improved service quality, ultimately enhancing passengers' trust and satisfaction with the airline's offerings.

Schultz et al. (2021) employed recurrent and convolutional neural networks to categorize airport performance by incorporating weather data from London-Gatwick Airport. Their research demonstrated that utilizing machine learning methodologies is an effective means to assess the relationship between reduced airport performance and the intensity of local weather events. The models they developed exhibited prediction accuracy exceeding 90% for departure movements.

Ogunsina and DeLaurentis (2022) presented a comprehensive and systematic approach aimed at achieving a swift and all-encompassing recovery of various aspects during the management of airline disruptions. They achieved this through the implementation of an intelligent multi-agent system that drew upon principles from both artificial intelligence and distributed ledger technology. Their findings suggest that their approach, which enables simultaneous recovery across multiple dimensions, operates efficiently within polynomial time. This effectiveness is particularly notable when dealing with disruptions affecting the entire airline route network, showcasing the potential of their paradigm for enhancing disruption management in the airline industry.

Degas et al. (2022) analyzed the current state of Artificial Intelligence (AI) within the aviation and Air Traffic Management (ATM) domain. They focused on various aspects, including a review of research conducted over the past decade in AI within ATM, identifying emerging trends and characteristics, and exploring the importance of Explainable Artificial Intelligence (XAI) in this context. The authors delved into the functioning of both general AI and ATM-specific XAI, examining where and why XAI is necessary, its current implementations, and the associated limitations. They synthesized their findings into a conceptual framework called the DPP (Descriptive, Predictive, Prescriptive) model. They also provided an example of how this model could be applied in a scenario set in the year 2030. The study concludes that AI systems within ATMs require further research and development to gain acceptance among end-users. Key challenges to address include the development of suitable XAI methods, along with their validation by relevant authorities and end-users, to ensure the safe and effective use of AI in air traffic management.

Soori et al. (2023) provided an extensive review of the latest advancements in Artificial Intelligence (AI), Machine Learning (ML), and Deep Learning (DL) within the realm of advanced robotics systems.

They explored a variety of applications for these systems in the modification of robots. The authors also recommended further research endeavors aimed at addressing gaps in the current literature and published papers concerning the utilization of AI, ML, and DL in advanced robotics systems. Their study emphasized that the integration of AI, ML, and DL with robotics holds substantial potential for creating a diverse range of applications that can deliver societal benefits in various ways.

Alltough there are studies which aimes to predict fuel consumption and flight delays (Horiguchi et al., 2017 ; Faiza and Khalil, 2023,; McCarthy et al, 2019 ; Manjunatha Kumar et al., 2022; Alharbi and Prince, 2020), to facilitate the planning of forthcoming airport terminals and to integrate technologies and resources that improve operational flexibility, increase capacity, and enhance the overall customer experience (Sims, 2019), for risk management on Airlines (Baydar and Dursun, 2019) and to summarize the potential applications of Artificial Intelligence in the airline industry, highlighting various areas for development by highlighting the design and management of airline communication networks, diagnostic systems for the maintenance of aircraft structures and engines, crew scheduling, airspace control, decision support for flight operations personnel, Defining of number of employees and fare quoting processes (McMullen, 1987 ; Pilon, 2023; Petrović et al, 2018), There is a notable absence of research that evaluates the superiority of one option among human, AI alone, and AI-human collaboration in the context of airlines, particularly concerning the negative aspects and strategic management implications of AI.

In that context, this book chapter delves into the potential risks associated with the incorporation of technology within the airline industry. The objective is to illuminate the most critical concerns by gathering insights from industry experts and passengers, to determine which option - human, AI alone, or AI-human collaboration - holds the upper hand.

METHODOLOGY

This study involves a literature review aimed at determining the optimal choice among AI usage, human involvement, or a combination of human and AI usage. The outcome of this review has led to the identification of four main criteria (Criterion 1: Cost, Criterion 2: Technological Competence, Criterion 3: User Acceptance, and Criterion 4: Ethical Considerations and Data Security), as well as three alternatives (Alternative 1: Artificial Intelligence Usage, Alternative 2: Human, Alternative 3: Human + AI Usage)((Gruetzemacher et al, 2020; Makridakis, 2017, Tao et al, 2019; Piotrowski, 2023; Stahl and Wright, 2018; Norori et al., 2021; Wach et al).

The authors determined each criterion and alternative through a comprehensive literature review and the authors have provided definitions for each criterion and alternative, which are outlined below.

Criteria

Cost: This criterion refers to the financial expenses associated with each alternative. It assesses the monetary implications of employing artificial intelligence (AI), relying solely on human labor, or adopting a combination of human and AI resources. Cost considerations may include initial investment, maintenance expenses, and potential cost savings or revenue generation over time.

Technological Competence: This criterion evaluates the level of technological proficiency required for each alternative. It assesses the capability of AI systems, human workers, or a combination of both to effectively perform tasks within the given context. Factors such as accuracy, reliability, adaptability, and scalability of technology are considered under this criterion.

User Acceptance: User acceptance refers to the willingness and satisfaction of stakeholders, including employees, customers, or end-users, with the chosen approach. It assesses how well AI systems, human workers, or a combination of both meet the expectations, needs, and preferences of the individuals involved. Factors such as usability, trust, ease of interaction, and user experience contribute to user acceptance.

Ethical Considerations and Data Security: This criterion focuses on ethical implications and data protection measures associated with each alternative. It examines the ethical principles, privacy concerns, and security protocols relevant to AI usage, human involvement, or a hybrid approach. Factors such as transparency, fairness, accountability, confidentiality, and compliance with regulations are considered under this criterion.

Alternatives

Artificial Intelligence (AI) Usage: This alternative involves the utilization of AI technologies to perform tasks autonomously or semi-autonomously without significant human intervention. AI systems leverage algorithms, machine learning, and other computational techniques to analyze data, make decisions, and execute actions based on predefined objectives or learning patterns.

Human: This alternative relies solely on human labor to accomplish tasks without the involvement of AI technologies. Human workers apply their knowledge, skills, experience, and cognitive abilities to perform various activities, tasks, or roles within the given context.

Human + AI Usage: This alternative combines human intelligence with AI technologies to achieve optimal outcomes. It involves collaborative efforts between human workers and AI systems, where each contributes its strengths to enhance performance, productivity, and decision-making processes. This approach leverages the complementary capabilities of humans and machines to achieve synergistic effects and overcome individual limitations.

With the determination of each criterion and alternative, the Analytic Hierarchy Process (AHP)-based Technique for Order of Preference by Similarity to the Ideal Solution (TOPSIS) approach has been selected. This method, recognized as one of the most widely used multi-criteria decision analysis techniques (de Farias Aires, and Ferreira, 2019), was initially introduced by Hwang and Yoon in 1981 and further refined by Zeleny in 1982. Subsequent developments by Lai and Liu in 1993 have enhanced its applicability (Özgüner and Özgüner, 2020). Given its suitability for the scope of this chapter, the AHP-based TOPSIS approach has been utilized.

This method is based on the idea that the selected best alternative should be the one closest to the positive ideal solution while being farthest from the negative ideal solution (Derse and Yontar, 2020). The best alternative is the one that is closest to the positive ideal solution (PIS) and farthest from the negative ideal solution (NIS). The PIS is a theoretical alternative that maximizes the benefit criteria (B) while minimizing the cost criteria (C) simultaneously. In contrast, the NIS maximizes the cost criteria and minimizes the benefit criteria. The ideal choice is the alternative with the smallest Euclidean distance from the PIS while being the farthest from the NIS, making it the most favorable option among all (de Farias Aires, and Ferreira, 2019; Chen and Tsao; 2008; Dymova et al, 2013). To achieve this objective, each step of the TOPSIS method has been applied sequentially (de FSM Russo and Camanho,2015; Ren et al., 2007; Pavić and Novoselac, 2013; Çelikbilek and Tüysüz, 2020; Chu and Lin, 2003; García-Cascales and Lamata, 2012)

Step One: Creating Matrix

As a result of the literature review and interview with the experts who work for airlines and passengers, a decision matrix has been created

To calculate the weight, the Analytical Hierciarcial Process (AHP) has been used. It is one of the multi-criteria decision analysis methods which was created by Saaty. In this chapter, it has been used to calculate Criterion Weight. Amon the criteria C1, C2, C4 benefit, and C3 is non-benefit.

Step Two: Normalizing the Decision Matrix

In this step, the normalized performance matrix can be obtained using the following transformation formula:

$$n_{ij} = z_{ij} / \sqrt{\sum\nolimits_{j=1}^{m} \left(z_{ij} \right)^2}, j = 1, \ldots \ldots, n, i = 1, \ldots \ldots \ldots, m.$$

The zij represents the performance values of "the alternatives" concerning some attribute/criterion. In this case, the result has been given in Table 2.

Step Three: Calculating the Weighted Normalized Decision Matrix

The calculation of the weighted normalized value proceeds as follows:

$$v_{ij=} w_{ij}.n_{ij}, j = 1, \ldots \ldots, n, i = 1, \ldots \ldots, m.$$

Table 1. Decision matrix

	User Acceptance	**Cost**	**Technological Competence**	**Ethical Considerations and Data Security**
Criterion Weight	0,31	0,19	0,15	0,35
AI	7,00	8,00	7,00	7,00
Human	9,00	7,00	5,00	8,00
AI+Human	10,00	9,00	6,00	9,00

Table 2. Normalized matrix

	C1	**C2**	**C3**	**C4**
Criterion Weight	0,31	0,19	0,15	0,35
A1	0,462	0,574	0,667	0,503
A2	0,593	0,503	0,477	0,574
A3	0,659	0,646	0,572	0,646

These weights can be derived through various methods, such as direct assignment or the Analytic Hierarchy Process (AHP), among others. In this chapter, it has been obtained by the AHP method.

In this chapter results of weighted normalized have been given in Table 3

Step Four: Determining the Positive Ideal and Negative Ideal Solutions

It is been calculated as:

$$A^+ = \left(a_{i1}^+, a_{i2}^+, \ldots, a_{im}^+\right), a_{ij}^+ = \max\left(a_{ij}\right), j = 1, 2, \ldots, m$$

$$A^- = \left(a_{i1}^-, a_{i2}^-, \ldots, a_{im}^-\right), a_{ij}^- = \max\left(a_{ij}\right), j = 1, 2, \ldots, m$$

A+ refers to ideal solution value while A- refers to negative ideal solution value

Step Five: Calculating the Separation Measures

Compute the separation measures using the n-dimensional Euclidean distance. The separation of each alternative from the positive ideal solution and negative ideal solution can be expressed as follows:

$$D_i^+ = \sqrt{\sum_{j=1}^{m} W_{j\left(a_{ij}^+ - a_{ij}\right)}2}$$

$$D_i^- = \sqrt{\sum_{j=1}^{m} W_{j\left(a_{ij}^- - a_{ij}\right)}2}$$

Table 3. Weigtened normalized matrix

	C1	C2	C3	C4
A1	0,14	0,11	0,10	0,18
A2	0,18	0,09	0,07	0,20
A3	0,21	0,12	0,09	0,23

Table 4. Positive ideal and negative ideal solutions

	C1	C2	C3	C4
A1	0,14	0,11	0,10	0,18
A2	0,18	0,09	0,07	0,20
A3	0,21	0,12	0,09	0,23
A+	0,18	0,12	0,07	0,23
A-	0,14	0,09	0,10	0,18

Table 5. Positive Ideal Solution and Negative Ideal Solution

	D_i+	D_i-
A1	0,07	0,01
A2	0,04	0,06
A3	0,03	0,09

In this case, it has been given in Table 5.

Step Six: Calculating the Relative Closeness or Ratio to the Ideal Solution

The relative closeness Ri to the ideal solution or ratio can be represented as follows:

$$R_i = \frac{D_i^-}{D_i^- + D_i^+} \quad i = 1, 2, \ldots, n$$

Step Seven: Ranking the Preference Order

In this step, the best alternatives have been ranked in descending order based on their Ri values, with the highest Ri in Table 6.

Data Analysis and Tools

After conducting a comprehensive literature review, we conducted it with 10 experts employed within the airline industry and 10 passengers via Zoom or Skype. During these interviews, participants were requested to rate the importance of each criterion on a scale from 1 to 9, which was developmental (Ji and Jiang, 2003), considering their relevance to the decision-making process. Following the interviews, the decision matrix has been created based on the insights gathered and given in Table 1. This matrix allowed for a more nuanced understanding of the significance of each criterion as perceived by both industry professionals and passengers.

Table 6. Ideal Solution or Ratio

	Ri
A1	0,155
A2	0,607
A3	0,771

SOLUTION AND RECOMMENDATION

In this chapter, our primary aim was to analyze the pros and cons related to the utilization of Artificial Intelligence (AI) in the airline industry. We have meticulously evaluated the impact of AI on various aspects of this dynamic sector, including safety, efficiency, customer service, and cost-effectiveness. Our systematic examination has offered valuable insights into the pivotal question of whether the preference should lean towards a fully automated AI-driven system, human operation, or a harmonious AI-human partnership within the airline industry.

Through our comprehensive analysis, we have found that there are pros and cons to each approach. A fully automated AI-driven system can excel in safety and efficiency but may lack the human touch necessary for superior customer service. Human operation offers a personal touch but may not be as efficient in certain aspects. A harmonious AI-human partnership appears to be the most promising path, combining the strengths of both AI and human operators. Table 8 illustrates that the most favored option is the AI-human partnership, with a value of 0.771, followed by the human-only approach (Alternative 2) with a value of 0.607. In contrast, Alternative 1 is the least preferred, with a value of 0.155.

Stuff who work for airlines and passengers choose the AI-human combination usage (AI-human partnership) over solely relying on humans or AI alone because the data from Table 8 indicates that the AI-human partnership provides the highest overall value (0.771). This suggests that it offers a well-balanced solution that leverages the strengths of both AI and human operators. The combination of AI's efficiency and data processing capabilities with human expertise and judgment likely results in a more effective and versatile approach. This preference is driven by the desire to optimize safety, efficiency, customer service, and cost-effectiveness, as highlighted in the comprehensive analysis.

In the realm of strategic management, the preference for the AI-human partnership in the airline industry aligns with the core principles of crafting a competitive advantage and achieving organizational goals. By selecting this approach, airline industry professionals are strategically leveraging their resources to optimize various critical factors, such as safety, efficiency, customer service, and cost-effectiveness. This strategic decision acknowledges the complementary strengths of AI and human operators, fostering an approach that not only enhances performance but also ensures adaptability in a rapidly evolving industry. Ultimately, it demonstrates a forward-thinking and strategic orientation that positions airlines for long-term success in a highly competitive and dynamic market.

FUTURE RESEARCH DIRECTIONS

While our analysis has shed light on the complexities and implications of implementing Artificial Intelligence (AI) in the aviation sector, several avenues for future research remain to be explored. These directions aim to further deepen our understanding and address emerging challenges in this rapidly evolving field:

Optimal Integration Strategies: Investigating optimal strategies for integrating AI technologies into existing aviation systems will be crucial. Future research could explore the most effective ways to transition from traditional methods to AI-driven systems while minimizing disruptions and maximizing benefits.

Human-AI Interaction Studies: Delving deeper into the dynamics of human-AI interaction within aviation operations is essential. Research focusing on human factors, cognitive workload, and decision-making processes in AI-enhanced environments can provide valuable insights into how to design interfaces and workflows for optimal performance and safety.

Ethical and Regulatory Considerations: As AI adoption in aviation raises ethical and regulatory concerns, future research should explore frameworks for ethical AI development and deployment. Addressing issues such as accountability, transparency, and bias mitigation will be crucial for fostering trust and ensuring responsible AI implementation.

Impact on Workforce and Training: Examining the impact of AI on the aviation workforce and training programs is imperative. Research could assess the skills and competencies needed for individuals working in AI-enabled environments and develop training curricula to prepare aviation professionals for the evolving landscape.

Long-Term Safety and Reliability: Assessing the long-term safety and reliability implications of AI adoption is vital. Future studies could employ predictive analytics and simulation models to anticipate potential risks and develop proactive strategies for maintaining safety standards in AI-driven aviation systems.

Socio-Economic Effects: Investigating the socio-economic effects of AI implementation on various stakeholders, including passengers, airlines, and regulators, is essential. Research could analyze factors such as accessibility, affordability, and job displacement to ensure that AI advancements benefit society as a whole.

By addressing these future research directions, understanding the implications of AI in the aviation sector, and paving the way for a future that harnesses the full potential of AI while ensuring the industry's continued excellence and sustainability can be furthered.

CONCLUSION

As the aviation industry embraces AI and emerging technologies, a new era of enhanced safety and operational efficiency dawns. The transformative potential of predictive maintenance, flight planning optimization, and AI-powered air traffic management holds great promise for airlines worldwide. However, to fully harness the benefits while mitigating potential risks, comprehensive regulatory frameworks and the integration of human expertise alongside intelligent machines will be instrumental in ensuring the safe and efficient functioning of the aviation industry. This book chapter aims to provide valuable insights to airlines, industry stakeholders, and policymakers, paving the way for a future where AI-driven advancements elevate the aviation industry to new heights. Our extensive analysis of the utilization of Artificial Intelligence (AI) in the airline industry has provided a nuanced understanding of the complex trade-offs involved in choosing between fully automated AI-driven systems, human operation, and a harmonious AI-human partnership. Through a meticulous examination, we have delineated the advantages and disadvantages across critical dimensions such as safety, efficiency, customer service, and cost-effectiveness. Our findings, as demonstrated in Table 8, have highlighted the AI-human partnership as the preferred alternative. This choice underscores the industry's recognition of the need for a well-balanced, strategic solution that effectively capitalizes on the strengths of both AI and human operators. The harmonious combination of AI's efficiency and data processing capabilities with human expertise and judgment offers a more versatile and resilient approach, aligning with the strategic principles of competitive advantage and goal attainment. Importantly, the strategic significance of the AI-human partnership extends beyond operational considerations. It is emblematic of a forward-thinking approach by industry professionals who are keen on navigating the complex and rapidly evolving aviation landscape. By selecting this approach, they position airlines to thrive in an intensely competitive and dynamic environment, ensuring sustained excellence and long-term success.

In this age of industry transformation, the airline sector's embrace of the AI-human partnership serves as a paradigm of strategic adaptability, signifying its commitment to not only meeting current demands but also thriving in an uncertain future. This chapter's analysis is based on the discovery that aligning technological combinations with strategic objectives and readiness for innovative adoption serves as a safeguard for industries aspiring to maintain a leading edge in terms of innovation and competitiveness.

REFERENCES

Alharbi, B., & Prince, M. (2020). A Hybrid Artificial Intelligence Approach to Predict Flight Delay. *International Journal of Engineering Research & Technology (Ahmedabad)*, *13*(4), 814–822. doi:10.37624/IJERT/13.4.2020.814-822

Alsheibani, S. A., Messom, D. C., Cheung, Y., & Alhosni, M. (2020). *Reimagining the Strategic Management of Artificial Intelligence: Five Recommendations for Business Leaders*. Research Gate.

Amariles, D. R., & Baquero, P. M. (2023). Promises and Limits of Law for a Human-centric Artificial Intelligence. *Computer Law & Security Report*, *48*, 105795. doi:10.1016/j.clsr.2023.105795

Andrei, A. G., Balasa, R., & Semenescu, A. (2022, February). Setting up New Standards in the Aviation Industry with the Help of Artificial Intelligence–Machine Learning Application. []. IOP Publishing.]. *Journal of Physics: Conference Series*, *2212*(1), 012014. doi:10.1088/1742-6596/2212/1/012014

Baumann, S., & Klingauf, U. (2020). Modeling of Aircraft Fuel Consumption Using Machine Learning Algorithms. *CEAS Aeronautical Journal*, *11*(1), 277–287. doi:10.1007/s13272-019-00422-0

Büyüközkan, G., Havle, C. A., & Feyzioğlu, O. (2020). A New Digital Service Quality Model and Its Strategic Analysis in the Aviation Industry Using Interval-Valued Intuitionistic Fuzzy AHP. *Journal of Air Transport Management*, *86*, 101817. doi:10.1016/j.jairtraman.2020.101817

Çelikbilek, Y., & Tüysüz, F. (2020). An In-depth Review of Theory of the TOPSIS Method: An Experimental Analysis. *Journal of Management Analytics*, *7*(2), 281–300. doi:10.1080/23270012.2020.1748528

Chang, S., Wang, Z., Wang, Y., Tang, J., & Jiang, X. (2019, August). Enabling Technologies And Platforms to Aid the Digitalization of Commercial Aviation Support, Maintenance, and Health Management. In *2019 International Conference on Quality, Reliability, Risk, Maintenance, and Safety Engineering (QR2MSE)* (pp. 926-932).IEEE 10.1109/QR2MSE46217.2019.9021222

Chen, T. Y., & Tsao, C. Y. (2008). The Interval-valued Fuzzy TOPSIS Method and Experimental Analysis. *Fuzzy Sets and Systems*, *159*(11), 1410–1428. doi:10.1016/j.fss.2007.11.004

Chu, T. C., & Lin, Y. C. (2003). A Fuzzy TOPSIS Method for Robot Selection. *International Journal of Advanced Manufacturing Technology*, *21*(4), 284–290. doi:10.1007/s001700300033

De, F. S. M., Russo, R., & Camanho, R. (2015). Criteria in AHP: A Systematic Review of Literature. *Procedia Computer Science*, *55*, 1123–1132. doi:10.1016/j.procs.2015.07.081

De Farias Aires, R. F., & Ferreira, L. (2019). A New Approach to Avoid Rank Reversal Cases in The TOPSIS Method. *Computers & Industrial Engineering*, *132*, 84–97. doi:10.1016/j.cie.2019.04.023

Degas, A., Islam, M. R., Hurter, C., Barua, S., Rahman, H., Poudel, M., Ruscio, D., Ahmed, M. U., Begum, S., Rahman, M. A., Bonelli, S., Cartocci, G., Di Flumeri, G., Borghini, G., Babiloni, F., & Arico, P. (2022). A Survey on Artificial Intelligence (AI) and Explainable AI in Air Traffic Management: Current Trends and Development with Future Research Trajectory. *Applied Sciences (Basel, Switzerland)*, *12*(3), 1295. doi:10.3390/app12031295

Derse, O., & Yontar, E. (2020). SWARA-TOPSIS Yöntemi ile En Uygun Yenilenebilir Enerji Kaynağının Belirlenmesi. *Endüstri Mühendisliği*, *31*(3), 389–419. doi:10.46465/endustrimuhendisligi.798063

Dymova, L., Sevastjanov, P., & Tikhonenko, A. (2013). A Direct Interval Extension of TOPSIS Method. *Expert Systems with Applications*, *40*(12), 4841–4847. doi:10.1016/j.eswa.2013.02.022

Ertel, W. (2009). *Introduction to Artificial Intelligence*. Springer.

Faiza, Khalil, K. (2023). Airline Flight Delays Using Artificial Intelligence in COVID-19 with Perspective Analytics. *Journal of Intelligent & Fuzzy Systems*, 1-23.

García-cascales, M. S., & Lamata, M. T. (2012). On Rank Reversal and TOPSIS Method. *Mathematical and Computer Modelling*, *56*(5-6), 123–132. doi:10.1016/j.mcm.2011.12.022

Gruetzemacher, R., Paradice, D., & Lee, K. B. (2020). Forecasting Extreme Labor Displacement: A Survey of AI Practitioners. *Technological Forecasting and Social Change*, *161*, 120323. doi:10.1016/j.techfore.2020.120323

Hallows, R., Glazier, L., Katz, M. S., Aznar, M., & Williams, M. (2022). Safe and Ethical Artificial Intelligence in Radiotherapy–Lessons Learned from the Aviation Industry. *Clinical Oncology*, *34*(2), 99–101. doi:10.1016/j.clon.2021.11.019 PMID:34922798

Hamet, P., & Tremblay, J. (2017). Artificial Intelligence in Medicine. *Metabolism: Clinical and Experimental*, *69*, S36–S40. doi:10.1016/j.metabol.2017.01.011 PMID:28126242

Horiguchi, Y., Baba, Y., Kashima, H., Suzuki, M., Kayahara, H., & Maeno, J. (2017, February). Predicting Fuel Consumption and Flight Delays for Low-cost Airlines. *Proceedings of the AAAI Conference on Artificial Intelligence*, *31*(2), 4686–4693. doi:10.1609/aaai.v31i2.19095

Hosny, A., Parmar, C., Quackenbush, J., Schwartz, L. H., & Aerts, H. J. (2018). Artificial Intelligence in Radiology. *Nature Reviews. Cancer*, *18*(8), 500–510. doi:10.1038/s41568-018-0016-5 PMID:29777175

Huang, M. H., & Rust, R. T. (2018). Artificial Intelligence In Service. *Journal of Service Research*, *21*(2), 155–172. doi:10.1177/1094670517752459

İpek, S. (2019). Yapay Zekanın Toplum Üzerindeki Etkisi ve Yapay Zekâ (AI) Filmi Bağlamında Yapay Zekaya Bakış. *Uluslararası Ders Kitapları ve Eğitim Materyalleri Dergisi*, *2*(2), 203–215.

İşler, B., & Kılıç, M. (2021). Eğitimde Yapay Zekâ Kullanımı ve Gelişimi. *Yeni Medya Elektronik Dergisi*, *5*(1), Ji, P., & Jiang, R. (2003). Scale transitivity in the AHP. *The Journal of the Operational Research Society*, *54*(8), 896–905.

Keding, C. (2021). Understanding The Interplay Of Artificial Intelligence And Strategic Management: Four Decades Of Research In Review. *Management Review Quarterly*, *71*(1), 91–134. doi:10.1007/s11301-020-00181-x

Konert, F. A. A., & Balcerzak, B. T. (2021, June). Legal And Ethical Aspects Of Rules For The Operation Of Autonomous Unmanned Aircraft With Artificial Intelligence. In *2021 International Conference On Unmanned Aircraft Systems (ICUAS)* (Pp. 602-609). IEEE. 10.1109/ICUAS51884.2021.9476822

Makridakis, S. (2017). The Forthcoming Artificial Intelligence (AI) Revolution: Its Impact on Society and Firms. *Futures*, *90*, 46–60. doi:10.1016/j.futures.2017.03.006

Manjunatha Kumar, B. H., Achyutha, P. N., Kalashetty, J. N., Rekha, V. S., & Nirmala, G. (2022). Business Analysis and Modelling of Flight Delays Using Artificial Intelligence. *International Journal of Health Sciences*, (I), 7897–7908. doi:10.53730/ijhs.v6nS1.6735

Martilla, J. A., & James, J. C. (1977). Importance-performance Analysis. *Journal of Marketing*, *41*(1), 77–79. doi:10.1177/002224297704100112

Mccarthy, N., Karzand, M., & Lecue, F. (2019, July). Amsterdam to Dublin Eventually Delayed? Lstm and Transfer Learning for Predicting Delays of Low-Cost Airlines. *Proceedings of the AAAI Conference on Artificial Intelligence*, *33*(01), 9541–9546. doi:10.1609/aaai.v33i01.33019541

Mcmullen, M. (1987). Artificial Intelligence in the Airline Industry. *IATA Review. International Air Transport Association*, (2), 16–18.

Molchanova, K. M., Trushkina, N. V., & Katerna, O. K. (2020). Digital Platforms and Their Application in the Aviation Industry. *Intellectualization of Logistics and Supply Chain Management*, *1*(3), 83–98. doi:10.46783/smart-scm/2020-3-8

Norori, N., Hu, Q., Aellen, F. M., Faraci, F. D., & Tzovara, A. (2021). Addressing Bias in Big Data and AI for Health Care: A Call for Open Science. *Patterns (New York, N.Y.)*, *2*(10), 100347. doi:10.1016/j.patter.2021.100347 PMID:34693373

Ogunsina, K., & Delaurentis, D. (2022). Enabling Integration And Interaction For Decentralized Artificial Intelligence In Airline Disruption Management. *Engineering Applications of Artificial Intelligence*, *109*, 104600. doi:10.1016/j.engappai.2021.104600

Özgüner, Z., & Özgüner, M. (2020). Entegre Entropi-TOPSIS Yöntemleri ile Tedarikçi Değerlendirme ve Seçme Probleminin Çözümlenmesi. *İstanbul Ticaret Üniversitesi Sosyal Bilimler Dergisi, 19*(37), 551-568.

Öztürk, L. S. (2019). *Tekstil Sektöründe Önem Performans Analizi Uygulaması ile Üretime Dayalı Stratejik Öncelik Alanlarının Belirlenmesi*. Yüksek Lisans Tezi, Pamukkale Üniversitesi Sosyal Bilimler Enstitüsü.

Pavić, Z., & Novoselac, V. (2013). Notes on TOPSIS Method. *International Journal of Research in Engineering and Science*, *1*(2), 5–12.

Pérez-campuzano, D., Ortega, P. M., Andrada, L. R., & López-lázaro, A. (2021). Artificial Intelligence Potential within Airlines: A Review on How AI Can Enhance Strategic Decision-making in Times of COVID-19. *Journal of Airline and Airport Management*, *11*(2), 53–72. doi:10.3926/jairm.189

Petrović, D., Puharić, M., & Kastratović, E. (2018). Defining of Necessary Number of Employees in Airline by Using Artificial Intelligence Tools. *International Review (Steubenville, Ohio)*, (3-4), 77–89. doi:10.5937/IntRev1804077P

Pilon, R. V. (2023). *Artificial Intelligence in Commercial Aviation: Use Cases and Emerging Strategies.* Taylor & Francis. doi:10.4324/9781003018810

Piotrowski, D. (2023). Privacy Frontiers in Customers' Relations with Banks. *Economics and Business Review EBR, 23*(1), 119-141. https://Doi.Org/10.18559/Ebr.2023.1.5

Rana, N. P., Chatterjee, S., Dwivedi, Y. K., & Akter, S. (2022). Understanding Dark Side of Artificial Intelligence (AI) Integrated Business Analytics: Assessing Firm's Operational Inefficiency and Competitiveness. *European Journal of Information Systems*, *31*(3), 364–387. doi:10.1080/0960085X.2021.1955628

Ren, L., Zhang, Y., Wang, Y., & Sun, Z. (2007). Comparative Analysis of a Novel M-TOPSIS Method and TOPSIS. *Applied Mathematics Research Express, 2007*, abm005.

Roadmap, A. I. (2020). A Human-centric Approach to AI in Aviation. European Aviation Safety Agency, 1.

Schulze-horn, I., Hueren, S., Scheffler, P., & Schiele, H. (2020). Artificial Intelligence in Purchasing: Facilitating Mechanism Design-Based Negotiations. *Applied Artificial Intelligence*, *34*(8), 618–642. doi:10.1080/08839514.2020.1749337

Shmelova, T., Sterenharz, A., & Dolgikh, S. (2020). Artificial Intelligence in Aviation Industries: Methodologies, Education, Applications, and Opportunities. In Handbook of Research on Artificial Intelligence Applications in the Aviation and Aerospace Industries (pp. 1-35). IGI Global.

Silling, U. (2019). Aviation of the Future: What Needs to Change to Get Aviation Fit for the Twenty-first Century. In *Aviation and Its Management-Global Challenges and Opportunities*. Intechopen. doi:10.5772/intechopen.81660

Sims, N. (2019). *Transforming The Future of Airports with Artificial Intelligence*. Machine Learning and Generative Design.

Sircar, A., Yadav, K., Rayavarapu, K., Bist, N., & Oza, H. (2021). Application Of Machine Learning and Artificial Intelligence in Oil and Gas Industry. *Petroleum Research*, *6*(4), 379–391. doi:10.1016/j.ptlrs.2021.05.009

Soori, M., Arezoo, B., & Dastres, R. (2023). Artificial Intelligence, Machine Learning and Deep Learning in Advanced Robotics, A Review. *Cognitive Robotics*.

Stahl, B. C., & Wright, D. (2018). Ethics And Privacy in AI and Big Data: Implementing Responsible Research and Innovation. *IEEE Security and Privacy*, *16*(3), 26–33. doi:10.1109/MSP.2018.2701164

Takeichi, N., Kaida, R., Shimomura, A., & Yamauchi, T. (2017). Prediction of Delay Due to Air Traffic Control by Machine Learning. In a *Modeling and Simulation Technologies Conference* (p. 1323). ARC. 10.2514/6.2017-1323

Tamer, H. Y., & Övgün, B. (2020). Yapay Zekâ Bağlamında Dijital Dönüşüm Ofisi. *Ankara Üniversitesi SBF Dergisi*, *75*(2), 775–803. doi:10.33630/ausbf.691119

Tao, B., Díaz, V., & Guerra, Y. (2019). Artificial Intelligence And Education, Challenges and Disadvantages for the Teacher. *Art Journal*, *72*(12), 30–50.

Vincent, N. C., Bhakar, R. R., Nadarajan, S. R., Syamala, A., & Varghese, J. (2021). Impact of Artificial Intelligence in the Aviation and Space Sector. In *Artificial Intelligence* (pp. 209–229). CRC Press. doi:10.1201/9781003095910-15

Wach, K., Duong, C. D., Ejdys, J., Kazlauskaitė, R., Korzynski, P., Mazurek, G., Paliszkiewicz, J., & Ziemba, E. (2023). The Dark Side Of Generative Artificial Intelligence: A Critical Analysis of Controversies and Risks of Chatgpt. *Entrepreneurial Business and Economics Review*, *11*(2), 7–24. doi:10.15678/EBER.2023.110201

Yu, K. H., Beam, A. L., & Kohane, I. S. (2018). Artificial Intelligence in Healthcare. *Nature Biomedical Engineering*, *2*(10), 719–731. doi:10.1038/s41551-018-0305-z PMID:31015651

Zupan, J. (1994). Introduction To Artificial Neural Network (ANN) Methods: What They Are and How to Use Them. *Acta Chimica Slovenica*, *41*, 327–327.

ADDITIONAL READING

Ivanov, D., Pelipenko, E., Ershova, A., & Tick, A. (2021, November). Artificial Intelligence in Aviation Industry. In *International Scientific Conference Digital Technologies in Logistics and Infrastructure* (pp. 233-245). Cham: Springer International Publishing.

Kabashkin, I., Misnevs, B., & Zervina, O. (2023). Artificial Intelligence in Aviation: New Professionals for New Technologies. *Applied Sciences (Basel, Switzerland)*, *13*(21), 11660. doi:10.3390/app132111660

Saraf, A. P., Chan, K., Popish, M., Browder, J., & Schade, J. (2020). Explainable artificial intelligence for aviation safety applications. In AIAA Aviation 2020 Forum (p. 2881). ARC. doi:10.2514/6.2020-2881

Shmelova, T., Sterenharz, A., & Dolgikh, S. (2020). Artificial intelligence in aviation industries: methodologies, education, applications, and opportunities. In *Handbook of research on artificial intelligence applications in the aviation and aerospace industries* (pp. 1–35). IGI Global. doi:10.4018/978-1-7998-1415-3.ch001

Shmelova, T., Yatsko, M., Sierostanov, I., & Kolotusha, V. (2023). Artificial Intelligence Methods and Applications in Aviation. In *Handbook of Research on AI Methods and Applications in Computer Engineering* (pp. 108–140). IGI Global. doi:10.4018/978-1-6684-6937-8.ch006

Ziakkas, D., & Pechlivanis, K. (2023). Artificial intelligence applications in aviation accident classification: A preliminary exploratory study. *Decision Analytics Journal*, *9*, 100358. doi:10.1016/j.dajour.2023.100358

Chapter 12
Artificial Intelligence:
Its Use for Creation of Value in Airports

Diogo Andrade Belejo
https://orcid.org/0009-0009-9500-4066
Universidade Lusófona, Portugal

José Carlos Rouco
https://orcid.org/0000-0002-8710-0367
Universidade Lusófona, Portugal

Lúcia Silva Piedade
https://orcid.org/0000-0003-1258-2530
Universidade Lusófona, Portugal

ABSTRACT

Nowadays, when it's a priority to support the recovery of the civil aviation industry, it is essential to consider the role played by technology, specifically artificial intelligence. The goal of this study is to dissect how this powerful tool can contribute to the growth of the airport sector, starting by raising the research question, "How can artificial intelligence add value to an airport?". It is within the scope of its application that the concept of performance is highlighted, based on measuring the efficiency level of operational activities, through principles such as consumer trust, service quality and opportunity for organizational cost reduction, driving the investment to critical value-creating elements for airport management. By exposing the presently known cases of AI application, it becomes necessary to address their level of expansion across the world, outlining their relationship with the responsible factors for value growth, and enabling the development of forecasts, regarding the investment in airport security, which is currently limited to only certain segments.

INTRODUCTION

It is in the aeronautics sector, technological development is a topic that is constantly on the agenda, and which undeniably contributes to the prominence, and consequent value creation, of various airports

DOI: 10.4018/979-8-3693-0908-7.ch012

around the world. Innovation does not rest and technology does not cease its evolution; one of the most highlighted topics in the area today is related to the concept of artificial intelligence (AI), broadly understood as the ability of a system to perform and learn from the executed tasks, similar to that performed by human beings. In this context, we intend to study the applicability of this remarkable innovation, describing its contact with passengers and its integration into the activities carried out by airport staff.

Since AI is a concept that has been around for relatively few years, the literature on its incorporation into organizations tends to be limited in volume, and the respective publications are more recent and mostly conceptual; nevertheless, there are already some perspectives and definitions inherent to the subject that contribute to the enrichment of studies already/ to be carried out and the technology in question is already heavily debated and has captured the attention of several researchers. It should also be noted that there are already several areas of application of AI in airports, such as baggage dispatch and handling, subtitling of systems used by passengers, air quality control, etc., to enhance the consumer experience and add value to the airport space, making it stand out from the rest.

The dimensions of AI, which are directly related to this study, are divided into two parts - the application in the various areas of an airport and the contact with passengers, working together to improve the efficiency and value of the area. It has therefore become crucial to explore the integration of technological innovation in order to understand in which areas its application is most relevant to the management of airport spaces.

Considering the factors mentioned above, this research project took the following into account:

- It aims to contribute to the literary approaches inherent to the presence of AI in airports.
- It aims to promote technological innovation and the use of AI in airports.
- It aims to disseminate the means of applying artificial intelligence.
- It aims to gain an in-depth understanding of how AI can enhance airport space.

Considering this context and based on the main idea that technological development contributes to the growth of the aviation industry, the starting question that will guide the study is: How can artificial intelligence add value to an airport?

As far as the research methodology is concerned, we opted for the qualitative approach advocated by Creswell (2014), which refers to understanding a phenomenon in its natural context; since, as described, the main object of the work is based on the incorporation of AI in airport spaces, its method encompasses a pure (theoretical) research, in terms of nature, exploratory, in terms of data collection, and documentary, in terms of procedures.

As there is no statistical data to analyze/corroborate and as this is a mostly conceptual investigation, this study aims, through the aforementioned methodology, to answer the starting question and the associated derived questions, a research design mechanism that is defended as the most appropriate, also according to Creswell.

This research aims to assess the presence, and consequent impact, of AI in airport spaces; it is in that context that the choice of theme to be developed is based on strengthening the literary approaches carried out, contributing to future studies on the subject, not only from a technological development perspective but also regarding a more efficient airport spaces management, two areas of great market value and with a very strong impact on the world economy.

The following figure illustrates the basic structure of the the project to better present and clarify the subject.

Figure 1. General structure of the research work

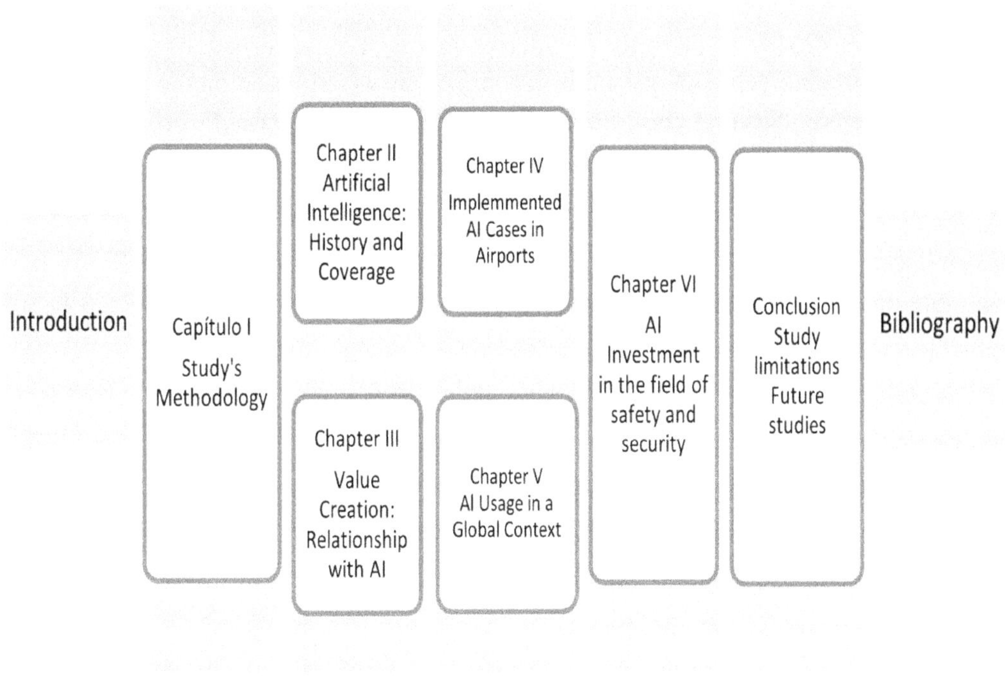

STUDY METHODOLOGY

Research Study Methodology

The research is divided into three parts: literary analysis, where the concepts of artificial intelligence are developed, including their historical context and the fields of knowledge covered, value creation, enabling a link between the advantages associated with technological innovation and the prominence of an organization concerning market competitors, and technological incorporation in airports, describing current cases of AI integration in the operational activity of the airport sector.

The main purpose of the methodology is essentially to highlight the data collection processes and the used instruments, and in the case of this study, according to the PRISMA Method, highlighted through the qualitative approach and the systematic literature review inherent to the subject. Through the method described below, the goal is to answer the study questions initially highlighted, thus fulfilling the objectives also emphasized, through the results obtained and their subsequent discussion, while also opening up the possibility of including themes to be developed in the future, directly related to what has been discussed (Urrútia & Bonfill, 2010).

According to Urrútia and Bonfill (2010), the PRISMA method is the most suitable for the development of systematized literature reviews, since it stands out for its justification of the covered topics, through data collection data from other researchers; it respects a series of aspects to be characterized and described, generally highlighted in the shape of a checklist which aims to substantiate the structure applied to the dissertation, while also allowing the creation of a complete process on the judgments and decisions made by the authors, based on the bibliographic survey used.

Drawing Up the Research Questions

According to Creswell (2014), as far as the qualitative approach is concerned, it is the responsibility of the researchers to formulate research questions that can be answered based on the bibliographic survey analyzed and the starting question emphasized. Therefore, the enumeration of the research questions considers three factors: (1) the possibility of being answered; (2) being related to existing knowledge and the addressed topic; and (3) fostering the saturation of each field of data collected. In this way, four derived research questions were identified:

Derived Question No. 1: What does artificial intelligence consist of?

Derived Question No. 2: What are the current known cases of artificial intelligence being used in airports?

Derived Question No. 3: What are the benefits of such integration?

Derived Question No. 4: Are there any other sectors where AI could be incorporated?

Flowchart According to the PRISMA Method

The following flowchart illustrates the stages of the scientific procedure according to which the research model used in this dissertation was defined, and which was structured according to the methodology of the authors cited. Its stages consist of an in-depth analysis of how to screen and select the data collected, after initial filtering, to systematize the content; it also includes a comprehensive analysis of published articles and the type of source used to gather the information.

ARTIFICIAL INTELLIGENCE

Introduction to the Concept of AI

In a world where technology is one of the most important tools for organizations, the emergence of artificial intelligence has an astronomical value and is already widely integrated into market sectors. To understand the influence of this technology on organizations, particularly in the aeronautics sector, we must first put its historical development into context and dissect its descriptive aspects. Briefly, some researchers describe AI as follows:

* Systems that behave like human beings.
* Rational thinking systems.
* Systems that operate rationally.

As a result, the approaches inherent in artificial intelligence tend to encompass the processes of reasoning and behavior and the success associated with the similarity between technological and human performance (Gomes, 2010). It remains to be seen, then, in what context AI arises.

Figure 2. Flowchart of the systematic review

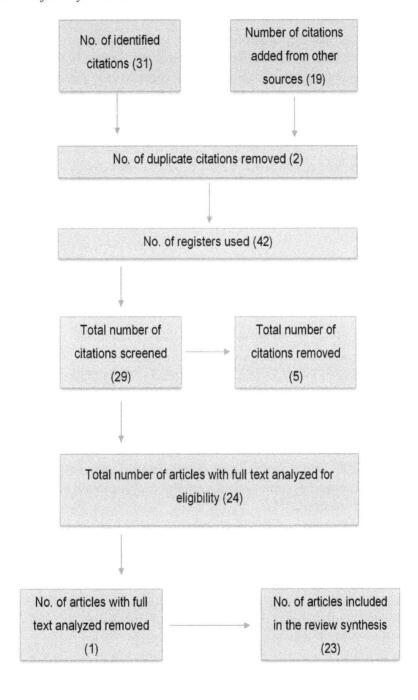

History of Artificial Intelligence

According to the mentioned author, the historical framework of artificial intelligence can be traced back to four phases of expansion: the creation of AI, enthusiasm and expectations, the knowledge-based system, and the transformation of the technology into an industry.

The first official approach to this technological innovation is based on the article Computing Machinery and Intelligence by Alan Turing in 1950; the researcher presented his test, known worldwide as the Turing Test, based on the inability to distinguish between a reasoning process and an answer given by both a human being and an artificial intelligence system; in other words, the machine is considered to be successful if a (human) participant, after submitting some written questions, is unable to identify whether the answer obtained was given by a person or not (X2id, 2023). What made this type of system even more intriguing was that grammatical and semantic errors were deliberately involved in the results provided, reinforcing the level of realism associated with technological performance. It could therefore be concluded that success in the test was not solely dependent on human reasoning or intelligence (Oxford Internet Institute, n.d). As a result of the impact caused by the emergence of artificial intelligence described above, its second period of expansion was marked by great expectations and associated enthusiasm; according to Gomes (2010), this period is between the 50s and 70s of the 20th century, where although no great progress was made, the technology was the subject of strong idealizations, and highly debated: McCarthy, Hyman, Minsky, Shannon, and Rochster were some of the minds that most actively participated in the discussion of the subject, and were responsible (along with six other participants) for organizing a two-month seminar at Dartmouth (1956), where outlines of artificial intelligence were presented, including the Logic Theorist reasoning program, by Allen Newell and Hebert Simon (Dartmouth, 2023).

The third moment of the rise of the technology under discussion was marked by the periods of testing/corroboration expectations and the creation of knowledge-based systems. The researchers responsible for studying artificial intelligence, mainly because it was a promising discovery, were very confident about their approaches to technological development: in the field of predictions, around the 1970s, there was even discussion about the possibility of a computer being autonomous enough to play chess and win championships, or even prove mathematical theorems, within the next ten years (Valéio, 2022). This kind of confidence associated with the future of artificial intelligence was naturally related to the ecstasy surrounding the success of the first developed systems; nevertheless, the first signs of technological deficiency emerged as soon as they were faced with solving more extensive or complex problems (Instituto de Engenharia, 2018).

Despite the obstacles encountered, there was never any doubt that the research would come to an end, and in 1969 the DENDRAL program was born; this system was developed by Stanford University to contribute to the identification and study of unknown organic molecules through mass spectrometry, using basic knowledge of chemistry (Edward & Bruce, 1990). Not only did this program contribute to scientific advances in the field of chemistry and molecular structures, but it also stood out mainly for its impact on the development of intelligent systems, since it represented the first successful knowledge-intensive program (Kornienko, Kornienko, Fofanov & Chubik, M., 2015).

From the 1980s onwards, a prosperous period for investment in technology, artificial intelligence began to be more and more integrated into organizations, its expansion never saw an end, and to this day it continues to be researched and developed. R1, the first successful commercial system, was created by Digital Equipment Corporation (DEC), which was responsible for configuring new computer program systems; by the mid-1980s, the company that owned the system already had annual revenues of forty million dollars, and two years later DEC's AI department had forty expert systems delivered and just as many in production phase (Schroer, 2023).

In the same decade, Japan presented the world with its "Fifth Generation" project, consisting of a ten-year forecast for the creation of intelligent computers based on the application of Prolog. As a major competing power, the United States of America introduced the Microelectronics and Computer Technology Corporation (MCC), a deliberate project to ensure its competitive power. These two major systems have thus contributed to the intensive use of AI, sustaining its investment and promoting the ongoing research inherent in the technology (Instituto de Engenharia, 2018).

The first ten years of the 21st century saw a restructuring of the way artificial intelligence was developed: more emphasis was placed on existing theories as a basis, particularly those highlighted in the historical context of the technology, and on substantiating the systems developed through intensive experimental practice, to corroborate the fidelity of the emerging programs (Cesce, 2017). As a result, the so-called technological innovation has begun to acquire greater clarity in terms of its capacity and projected level of growth, being increasingly incorporated into the various market sectors, and making a strong contribution to the expansion and success of companies across the globe.

Applying Artificial Intelligence

Before describing where artificial intelligence has been and is being, incorporated into the airport context, its areas of coverage should be highlighted, considering its history and development within the various fields of knowledge.

According to Gomes (2010), not only is AI an integral technology of the programming sector, but it is also directly related to engineering, mathematics, psychology, and even philosophy. The following diagram highlights the different areas of knowledge inherent in technological innovation:

CREATING VALUE IN BUSINESS

The Performance Concept

The concept of performance is generally associated with the fields of economics and management when evaluating an organization's operational activity. Its definition can be dissected in various ways, and performance can not only be measured through financial indicators but also based on factors relating to effectiveness and efficiency (Russo, 2014). According to Scherer (1980), good performance in the organizational context can be achieved through three key factors:

- Efficient use of resources to produce high-quality products.
- Integration of policies with macroeconomic goals and fair income distribution.
- Keeping abreast of scientific and technological developments, with a focus on improving the offered products and services.

Regarding this last point, it is possible to establish a link between high-quality performance and artificial intelligence, insofar as performance can be understood through the execution of tasks by companies whose purpose is to "measure, evaluate and improve" (Russo, 2014).

In the context of associating performance measures with the concepts of effectiveness and efficiency, it is also necessary to describe how they are characterized; according to Santos (2008), effectiveness can be presented under the pretext of doing the right things, while efficiency can be described as doing things

Figure 3. AI's fields of influence

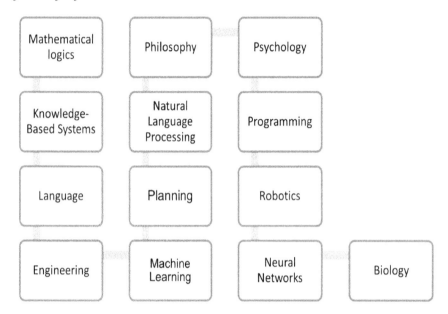

right. It should also be noted that company objectives must be considered to measure an organization's performance (through effectiveness and efficiency).

In short, it should be noted that performance evaluation is subjective in its genesis since performance is made up of a series of external and internal factors that condition the results obtained, given the proper functioning of companies (Russo, 2014).

The Value Creation Concept

The concept of value translates into the usefulness of certain goods, or the purchasing power associated with their possession, whereby products with a high use value may have a lower exchange value (the case of water, as an essential good for human life, with a high use value). In this way, it is possible to delimit the level of wealth through the ability to satisfy needs or conveniences; in other words, in an organizational context, the performed work is the greatest measure of exchange value, and consequently the greatest driver of value creation for companies (Leal, 2010).

With that said, value creation can be described as the relationship between the investment made to obtain a financial return and the need or importance attributed to the good, or in the case of AI, service offered (Leal, 2010).

Artificial intelligence is then inserted into the realm of value creation, through the amount of third-party work that a single system is capable of covering, efficiently meeting the needs of consumers and the importance it represents for companies, exponentiating the degree of wealth associated with it.

Value Creation and Artificial Intelligence

As a way of adapting to the latest era, companies tend to attach more and more importance to their customers, to be able to provide superior experiences and stand out from their competitors in the market.

Artificial intelligence has allowed this means of operation to evolve, since analytical tools and technological development can be used together to allow more personalized treatment of companies' consumers, and consequently provide outputs that best suit their needs (Business Analytics Portugal, 2018).

There are several advantages associated with the integration of artificial intelligence in the business context: in addition to issues related to the customer experience itself, it should be noted that the automation of services makes it possible to speed up the processes of collecting and processing information, leading to more efficient response times and a reduction in operating costs and associated human resources (Negrão, 2019).

That said, it is important to analyze the role of emerging technology in business to corroborate the relationship between technological development and the creation of value for organizations, from customer contact to the effects on the organizational body.

Customer's Trust

In the business context, and the relationship established between company and consumer, trust can be understood as the driving factor for better communication, contributing to a higher level of reciprocity and fostering the creation of value between both sides. This type of relationship base plays a key role for companies since such construction allows a commitment from both parties, valuing and satisfying organizational goals while providing the possibility of a long-term relationship, which represents an extremely beneficial factor from a business perspective (ECO, 2021).

Service Quality

As has already been widely mentioned, the evolution of companies has been aligned with factors such as globalization and technological development; it is important to note that not only is their growth in the organizational context but also from the perspective of consumer behavior. In today's market, customers tend to be increasingly demanding of the goods and services available to them, always looking for the best possible quality and the most competitive prices. As such, the best way to strengthen the relationship with customers and gain their trust is to invest in the services offered, always aiming to exceed their expectations (Negrão, 2018).

The use of artificial intelligence tools allows for a better understanding of customers and their preferences, in order to better meet their needs and their degree of demand and expectations regarding services. It is to this extent that the criteria by which a service is evaluated should be prioritized to create a positive perception for consumers along the value chain (Negrão, 2018).

Process Efficiency and Customer Response

As a result of major technological advances and their consequent implementation in companies, they are forced to adapt their management models to achieve a higher level of consumer satisfaction. Artificial intelligence is taking its place, insofar as it makes it possible to respond to the need to increase the quality of services, through the development of computers whose ability resembles human behavior; examples of this type of performance are based on Machine Learning (characterized by the ability to learn from data processing) and Robotic Process Automation, or RPA (described by the ability to memorize and repeat initially programmed processes). By incorporating this field of IT into business management, and the consequent joint operation of both RPA and Machine Learning, the optimization of organizational processes becomes a possibility, thus contributing to their enhancement (ECO, 2021).

It is also based on the processes of learning and automation of the tasks performed, that emerging intelligent systems also allow for a next step, related to decision-making; in an organizational context, this factor is of the utmost importance. However, through the data patterns that are analyzed, artificial intelligence makes it possible to make a choice, aiming to maximize the level of efficiency, resulting in a reduction in the response time to consumers (Lucas, 2023).

Costs Reduction

In order to contribute to the value creation effect, and as already mentioned, organizations increasingly tend to adapt their means of operation according to the technology developed and the needs of users. In addition to existing expectations and forecasts regarding the use of automated systems to carry out audits and create new business models, it is also argued that the association between data processing and the integration of AI in companies can result in strong benefits, namely the reduction of operating costs: not only does efficient information analysis become possible, but it also paves the way for predicting customer behavior, predicting possible losses for the organization, market trends, and risk management; thus, there is the emergence of conditions that allow for superior management of business costs (ECO, 2021).

Combining Factors

To address the last four factors discussed, relating to the role that artificial intelligence plays in the context of value creation, it is important to highlight the most relevant results to be presented, so a succinct yet complete understanding of the extent to which AI is incorporated into organizations can be obtained.

The following capabilities should therefore be emphasized:

- Automation of tasks.
- Decision making.
- Development of new products.
- Customization of Services.
- Improving Customer's Experience.

INCORPORATING ARTIFICIAL INTELLIGENCE INTO AIRPORTS

Now that we have broadly described the responsible factors for creating value for organizations (related to the artificial intelligence integration), we must also characterize the existing cases of its application, in order to be able to understand more precisely the advantages associated with the use of technology within companies.

In this way, it is not only possible to summarize existing events relating to the incorporation of technological innovation in airport spaces, but it is also possible to produce an analysis of its application at a global level and therefore discuss the subject, establishing a linking the occurrences currently projected and/or known and the elements that create value for companies, mentioned above.

Automatic Scheduling

Although there is reportedly a strong use of technology at airports, the human factor is also essential for their smooth running. There should be the best possible coordination when it comes to creating timetables for airport staff, so that everyone as a representative body of the sector can maintain their tasks in a positive manner. Creating these schedules, however, is an overly complex activity with high operational costs. To this end, the handling company Swissport is developing a task automation program based on artificial intelligence, the aim of which is to efficiently manage the shifts of each employee, regenerating itself, considering the impartial and rapid distribution of working hours (ZHAW, n.d).

Swissport is the world's largest ground handling company, responsible for providing handling services to more than 265 million passengers and 4.7 million tons of cargo every year. One of its main organizational goals is to provide the best possible service at the guaranteed minimum price. Hubs that receive a high volume of average movements per hour also end up with extensive peaks in capacity throughout the day, making the activity of providing assistance more difficult; the numerous tasks to be carried out, and the hours of continuous work associated with them, require the involvement of hundreds of shifts and thousands of employees, thus outlining the complexity of the task of distribution between employees (ZHAW, n.d).

As a response to the monthly task of creating so many shifts and managing staff, the company is developing a software optimization model to make it possible to schedule shifts automatically, using a database that contain and evaluate information about each employee's contractual terms and personal preferences, enabling maximum efficiency in the operation and the satisfaction of each employee.

Predictive Analytics

Delays at airports every year represent a loss of millions of dollars for airlines; this phenomenon is often predictable, but unfortunately unavoidable. Many airlines tend to concentrate their operations in a small number of hubs and, as a result, delays end up spreading throughout their movements. For example, a two-hour delay on a flight at 8am can cause up to eight hours of delays throughout the day (International Business Machines Corp., 2017).

During peak capacity periods, it is crucial to have efficient management and therefore limitation of waiting patterns and long cab times. The opportunity that exists to mitigate this phenomenon lies in the possibility of combining operational data, airport history, flight reports and weather forecasts into a single system that can analyze information on congestion, speeding up decision-making processes. The application of this technological innovation can be illustrated through the meteorological factor: when adverse weather conditions arise, airlines are allowed to analyze the expected behavior of the airport, in terms of congestion patterns and runway configuration, in order to develop appropriate planning for delays, increasing the efficiency of operations (International Business Machines Corp., 2017).

According to the same author, some of the characteristics associated with this system should also emphasized, namely:

- Visualizing the planned capacity at airports and future demand for flights.
- Predicting congestion levels, based on a database revised in cyclical periods of fifteen minutes.
- Display the current and future configuration of runways.
- Present a schedule containing the changes to the runway configuration over a twelve-hour period.

- Use individual flight records in relation to congestion and airport conditions.
- Consider the position of terminals and the location of runways.~

Ground Operations

In order to reduce aircraft downtime, Latam Airlines already operates cameras based on artificial intelligence systems at São Paulo International Airport (IATA code: GRU); the aim of which, is to monitor the punctuality, quality and consequent efficiency of ground operations in real time (Cardoso, 2023).

This modern system is characterized by tracking all operations carried out around the aircraft, providing a perceptive analysis of take-off times and connection times with the power supply unit. The action of artificial intelligence begins as soon as a Latam Airlines aircraft is detected approaching its gate, making it possible to provide a realistic, fast, complete and efficient record of events related to ground operations (Cardoso, 2023).

Virtual Agents and Chatbots

Airports are places where people move around a lot, coming from all over the world, with different native languages and different needs. Providing a personalized service to a large number of customers is an extremely complex activity, and a number of studies have been carried out to increase the efficiency of this task.

Launched in 2022, the Science and Technology Park of the University of Porto, developed a platform characterized by the use of artificial intelligence capable of responding immediately to passenger questions related to airport spaces, and has already been implemented in forty airports around the world. The startup focused on air tourism continues to grow and currently incorporates eleven different languages into its system, with its initial commercial expansion in Europe, including countries such as Portugal, Spain, Germany and Switzerland as clients (Silva, 2022).

The solution developed uses a range of social media, including Twitter, Instagram, Facebook Messenger, Google voice assistants, or even existing airport applications, in order to be accessible to as many travelers as possible, providing the answer that best suits the questions raised. The great advantage of this platform is that it provides a free and customizable service, targeting its performance at questions related to stores, restaurant areas, flight information, among other passenger FAQs (Silva, 2022).

It should be noted that the importance of this technological innovation is not only highlighted by the level of efficiency it brings, but it also allows for easy adaptation to the evolution of the airport sector and a closer relationship with costumers.

Automatic Translation Systems

Developed through collaboration between Priberam and the Deutsche Welle (DW) media group, the "Plain X" platform was created, a system based on the use of Human Language Technology (HLT), focused on processes related to linguistics, or whose purpose is the automatic production of subtitles for the news displayed on the hundreds of screens spread throughout an airport. The projection of such a discreet, yet important, technology is already a reality, and its incorporation has been recorded on around two hundred monitors at Frankfurt am Main Airport (IATA code: FRA) (Santos, 2021).

The "Plain X" system, while characterized by its linguistic capabilities, is assisted by the integration of artificial intelligence in the tasks of translation, transcription and automatic production of subtitles and/or voiceover. In the currently known case, concerning Frankfurt am Main Airport, the technology uses submitted scripts, synchronizes them with the video broadcasts to be subtitled, creates files (where the subtitles are contained) and stores them in pre-programmed folders; the last step in the process is to send the complete and already subtitled files to the airport's servers, where the final, adapted content is displayed. It is also worth mentioning that, despite being highly detailed and having a considerable number of steps to take, the entire process of the platform is automated (Santos, 2021).

Targeted Advertising

Approaching a concept of projection and expectations, artificial intelligence, as an innovation that resembles human behavior, which has been growing intensively and rapidly; currently, with the developments that have taken place, there is even the capacity for computerized replication of creativity, a trait that was considered to be exclusively human. Allied to this factor, the marketing sector has been undergoing a restructuring of its operation, making the automatic production of entire campaigns an easily accessible possibility (Dawes, 2023).

In the airport context, AI makes it possible to improve the organization of internal and surrounding spaces; by creating advertising targeted at each consumer, it becomes possible to predict behavior, identify a audience to be reached and customize advertising strategies according to region/buying power. The main goal of this type of approach is to drive passenger consumption levels, encouraging greater use of airport spaces and strengthening the relationship established between the organization and the consumer (Dawes, 2023).

Lost Baggage Handling

Thousands and thousands of belongings are lost every day at airports around the world; from documentation, to backpacks, suitcases and handbags, items of clothing, accessories, among a wide variety of objects, these end up in the lost and found section, which naturally requires a whole process of cataloging and inventory management of some difficulty, due to the number of daily users of airports, and their respective lost goods, subsequently delivered (Baskas, 2023).

The entry of the startup Boomerang into the context of handling lost luggage marks its position through the use of artificial intelligence to increase the efficiency of the registration process and therefore the management of lost belongings in airport spaces (Boomerang, 2023).

When an object considered lost is handed over to the dedicated section at airports, the staff in charge of it will only have to record it photographically and make a brief report on the event, trying to address a few key points, such as the date of delivery, the characterization of the item and a brief description of its condition, in terms of existing damage or other factors that promote the item's individuality. What gives AI its importance in this process comes in the following moments: by entering these reports into an up-to-date database, and in accordance with the Machine Learning characterization, passengers looking to recover their lost objects can make an online request (at the lost and found department of airports), describing the goods in as much detail as necessary and, if possible, uploading a photograph of them (Batista, 2023).

Immediately after submitting the request, the developed AI works by comparing the belongings described by passengers with those known to the system; in other words, through direct access to the lost and found database, it becomes possible to find the lost object in a matter of minutes. If this is indeed the case, the passenger is immediately notified of the next processes to be carried out, until the goods are actually delivered; it is also worth mentioning that an innovation is planned for the continuity of the platform in question, which will allow for the automatic labeling of lost objects, in the event of a home delivery request from the passengers holding the luggage that was initially lost (Boomerang, 2023).

Having this settled, it is important to add that the introduction of such a skillful technology, in an area where the speed of processes should be the main priority, due to passenger dissatisfaction with an initial loss, greatly speeds up the baggage recovery process, mainly boosting user satisfaction (Batista, 2023).

Smart Scanners

It is common knowledge that security is the primary and most actively represented value in the operations of the entire aviation industry. Within the airport space (in the sectors of direct contact with the user), passing through security control is usually one of the most time-consuming and human-intensive processes, from arrival at the airport to boarding. The main cause of congestion in the passenger flow is related to the meticulousness and attention that must be considered throughout this stage of a flight operation. Although it can also be a phase that causes travelers some embarrassment, the body analysis carried out using existing technological means, makes it possible to accurately detect any type of prohibited objects that may be being carried, such as narcotics, explosives, undeclared monetary possessions, etc (European Comisson, 2009).

Once one of the cases mentioned is suspected or detected, passengers are subjected to a highly rigorous inspection, depending on the case in question, either at the security checkpoint or in designated areas; this type of circumstance inevitably causes a delay for other users, which subsequently translates into a substantial reduction in the level of efficiency of operations (Alecrim, 2023).

Of the solutions that have been discovered and are in the process of development, the startup Evolve Technology stands out; the key point of this technological innovation, naturally based on artificial intelligence, lies in the fluidity with which it passes through the body scanners and in the application of the Machine Learning concept to the data obtained. By using equipment similar to the ones we know, it becomes possible to analyze, create and permanently store patterns corresponding to reported cases of carrying unauthorized objects. The difference between this type of technological integration and the means conventionally used is highlighted through the deconstruction of the radiographic analysis carried out, giving way to a radar-type assessment (Alecrim, 2023).

In this way, it is estimated that with the ease provided by the automated performance of the system developed, up to eight hundred passengers can be processed per hour, resulting in a considerable increase in the degree of efficiency associated with such a detailed task. It is also worth noting that with an intensive study of the platform, it will become possible to "train" the system so that it is autonomous enough to distinguish what is or is not suspicious, thus saving users the action of removing a belt with a metal buckle, or coins from their pockets, for example (Harris, 2016).

Figure 4. Application of AI in airports worldwide
Source: Statista, 2023 (adapted)

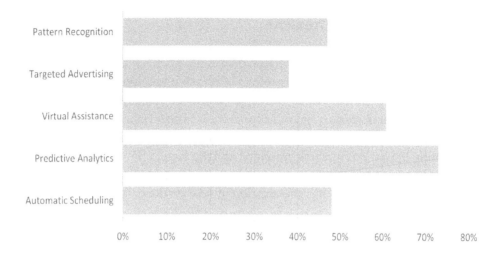

THE USE OF AI IN A GLOBAL CONTEXT

Application of AI in Airports Worldwide

The presented graph, as the title suggests, highlights the level of artificial intelligence application in the airport sector within a global analysis. It is from the information it provides that it is possible to establish a relationship between the areas in which the technology is being incorporated and the existing cases, or those in the development process, highlighted above.

Thus, based on the types of technological innovations described, it can also be seen that there is a tendency for organizations to increase the level of AI integration in the performance of their tasks over the next few years, maximizing all operations efficiency level (Srivastava, 2023).

Regarding the first category, "Automatic Scheduling", its global application stands at 48% and the existing case associated with it is present in "Automatic Scheduling ", presented in Chapter Four. The second division, "Predictive Analytics", consists of 73% of application throughout the world's airports, representing the highest percentage of AI integration in the aeronautical sector; of the known cases of its use, we emphasize "Predictive Analysis" and "Ground Operations", mentioned above. The third set of results, related to "Virtual Assistance", has an overall application percentage of 61%, a slightly lower figure than the second class; in the context of the relationship with the developed platforms, already characterized, we should highlight not only "Virtual Agents and Chatbots", but also "Automatic Translation Systems". As for the fourth category declared, "Targeted Advertising", this has a percentage of integration in the industry of 38%, the lowest figure recorded, and its application can be portrayed through the "Targeted Advertising", emphasized earlier. The fifth and final division, which consists of "Pattern Recognition", has an incorporation value in the airport field of 47%, a similar percentage to the first category; this effect can be translated into the relevance of the human factor in these areas of the sector, which continues to play a crucial role in the smooth running of organizations. In addition to this figure, "Lost Baggage Handling" and "Smart Scanners" stand out, two technologies directly related to airport security measures.

The Relationship With Value Creation

In addition to being able to establish a link between the results obtained and the technologies that exist or are projected for future years, it is also possible to establish a relationship between the innovations described and the elements that create value for companies, as outlined in Chapter Three.

Based on the concept of performance and value creation, amd on levels of effectiveness and efficiency, dissected in accordance with the insertion of AI in organizations, it is therefore justifiable to build a model capable of aggregating the various systems presented and the factors previously mentioned, relating to the use of qualitative measures to enhance organizational conduct, which translates to elements such as the automation of tasks, decision-making, the creation of new products, among others.

ARTIFICIAL INTELLIGENCE IN THE SECURITY FIELD

Following the results obtained, regarding the worldwide application of technology, it was possible to highlight that the factor associated with security, "Pattern Recognition", only has an overall application percentage of 47%, the second lowest figure compared to the other categories. Although it does not cover the entire area of security in the domain, the percentage figure shown reflects the need for investment in this area and encourages the development of new technologies that actively act as a means of preventing and responding to the appearance of flaws on the human factor part.

As mentioned, the issue of security is extremely important in the airport industry. Airports are places subject to a wide variety of risks, from minor events to attacks that cause human lives to be at stake;

Figure 5. Artificial intelligence and value creation

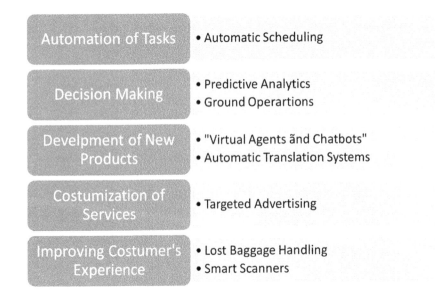

measures are constantly being implemented and updated to mitigate the risks associated with the sector's operation, and in recent years protection requirements have intensified, leading organizations to take advanced defensive measures. In addition to this adversity, and as has been pointed out, costumers also tend to increase their level of demand in terms of the quality and ease of access to the services provided, which ends up being an added challenge for companies. The response to these situations essentially involves adapting management models to technological developments, which have become increasingly important, boosting the efficiency of all operational processes (Aly & Hammoud, 2023).

Throughout the world, and especially in the aeronautical sphere, systems based on artificial intelligence have continuously marked the functioning of spaces, which allows for the fostering of a means of cooperation between technology and airport security bodies (Aly & Hammoud, 2023). As an example, according to Himanshu & Sonia (2021), the AI market, allied to the aerospace sector, was valued at 374 million dollars in 2020, projected to reach 5826 million dollars in the following eight years, illustrating a CAGR rate of approximately 43%. The primary reason for this level of growth is naturally related to the benefits of incorporating AI into organizational systems, so it remains to be analyzed how this valuable technological innovation can be used to optimize safety processes and improve operational efficiency in airport management.

Optimizing Surveillance Systems

One of the main responsibilities for airport management is to guarantee maximum security for all users; this naturally implies the existence of a surveillance system capable of monitoring the course of all events both inside and in the surrounding areas of the airport. This type of task is presumably highly complex, as it covers an extensive area, including several terminals, parking lots and numerous entries and/or exit points. This is where some kind of deficiency in the performance of the human factor can be registered, since the operators responsible for monitoring hundreds of cameras may inevitably feel tired or overwhelmed; as an effect of these circumstances, a simple lack of attention at a given critical moment can lead to an inability to respond to dangerous situations in a timely manner (Hussain, 2023).

The use of AI contributes to mitigating these risk factors, being able to optimize surveillance action by providing information in real time and automating alert systems when some kind of threat arises. In addition to these advantages, it is also able to communicate with camera operators when extra attention is required, or immediate intervention is needed. To summarize, the solution presented for improving the functioning of the operation is part of the transformation of conventional equipment into reactive security systems, capable of predicting or recognizing any type of danger to airport security (Hussain, 2023).

Perimeter Protection

Following the logic of control over the airport area, with the flow of users in the spaces, both the entry and/or exit points and respective passenger terminals, as well as the buildings designated for authorized personnel only, are inevitably subject to any type of attack. It is true that the identification, or just the prevention, of a trespassing attitude is a concern for security organizations, and it is necessary to confront this type of situation with the appropriate solutions (Isarsoft, 2023).

As such, the creation of technologies based on artificial intelligence systems enables the ability to respond to these challenges, or even predict their occurrence: the use of smart cameras also makes it possible to identify and track suspicious objects or users. It should be noted that sending an immediate alert to the competent authorities regarding risky behavior or access violations optimizes the speed with which threats are dealt with and raises awareness of the entire airport perimeter (Isarsoft, 2023).

Unauthorized Entry Control

As mentioned, access control is a part of airport security; it is imperative that there is efficient management of access to restricted areas, such as the air traffic control tower, the courtyard, or other places designated for employees only. In addition to this, it must also be ensured that the entry of people authorized to circulate in the places in question is carried out smoothly, at any time of the day, regardless of the circumstances (Isarsoft, 2023).

Although the use of ID cards is a widely implemented security measure in many organizations, with the technological development that exists, this type of defense factor is now considered almost obsolete, not to mention that it can generate risk for companies through events associated with misplacement, theft or loss (Scylla Technologies Inc., 2023).

Artificial intelligence is the answer to this problem, based on the integration of biometric control, which makes it possible to identify an employee through non-transmissible characteristics and also allows an alert to be sent to the competent authorities in the event of an attempted breach (Scylla Technologies Inc., 2023).

Foreign Object Debris

Foreign Object Debris represents a problem with which the aviation sector is very familiar; it consists of pieces of tires, screws or pieces of sidewalk, among other debris, which compromise a flight operation. The damage caused by this type of adversity amounts to almost thirteen billion dollars a year worldwide, based on technical problems, workplace injuries, flight delays, etc. One of the reasons for the existence of this major obstacle is the daily manual runway inspections, which only increase the risk inherent in the circumstances described (Papadopulos & Gonzalez, 2021).

Once again, through intelligent surveillance systems, the use of AI can contribute to a substantial reduction in the damage caused by FOD, based on solutions that provide automatic and constant monitoring of runways, in any weather condition or desired area. Such a change represents a significant increase in safety standards and the level of efficiency of operations, as it works to prevent a possible runway closure and reduce downtime (Papadopulos & Gonzalez, 2021).

Identifying Passenger Falls and Injuries

Accidents resulting from passengers slipping or falling are extremely common and are one of the most well-known causes of injuries in airport spaces. Derived from the construction of the infrastructure, spilled liquids, or the rush with which people often circulate, there are thousands of occurrences every year, which require special attention on the part of medical care regarding the behavior of users (Scylla Technologies Inc., 2023).

Through automated surveillance systems, artificial intelligence makes it possible to identify falls by any individual in real time, being able to alert security teams, who in turn activate the appropriate protocols in order to act quickly to safeguard human life and reduce the likelihood of serious consequences (Isarsoft, 2023).

Lost/Abandoned Luggage Identification

The abandonment or lack of supervision of passengers' luggage can constitute a threat to the security of the airport sector, since they may contain explosives or other objects that pose a risk to physical integrity; incidents of this nature generally require a lengthy investigation and resolution, which can result in the loss of millions of dollars for the organizations responsible, in addition to the eventual end of human lives (Scylla Technologies Inc., 2023).

Artificial intelligence implementation solutions act insofar as they allow the identification of suitcases, or even bags placed in certain locations, not moved during a certain period and automatically notify airport security bodies, leading to rapid action and in accordance with the alert level (Isarsoft, 2023).

Another relevant issue is associated with the theft of luggage or belongings; with the integration of AI-based surveillance systems, when there is a report of theft, it is projected that it will be possible to automatically monitor the activity of passengers before, during and after the occurrence is reported, speeding up the entire case resolution process, recovering, if possible, the property sought (Scylla Technologies Inc., 2023).

Temperature Tracking

Although we live in a post-pandemic period, where restrictions on passenger freedom have already been partly lifted, public health remains a constant concern for the airport industry, with millions of passengers moving between different parts of the world every day, enabling the spread of diseases of all kinds.

Artificial intelligence will help to improve the screening of airport users by automatically analyzing skin temperature, assessing appropriate social distancing and verifying the use of a mask, if required by the national health authorities. The identification of non-compliance with the imposed standards also makes it possible to send an alert to the competent authorities, who can intervene if necessary (Kritikos, 2020).

Increasing Operational Efficiency

Some parts of airports are prone to phenomena such as congestion or overcrowding. These types of situations, which are generally unavoidable, cause losses for organizations, since prolonged queues or overcrowding result in consumer dissatisfaction and a lack of enjoyment of the flight experience. It should be emphasized that the time required to pass through security, for example, can lead to less time spent in the retail sector, an essential contributor to the financial stability of the aviation industry - around 40% contribution to total airport revenue (Scylla Technologies Inc., 2023).

The integration of artificial intelligence to mitigate this phenomenon translates into a reduction in waiting times and a consequent increase in customer satisfaction. The solutions fall mainly under the intelligent monitoring of the flow of users in the space, identification of patterns of circulation volumes, and subsequent creation of estimates, in order to optimize the management of existing queues; an interesting use case of this technological means could be to provide a personalized approach to the times of greatest flow of people, to passengers who require a higher quality service (Aguiar-Costa, Cunha, Silva, & Abreu, 2022).

Another issue related to increasing the level of efficiency of operations is linked to the evolution of security screening equipment, already described in Chapter Four. The combination of this system with the proper processing of biometric data in the check-in, baggage check and boarding processes makes it possible to considerably increase passenger satisfaction with their experience on the ground. It is no longer imperative to present a passport at the last moment before boarding the aircraft, since facial recognition allows the database of everyone's documentation to be checked; this type of innovation once again reduces the time spent in queues and results in the transformation of airport spaces into highly efficient places (Scylla Technologies Inc., 2023). It is also worth mentioning that the emergence of innovations of this nature naturally involves intensive study, not only because of the highly detailed regulations governing the airline industry, but also because of the elements relating to privacy rights and the correct storage and processing of passenger data.

CONCLUSION, LIMITATIONS, AND FUTURE RESEARCH

This applied project in aeronautical management has enabled a complete exploration of the areas inherent in the content learned over the last three years, where it has been possible to relate some areas of extreme relevance, such as business management, the criteria for creating value, the adaptation of organizations to technological development and the operation of airports.

Through the carried-out research, it became feasible to answer the questions initially raised, always highlighting the importance of organizational efficiency as the biggest driver in the face of market competitors.

So, the answer to the starting question, "How can artificial intelligence add value to an airport?" is: By investing in and incorporating emerging technologies in the sector, in order to increase consumer satisfaction and transform airport spaces into safer and more efficient place.

It was also possible, based on the presentation of known cases about the integration of technology in industry, to expose its extent of application in the global context, leading to the establishment of a link between the technological events already applied, or in the process of development, and the factors responsible for improving the performance of organizations, these being the automation of tasks, decision-making, the development of new products, the personalization of services and the improvement of the customer experience.

Also based on the obtained results demonstration, it was possible to emphasize the level of integration of artificial intelligence within the scope of airport security, describing some of the existing expectations regarding the future of its operation, based on the importance that this area entails for the conduct of all operations in the aeronautical field.

In terms of limitations to the development of the project, we must highlight the small number of published articles on the subject, mainly because it is a recent subject, and some of the information explored for the study involved the use of other types of sources, namely online news.

For future research, technological investment in security control is proposed, since, as mentioned, it represents the greatest value in aviation, and updating systems or measures to defend airport spaces should be a priority, in order to always offer the best experience to its users, with maximum protection of their lives and rights.

REFERENCES

Aerospace Artificial Intelligence Market Size. Growth, Research - 2028. (n.d.). Allied Market Research. https://www.alliedmarketresearch.com/aerospace-artificial-intelligence-market-A11337

Agarwal, A. (2023, January 10). *Travel Marketing Poised for Reboot From Generative AI.* Skift. https://skift.com/2023/01/10/travel-marketing-poised-for-reboot-from-generative-ai/

Aguiar-Costa, L., Cunha, C., Silva, W., & Abreu, N. (2022). *Customer satisfaction in service delivery with artificial intelligence: A meta-analytic study.* Mackenzie. https://www.redalyc.org/journal/1954/195473680001/html/

Alecrim, E. (2023). Scanners de aeroportos serão menos constrangedores graças à inteligência artificial. *Tecnoblog.* https://tecnoblog.net/especiais/scanner-aeroporto-evolv/

Aly, M., & Hammoud, G. (2023). *Impact of applying the artificial intelligence in airports' operations (applied in capital international airport).* Helwan University. https://www.eurchembull.com/uploads/paper/1a04d6acd90bc133444961d591becacc.pdf

Appinventiv. (2023, March 3). *Influence of AI in the Aviation Industry.* Appinventive. https://appinventiv.com/blog/ai-in-aviation/#:~:text=AI%20for%20aviation%20in%20the,implementing%20such%20cutting%2Dedge%20technologies

Automated Airport Staff Scheduling. (n.d.). ZHAW Institute of Data Analysis and Process Design IDP. https://www.zhaw.ch/en/engineering/institutes-centres/idp/research/optimization-and-simulation/automated-airport-staff-scheduling/

Baskas, H. (2023, January 25). Airports turn to AI and other tech tools to hunt for lost bags amid travel meltdowns. *NBC News.* https://www.nbcnews.com/tech/travel/airports-turn-ai-tech-tools-hunt-lost-bags-rcna65335

Batista, D. A. (2023). *Aeroporto usa inteligência artificial para devolver rapidamente malas e objetos perdidos.* Melhores Destinos. https://www.melhoresdestinos.com.br/inteligencia-artificial-aeroporto.html

Boomerang. (2023). *Why Boomerang?* Boomerang. https://thanksboomerang.com/for-partners

Business Analytics. (n.d.). *Inteligência Artificial: melhorar a experiência do cliente.* Business Analytics Portugal. http://businessanalytics.pt/inteligencia-artificial-melhorar-experiencia-dos-clientes/

Cardoso, P. M. (2023, March 31). Inteligência artificial já está sendo usada em um aeroporto brasileiro. *AERO Magazine.* https://aeromagazine.uol.com.br/artigo/inteligencia-artificial-ja-esta-sendo-usada-em-um-aeroporto-brasileiro.html

Cesce (n.d). *Breve historia de la inteligencia artificial: el camino hacia la empresa.* Cesce. https://www.cesce.es/es/w/asesores-de-pymes/breve-historia-la-inteligencia-artificial-camino-hacia-la-empresa

Chakraborty, K. (2022b). *How Automated Threat Recognition Technology Enhances Airport Security.* Techopedia. https://www.techopedia.com/how-automated-threat-recognition-technology-enhances-airport-security/2/34779

Creswell, J. (2014). *Investigação qualitativa e projeto de pesquisa: Escolhendo entre cinco abordagens. 3*. Penso.

Dartmouth. (2023). *Artificial Intelligence Coined at Dartmouth.* Dartmouth. https://home.dartmouth.edu/about/artificial-intelligence-ai-coined-dartmouth

ECO. (2021). Criação de valor com a IA. SAPO. https://eco.sapo.pt/2021/12/15/criacao-de-valor-com-a-ia/

European Commission. (2009, February 11). *The impact of the use of body scanners in the field of aviation security on human rights, privacy, personal dignity, health and data protection.* EC. https://ec.europa.eu/justice/article-29/documentation/other-document/files/2009/2009_05_11_annex_consultation_letter_chairman_art29wp_daniel_calleja_dgtren_en.pdf

Gomes, D. (2009). *Inteligência Artificial: Conceitos e Aplicações.* Universidade Federal Fluminense. https://www.professores.uff.br/screspo/wp-content/uploads/sites/127/2017/09/ia_intro.pdf

Harris, M. (2016, October). AI-powered body scanners could soon be inspecting you in public places. *The Guardian.* https://www.theguardian.com/technology/2016/oct/25/airport-body-scanner-artificial-intelligence

Hussain, A. (2023). *How artificial intelligence can help airports in the areas of safety and security.* LinkedIn. https://www.linkedin.com/pulse/how-artificial-intelligence-can-help-airports-areas-safety-hussain/

Instituto de Engenharia. (2018). *A história da inteligência artificial.* Instituto de Engenharia. https://www.institutodeengenharia.org.br/site/2018/10/29/a-historia-da-inteligencia-artificial/

Isarsoft. (2023a, July). *AI in Airports.* Isarsoft. https://www.isarsoft.com/article/ai-in-airports

Kornienko, A., Kornienko, A., Fofanov, O., & Chubik, M. (2015b). *Knowledge in Artificial Intelligence Systems: Searching the Strategies for Application.* ScienceDirect. https://www.sciencedirect.com/science/article/pii/S1877042814067160?ref=pdf_download&fr=RR-2&rr=81647240fbcd384e

Kritikos, M. (2020). *What if AI could improve thermal imaging, to help fight coronavirus?* European Parliament. https://www.europarl.europa.eu/RegData/etudes/ATAG/2020/656299/EPRS_ATA(2020)656299_EN.pdf

Leal, V. (2010b, October). *A Criação de Valor em Portugal.* Instituto Superior Técnico. https://fenix.tecnico.ulisboa.pt/downloadFile/395142108129/DISSERTA%C3%87%C3%83O.pdf

Lucas, J. (2023, July). *O processo de tomada de decisão através da inteligência artificial.* LinkedIn. https://www.linkedin.com/pulse/o-processo-de-tomada-decis%C3%A3o-atrav%C3%A9s-da-intelig%C3%AAncia-orzzi-lucas/?originalSubdomain=pt

Machado, M. (2021). *Método de pesquisa qualitativa: O que é e como fazer?* Academica. https://www.academica.com.br/post/m%C3%A9todo-qualitativo-como-fazer

Negrão, C. (2018). *Influência Da Inteligência Artificial Na Criação De Valor Nos Processos De Negócio Das Organizações.* ISEG. https://www.repository.utl.pt/bitstream/10400.5/19612/1/DM-CSMN-2019.pdf#page16

Papadopoulos, E., & Gonzalez, F. (2020). *UAV and AI Application for Runway Foreign Object Debris (FOD) Detection.* IEEE. https://ieeexplore.ieee.org/stamp/stamp.jsp?tp=&arnumber=9438489

Russo, A. (2014). *Criação de Valor.* Instituto Politécnico De Setúbal. https://core.ac.uk/download/pdf/62696164.pdf

Santos, M. (2021). *Tecnologias de Inteligência Artificial da Priberam já em funcionamento no aeroporto de Frankfurt.* Ecommercenews PT. https://ecommercenews.pt/tecnologias-de-inteligencia-artificial-da-priberam-ja-em-funcionamento-no-aeroporto-de-frankfurt/

Schroer, A. (2023, July). *What Is Artificial Intelligence?* Builtin. https://builtin.com/artificial-intelligence

Scylla. (n.d.). *How Leveraging AI Helps Optimize Safety and Security for Airports.* Scylla. https://www.scylla.ai/how-leveraging-ai-helps-optimize-safety-and-security-for-airports/

Silva, I. M. (2022). *Plataforma made in UPTEC esclarece dúvidas de viajantes nos aeroportos. Notícias* U.Porto. https://noticias.up.pt/plataforma-made-in-uptec-esclarece-duvidas-de-viajantes-nos-aeroportos/

Statista. (2023, February 6). *Use of AI at airports 2022.* Statista. https://www.statista.com/statistics/666275/adoption-of-operational-intelligence-capabilities-at-airports/

Teste de Turing. (n.d.). *Explicando IA.* A to Z FAI. https://atozofai.withgoogle.com/intl/pt-BR/turing-test/

The History of Artificial Intelligence - Spotlight at Stanford Search Results. (1990). Stanford Libraries. https://exhibits.stanford.edu/ai/catalog?f%5Btopic_facet%5D%5B%5D=DENDRAL

Urrútia, G., & Bonfill, X. (2009). *PRISMA declaration: A proposal to improve the publication of systematic reviews and meta-analyses.* BMJ. https://bmjopen.bmj.com/content/bmjopen/suppl/2013/06/10/bmjopen-2012-002330.DC1/bmjopen-2012-002330supp_PRISMA-2010.pdf

Valério, J. (2022). *Inteligência Artificial: A origem [1/7].* Diferencial. https://diferencial.tecnico.ulisboa.pt/ciencia/inteligencia-artificial-a-origem-1-7/

X2id. (2023). *História da Inteligência Artificial.* X2ID. https://x2inteligencia.digital/2020/02/20/historia-da-inteligencia-artificial-2

KEY TERMS AND DEFINITIONS

Artificial Intelligence: Defined as the machine's ability to simulate human behavior in the performance of programmed tasks.

Biometric Identification: The use of biometric signature for different purposes, such as the self check-in process or the control over staff-only entry points; an example of this type of signature system is the fingerprint scanning or face recognition.

Compound Annual Growth Rate: As the name suggests, is described as evaluation of the annual growth of a said investment to analyse its level of viability.

Foreign Object Debris: Named after any type of found objects, located at inconvinient places, such as the airport runways, that can be responsible for equipment damaging or staff injuring, resulting in a loss for the associated organization.

Human Language Technology: Defined as how programmed systems, receive, analyze, and modify the submitted request, to repond to a need of its user; an example of that is the the automated translation systems.

IATA: also known as International Ait Transport Association, is the grater support for the aviation sector as it helps improving its level of efficiency and participates on the formuling of the industry policy.

Chapter 13
Comparative Analysis of Seasonality Patterns in Faro Airport (Portugal)

Jorge Abrantes
ⓘ https://orcid.org/0000-0003-4692-907X
Estoril Higher Institute for Tourism and Hotel Studies, Portugal & Universidade Aberta, Portugal

Rui Castro e Quadros
ⓘ https://orcid.org/0000-0003-0685-259X
Instituto Superior de Educação e Ciências, Portugal & Escola Superior de Hotelaria e Turismo do Estoril, Portugal

António Rodrigues
ISG - Business & Economics School, Lisboa, Portugal

ABSTRACT

Seasonality is a reality in leisure tourist destinations such as the Mediterranean and the Algarve (Portugal) Region in Europe. The objective of the present investigation is to evaluate the seasonal effects on passenger air operations to/from Faro airport (Algarve), based on a comparative analysis that takes into account a period of low season (February) and a period of high season (August). In methodological terms, the analysis will be exploratory, descriptive, and qualitative although based on quantitative elements, taking into account the origin destinations of the traffic, the airlines and their operations and the respective number of flights. The results obtained show the strong incidence of seasonality at Faro airport, both with an increase in the number of flights operated in high season, as well as a greater number of airlines and destinations (some of them operated exclusively seasonal).

INTRODUCTION

Seasonality is a phenomenon the tourism sector has to live with and which is unlikely to be eliminated, especially in tourist destinations in southern Europe, where the beaches and the weather are the main

DOI: 10.4018/979-8-3693-0908-7.ch013

reasons for a vacation (Sun & Sea). Its scope impacts means of transport, airports, destinations and tourism products, public and private companies and all other sectors and activities that directly or indirectly intersect with the tourism value chain (Mathieson & Wall, 1982).

As a universally recognized phenomenon, seasonality has been a challenge for different decision-makers over the years. Even though it has become one of the most distinctive and determinant characteristics of the tourism industry (as well as for the transport sector) it is also a misunderstood phenomenon (Corluka, 2019; Cunha, 2009). Even so, it is recognized that seasonality presents a stable and well-defined pattern over time, not being confused with specific phenomena or occasional events (Ferrante, Lo Magno, & De Cantis, 2018; Witt & Moutinho, 1995).

Butler (2014) considers four inherent characteristics of seasonality: it is a phenomenon with a constant pattern, usually felt at the same time year after year, it is present in several sectors of activity (which includes tourism and transport), it is influenced by endogenous and exogenous factors and, it is essential to know the offer and demand of the region to mitigate its effect.

Looking more particularly to the aviation sector, seasonality directly affects airports and airlines (Dobruszkes, Decroly, & Suau-Sanchez, 2022) where demand for air travel is derived from activities such as business, visiting friends and relatives, and tourism. The authors go further by stating that in commercial aviation investigations into the impacts of seasonality are mainly related with airports, airlines or routes.

As many of the moments of leisure and holiday travelers in Europe are concentrated in the summer months, either because of school or work holidays but also because of better weather conditions, the seasonal effects are more pronounced in these periods. As demand for tourism and holiday travel tends to be seasonal, air transport demand by leisure and vacation travelers also tends to vary seasonally (Merkert & Webber, 2018; Zou, Reynolds-Feighan, & Yu, 2022).

The objective of this investigation was to evaluate the effects of seasonality in the Algarve (Portugal), more specifically in air operations at Faro airport, the main gateway for international tourism in this region. For this purpose an analysis was carried during two observation moments in the year 2023. The first assessment took into account the flights made during a week to the airport in February 2023, a period traditionally of more limited demand (low season), and a second observation was done during a week in August 2023, a month traditionally with strong touristic demand (high season).

With this investigation, the aim was to find out how airline companies and their respective flights to the Algarve region behave and during these two seasons and how the increase in demand is achieved. Was it obtained with more flights in already operated markets (from existing companies)? Was it based on new operations to new destinations (by the same airlines or by airlines that did not operate in low season)? Or was it a combination of factors (more airlines, more flights and more destinations)?

LITERATURE REVIEW

Travel is one of the most ancient and common aspects of human life and it can be traced back to mythical times (Rabotić, 2014, p. 29). Seasonality is also a reality and a phenomenon that dates back to those ancient times.

Page and Connell (2009, p. 25) mentioned in Rabotić (2014, p. 104) in a reference to Roman Era expressed that "seaside resorts... where the upper classes and the masses locked each summer to get away from the overcrowded and unhealthy conditions in Rome". In the same way, Sánchez (2021, p. 57) reaffirms that "the richest Romans spent their leisure time during the unbearable summer months of Rome in luxurious *villae* located in the Bay of Naples (…)". During the Grand Tour, some references to seasonality are also recurrent especially by Black (1992) in his work about "The British Abroad: The Grand Tour in the Eighteenth Century". Reilly (2021) makes clear the seasonal effects in Rome during these periods as the city was "probably the most visited European travel destination well into the nineteenth century". According to Reilly (2021) "Rome was not just a city, it was the caput mundi, the head of the world". Based on itineraries of 271 travelers to Italy from 1400 to 1850, it concludes that northern European travel to Italy was highly seasonal. As mentioned "Northern travelers tended to enter Italy in the winter, and typically left in late spring, thus minimizing exposure to endemic malaria infection" (Reilly, 2021, p. 70), due to 'Roman fever' during the malarial summer season.

Even being an intrinsic phenomenon in the tourism sector, it is only more recently that the study of seasonality as a social phenomenon has begun to be faced. Cannas (2012) makes it clear by stating about tourism that "seasonality is a critical topic in academic literature".

BarOn (1972, 1973), one of the pioneers in this field, defined seasonality as an incomplete and unbalanced use of the means available to the economy. Later, BarOn (1975) was more conclusive in his definition by including the effects that occur systematically due to the state of the weather, calendar restrictions (holidays, festive seasons), special attractions (for example, festivals) or just by personal lifestyle.

Allcock (1989) also considers that seasonality corresponds to a concentration of tourist flows in certain traditionally short periods, while Butler (1994) defines it as a temporal imbalance in the tourist phenomenon which can be expressed in terms of the dimension of elements such as the number of visitors, visitor spending, road traffic and in other means of transport, and employment, among others.

These authors list as natural seasonality those that result from calendar factors (holidays and religious festivals, among others) and, no less important those that derive directly or indirectly from the decisions of economic agents at the economic level, at school holidays or in companies, all of them with an impact on tourism consumption. BarOn (1972) and Hinch and Hickey (1996) reinforced this understanding by characterizing as institutional seasonality the seasonality that also depends from religious, cultural, social, ethnic and organizational factors.

Hylleberg (1992) also points out some of its main causes, such as those derived from climatic phenomena and the seasons of the year (temperatures, hours of exposure to sunlight, precipitation, snow, etc.). Andriotis (2005) makes clear in his characterization that summer is the primary season for most tourist destinations as well as winter is the primary season for ski resorts, typically located in mountain areas, as defended by Suau-Sanchez and Voltes-Dorta (2019).

In turn, Cooper, Fletcher, Fyall, Gilbert, and Wanhill (2005), as well as Rosselló and Sansó (2017), point to a definition based on the temporality of fluctuations in tourist flows on a daily, weekly, monthly or even annual basis, leading to seasonality being considered, once again, as a pattern of visitors that happens every year, as later reinforced by Butler (2014). Similarly, demand at airports presents temporal imbalances on an hourly, daily or monthly basis, since they rarely present a harmonious distribution throughout the year (Ashford, Stanton, & Moore, 1997).

Based on its annual cycle, Butler and Mao (1997) identified several possible seasons: one peak season, very characteristic of sun and sea destinations (which includes the Algarve); two peaks season, especially in mountain areas and winter sports; and, non-peak season, verifiable in many tropical and urban regions, with minimal fluctuations in terms of seasonality.

At this level, it is important to mention the very comprehensive investigation carried out by Dobruszkes, Decroly, and Suau-Sanchez (2022) in terms of seasonality of regular worldwide air services at the airport level. Based on a sample of 3,303 airports, the authors concluded that 2,111 airports are no-peak airports, given the stable pattern throughout the year. These are the airports that usually serve big cities, with significant business travel, and being less affected by seasonality than leisure tourism. The selection of the remaining 1,192 peak airports allowed to define a summer/winter profile and spring/autumn seasonal pattern profile, with the summer/winter profile being more pronounced than spring/autumn profile. At this level, the regions with the highest seasonality patterns are located in the Mediterranean region (summer peak) and in the Florida-Caribbean axis (winter peak).

Lim and McAleer (2001) also defined seasonal effects but based on quantifiable patterns. As long as the months have average indices greater than 1.0, this means an increase in the number of tourists above the normal pattern and an increase in cyclical seasonal trend. Regarding aviation, many of these investigations are based on the application of indexes – mostly the Gini index – as is the case of Reynolds-Feighan (2021), mentioned in Dobruszkes, Decroly, and Suau-Sanchez (2022), evaluating over a period of 12 months movements in air traffic and seasonality by business model (full service carrier / low cost carrier), by airport and urban area. Also Halpern (2011) used Gini indexes to investigate seasonal dynamics of passenger demand at airports in Spain and concluded that these dynamics are higher at airports that serve holiday destinations.

From the perspective of supply, seasonality can be described as a temporal imbalance, with a strong concentration on the use of equipment and activities of certain tourist products (López & López, 2006), leading to imbalances and inefficiencies with the overuse of infrastructures in certain periods, in contrast to its underutilization in other periods of less activity (Manning & Powers, 1984). These imbalances and inefficiencies are felt with greater urgency in periods of low season, given the lower demand and less use of resources and with direct economic effects on the exploration and results generated in companies in terms of their profitability and profits (Manning & Powers, 1984; Williams & Shaw, 1991).

Service companies with high fixed costs, such as hotels and tourism in general – as well as air transport and airport infrastructure – have direct economic effects on the weight average cost of capital and on the ability to finance the activity (Chung, 2009; Cooper et al., 2005; Mathieson & Wall, 1982). Many of the airlines operate at maximum capacity in times of higher demand and reduce their operating activity in periods of lower demand, as well as, some airports are extremely busy at some times of the year, but operate well below their capacity in other periods (Dobruszkes, Decroly, & Suau-Sanchez, 2022; Zou, Reynolds-Feighan, & Yu, 2022).

This inadequacy of capacity and its optimization represents additional problems for airports in terms of congestion, waiting times and the provision of lower quality services (Grbčić, Hess, Hess, and Krljan, 2021; Halpern, 2011). As mentioned by Grbčić, Hess, Hess, and Krljan (2021) seasonality is the major cause of under-capacity or overcapacity at smaller airports, in the same way as for De Neufville and Odoni (2003) the degree of seasonal concentration will be bigger in smaller airports and at airports serving holiday areas.

The socio-cultural impacts are also evident, with a concentration of tourists during the high season, causing enormous pressure on infrastructure, with congestion, overcrowded streets and equipment (museums and other attractions), queues, among other aspects (Allcock, 1989; Chung, 2009; Koenig-Lewis & Bischoff, 2005). In some destinations, even those of a tourist nature, this new reality – overtourism – begins to have negative reactions from local populations, due to the loss of identity of their neighborhoods due to the excess of visitors, pollution, overcrowding and overload of these territories, in terms of environmental impacts, and, as such, excessive use of infrastructure and degradation of its quality (Dodds & Butler, 2019; Jordan, Pastras & Psarros, 2018; Manning & Powers, 1984). Airports can also experience problems during their peak season, not only in terms of resource allocation, quality of service, congestion (air navigation or passengers), noise and air pollution (Halpern, 2011). With the return of commercial aviation to levels before COVID-19 pandemic, Frost (2003) foresee a "return to travel chaos", "as the aviation industry warns of overloaded airports, crowded skies and longer flight times".

Just as the causes of seasonality are diverse and complex, the impacts of seasonality also tend to be important in their different dimensions (Koenig-Lewis & Bischoff, 2005). If it is recognized that the concentration of means during the period of greater demand causes pressure in the territories and infrastructures, it is also known that in periods of lower demand many of the infrastructures may be closed and many of the services unavailable. A balance is necessary to guarantee the sustainability of the territories and their populations, in favor of a harmonious development of tourism and related territories.

In commercial aviation, balancing demand and capacity poses also a major challenge for airlines with significant seasonal markets and operations. The lack of demand means that airlines also have to adjust their resources in terms of airline capacity, particularly the fleet and employee needs. The limited flexibility within each seasonal cycle means that many airlines have to park a considerable part of their fleet during the off-season months (Zou, Reynolds-Feighan, & Yu, 2022).

According to Halpern (2011), when studying the seasonal concentration of passengers at the 48 Spanish airports operated by AENA (Aeropuertos Españoles y Navegación Aérea) concluded that seasonality is generally higher at airports that serve holiday regions (with the exception of the Canary Islands which tend to exhibit no-peak airport behavior). However, Halpern (2011) argues that country of origin may determine seasonal concentration with greater concentration during the summer of passengers from northern European countries travelling to southern/Mediterranean holiday areas in Europe, because travel may be particularly motivated by climate (sun).

Also Ashford, Stanton, and Moore (1997) suggest that charter airlines tend to have a higher level of seasonal concentration at an airport. Charter airlines only fly in periods of greater tourist demand/ holiday periods in opposition to regular models that tend to present a more stable operation providing year-round services. This same assumption is evidenced by Brilha (2008) in relation to the low cost airlines that came to contribute to a flatter demand curve at airports since scheduled low cost carriers provide a year-round service that are more predictable than the seasonal operation of charter carriers.

Kraft and Havlíková (2016) compare the number of flights in the months of February and June of 2014 operated from 10 of central Europe's airports - Vienna and Salzburg (Austria), Prague, Brno and Pardubice (Check Republic), Warsaw (Poland), Frankfurt-Hahn and Rostock-Laage (Germany), Bratislava (Slovakia), and Debrecen (Hungary). The researchers find three main profiles at the airport level from summer peak, winter peak and no seasonality pattern, although there is a lot of heterogeneity in the different airports, whether in terms of size, the range of flights offered by the airlines and the destinations operated. The research also led to the conclusion that smaller airports show a stronger specialization in selected destinations and/or specific segments of the customer market (e.g. charter flights), while other airports show a very strong presence of one or two airlines, traditionally low cost carriers.

Garrigos-Simon, Narangajavana, and Gil-Pechuan (2010) also evaluated the effects of seasonality on the Alicante-London route, based on observations of traffic and prices in April and August and concluded by the relevance of seasonality and competitiveness in the price strategies.

Zou, Reynolds-Feighan, and Yu (2022), based on research of 9 low cost carriers in the United States of America and Europe from 2004 to 2017, concluded that there was a pattern of greater seasonality in Europe representing lower fleet utilization or reducing seasonal traffic during low season periods. In turn, Wu, Liao, Zhang, Luo, and Zhang (2020) evaluated the networks of 5 low cost airlines in China during the period from 2008 to 2017 and concluded that these airline models are affected by seasonal variations, especially for the routes to tourism destinations. In the same way, in an analysis of monthly flights during 2018 in 222 airports in China, Wang, Xiao, Dobruszkes, and Wang (2023) found that seasonality is high in cities that are tourism destinations as well as in small airports serving remote places, mainly due to the country's vast territory.

There are several strategies that are used to deal with the effects of seasonality, whether at the level of destinations, tourism companies, as well as airlines and airports. As already mentioned in terms of airlines, these tend to operate at their maximum capacity in the high season, including additional capacity through leasing contracts, and to reduce their operations including aircraft parking or carrying out heavy maintenance programs during low season (Aviation Week, 2023; Zou, Reynolds-Feighan, & Yu, 2022). Alternatively, in scheduled models, the strategy can also involve extending seasonal operations to winter with a reduction in the number of flights operated and/or smaller capacity planes (Dobruszkes, Decroly, & Suau-Sanchez, 2022). On the airport side, the analysis of used capacity allows for better planning, design and adjustment of installed capacity in order to avoid additional investments and unnecessary costs (Grbčić, Hess, Hess, & Krljan, 2021).

From the tourist point of view, but with an impact on transport needs, Butler (2001) indicated the following approaches to mitigate seasonality: market diversification, differentiated prices and tax incentives, encourage domestic tourism in low seasons, greater distribution of vacations throughout the year, and focuses on off-season activities, such as festivals and conferences. Likewise, Weaver, and Lawton (2002) consider six strategies with the potential to mitigate seasonality, in terms of redistributing demand, reducing supply, reorganizing supply, restructuring supply, and containing demand in high season and its expansion to periods of lower demand, outside the high season. From a more comprehensive perspective, Farraró (2023) analyzed the evolution of seasonality at European level (EU-15 comprising Austria, Belgium, Denmark, Finland, Germany, Greece, Italy, Luxembourg, Netherlands, Portugal, Spain, Sweden and United Kingdom), between 2001 and 2017, concentrating on the most significant touristic countries. The author defined eight areas to analyze seasonality (capital areas, including Lisbon; Atlantic islands; Coastal Mediterranean areas; Mountain areas; business areas; Atlantic Coast, where Algarve is included; and, other areas). The utilization of Gini values per group of regions showed that "capital and business regions" (as is the case of Lisbon) report a "seasonality value lower than 0.2. This indicates that those areas receive tourists throughout the year, and they do not see any great differences between the low and peak seasons". In turn, Algarve located on the Atlantic coast and a common destinations for summer tourism displayed a seasonality rate of around 0.3, due to a high activity during the summer around the Atlantic coast (Farraró, 2023).

In this way, the different participants in the tourism and transport sector must know the characteristics of the destination and what tourists are looking for, so the strategies and/or actions to be implemented permit to mitigate and minimize the negative effects of seasonality.

FARO AIRPORT AND SEASONALITY

Faro airport opened in July 1965 and has been over the years, the main gateway to the Algarve region. On that day, the inaugural operation was carried out by a Douglas DC-3 plane from the General Directorate of Civil Aviation (DGAC) followed by a TAP flight from Lisbon with a Super Constellation plane, carrying 84 passengers (Viegas, 2015). In that inaugural year, 58,585 passengers were transported, and in 1970, its value already exceeded 336,800 passengers (Pordata, 2022; Viegas, 2015)

With the inauguration of the airport and the Ponte Salazar in Lisbon (currently called Ponte 25 de Abril) in 1966, the conditions were created for the growth of tourism in the Algarve. The 1960s "was the beginning of the tourism boom in the Algarve and the massive arrival of foreign tourists, mainly Europeans, to the country." (Martins, 2011, p. 49). The inauguration of Faro airport made it possible to integrate the Algarve into international tourist circuits and bring it closer to the centers that emit tourists, in particular the countries of Western Europe (Martins, 2011), with a development of urban spaces based on a territorial model of "Sun and Sea".

Being a tourist airport whose passengers use the structure looking for leisure (Sun and Sea), Faro airport also works as a gateway for tourists to the region, including Andalusia (Spain). According to Almeida (2009), this airport present a particular constraint due to the strong seasonality marked by peaks in demand in the summer months, and a decrease during the winter, implying a set of adaptations to the productive structure of the Algarve region. More recently Martín-Martín, Serdeira-Azevedo, Puertas-Medina and Guaita-Martínez (2023) carried out a comparative analysis of seasonality in the border destinations of the Algarve and Huelva, between 2015 and 2019, concluding that in both regions the seasonality of national tourism is greater than abroad, mainly in the Algarve. However, the analysis also shows that the seasonality of foreign markets, as well as hotel reservations, is more intense in the Spanish region rather than in the Algarve.

The strong vocation for tourist traffic has led the airport to follow the evolution of the different business models in commercial aviation. In 1990, with a total of 2,757,549 passengers carried, more than 80% of the traffic carried was on charter airlines (80.6%). In 1996, this value reached 86.3% of the total number of passengers processed at Faro airport, with 12.5% in traffic from traditional airlines. In that year, low cost airlines accounted for only 1.2% (Almeida, Ferreira & Costa, 2008; Pordata, 2022). However, in 2011, around 83% of all regular movements and around 87% of all passengers transported at Faro airport were already flights carried out by low cost carriers (INAC, 2012).

More recent data published quarterly by ANAC (Portuguese Civil Aviation Authority) show the consolidation of the weight of low cost carriers in the Algarve, with traditional airlines (TAP, British Airways and Lufthansa) representing cumulatively a market share of 11% (ANAC, 2023a). In 2019, Faro airport surpassed, for the first time, the threshold of 9 million passengers (9,010,860 passengers). The rapid post-pandemic recovery of traffic and tourism for the Algarve in 2023 permitted a record year with 9,640,270 passengers, representing a growth of 18% compared to the previous year and 7% when associated with 2019. All months of 2023 were above the values recorded monthly in 2019, with the last quarter of 2023 recording double-digit growth compared to that pre-pandemic year.

Faro airport was the third largest national airport in terms of passengers in 2023, led by Lisbon (33.6 million passengers) and Porto (15.2 million passengers) (ANA, 2024). Due to their city pattern, these two airports have lower levels of seasonality as business tourism, as a complement to leisure tourism, reduces the typical seasonality of the leisure tourism by prolonging the tourism season (Farraró, 2023; Pinho & Marques, 2021).

This strong tourist motivation, as mentioned above, also leads to a strong demand in the summer and a reduced demand in the winter months, as mentioned by Almeida (2009).

The monthly evolution of traffic between 2017 and 2023 shows a very similar pattern over the years. The years 2020 and 2021 show the effects resulting from the pandemic, with values distorting the seasonal figures displayed in the remaining years. Figures can be found in Annex 1.

The figure above shows a typical pattern of a leisure destination, with greater demand in the summer months and lower levels of passengers in the winter months.

Figure 1. Seasonality in Faro airport (2017-2023): Passengers
Source: Own elaboration based on ANAC (2023b)

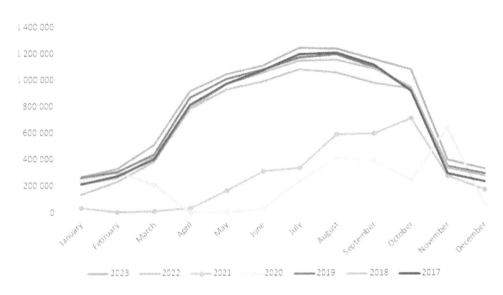

This same behavior is evidenced by the number of non-residents tourists in the Algarve for the same period (2017-2023). The correlation between the number of passengers processed at Faro airport and the number of non-resident tourists in the Algarve, between 2017 and 2022, stands at 98.07%. Information for 2023 only shows a correlation coefficient of 99.63%, showing a global correlation of 98.33% between 2017 and 2023. Information regarding non-resident tourists can be found in Annex 2.

METHODOLOGY

Seasonality, as assessed during the theoretical context and in its characterization and framework in relation to Faro airport, is a phenomenon that affects the tourism and transport value chain, whether in terms of markets, destinations, means of transport and airport infrastructure, accommodation, among others.

In order to better understand this phenomenon, the present investigation focuses on Faro airport, whose main objective will be to understand how the airlines that operate to this airport plan their activity in order to satisfy the increase in demand in the summer months.

The study was based on the collection of information on the ANA – Aeroportos de Portugal website, on the number of flights departed from Faro airport during a week, including a low season period (February) and a high season period (August). The information will take into account flights departing from the airport regardless of aircraft capacity and potential commercial agreements established between airlines. Data were collected between 6th and 12th of February (low season) and between 7th and 13th of August (high season).

In methodological terms, the analysis will be exploratory, descriptive, and qualitative although based on quantitative elements, taking into account the airlines and their operations and the respective number of flights, the origin of the traffic (by airport), and respective comparison in these two moments of observation.

Comparative analysis is the process to determine and quantify relationships of observing and comparing similarities and differences of outcomes items to one another (Bukhari, 2011; Drobnič, 2014; Indeed, 2021). Comparative analysis makes it possible to compare several items trying to find similarity and variance among them and identify common points and differences that help to give a better explanation of the phenomena under study. As mentioned by Azarian (2011, p. 117) "it enables us to see better the implicit and often taken-for-granted basis of our own practices and phenomena".

Methods of comparison can be qualitative or quantitative (Bolbakov, Sinitsyn, & Tsvetkov, 2020), and in the present investigation qualitative analysis will be privileged even if based on quantitative data. This comparison will make it possible to assess the existing differences in these two moments of observation at Faro airport, regarding the airlines, the number of flights operated and the destinations served.

According to Pickvance (2001) there are several reasons for the use of comparative analysis such as: a) To explore a theoretically postulated relationship; b) To examine whether a relationship reported in a study in one society also holds in another; c) To examine whether a condition which is given or fixed for one society is influential or not; d) To examine a small number of empirical cases holistically to grasp the causal processes leading to observed similarities and differences.

The comparative analysis will focus as mentioned on the number of airports served and the number of flights operated to these destinations, in February and in August, to understand if there were significant changes in the number of flights operated by airline between these two periods, as well as in terms of potential new destinations and new airlines.

ANALYSIS AND RESULTS

The information collected during a week in February and August 2023, as previously mentioned, allows validating the strong impact of seasonality in the Algarve region measured through the number of flights departing from Faro airport.

The main conclusions are summarized below, whose detailed information by airport and airline can be found in Annex 3:

- In February 2023, the number of flights operated during that week reached 294 flights (from 55 airports), a value that rose to 846 flights operated from 83 airports during the week in August, almost tripling (2.88 times) the movement at Faro airport.
- Low cost airlines dominate the commercial operation for Faro airport, being reduced to the presence of traditional airlines. Charter flights have almost disappeared.
- The main market in February was London Gatwick (36 flights), followed by Lisbon (22) and Paris Orly (14 flights). In turn, in August London Gatwick remained the main issuer (71 flights), with Dublin (53) and Manchester (39 flights) the following markets, respectively.
- Dublin was the fastest growing market in absolute value with +41 flights in August 2023. London Gatwick (+35 flights) and Manchester (+26 flights) were the next markets with the highest growth in the number of flights.
- 31 new destinations were operated in August, with 3 markets (Gothenburg and Helsinki in the Nordics and Paderborn in Germany) no longer being operated in summer. These destinations were operated with a weekly flight during the low season. Of the new destinations, the East Midlands

stand out with 24 weekly flights, followed by Geneva and London Gatwick with 14 weekly flights each.

- Only 5 airports maintained their operations during the two observation periods, 3 of which were operated by Ryanair. In terms of countries, Germany (Frankfurt-Hahn and Nuremberg, operated by Ryanair and Hannover by Tui Fly) and the United Kingdom (Cardiff by Ryanair) were the European markets that maintained the operation. Also the long haul operation to Canada (Toronto) operated by Air Transat maintains a weekly flight throughout the year.

- In February, five destinations were operated based on a weekly operation, a figure that increased to eight in August. Only the Air Transat operation remained with a weekly flight in the two observation periods, representing 7 new summer destinations, even if with a weekly flight only.

- The main outbound market for the Algarve was the United Kingdom with 26 airports, followed by Germany (15 airports) and France (10 airports). London is the city with the largest number of airports, and in August it had flights from all its airports (City, Gatwick, Heathrow, Luton, Southend, and Stansted).

- Globally, Faro airport received flights from 19 countries (all European with the exception of the Air Transat flight from Canada).

- Domestic operations can be resumed to flights from TAP (to/from Lisbon to feed its hub) and from Porto with Ryanair flights. The Air Transat flight in winter allows the airline to benefit from cabotage rights (eighth freedom of the air) between Lisbon and Faro.

- Ryanair is the main airline in the Algarve market, followed by easyJet. In February Ryanair operated 79 flights to 28 airports, with easyJet operating 64 flights to 13 airports. In August Ryanair increased its presence with 270 flights operated during a week to 47 airports, while easyJet increased its operation to 161 weekly flights to 21 airports.

- While Ryanair favors a more diversified network of flights (in February, 21 of the 28 airports operated with two weekly flights), easyJet invests on a more densified network (only 3 of the 13 airports operated with two weekly flights). In August, Ryanair reinforced some of its traditional destinations but maintained, even so, 15 destinations based on two weekly flights while easyJet operated only 3 airports with two weekly flights.

- The main focus of both companies is on the London market. easyJet operated 24 flights in winter - 17 from Gatwick and 7 from Luton - while Ryanair operated 16 flights to/from Stansted (11 flights) and Luton (5 flights). In the high season, easyJet substantially expanded its operation in London with 65 weekly flights (representing more than 40% of the airline's network to Faro airport), especially to/from Gatwick (42 flights), Luton (21 flights) and Southend (2 weekly flights). Ryanair operated 28 flights with an increased presence at Stansted (23 flights) but maintaining the same operation at Luton (5 flights).

The biggest operational activity in August at Faro airport led to an increase in tourism in the region, as the statistics shown, as well as the correlation coefficient between flights operated and foreign tourists to the region.

CONCLUSION

As mentioned by Dobruszkes, Decroly, and Suau-Sanchez (2022, p. 15) "Seasonality in aviation has significant impacts on the efficient use of airport capacity and capital. Seasonality creates problems in terms of capital funding and the recovery of costs, as well as excessive costs during off-peak periods and problems of supply and level of service during peak periods".

However, it is these "problems" that allow leisure destinations to continue to grow and receive more tourists throughout the year. The effects of the COVID-19 pandemic had a devastating effect on the service sectors, in particular aviation and tourism, in addition to airports, to which the Algarve and Faro airport were no exception. However, 2023 showed a strong recovery in air traffic with values above the records obtained in 2019, with more than 9.64 million passengers in Faro.

The results obtained clearly show the effects of seasonality in the region, with an increase in tourist activity in the summer and sunny months. Dependence on the English market is evident and is still very present in the Algarve, despite the many efforts on market diversification. In this way, the Algarve, as a mature Sun and Sea destination, with over fifty years of experience in tourism, also had to reinvent itself in ways that not only bring tourists closer to its beaches, nightlife and consumption (Martins, 2015). Investments in golf, events, meetings and incentives, sport fishing, among others, are the way to tourist diversification and that allow the region to minimize and mitigate seasonal effects.

The present investigation has some limitations. To have only two periods of operation (one in low season and another in high season) may not incorporate all the market effects, either in airports or in its tourist effects. It was also decided to carry out the analysis based only on flights departing from Faro airport, but the operation on short haul flights in Europe and operated mainly by low cost carriers are based on point to point and round trip flights. On the other hand, the identification of the aircraft capacity would help to give more knowledge of the potential volumes of traffic to/from the inbound markets. It is true that the correlations obtained between passengers carried in flights operated at the airport and foreign tourists to the Algarve show high values and highlight the strong robustness of the data correlated.

The present investigation is expected to have made a contribution to the assessment of the seasonality and dependence of tourism on certain markets, with the risks that are inherent to it in the event of fluctuations in those of these inbound markets. This research could also be applied to other national airports with a strong tourist attraction, so that seasonality can be studied and compared and that possible actions can be implemented to reduce its effect in times of lower demand. Despite the aforementioned limitations, an analysis of the different aviation business models and what measures could be taken regionally, including tourism authorities and tourism sector associations, to mitigate the effects of seasonality itself, should be addressed. No less important, what impacts will climate change and drought have on the region and what impacts in seasonality patterns and in tourism flows and incoming markets in the near future? According to the report "Regional impact of climate change on European tourism demand" (Matei et al., 2023, p. 4) "Seasonality patterns are also expected to undergo substantial changes, with varying impacts across regions. (…) Southern coastal regions are projected to lose significant amounts of summer tourists (-10%) compared to the present, particularly in warmer climate scenarios (3°C and 4°C). In these regions, the decline in summer demand is partially offset by increases in spring, autumn, and winter.". This new challenge will certainly deserve future monitoring and follow-up to avoid significant losses in the region.

REFERENCES

Allcock, J. (1989). Seasonality. In S. Witt & L. Moutinho (Eds.), *Tourism Marketing and Management Handbook* (pp. 387–392). Prentice Hall.

Almeida, C. (2009). *Aeroportos e turismo residencial: do conhecimento às estratégias* [Airports and residential tourism: from knowledge to strategies]. Tese de Doutoramento [PhD Thesis], Departamento de Economia, Gestão e Engenharia Industrial, Universidade de Aveiro, Portugal.

Almeida, C., Ferreira, A. M., & Costa, C. (2008). A importância das companhias aéreas de baixo custo no desenvolvimento de segmentos de mercado turístico: O caso do turismo residencial no Algarve [The importance of low-cost airlines in the development of tourism market segments: The case of residential tourism in the Algarve]. *Revista Portuguesa de Estudos Regionais*, *19*(19), 7–21. doi:10.59072/rper.vi19.261

ANA. (2024). *Vinci Airports – Tráfego até 31 de Dezembro de 2023 [Vinci Airports – Traffic until December 31, 2023].* ANA – Aeroportos de Portugal. https://pt.newsroom.ana.pt/assets/vinci-airports-trafego-2023-3595-4a6c7.html

ANAC. (2023a). *Boletim Estatístico Trimestral nº 56* [Quarterly Statistical Bulletin nº 56]. Autoridade Nacional de Aviação Civil. https://www.anac.pt/SiteCollectionDocuments/Publicacoes/BET/BET_56_4TRIM_22.pdf

ANAC. (2023b). *Newsletters de tráfego* [Traffic Newsletters]. Autoridade Nacional de Aviação Civil. https://www.anac.pt/vPT/Generico/PublicacoesINAC/newslettersdetrafego/Paginas/NewslettersdeTrafego.aspx

Andriotis, K. (2005). Seasonality in Crete: Problem or a way of life? *Tourism Economics*, *11*(2), 207–224. doi:10.5367/0000000054183478

Ashford, N., Stanton, H. P. M., & Moore, C. A. (1997). *Airport operations* (2nd ed.). McGraw-Hill.

Aviation Week. (2023, April 27th). *Air Serbia To Increase Fleet By Half For Summer Season*. Aviationweek.com. https://aviationweek.com/air-transport/airlines-lessors/air-serbia-increase-fleet-half-summer-season

Azarian, R. (2011). Potentials and Limitations of Comparative Method in Social Science. *International Journal of Humanities and Social Science*, *1*(4), 113–125.

BarOn, R. (1972). Seasonality in tourism – part I. *International Tourism Quarterly*, *4*, 40–64.

BarOn, R. (1973). Seasonality in tourism – part II. *International Tourism Quarterly*, *1*, 51–67.

BarOn. R. (1975). Seasonality in tourism: a guide to the analysis of seasonality and trends for policy making. Economist Intelligence Unit.

Black, J. (1992). *The British Abroad: The Grand Tour in the Eighteenth Century*. St. Martin's Press.

Bolbakov, R. G., Sinitsyn, A. V., & Tsvetkov, V. Ya. (2020). Methods of comparative analysis. *Journal of Physics: Conference Series*, *1679*(5), 052047. doi:10.1088/1742-6596/1679/5/052047

Brilha, N. (2008). Airport requirements for leisure travelers. In A. Graham, A. Papatheodorou, & P. Forsyth (Eds.), *Aviation and Tourism: Implications for the Leisure Travel* (pp. 167–176). Ashgate Publishing Limited.

BukhariS. (2011). What is Comparative Study?. SSRN. doi:10.2139/ssrn.1962328

Butler, R. (1994). Seasonality in Tourism: Issues and Problems. In A. Seaton (Ed.), *Tourism: The state of Art* (pp. 332–339). John Wiley & Sons, Ltd.

Butler, R. (2001). Seasonality in Tourism: Issues and Implications. In T. Baum & S. Lundtorp (Eds.), *Seasonality in Tourism* (pp. 5–23). Pergamon. doi:10.1016/B978-0-08-043674-6.50005-2

Butler, R. (2014). *Addressing Seasonality in Tourism: The Development of a Prototype – Conclusions and Recommendations resulting from the Punta del Este Conference*. World Tourism Organization.

Butler, R., & Mao, B. (1997). Seasonality in tourism: problems and measurement. In P. E. Murphy (Ed.), *Quality management in urban tourism* (pp. 9–24). John Wiley & Sons, Ltd.

Cannas, R. (2012). An Overview of Tourism Seasonality: Key Concepts and Policies. *Alma Tourism - Journal of Tourism. Culture and Territorial Development*, 5, 40–58.

Chung, J. Y. (2009). Seasonality in Tourism: A Review. *e-Review of Tourism Research, 7*(5), 82-96.

Cooper, C., Fletcher, J., Fyall, A., Gilbert, D., & Wanhill, S. (2005). *Tourism Principles and Practice* (3rd ed.). Pearson Education.

Corluka, G. (2019). Tourism Seasonality – An overview. *Journal of Business Paradigms, 4*(1), 21–43.

Cunha, L. (2009). *Introdução ao turismo* [Introduction to tourism] 4th ed.). Editorial Verbo.

De Neufville, R., & Odoni, A. R. (2003). Airport systems: Planning. McGraw-Hill.

Dobruszkes, F., Decroly, J.-M., & Suau-Sanchez, P. (2022). The monthly rhythms of aviation: A global analysis of passenger air service seasonality. *Transportation Research Interdisciplinary Perspectives, 14*, 100582. doi:10.1016/j.trip.2022.100582

Dodds, R., & Butler, R. (2019). The phenomena of overtourism: A review. *International Journal of Tourism Cities, 5*(4), 519–528. doi:10.1108/IJTC-06-2019-0090

Drobnič, S. (2014). Comparative Analysis. In A. C. Michalos (Ed.), *Encyclopedia of Quality of Life and Well-Being Research*. Springer., doi:10.1007/978-94-007-0753-5_492

Farraró, A. V. (2023). *Tourism Issues: Seasonality and Economic Structure*. [Doctoral Thesis], Faculty of Geography and Tourism, Department of Geography, Universitat Rovira i Virgili, Vilaseca, Tarragona, Spain.

Ferrante, M., Lo Magno, G., & De Cantis, S. (2018). Measuring tourism seasonality across European countries. *Tourism Management, 68*(1), 220–235. doi:10.1016/j.tourman.2018.03.015

Frost, R. (2023, 5th July). Return to travel chaos? Air passengers warned they could face a 'challenging' summer. *Euronews.com*. https://www.euronews.com/travel/2023/07/05/return-to-travel-chaos-air-passengers-warned-they-could-face-a-challenging-summer

Garrigos-Simon, F., Narangajavana, Y., & Gil-Pechuan, I. (2010). Seasonality and price behaviour of airlines in the Alicante-London market. *Journal of Air Transport Management, 16*(6), 350–354. doi:10.1016/j.jairtraman.2010.05.007

Grbčić, A., Hess, S., Hess, M., & Krljan, T. (2021). The impact of seasonality on efficient airport capacity utilization. *Scientific Journal of Maritime Research, 35*(2), 215–223. doi:10.31217/p.35.2.3

Halpern, N. (2011). Measuring seasonal demand for Spanish airports: Implications for counter-seasonal strategies. *Research in Transportation Business & Management, 1*(1), 47–54. doi:10.1016/j.rtbm.2011.05.005

Hinch, T., & Hickey, G. (1996). Tourism attractions and seasonality: spatial relationships in Alberta. In K. Mackay & K. Boyd (Eds.), *Tourism for All Seasons: Using Research to Meet the Challenge of Seasonality* (pp. 69–76). University of Manitoba.

Hylleberg, S. (1992). *Modelling Seasonality*. Oxford University Press. doi:10.1093/oso/9780198773177.001.0001

INAC. (2012). *Impacto das Transportadoras de Baixo Custo no Transporte Aéreo Nacional* [Impact of Low-Cost Carriers on National Air Transport]. Instituto Nacional de Aviação Civil.

Indeed (2021). *What Is Comparative Analysis and How Is It Used?* Indeed. https://www.indeed.com/career-advice/career-development/comparative-analysis

INE. (2023). *Hóspedes não residentes nos estabelecimentos de alojamento turístico, segundo a NUTS II* [Non-resident guests in tourist accommodation establishments, according to NUTS II]. Instituto Nacional de Estatística.

Jordan, P., Pastras, P., & Psarros, M. (2018). *Managing Tourism Growth in Europe: The ECM toolbox.* European Cities Marketing & Toposophy.

Koenig-Lewis, N., & Bischoff, E. (2005). Seasonality research: The state of the art. *International Journal of Tourism Research, 7*(4-5), 201–219. doi:10.1002/jtr.531

Kraft, S., & Havlíková, D. (2016). Anytime? Anywhere? The seasonality of flight offers in Central Europe. *Moravian Geographical Reports, 24*(4), 26–37. doi:10.1515/mgr-2016-0020

Lim, C., & McAleer, M. (2001). Monthly seasonal variations – Asian tourism to Australia. *Annals of Tourism Research, 28*(1), 68–82. doi:10.1016/S0160-7383(00)00002-5

López, J., & López, L. (2006). La concentración estacional en las regiones españolas desde una perspectiva de la oferta turística [The seasonal concentration in the Spanish regions from a perspective of the tourist offer]. *Revista de Estudios Regionales, 3*(1), 77–104.

Manning, R., & Powers, L. (1984). Peak and off-peak use: Redistributing the outdoor recreation/tourism load. *Journal of Travel Research, 23*(2), 25–31. doi:10.1177/004728758402300204

Martín-Martín, J. M., Serdeira-Azevedo, P., Puertas-Medina, R. M., & Guaita-Martínez, J. M. (2023). Análisis comparativo de la estacionalidad turística en dos destinos fronterizos: Algarve (Portugal) – Huelva (España) [Comparative analysis of tourist seasonality in two border destinations: Algarve (Portugal) – Huelva (Spain)]. *Journal of Tourism Analysis*, *30*(2), 26–50. doi:10.53596/r0y74q81

Martins, J. (2015). *Algarve, da Urbanização Turística à Metropolização Sazonal 1960/2013 [Algarve, from Tourist Urbanization to Seasonal Metropolization 1960/2013]*. [PhD Thesis in Sociology], Faculdade de Ciências Sociais e Humanas, Universidade Nova de Lisboa, Portugal.

Martins, P. (2011). *Contibutos para uma história do ir à praia em Portugal [Contributions to a history of going to the beach in Portugal]*. [Master Dissertation, Faculdade de Ciências Sociais e Humanas, Universidade Nova de Lisboa].

Matei, N., Garcia Leon, D., Dosio, A., Batista e Silva, F., Ribeiro Barranco, R., & Ciscar Martinez, J. C. (2023). *Regional impact of climate change on European tourism demand*. Publications Office of the European Union.

Mathieson, A., & Wall, G. (1982). *Tourism, Economic, Physical and Social Impacts*. Longmann.

Merkert, R., & Webber, T. (2018). How to manage seasonality in service industries – The case of price and seat factor management in airlines. *Journal of Air Transport Management*, *72*, 39–46. doi:10.1016/j.jairtraman.2018.07.005

Pickvance, C. G. (2001). Four varieties of comparative analysis. *Journal of Housing and the Built Environment*, *16*(1), 7–28. doi:10.1023/A:1011533211521

Pinho, M., & Marques, J. (2021). Business tourism in Porto: An empirical investigation of its potentialities and development challenges. *International Journal of Tourism Cities*, *7*(1), 1–12. doi:10.1108/IJTC-05-2019-0071

Pordata (2022). *Tráfego de passageiros nos principais aeroportos: Lisboa, Porto e Faro. [Passenger traffic at the main airports: Lisbon, Porto and Faro]*. Pordata. https://www.pordata.pt/portugal/trafego+de+passageiros+nos+principais+aeroportos+lisboa++porto+e+faro-3248

Rabotić, B. (2014). Special-Purpose Travel in Ancient Times: "Tourism" before Tourism? In M. Skakun (ed.), *Proceedings Book of the 2nd Belgrade International Tourism Conference (BITCO 2014): Thematic Tourism in a Global Environment: Advantages, Challenges and Future Developments* (pp. 99-114). Belgrade: College of Tourism.

Reilly, B. (2021). Seasons in Italy: Northern European travelers, Rome, and malaria. *Journal of Tourism and Cultural Change*, *19*(1), 59–78. doi:10.1080/14766825.2019.1693582

Rosselló, J., & Sansó, A. (2017). Yearly, monthly and weekly seasonality of tourism demand: A decomposition analysis. *Tourism Management*, *60*, 379–389. doi:10.1016/j.tourman.2016.12.019

Sánchez, J. G. (2021, November). Roma de Férias – os turistas da antiguidade [Rome on Holiday – tourists from ancient times]. *National Geographic História*, *1*(1), 57–69.

Suau-Sanchez, P., & Voltes-Dorta, A. (2019). Drivers of airport scheduled traffic in European winter tourism areas: Infrastructure, accessibility, competition and catchment area. *Journal of Air Transport Management*, *81*, 101723. doi:10.1016/j.jairtraman.2019.101723

Viegas, D. (2015). Aeroporto de Faro foi inaugurado há 50 anos [Faro Airport was opened 50 years ago]. *Jornal do Algarve*. https://jornaldoalgarve.pt/aeroporto-de-faro-foi-inaugurado-ha-50-anos-2/

Wang, J., Xiao, F., Dobruszkes, F., & Wang, W. (2023). Seasonality of flights in China: Spatial heterogeneity and its determinants. *Journal of Air Transport Management*, *108*, 102354. doi:10.1016/j.jairtraman.2022.102354

Weaver, D., & Lawton, L. (2002). *Tourism Management* (2nd ed.). John Wiley & Sons, Ltd.

Williams, A. M., & Shaw, G. (1991). *Tourism and Economic Development. Western European Experiences* (2nd ed.). John Wiley & Sons, Ltd.

Witt, S. F., & Moutinho, L. (1995). *Tourism Marketing and Management Handbook*. Prentice Hall.

Wu, C., Liao, M., Zhang, Y., Luo, M., & Zhang, G. (2020). Network development of low-cost carriers in China's domestic market. *Journal of Transport Geography*, *84*, 102670. doi:10.1016/j.jtrangeo.2020.102670

Zou, L., Reynolds-Feighan, A., & Yu, C. (2022). Airline seasonality: An explorative analysis of major low-cost carriers in Europe and the United States. *Journal of Air Transport Management*, *105*, 102272. doi:10.1016/j.jairtraman.2022.102272

APPENDIX

Appendix One

Figure 2. Number of passengers at Faro Airport (2017 – 2023)
(Source: Own elaboration based on ANAC (2023b)

Months/Years	2023	2022	2021	2020	2019	2018	2017	Var. 23/22	Var 23/19
January	269 179	141 120	33 827	240 990	264 617	217 011	218 594	90,74%	1,72%
February	329 568	235 113	8 612	307 458	306 634	263 064	278 196	40,17%	7,48%
March	511 709	385 673	12 583	213 879	442 476	422 823	405 271	32,68%	15,65%
April	917 375	787 040	37 534	408	869 806	789 978	813 037	16,56%	5,47%
May	1 044 046	927 477	167 928	1 043	1 009 788	971 170	970 910	12,57%	3,39%
June	1 109 033	989 107	313 032	35 130	1 080 814	1 057 629	1 073 802	12,12%	2,61%
July	1 242 881	1 084 247	339 441	239 821	1 172 139	1 147 594	1 194 006	14,63%	6,04%
August	1 236 946	1 058 311	589 542	410 759	1 193 256	1 156 244	1 207 310	16,88%	3,66%
September	1 161 930	981 179	595 644	383 795	1 099 475	1 089 793	1 115 196	18,42%	5,68%
October	1 083 360	937 033	715 162	244 577	929 684	951 314	919 051	15,62%	16,53%
November	401 428	345 864	279 047	641 325	347 944	339 535	293 133	16,07%	15,37%
December	332 815	298 551	173 302	66 091	294 227	278 746	234 153	11,48%	13,12%
Total	9 640 270	8 170 715	3 265 654	2 785 276	9 010 860	8 684 901	8 722 659	17,99%	6,99%

Appendix Two

Figure 3. Non-resident guests in tourist accommodation establishments (2017 – 2023)
(Source: Own elaboration based on INE (2023))

Months/Years	2023	2022	2021	2020	2019	2018	2017	Var. 23/22	Var 23/19
January	99 010	50 620	10 975	96 172	91 790	78 638	79 343	95,59%	7,87%
February	138 056	101 728	4 251	145 363	131 273	114 166	118 310	35,71%	5,17%
March	215 501	161 904	4 679	79 647	197 018	199 669	171 898	33,10%	9,38%
April	369 648	314 833	12 921	893	337 269	296 377	322 636	17,41%	9,60%
May	409 356	381 307	79 596	1 719	412 944	387 858	374 502	7,36%	-0,87%
June	411 153	387 693	137 248	12 864	416 265	392 010	388 355	6,05%	-1,23%
July	452 329	444 197	135 009	91 359	455 550	431 557	422 283	1,83%	-0,71%
August	469 569	434 838	244 088	182 160	484 068	449 029	430 886	7,99%	-3,00%
September	441 548	399 813	244 124	161 635	445 689	428 838	412 160	10,44%	-0,93%
October	417 912	370 415	281 758	108 532	372 723	363 079	350 192	12,82%	12,12%
November	163 118	137 850	115 371	24 586	142 874	131 639	119 665	18,33%	14,17%
December	114 670	95 704	59 675	19 508	104 978	96 292	83 758	19,82%	9,23%
Total	3 701 870	3 280 902	1 329 695	924 438	3 592 441	3 369 152	3 273 988	12,83%	3,05%

Appendix Three

Figure 4. Flights operated from Faro Airport – February and August 2023
(Source: Own elaboration based on ANA – Aeroportos de Portugal website flight information)

Airport	Country	Flights in February 2023 by airline	Number of weekly flights	Flights in August 2023 by airline	Number of weekly flights
Aarhus	Danmark			Ryanair (2)	2
Aberdeen	UK			Ryanair (2)	2
Amsterdam	Netherlands	Transavia (10), easyJet (2)	12	Transavia (18), easyJet (3)	21
Barcelona	Spain	Vueling (1)	1	Vueling (3), easyJet (2), Ryanair (2)	7
Basel	Switzerland	easyJet (4)	4	easyJet (7)	7
Belfast	UK	easyJet (3)	3	easyJet (14), Jet 2 (4), Ryanair (4)	22
Berlin Brandenburg	Germany	Ryanair (2)	2	Ryanair (5), easyjet (3)	8
Bilbao	Spain			Volotea (2), Vueling (2)	4
Billund	Danmark			Jettime (1)	1
Birmingham	UK	Jet 2 (4), Ryanair (3)	7	Jet 2 (10), Ryanair (10), easyJet (2), Tui Airways (2)	24
Bordeaux	France	Ryanair (2)	2	easyJet (4), Ryanair (4)	8
Bournemouth	UK	Ryanair (2)	2	Ryanair (5)	5
Bristol	UK	easyJet (9), Jet 2 (2), Ryanair (2)	13	easyJet (18), Jet 2 (6), Ryanair (6)	30
Brussels	Belgium	Brussels Airlines (2), Transavia (2)	4	Brussels Airlines (7), Transavia (6), Tui Belgium (3)	16
Brussels Charleroi	Belgium	Ryanair (3)	3	Ryanair (11)	11
Cardiff	UK	Ryanair (2)	2	Ryanair (2)	2
Cologne-Bohn	Germany	Eurowings (2)	2	Ryanair (4), Eurowings (3)	7
Copenhaguen	Danmark			Norwegian Air (2), Ryanair (2), SAS (1)	5
Cork	Ireland	Ryanair (2)	2	Ryanair (8), Aer Lingus (6)	14
Dublin	Ireland	Rynair (10), Aer Lingus (2)	12	Ryanair (29), Aer Lingus (24)	53
Durham Tees Valley (Teeside)	UK			Ryanair (2)	2
Dusseldorf	Germany	Eurowings (4), Tui Fly (2)	6	Eurowings (7), Condor (3), Tui Fly (2)	12
Dusseldorf Weeze	Germany	Ryanair (2)	2	Ryanair (3)	3
East Midlands (Nottingham)	UK			Ryanair (13), Jet 2 (8), Tui Airways (3)	24
Edimburg	UK	Jet 2 (2), Ryanair (2)	4	Ryanair (7), Jet 2 (4)	11
Eindhoven	Netherlands	Transavia (7), Ryanair (4)	11	Transavia (8), Ryanair (7)	15
Exeter	UK			Ryanair (2)	2
Frankfurt	Germany	Lufthansa (3), Tui Fly (2)	5	Lufthansa (10), Condor (3), Tui Fly (2)	15
Frankfurt Hahn	Germany	Ryanair (2)	2	Ryanair (2)	2
Geneva	Switzerland			easyJet (11), Swiss (3)	14
Glasgow International	UK	easyJet (3)	3	easyJet (5), Jet 2 (4)	9
Glasgow Prestwick	UK			Ryanair (5)	5
Gothenburg	Sweden	SAS (1)	1		
Hamburg	Germany	Eurowings (3)	3	Eurowings (5), Marabu (3)	8
Hannover	Germany	Tui Fly (2)	2	Tui Fly (2)	2
Helsinki	Finland	Jettime (1)	1		
Jersey	UK			British Airways (1)	1
Karlsruhe	Germany	Ryanair (2)	2	Ryanair (3)	3
Katowice	Poland			Enter Air (1), LOT (1)	2
Kerry County	UK			Ryanair (2)	2
Knock	Ireland			Ryanair (3)	3
Leeds	UK	Jet 2 (4), Ryanair (2)	6	Jet 2 (13), Ryanair (4)	17
Leipzig	Germany			Condor (1)	1
Lille	France			Volotea (2)	2
Lisbon	Portugal	TAP (20), Air Transat (1), Transavia (1)	22	TAP (28)	28
Liverpool	UK	easyJet (2), Ryanair (2)	4	easyJet (16), Ryanair (3)	19
London City	UK			British Airways (5)	5
London Gatwick	UK	easyJet (17), British Airways (14), Wizz Air (UK) (5)	36	easyJet (42), British Airways (16), Wizz Air (UK) (11), Tui Airways (2)	71
London Heathrow	UK			British Airways (14)	14
London Luton	UK	easyJet (7), Ryanair (5)	12	easyJet (21), Ryanair (5)	26
London Southend	UK			easyJet (2)	2
London Stansted	UK	Ryanair (11), Jet 2 (2)	13	Ryanair (23), Jet 2 (12)	35
Luxemburg	Luxemburg	Luxair (3), Ryanair (2)	5	Luxair (5), Ryanair (2)	7
Lyon	France	easyJet (3)	3	easyJet (3), Transavia (2), Volotea (2)	7
Madrid	Spain	Ryanair (2)	2	Iberia (7), Ryanair (6)	13
Manchester	UK	Jet 2 (5), Ryanair (5), easyJet (3)	13	Ryanair (18), Jet 2 (11), easyJet (7), TUI Airways (3)	39
Marseille	France	Ryanair (2)	2	Ryanair (5)	5
Memmingen	Germany	Ryanair (2)	2	Ryanair (3)	3
Milan Bergamo	Itlay	Ryanair (2)	2	Ryanair (7)	7
Milan Malpensa	Italy			easyJet (1)	1
Munich	Germany	Lufthansa (2)	2	Lufthansa (7), Marabu (3)	10
Nantes	France	Transavia (3), easyJet (2)	5	easyJet (4), Volotea (3), Transavia (2)	9
Newcastle	UK	Jet 2 (2), Ryanair (2)	4	Jet 2 (9), Ryanair (3)	12
Newquay	UK			Ryanair (3)	3
Nuremberg	Germany	Ryanair (2)	2	Ryanair (2)	2
Oslo	Norway	Norwegian Air (1)	1	Norwegian Air (4), SAS (2)	6
Paderborn	Germany	Eurowings (1)	1		
Paris Beauvais	France	Ryanair (2)	2	Ryanair (5)	5
Paris Charles de Gaulle	France	easyJet (5)	5	Air France (4), easyJet (3), ASL Air (1)	7
Paris Orly	France	Transavia (10), easyJet (4)	14	Transavia (21), easyJet (7)	28
Porto	Portugal	Ryanair (6)	6	Ryanair (21)	21
Prague	Check Republic			Smartwings (1)	1
Rome Fiumicino	Italy			Ryanair (2)	2
Rotterdam	Netherlands	Transavia (7)	7	Transavia (13)	13
Shannon	Ireland			Ryanair (4)	4
Southampton	UK			British Airways (1)	1
Stockholm	Sweden	Norwegian Air (1), SAS (1)	2	Eurowings (2), Norwegian Air (2), SAS (2)	6
Strasbourg	France			Volotea (1)	1
Stuttgard	Germany	Eurowings (2), Tui Fly (1)	3	Eurowings (5), Tui Fly (2)	7
Toronto	Canada	Air Transat (1)	1	Air Transat (1)	1
Toulouse	France			easyJet (2), Ryanair (2), Volotea (2)	6
Valencia	Spain			Ryanair (2)	2
Vienna	Austria	Ryanair (2)	2	Ryanair (3)	3
Warsaw	Poland			LOT (2), Smartwings Poland (1)	3
Warsaw Modlin	Poland			Ryanair (2)	2
Zurich	Switzerland			Edelweiss (4)	4

Chapter 14
Future of Humanity:
New Era Space Economy

Fırat Cem Doğan

https://orcid.org/0000-0002-2398-1484
Hasan Kalyoncu University, Turkey

Mehmet Hanifi Aslan
Hasan Kalyoncu University, Turkey

ABSTRACT

The study aims to reveal the possible economic, social, and technological consequences of these activities and make projections and evaluations regarding the space economy for the future of humanity. It also aims to create a futuristic perspective on what space could bring to humanity, which has been a subject of great curiosity. Within this study, space and space economy will also be evaluated in terms of addressing the problems that may arise from the depletion of natural resources on Earth in the future. The study examines the space activities of both the public sector and private enterprises in various countries using numerical data. For example, the budget of the (NASA) of the United States alone reached $57.69 billion in 2022, more than two and a half times the amount in 2009. It is estimated that the size of the global space economy will reach approximately $641.2 billion by 2030. As activities related to all components of the space economy continue to increase through public and private initiatives, the dream of a future in space for humanity is closer than ever before.

INTRODUCTION

Ideas and concepts related to the exploration of space and space travel, which have intrigued humanity since ancient times, were depicted in the literary works of the French writer Cyrano de Bergerac in the 17th century, particularly in his Sun and Moon travel narratives. Two hundred years later, Jules Verne's inspiring book "From the Earth to the Moon" and Herbert George Wells' "Tales of Space and Time" portrayed space travel and extraterrestrial beings in a futuristic and imaginative manner. Fictional, imaginative, and futuristic texts about space journeys began to materialize with the advancement of

DOI: 10.4018/979-8-3693-0908-7.ch014

technology in the 20th century, and as a result, a significant space economy has emerged at the present stage (Ekşi vd., 2019: 499).

The concept of space economy encompasses a wide range of activities related to the design, production, and research and development (R&D) of artificial spacecraft; their manufacturing, launch, maintenance, and operations in orbit and on the ground; their utilization for scientific, economic, and societal purposes; the provision of services to Earth using these devices; the extraction, exploration, transportation, sale, and utilization of minerals and resources from celestial bodies in space; and the transportation and logistics services for space missions. It represents an economy that extends across a broad spectrum of activities. Space economy is sometimes referred to as "space-based economy," "orbital economy," "orbital economy," or "extraterrestrial space economy." It encompasses the delivery of services produced in space and offered to relevant firms and consumers, future endeavors and activities in advanced space technologies and research, and industries where multiple companies operate in an integrated manner. In other words, the scope of the space economy includes the goods, services, and other activities derived from scientific, economic, social, and military endeavors conducted beyond the Earth's atmosphere, covering the entire globe (Suleymanlı, 2009: 30-43).

As evident, space economy encompasses all industries involved in activities ranging from R&D to space infrastructure (launch vehicles, satellites, and ground stations) and products and services related to space (meteorological services, satellite phones, navigation devices, etc.). According to the National Aeronautics and Space Administration (NASA) of the United States, the concept refers to all economic activities related to the production and delivery of components that go into Earth's orbit or beyond (NASA, 2022).

In the not-too-distant future, it is believed that scientific research and applications conducted for an advanced space infrastructure will be highly important for interstellar travel. The outcomes and outputs of future space activities are expected to be utilized in many areas. For instance, water resources discovered through scientific activities on the surfaces of Mars and the Moon can be used for drinking water and other needs of space crews and personnel. On the other hand, R&D efforts for space activities will contribute to the provision and improvement of water resources such as oxygen and hydrogen, which are necessary for rocket fuel used in the development of new and enhanced satellites, space stations, next-generation space telescopes, and exploration missions beyond the solar system (Crawford vd., 2016: 59; Spudis ve Lavoie, 2011: 1-24).

The history of space economy extends back to the period immediately following World War II, until the year 1945 when the United States and the Soviet Union, which emerged as powerful nations from the war, established a bipolar world order. During this new system, known as the "Cold War," there were no direct wars or hot conflicts between the two superpowers, but numerous wars and internal conflicts were witnessed in various regions around the world. This new state of the world brought forth many different situations and debates. The most significant development during this period, which saw a balance of power between the United States and the Soviet Union, was the "space race" between the two countries (Smith, 1998: 19; Betts, 1987: 22-82).

The efforts to explore and conquer space, which have grown significantly and reached monumental proportions in the present day, have important economic dimensions and consequences. Although the initial aim of the space race between the USSR and the US was to prove their superiority to the world, considering the risky nature of space investments, it can easily be said that there was a significant competition at that time (Petroni and Bigliardi, 2019: 1). Just like commercial flights that began shortly after World War II rapidly increased air transportation within a decade, and the internet that started in the 1990s quickly enabled computers to perform most of our tasks, space economy has also rapidly changed and will continue to change people's lifestyles and work patterns. The activities of private companies such as SpaceX, Blue Origin, and others, launching their own rockets and establishing a presence in space, provide hints about the upcoming changes. Space activities, which were once primarily the domain of government institutions, now offer significant opportunities for the private sector due to technological advancements in manufacturing, propulsion, and launch, making space travel and mission execution easier, faster, and cheaper. Low costs have opened doors for new start-ups and encouraged established aerospace companies to explore opportunities that were previously considered expensive or difficult. Technological advancements have also attracted investor interest and led to a significant increase in financing space activities and investments in the past five to ten years (Brukardt, 2022: 1).

In the 21st Century global economy, innovations have become the key to creating competitive advantage among countries, driving economic growth, and improving the quality of life for humanity. Artificial intelligence, quantum computing, robotics, and nanotechnologies have advanced, becoming an indispensable part of our daily lives through their applications in monitoring climate and environmental changes, weather forecasting, air traffic management, global communication and broadcasting, agriculture, telemedicine, and banking cards. These technologies have transformed various aspects of our daily lives and have contributed to advancements in sectors such as artificial intelligence, quantum computing, robotics, hydrogen fuel cells, and nanotechnologies. (OECD, 2007: 17; OECD, 2008).

While space activities, which were highly prestigious but costly, were carried out by only a few pioneering countries in the 20th century, space exploration underwent a transformation starting from the 2000s. With technological advancements, the paradigms of space changed, and activities related to space began to be pursued not only in a few countries but in many countries, and not only in the public sector but also in the private sector, thanks to the new possibilities brought by technology (STM ThinkTech, 2020).

While harnessing energy and material resources from the Sun system is crucial to developing the necessary infrastructure for a sustainable space economy, activities such as mining on the lunar surface, space tourism, and resources from asteroids will contribute significantly to the space economy. The evolving space infrastructure will pave the way for future manned and unmanned space journeys within the solar system, construction of large space telescopes, and the establishment of stations for scientific research on the surfaces of Mars and the Moon (Crawford, 2016: 59).

SPACE EXPLORATION FROM PAST TO PRESENT

The first artificial satellite launched into space, Sputnik-1, by the Soviet Union on 4 October 1957, was the initial attempt in the space race. Shortly after that, on November 3, 1957, the satellite Sputnik-2 was sent into Earth's orbit with the passenger dog named Laika. Four months later, in January 1958, the Soviet Union launched Explorer-1 into space, and on January 2, 1959, Luna-1 became the first satellite to venture beyond Earth's orbit. In contrast, during this period, the Pioneer satellites (1, 2, 3, 4, 5, 6) developed by NASA for lunar missions were unable to reach the Moon due to launch failures (Pedroni vd., 2009: 51).

On 12 April 1961, Soviet cosmonaut Yuri Gagarin became the first person to reach space aboard the vehicle named Vostok-1. The 'space race' period was dominated by the Soviet Union's superiority over the United States until the late 1970s. In order to establish dominance over the Soviet Union, the United States increased its space expenditures and efforts. As a result of these endeavors, American astronaut

Neil Armstrong became the first human to set foot on the Moon with the spacecraft Apollo 11 on July 16-24, 1969. From that point on, the United States took the lead in the space race against the Soviet Union. (Yılmaz, 2013: 5; Greene, 2004: 17).

After the completion of the Apollo missions in 1972, NASA produced the Columbia spacecraft in 1981. This vehicle subsequently carried out over a hundred successful flights, making significant contributions to both the construction of the International Space Station and the Hubble Space Telescope in the following years. However, due to the high costs associated with space activities and the tragic explosion of the Challenger space shuttle 73 seconds after liftoff from the Kennedy Space Center in Florida in 1986, resulting in the loss of all seven crew members, NASA suspended the Space Shuttle Program (Crane vd., 2020: 7).

In order to conduct scientific research in space, the European Space Research Organisation (ESRO) was established in 1964 by ten countries in Europe. In 1975, it merged with the European Launcher Development Organisation to form the European Space Agency (ESA), which continues to carry out space missions to this day (Martin vd., 2005: 32).

In the late 1990s, the commercialization of space activities accelerated, and private enterprises started engaging in space ventures alongside the public sector. The first private space initiative occurred in 1999 when Motorola launched Iridium, a constellation of 66 satellites, into Low Earth Orbit to provide mobile phone communication. However, despite the expected revenue, Iridium failed to generate the projected income of $5 billion, leading to Motorola facing an economic crisis and filing for bankruptcy. Nevertheless, even though the revenue target was not achieved, the operational and technical objectives of the Iridium project were met, showcasing the potential of private enterprises in the field of space exploration (Morgen ve Behrens, 2009: 14).

In 1982, U.S. President Ronald Reagan established a new space commission called the Rogers Commission to explore the commercialization of space activities and review space policies. Following this, space exploration efforts further accelerated. In 2000, billionaires such as Elon Musk, Jeff Bezos, and Richard Branson began investing in the space industry to expand their power and wealth. Elon Musk, who founded PayPal in 2002, sold the venture to eBay for $1.5 billion and used $100 million to establish SpaceX, a company dedicated to space exploration. On September 28, 2008, SpaceX became the first privately financed company to launch a liquid-fueled Falcon rocket into space, and on December 9, 2010, it became the first private space company to successfully place the Dragon spacecraft into orbit around the Earth and return it safely. In 2016, SpaceX successfully landed its spacecraft on a mobile platform in the ocean and introduced the Starlink satellite, which provides ultra-high-quality broadband internet service, in 2019. Elon Musk initiated the Starlink project by launching 60 satellites into space using the Falcon 9 rocket. The main goal of the project is to increase internet speed and reduce the costs of information services. In fact, while the average cost of fiber optic cables necessary for the transition to 5G internet in the United States is around $150 billion, SpaceX has spent only $10 billion on the Starlink Project (Thompson, and Smith 2009: 12; SpacecampTurkey, 2022).

CURRENT STATE OF THE SPACE ECONOMY

In the 21st century, space activities conducted by countries have been both prestigious and economically beneficial. With the advancement of technology, public and private organizations involved in space exploration have created a new space ecosystem. This space ecosystem holds high potential as it encompasses emerging fields such as space mining, space tourism, small satellite projects, and in-space manufacturing. Future predictions regarding the space economy are highly optimistic in this context. The high potential of the space economy encourages many countries to initiate and develop their space programs. At this stage, influential new trends have emerged in the space economy, including the strong relationship between space and climate change, increased capital formation, reduction of orbital debris, the connection between space and security, satellite internet, asteroid mining, space tourism, and space research (STM, 2020: 4; Space Economy Academy, 2022).

In the late 1990s, the process of commercialization in the space economy and space industry gained further momentum. Innovations in digital data processing in the computer environment increasingly made advanced space technologies and assets crucial in various fields such as navigation, communication, meteorology, broadcasting, and Earth observation. The rising trend of the space economy gained traction in 2007 with the invention of smartphones, marking the beginning of a mass technology, internet, and communication era facilitated by wide mobile broadband and satellite communication applications (Suleymanlı, 2009: 32; Weinzierl, 2018).

In addition to the benefits of productivity, efficiency, increased number of firms, and the emergence of new industries, as well as job creation at the state level, the space economy has macroeconomic effects in terms of employment growth and savings. The space economy also impacts various sectors and industries in the economy (Henry, 2016: 6; Suleymanli, 2009: 33). Industries such as transportation, healthcare, environmental management, climate monitoring, agriculture, urban planning, education, energy, telecommunications, meteorology, mining, high-tech industries, finance and insurance, defense and security, R&D, tourism and entertainment, data analysis, and disaster management benefit from the ripple effects triggered by space activities (Weinzierl, 2018).

Despite significant uncertainties surrounding space, experts in the field appear to be optimistic about the space economy. They believe that with advancements in existing and new application areas, the space economy will reach a trillion-dollar volume in the future. The current favorable technological and economic environment is also encouraging an increase in space investments (Brukardt, 2022: 4).

In recent years, not only the United States, Russia, and other pioneering countries but also developing nations have allocated budgetary funds for space activities. As of 2021, the shares of G-20 countries' budgets allocated to space activities and the expenditures made by some leading countries for their space programs can be seen in Figure 1.

According to Figure 1, as of 2021, the United States ranks first with a share of 0.25% of its public budget allocated to space activities, followed by Russia in second place with 0.21%. Mexico allocates the smallest share to space activities, with 0.002%, followed by Brazil with 0.003%.

The expenditures of some leading countries for space programs as of 2021 are shown in Figure 2.

Figure 2, which displays government expenditures on space programs in leading countries in 2020 and 2021, shows that in 2021, the United States ranked first with $54.59 billion invested in these programs. It was followed by China with $10.29 billion and Japan with $4.21 billion. The European Union allocated $2.57 billion from its budget for space programs. The graph demonstrates the ambition and competition among countries like the United States, China, Japan, France, and Russia to become leaders in space in the future.

Since the Cold War era, the United States has supported space exploration through NASA. Figure 3 illustrates the budget of NASA over the years.

According to Figure 3, in 1961, when then US President John F. Kennedy announced the goal of sending humans to the moon by the end of the 1960s, NASA's budget was only $6.58 billion. By the

Figure 1. Shares of G-20 countries' budgets allocated to space activities (as a Percentage of GDP)
Source: *Compiled from 2021 OECD Economy for People, Planet and Prosperity.*

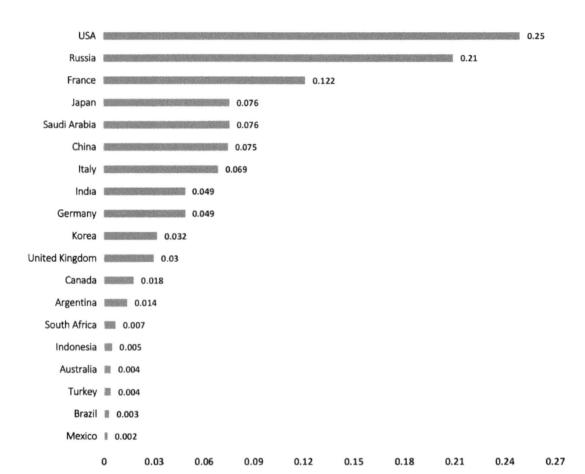

year 1965, when the first spacewalk took place, NASA's space expenditures had increased more than fivefold compared to 1961, reaching $34.02 billion. In 1969, when American astronaut Neil Armstrong set foot on the moon with Buzz Aldrin, NASA's budget stood at $22.71 billion. The NASA budget, which was $20.41 billion in 1989, increased to $22.61 billion in 2009 and reached $57.69 billion in 2022. The acceleration of the budget increase since 2021 is noteworthy.

In Figure 4, it can be observed that the share of GDP allocated to NASA in the United States rapidly increased from 1959, the year when the space race with Russia began after World War II, to 1968. Between 1974 and 2016, NASA's budget displayed a stable trend. However, in the last four years spanning from 2019 to 2022, the share allocated to NASA from the GDP has once again entered an increasing trend.

In the last decade, the number of international private companies involved in space activities has grown exponentially alongside the public sector, leading to a rapid increase in space investments. For instance, while the public sector spending on space activities in 2019 amounted to $79 billion, representing the majority of the financing used for space research, this amount is a reflection of the substantial monetary value of the various benefits provided by space activities. As seen in Figure 5, space investments offer a

Figure 2. Government expenditures on space programs in leading countries in 2020 and 2021 (Billion $)
Source: *statista.com https://www.statista.com/statistics/745717/global-governmental-spending-on-space-programs-leading-countries/*

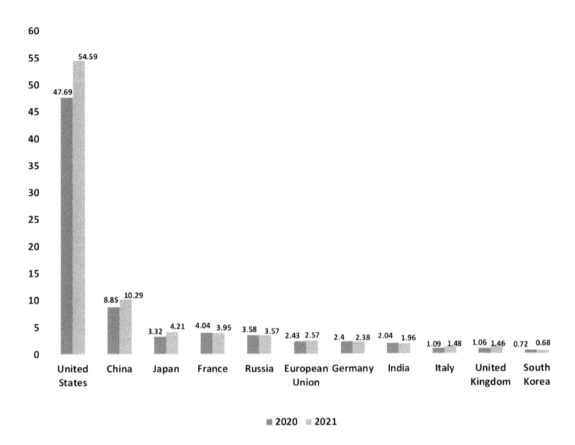

range of micro and macroeconomic benefits to countries and private companies, including commercial revenues, employment, productivity, social welfare, savings, and contributions to science and technology (OECD Space Forum, 2020).

The monetary values of the benefits derived from space investments are shown in Figure 5.

The most significant benefit derived from space investments, as indicated in Figure 5, is a commercial revenue of $15.4 billion, while the least benefit amounts to $3.4 billion in terms of reputation and inspiration.

It is expected that the space economy will further grow in the coming periods, and the projections for the future in this regard can be seen in Figure 6.

In Figure 6, contains projections for the future of the space economy between 2021 and 2030. According to these projections, the size of the space economy will increase each year. In 2021, it was $370 billion, and by 2030, it is expected to reach approximately $641.2 billion, representing a growth of around 75% compared to 2021.

The number of private companies (start-ups) involved in space programs in Europe, as well as their budgets, can be seen in Figure 7.

Figure 3. NASA budget from 1961 to 2022 (Billion $)
Source: *statista.com https://www.statista.com/statistics/264494/nasas-budget/*

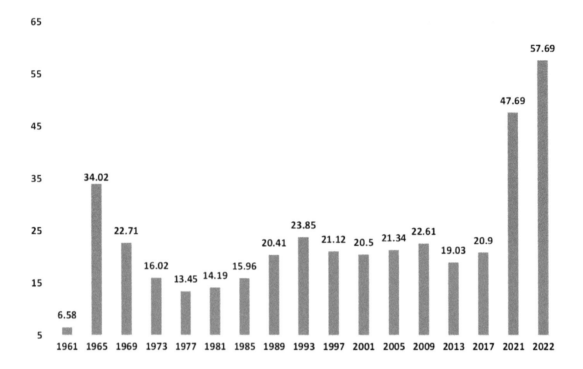

On the left side of Figure 7, there are total investments in Euros, and on the right side, the number of start-up applications is displayed. In 2014, the number of start-ups engaged in space activities in Europe was 20, with a total budget of only 20 million Euros. By 2017, the number of start-ups increased to 59, and their total budget grew 11 times compared to 2014, reaching 220 million Euros. In 2022, the number of start-ups rose to 88, with a budget of 610 million Euros.

Since the year 2000, the space tourism industry, supported by private ventures, has gained significant momentum. Billionaires like Richard Branson (Virgin Galactic), Jeff Bezos (Blue Origin), and Elon Musk (SpaceX) are striving to make space travel more frequent and affordable through private initiatives. While space tourism represents an emerging industry, it also has the potential to generate annual revenues in the billions of dollars, considering employment opportunities, tax revenue, and space-related benefits for national economies (Cohen ve Spector, 2019; Chang, 2020).

On 30 May 30 2020, Elon Musk's SpaceX became the first private venture to successfully carry out a tourist-oriented space travel on Earth. The company conducted a three-day trip to Earth's orbit for the first space tourists using the Crew Dragon capsule. The crewed commercial space journey, carried out by SpaceX's spacecraft called Crew Dragon 2, in Hawthorne, California, demonstrated the potential and capability of private companies to transport humans beyond the Earth's atmosphere (Suleymanlı, 2022: 43; Lerner ve Gorog, 2021).

Table 1 provides detailed information about the areas of operation, establishment years, number of employees, and products/services offered by private companies engaged in space activities worldwide.

Figure 4. Share of budget allocated to NASA (%), 1959-2022
Source: *Aerospace (2023) https://aerospace.csis.org/*

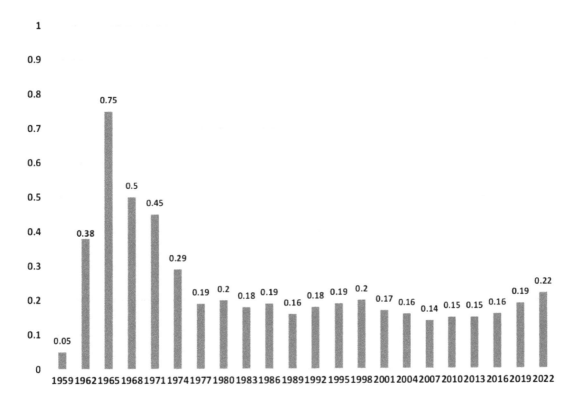

In Table 1, it can be observed that private companies engaged in space activities were mostly established and began their operations after the year 2000. When examining the products and services provided by these companies, a wide range of offerings is evident. These include low Earth orbit transportation, spacecraft, rocket, and satellite launches, engine and radar production, manned spaceflight, space tourism, space transportation, Earth observation, data collection, and video imaging services, planetary exploration, space mining, space debris removal, and even production of various goods in space colonization.

Space travel, carried out for various reasons, has been supported not only by the government but also through private sector involvement since the 2000s. The number of individuals visiting space through government and private ventures between 1961 and 2021 is illustrated in Figure 8.

As seen in Figure 8, the Freedom 7 spacecraft, developed and launched by the United States in 1961, successfully returned to Earth with four individuals onboard. In 1969, the Apollo 11 spacecraft carried a total of 23 individuals, including American astronaut Neil Armstrong and Buzz Aldrin, who famously set foot on the Moon. In 1985, 63 individuals traveled to space, followed by 58 in 1997, 46 in 2009, and 7 in 2021.

One of the significant elements of the space economy is space mining. The scarcity of natural resources, coupled with the increasing population, has become one of the most crucial challenges for the world economies in the 21st century. Excessive industrial production, overvaluation of minerals leading to increased production costs, environmental and ecological damage, energy insufficiency, and the depletion of traditional energy sources are among the problems faced by the Earth. In the face of these

Figure 5. Monetary values of benefits derived from space investments ($)
Source: *Compiled from OECD's "The Space Economy in Figures: How Space Contributes to the Global Economy" report published in 2019.*

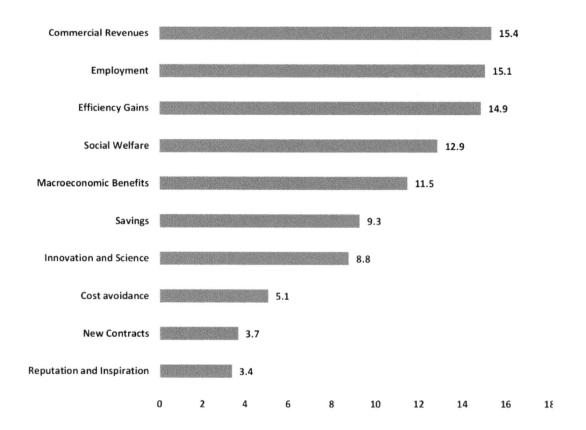

challenges, space mining is seen as a ray of hope. It is considered a potential solution to address issues such as the scarcity of natural resources and the damaging effects on the environment and nature. Moreover, it offers a promising opportunity to overcome energy shortages and the depletion of traditional energy sources (Bebitova, 2020).

At the core of NASA's vision for new space technologies, as the driving force of the space industry on Earth, are various futuristic services and industries. These services include new areas such as space agriculture, space tourism, and asteroid mining (Friel, 2019).

Space mining, in a narrow sense, involves extracting valuable minerals from planets near Earth, and in a broader sense, it encompasses the extraction of valuable minerals, metals, and gases from celestial bodies in both space and on Earth for use. Therefore, space mining holds significant importance for both the space-related and Earth-related aspects of the space economy. Since 2012, nearly 1,000 asteroids have been discovered in space each year, and by 2021, almost 9,000 asteroids had been found. It is believed that in the future, the valuable minerals, metals, and gases obtained from these asteroids will be highly important for national economies (Bebitova, 2020).

As of 2021, the values of asteroids in terms of minerals, metals, and gases are shown in Figure 9. According to the graph, the asteroid named Davide is the most valuable asteroid with a value of 26.99

Figure 6. Projection of space economy for the period 2021-2030 (in billion $)
Source: *The compilation is derived from the 2022 report titled "Space Economy Liftoff: Into the Final Frontier" by Klecha & Co.*

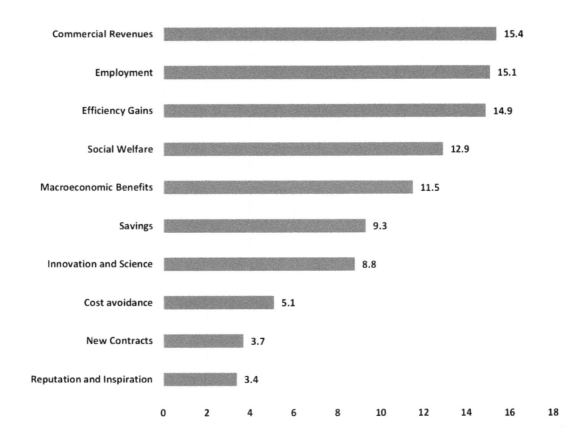

quintillion dollars, which is approximately 100 times the Gross Domestic Product (GDP) of the United States in 2021 (23 trillion dollars).

Space economy and its sectors and industries have not only economic impacts but also social benefits. Satellites launched into Earth's orbit sustainably support vital services such as weather forecasting, navigation, and communication. This economy performs a significant social function by providing high-capacity connectivity in vast and inaccessible areas, including deserts, mountains, islands, rainforests, or wetlands, thanks to state-of-the-art satellites. For instance, the majority of fundamental climate changes on Earth can be observed from space, enabling early precautions for potential climate changes in the coming years. Through satellites, the illegal activities of deforestation, fishing, and wildlife trade, amounting to approximately $73 billion annually, can be prevented. Space technologies can improve the quality of solar energy production forecasts by 30%, while also providing spatial opportunities for water and food production, precision irrigation, and agricultural techniques. Observing the world through satellite instruments allows for real-time mapping of infectious disease locations and hotspots, facilitating disease detection based on regional data (WEF, 2020: 1-4).

There are significant barriers and challenges related to space activities. The inadequacy of the existing legal system regarding space law poses a significant obstacle to the acceleration and commercializa-

Figure 7. Number of start-ups and budgets of private ventures investing in space in Europe
Source: *Compiled from the 2021 European Investment Bank (EIB) report.*

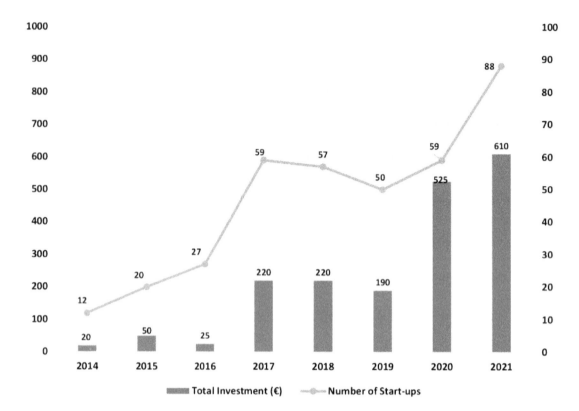

tion of space mining activities. The lack of solid legal foundations for the marketing, sales, accounting, sharing, taxation, and auditing of products obtained from space mining is one of the most serious issues facing the space mining sector (Mallick ve Rajagopalan, 2019).

Space law, as a field, encompasses the fundamental legal framework and regime for space and space activities, which are determined by international treaties, principles, and other non-binding regulations. The roots of space law are based on international public law, and its norms generally form a part of this branch of law. Establishing a modern and up-to-date space law that is relevant to the era can address existing and future issues (Kuzu vd., 2018: 109).

RESULT

In this article, the space economy, which has its roots in the space race of the 1950s, gained momentum from the late 1960s and early 1970s, and has taken on new and immense dimensions in the 21st century with the acceleration of technological advancements, is examined in terms of its conceptual and historical development, establishment, and transformation into a comprehensive economy and a sector consisting of dozens of complementary industries. The article also discusses the future perspectives of the space economy.

Table 1. Summary of companies engaged in space activities worldwide and their fields of operation

Research Area	Companies	Year of Establishment	Number of Full-Time Employees	Products/Services
Access to Space	Astrobotic	2008	11–50	Transportation to the Moon
	Blue Origin	2000	875	Launch vehicles and engines, space tourism
	Boeing Aerospace	1978	2,8	Crewed LEO transportation
	Masten Space Systems	2004	11–50	Suborbital launches of small payloads
	Sierra Nevada Corp.	1963	3,094	Cargo and crewed LEO transportation
	Space Adventures	1998	17	Crewed LEO, lunar transport, and tourism
	SpaceX	2002	5,42	Reusable launch vehicles, colonization
	Stratolaunch Systems	2011	501–1000	Air-launched orbital launch services
	World View Enterprises	2012	11–50	High-altitude private spaceflight balloons
	United Launch Alliance	2006	4000	Orbital launch services
	Virgin Galactic	2004	200	Space tourism; rapid commercial flight
Remote Sensing	Spire Global Inc	2012	11–50	Synthetic aperture radar remote sensing
	Iceye	2010	251–500	Earth imaging and video, data provision
	Planet	2006	101–250	Data gathering; Earth observation network
Satellite Data Access and Analysis.	Analytical Space	2016	10	Optical LEO comms network, full service
	Astroscal	2013	11–50	Space Debris Removal
	OneWeb	2012	101–250	Large-scale satellite constellation
Habitats and Space Stations.	Axiom	2015	11–50	Commercial space station building off ISS
	Bigelow Aerospace	1999	135	Inflatable space habitats
	Made in Space	2010	50	Additive manufacturing in space
	Nanoracks	2009	40	Payload transport, deployment hardware
	Space Tango	2014	5–10	Microgravity research platforms
Beyond Low Earth Orbit	Deep Space Industries	2012	11–50	Asteroid mining
	Golden Spike	2010	11–50	Human lunar expeditions
	Mars One	2011	11–50	Mars colonization
	Moon Express	2010	51–100	Moon exploration and mining
	Planetary Resources, Inc.	2010	11–50	Asteroid mining

Source: (Weinzierl, 2018: 178).

Figure 8. Number of human visits to space (annual count) between 1961 and 2021
Source: *Compiled from the 2022 report of the Center for Strategic and International Studies- Aerospace Security Project.*

Research Area	Companies	Year of Establishment	Number of Full-Time Employees	Products/Services
Access to Space	Astrobotic	2008	11–50	Transportation to the Moon
	Blue Origin	2000	875	Launch vehicles and engines, space tourism
	Boeing Aerospace	1978	2,8	Crewed LEO transportation
	Masten Space Systems	2004	11–50	Suborbital launches of small payloads
	Sierra Nevada Corp.	1963	3,094	Cargo and crewed LEO transportation
	Space Adventures	1998	17	Crewed LEO, lunar transport, and tourism
	SpaceX	2002	5,42	Reusable launch vehicles, colonization
	Stratolaunch Systems	2011	501–1000	Air-launched orbital launch services
	World View Enterprises	2012	11–50	High-altitude private spaceflight balloons
	United Launch Alliance	2006	4000	Orbital launch services
	Virgin Galactic	2004	200	Space tourism; rapid commercial flight
Remote Sensing	Spire Global Inc	2012	11–50	Synthetic aperture radar remote sensing
	Iceye	2010	251–500	Earth imaging and video, data provision
	Planet	2006	101–250	Data gathering; Earth observation network
Satellite Data Access and Analysis.	Analytical Space	2016	10	Optical LEO comms network, full service
	Astroscal	2013	11–50	Space Debris Removal
	OneWeb	2012	101–250	Large-scale satellite constellation
Habitats and Space Stations.	Axiom	2015	11–50	Commercial space station building off ISS
	Bigelow Aerospace	1999	135	Inflatable space habitats
	Made in Space	2010	50	Additive manufacturing in space
	Nanoracks	2009	40	Payload transport, deployment hardware
	Space Tango	2014	5–10	Microgravity research platforms
Beyond Low Earth Orbit	Deep Space Industries	2012	11–50	Asteroid mining
	Golden Spike	2010	11–50	Human lunar expeditions
	Mars One	2011	11–50	Mars colonization
	Moon Express	2010	51–100	Moon exploration and mining
	Planetary Resources, Inc.	2010	11–50	Asteroid mining

Since the creation of Earth, humanity has been fascinated by the sky and has had a desire to explore and travel beyond the Earth's atmosphere. Throughout history, various civilizations and nations have spent many years studying lunar eclipses, examining planets in the solar system, and developing a broad

Figure 9. Most valuable asteroids in the asteroid belt based on mineral and element content as of 2021 in Quintillion $)
Kaynak: *statista.com https://www.statista.com/statistics/656143/mineral-and-element-value-of-selected-asteroids/*

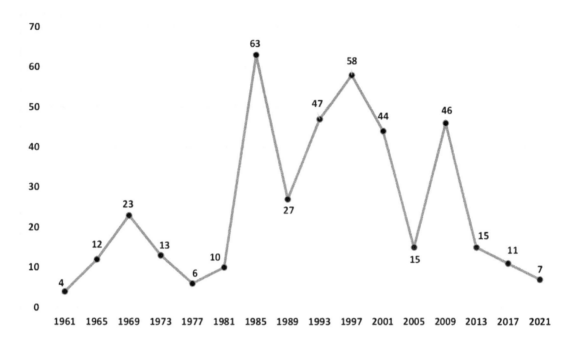

understanding of space and the Milky Way galaxy. In summary, a significant source of motivation for space exploration is the curiosity of humankind.

After World War II, the Soviet Union and the United States emerged as the new superpowers of the world, leading to a bipolar world during the period known as the "Cold War." One of the most significant developments during this period was the "space race" between the two countries. On October 4, 1957, the Soviet Union launched the first artificial satellite, Sputnik-1, followed by sending a dog named Laika into Earth's orbit on November 3, 1957. In 1969, the United States achieved the milestone of landing on the Moon with the Apollo-11 spacecraft. These events marked a significant acceleration in space activities.

To overcome critical future challenges on Earth, countries are actively seeking new resources. Therefore, they are investing in space activities beyond the Earth's atmosphere to explore energy sources and minerals. These investments also have numerous positive impacts on national economies. The high potential of the space economy encourages many countries and private companies to initiate space programs and engage in extensive research and development activities. Investments in space research provide countries and private enterprises with benefits such as commercial revenue, employment opportunities, social welfare, productivity gains, cost savings, innovation, and enhanced reputation.

It is expected that space activities will positively impact various industries in the short and medium term, including research and development (R&D), transportation, tourism, defense and security, climate monitoring, data analysis, disaster management, agriculture, environmental management, energy, tele-communications, healthcare, urban planning, education, and high-tech industries.

Countries such as the United States, China, Russia, and Japan, which are leading players in space activities, provide support through their allocated shares from the public budget. NASA's budget has increased from $20.41 billion in 1989 to $57.69 billion in 2022. Projections covering the years 2021-2030 indicate that the space economy will grow each year. Accordingly, the size of the space economy was $370 billion in 2021 and is projected to reach approximately $641.2 billion in 2030, representing a growth of around 75% compared to 2021. It is evident that R&D efforts and technological advancements in space activities, as well as the budgets allocated to these endeavors, are increasing day by day, fostering the growth of startups in the field.

In summary, the space economy has captured significant interest from both public and private entrepreneurs and represents a rapidly evolving field. With technological advancements driving cost reductions, it is expected that entrepreneurial activities and investments will increase in the coming years. This, in turn, will enable the exploration of new frontiers and the realization of benefits through the deployment of next-generation satellites. Today, humanity's dream of building a future beyond the Earth's atmosphere is much closer to reality than ever before.

ACKNOWLEDGMENT

This research received no specific grant from any funding agency in the public, commercial, or not for profit sectors.

REFERENCES

Aerospace. (2023). *Nasa Budget (GSMH %)*. Aerospace.com. https://aerospace.csis.org/

ASP. (2022). Center for Strategic and International Studies-Aerospace Security Project. https://www.csis.org/programs/international-security-program/aerospace-security-project

Bebeitova, M. (2020). Space Economy and the Concept of Space Mining. *M.A. Thesis, Kocaeli University Institute of Social Sciences*, Kocaeli, Turkey.

Betts, R. K. (1987). Nuclear Blackmail And Nuclear Balance, (1. Edition). The Brookings Instition, Washington.

Brukardt, R. (2022). How Will The Space Economy Change The World? *McKinsey Quarterly*.

Chang, E. Y. (2020). From Aviation Tourism to Suborbital Space Tourism: A Study on Passenger Screening And Business Opportunities. *Acta Astronautica*, *177*, 410–420. doi:10.1016/j.actaastro.2020.07.020

Cohen, E., & Spector, S. (2019). Space Tourism: The Elusive Dream, (1. Edition). Emerald Group Publishing, United Kingdom.

Crane, K. W., Linck, E., Lal, B., & Wei, R. Y. (2020). *OECD Measuring the Space Economy: Estimating the Value of Economic Activities in and for Space*. Science and Technology Institute for Defense Analyses., doi:10.1787/c5996201-

Crawford, I. A. (2016). The Long-Term Scientific Benefits of a Space Economy. *Space Policy*, *37*(2), 58–61. doi:10.1016/j.spacepol.2016.07.003

Dormehl, L. (2018). Asteroid Mining is Almost Reality. What to Know About the Gold Rush in Space. *Science Buddies.* https://www.sciencebuddies.org/

EIB. (2021). *The Future of The European Space Sector How to Leverage Europe's Technological Leadership and Boost Investments for Space Ventures.* EIB. https://www.eib.org/attachments/thematic/future_of_european_space_sector_en.pdf

Ekşi İ, G, Boztepe İ, Kurban D, Özcan L, Uçar İ, Bilgin K. B., & Öztürk Ö. (2019). Space and Medicine Where Are We? What Should We Do?. *Med J SDU.* 26(4), 498-504.

Friel, P. J. (2019). Space-Based Ballistic Missile Defense: An Overview of the Technical Issues. Laser Weapons in Spac. Routledge, New York. DOI: doi:10.4324/9780429050053

Greene, B. (2004). The Fabric of The Cosmos: Space, Time, and The Texture of Reality. Knopf. (1. Edition). Vintage Books, New York.

Henry, L. W. (2016). Leadership, Change, and Public-Private Partnerships: A Case Study of Nasa and the Transition From Space Shuttle to Commercial Space Flight. *IBM Center for the Business of Government*, (pp. 1-51). IBM.

Klecha & Co. (2022). *Space Economy Liftoff: Into the Final Frontier.* Klecha & Co. https://www.klecha-co.com/last-research/space-economy-lift-off-into-the-final-frontier/

Lerner, D. J., & Gorog, J. M. Jr. (2021). How "Rad" is A Trip to Space? A Brief Discussion of Radiation Exposure in Suborbital Space Tourism. *Journal of the American College of Radiology*, 18(1), 225–228. doi:10.1016/j.jacr.2020.06.020 PMID:33413908

Mallick, S. and Rajagopalan, R. P. (2019). If Space is 'the Province of Mankind', Who Owns its Resources? An Examination of the Potential of Space Mining and its Legal Implications. *Observer Research Foundation.* 1-27.

Martin, D. C., Fanson, J., Schiminovich, D., Friedman, P. D., Barlow, T. A., & Wyder, T. K. (2005). The Galaxy Evolution Explorer: A Space Ultraviolet Survey Mission. *The Astrophysical Journal*, 619(1), 1–6. doi:10.1086/426387

NASA. (2022). *Astrobotic Technology Reveals Design for Robot to Prospect at Moon's Poles.* NASA. Https://Sservi.Nasa.Gov/Articles/Astrobotic-Technology-Reveals-Design-For-Robot-To-Prospect-At-Moons-Poles/ Access date: 16.12.2022

OECD. (2007). *The Space Economy at a Glance 2007*, OECD Publishing, Paris..doi:10.1787/9789264040847-en

OECD (2008). *Space Technologies and Climate Change: Implications for Water Management, Marine Resources and Maritime Transport*, OECD Publishing. , doi:10.1787/9789264054196-en

OECD (Ed.). (2019). *The Space Economy in Figures: How Space Contributes to the Global Economy.* OECD. https://www.oecd.org/innovation/the-space-economy-in-figures-c5996201-en.htm

OECD (2019). *The Space Economy in Figures: How Space Contributes to the Global Economy.* OECD Publishing. . doi:10.1787/c5996201-en

OECD. (2021). *Economy for People, Planet and Prosperity 2021 Report.* OECD. https://www.oecd.org/sti/inno/space-forum/space-economy-for-people-planet-and-prosperity.pdf

Pedroni, G., Venturini, K., & Cantarello, S. (2019). Discovering the Basic Strategic Orientation of Big Space Agencies. *Space Policy, 25*(1), 45–62. doi:10.1016/j.spacepol.2008.12.010

Petroni, G. ve Bigliardi, B. (2019). The Space Economy: From Science to Market. (First Edition). Cambridge Scholars Publishing, United Kingdom.

Smith, J. A. (1998). *The Cold War 1945-1991* (2nd ed.). Blackwell Publishers.

Soysal, M., Doğan, G., & Kuzu, L. (2018). Sources of International Law Regarding Space Activities and the Role of the United Nations. *Çukurova University Faculty of Law Journal, 3*(2), 101-133.

Space Economy Academy. (2022). *Top 8 Drivers in Space Economics.* SEAC. https://seac-space.com/top-8-drivers-in-space-economics/ Access date: 03.04.2023

SpacecampTurkey. (2022). Starlink, SpaceX and Elon Musk. https://www.spacecampturkey.com/starlink-spacex-ve-elon-musk Access date: 16.12.2022

Spudis, P. D., & Lavoie, A. R. (2011). *Using The Resources of The Moon to Create a Permanent Cislunar Space Faring System. Proceedings of the American Institute of Aeronautics and Astronautics Space Conference.* Research Gate. 10.2514/6.2011-7185

Statista (2022). *Government Expenditures on Space Programs.* Statista. https://www.statista.com/statistics/745717/global-governmental-spending-on-spaceprograms-leading-countries/

Statista (2022). *Valuable Minerals Discovered in Space and Their Values.* Statista. https://www.statista.com/statistics/656143/mineral-and-element-value-of-selected-asteroids/

STM. (2020). The New Space Age: Space Strategies in Light of Selected Countries' Space Programs in the 21st Century, Cosmic Competition II. *STM Technological Thought Center, Research Report.* https://thinktech.stm.com.tr/tr/yeni-uzay-cagi-21inci-yuzyilda-kozmik-rekabet-ii-secili-ulkelerin-uzay-programlari-isiginda-uzay-stratejileri

Suleymanlı, J. (2022). *An Econometric Model Attempt on Space Economy and Determinants of Space Economy Revenues.* [Ph. D. Thesis, Istanbul University Institute of Social Sciences, Istanbul, Turkey].

Thompson, S., & Smith, G. P. (2009). *Space Policy Development via Macro-Economic Analysis.* NASA. https://www.nasa.gov/pdf/368983main_Applying%20a%20MacroEconomic%20Analysis%20to%20Space%20Policy%202009_06_09.pdf

Weinzierl, M. (2018). Space, the Final Economic Frontier. *The Journal of Economic Perspectives, 32*(2), 173–192. doi:10.1257/jep.32.2.173

World Economic Forum. (2020). *Six Ways Space Technologies Benefit Life on Earth.* Global Future Council on Space Technologies. Briefing Papers, September 2020. www3.weforum.org/docs/wef_gfc_six_ways_space_technologies_2020.pdf

Yılmaz, S. (2013). *Space Security* (1st ed.). Milenyum Publications.

ADDITIONAL READING

Anderson, C. (2023). *The Space Economy* (1st ed.). Wiley Publishing.

Bacon, J. J. (2018). *Space Commerce: An Industry Assessment*. Springer.

Davenport, C. (2018). *The Space Barons: Elon Musk, Jeff Bezos, and the Quest to Colonize the Cosmos*. PublicAffairs.

Dittmar, M. L. (2018). *Space Resources: Breaking the Bonds of Earth*. Springer.

Jacobson, R. C. (2019). *Space is Open for Business: The Industry That Can Transform Humanity*. Columbia University Press.

Lewis, J. S. (1996). *Mining the Sky: Untold Riches from the Asteroids, Comets, and Planets*. Addison-Wesley Publishing Company.

Lyall, F., & Larsen, P. B. (2018). *Space Law: A Treatise*. Routledge.

Pullen, G., & Williams, S. (2020). *Blockchain & The Space Economy (The Space Economy Series)*. Independently Published.

Sercel, J., & Lopez-Alegria, M. (Eds.). (2019). The Economics of Space: An Industry Ready to Launch. Springer O'Neill, G. K. (1977). The High Frontier: Human Colonies in Space. William Morrow & Co.

Zubrin, R. (2019). *The Case for Space: How the Revolution in Spaceflight Opens Up a Future of Limitless Possibility*. Prometheus Books.

KEY TERMS AND DEFINITIONS

NASA: The National Aeronautics and Space Administration, is the United States government agency responsible for the nation's civilian space program and for aeronautics and aerospace research. It was established on July 29, 1958, and has been involved in various space missions, scientific research, and space exploration endeavors. To reach for new heights and reveal the unknown for the benefit of humankind. We have an extraordinary mission: to drive advances in science, technology, aeronautics, and space exploration in order to enhance knowledge, education, innovation, economic vitality, and stewardship of Earth.

R&D: R&D stands for Research and Development. It refers to the systematic and investigative activities undertaken to develop new knowledge, technologies, products, or processes or to improve existing ones. R&D is a crucial aspect of innovation and progress in various fields, including science, engineering, technology, medicine, and business.

Space Mining: Space mining, also known as asteroid mining or extraterrestrial mining, refers to the concept of extracting valuable resources from celestial bodies such as asteroids, comets, the Moon, and other planets. The idea behind space mining is to tap into the vast reserves of minerals, metals, and other valuable materials that exist in space to support human exploration and colonization efforts, as well as to meet the resource needs of Earth and potential future space industries.

Space: The term "space" can have different meanings depending on the context in which it is used. In general, space refers to the vast, seemingly infinite expanse that exists beyond Earth's atmosphere, where celestial bodies like stars, planets, moons, and galaxies exist.

SpaceX: SpaceX is a private aerospace manufacturer and space transportation company founded by entrepreneur Elon Musk in 2002. The company's full name is Space Exploration Technologies Corp. SpaceX's primary mission is to reduce the cost of space travel and make it possible for humans to live on other planets. To achieve this, the company has developed a family of reusable rockets and spacecraft, with a focus on improving the reliability and efficiency of space travel.

Compilation of References

Abate, M., Christidis, P., & Purwanto, A. J. (2020). Government support to airlines in the aftermath of the COVID-19 pandemic. *Journal of Air Transport Management*, *89*, 101931. doi:10.1016/j.jairtraman.2020.101931 PMID:32952317

Abrantes, J. (2017). Turismo e Transportes: Impactos na Acessibilidade aos Destinos Turísticos. In F. Silva, F. & J. Umbelino (Eds.), Planeamento e Desenvolvimento Turístico (pp. 135-147). Lidel.

Abrantes, J., & Quadros, R. (2022). Impacts caused by COVID-19 on airports and tourism in the main islands of the Autonomous Region of the Azores. In: *XIII International Tourism Congress. 27-29 October. Book of Proceedings*, Estoril Portugal.

ACI. (2021a). *The impact of COVID-19 on the airport business and the path to recovery*. ACI World. https://bit.ly/3rpRI6K

ACI. (2021b). *World data reveals COVID-19's impact on world's busiest airports*. ACI World. https://aci.aero/news/2021/04/22/aci-world-data-reveals-covid-19s-impact-on-worlds-busiest-airports/

AED Cluster Portugal. (2023a, September 2). *About us*. AED Cluster Portugal. https://www.aedportugal.pt/en/about/

AED Cluster Portugal. (2023b, September 2). *Capabilities Matrix*. AED Cluster Portugal. https://www.aedportugal.pt/wp-content/uploads/2023/05/AED-Capabilities-Matrix-1.pdf

AED Cluster Portugal. (2023c, September 2). *Cluster Network Members*. AED Cluster Portugal. https://www.aedportugal.pt/wp-content/uploads/2023/04/Catalogue-AED-Cluster-Portugal-long-version-2023-06.pdf

Aeroportodamadeira.pt. (2022). Informação de Chegadas e Partidas. *Aeroporto da Madeira*. Available at: https://www.aeroportomadeira.pt/pt/fnc/voos-e-destinos/encontrar-voos/partidas-em-tempo-real

Aerospace and Defense Industries. (2015). *Facts & Figures*. ASD. https://nag.aero/wp-content/uploads/2022/01/ASD-Key-facts-figures-2015.pdf

Aerospace Artificial Intelligence Market Size. Growth, Research - 2028. (n.d.). Allied Market Research. https://www.alliedmarketresearch.com/aerospace-artificial-intelligence-market-A11337

Aerospace. (2023). *Nasa Budget (GSMH %)*. Aerospace.com. https://aerospace.csis.org/

Agarwal, A. (2023, January 10). *Travel Marketing Poised for Reboot From Generative AI*. Skift. https://skift.com/2023/01/10/travel-marketing-poised-for-reboot-from-generative-ai/

Agrawal, A. (2021). Sustainability of airlines in India with Covid-19: Challenges ahead and possible way-outs. *Journal of Revenue and Pricing Management*, *20*(4), 457–472. doi:10.1057/s41272-020-00257-z

Ağraz, S. (2006). Havayolu işletmelerinin istihdama katkısı. [Çalışma Ekonomisi ve Endüstri İlişkileri Anabilim Dalı PhD, İstanbul Üniversitesi, İstanbul].

Aguiar-Costa, L., Cunha, C., Silva, W., & Abreu, N. (2022). *Customer satisfaction in service delivery with artificial intelligence: A meta-analytic study*. Mackenzie. https://www.redalyc.org/journal/1954/195473680001/html/

Aksen, U., Göker, Ü. D., Timoçin, E., Akçay, Ç., & İpek, M. (2024). The effects of geomagnetic storms on air crash events between the years 1919-2023. *Advances in Space Research*, *73*(1), 807–830. doi:10.1016/j.asr.2023.11.008

Alamdari, F. (1999). Airline In-Flight Entertainment: The Passengers' Perspective. *Journal of Air Transport Management*, *5*(4), 203–209. doi:10.1016/S0969-6997(99)00014-9

Albers, S., & Rundshagen, V. (2020). European airlines' strategic responses to the COVID-19 pandemic (January-May, 2020). *Journal of Air Transport Management*, *87*, 101863. doi:10.1016/j.jairtraman.2020.101863 PMID:32834690

Alberti, F. G., & Pizzurno, E. (2015). Knowledge exchanges in innovation networks: Evidence from an Italian aerospace cluster. *Competitiveness Review*, *25*(3), 258–287. doi:10.1108/CR-01-2015-0004

Alecrim, E. (2023). Scanners de aeroportos serão menos constrangedores graças à inteligência artificial. *Tecnoblog*. https://tecnoblog.net/especiais/scanner-aeroporto-evolv/

Alfaro, L., Chari, A., Greenland, A. N., & Schott, P. K. (2020). *Aggregate and firm-level stock returns during pandemics, in real time (No. w26950)*. National Bureau of Economic Research. doi:10.3386/w26950

Alharbi, B., & Prince, M. (2020). A Hybrid Artificial Intelligence Approach to Predict Flight Delay. *International Journal of Engineering Research & Technology (Ahmedabad)*, *13*(4), 814–822. doi:10.37624/IJERT/13.4.2020.814-822

Alinezhad, A., & Khalili, J. (2019). COPRAS Method. *International Series in Operations Research and Management Science*, *277*, 87–91. doi:10.1007/978-3-030-15009-9_12

Alkan, A. D. (2022). The effects of COVID-19 on human resource management in aviation companies: The case of Europe. Digitalization and the Impacts of COVID-19 on the Aviation Industry (Eds. S. âurnaz & E. Argin), pp. 225-243. doi:10.4018/978-1-6684-2319-6.ch012

Allcock, J. (1989). Seasonality. In S. Witt & L. Moutinho (Eds.), *Tourism Marketing and Management Handbook* (pp. 387–392). Prentice Hall.

Almeida, C. (2009). *Aeroportos e turismo residencial: do conhecimento às estratégias* [Airports and residential tourism: from knowledge to strategies]. Tese de Doutoramento [PhD Thesis], Departamento de Economia, Gestão e Engenharia Industrial, Universidade de Aveiro, Portugal.

Almeida, C., Ferreira, A. M., & Costa, C. (2008). A importância das companhias aéreas de baixo custo no desenvolvimento de segmentos de mercado turístico: O caso do turismo residencial no Algarve [The importance of low-cost airlines in the development of tourism market segments: The case of residential tourism in the Algarve]. *Revista Portuguesa de Estudos Regionais*, *19*(19), 7–21. doi:10.59072/rper.vi19.261

Almeida, H., Campello, M., & Weisbach, M. S. (2004). The cash flow sensitivity of cash. *The Journal of Finance*, *59*(4), 1777–1804. doi:10.1111/j.1540-6261.2004.00679.x

Alola, U. V., & Alafeshat, R. (2021). The impact of human resource practices on employee engagement in the airline industry. *Journal of Public Affairs*, *21*(1), 1–12. doi:10.1002/pa.2135

Alsheibani, S. A., Messom, D. C., Cheung, Y., & Alhosni, M. (2020). *Reimagining the Strategic Management of Artificial Intelligence: Five Recommendations for Business Leaders*. Research Gate.

Altig, D., Baker, S., Barrero, J. M., Bloom, N., Bunn, P., Chen, S., & Thwaites, G. (2020). Economic uncertainty before and during the COVID-19 pandemic. *Journal of Public Economics*, *191*, 104274. doi:10.1016/j.jpubeco.2020.104274 PMID:32921841

Aly, M., & Hammoud, G. (2023). *Impact of applying the artificial intelligence in airports' operations (applied in capital international airport)*. Helwan University. https://www.eurchembull.com/uploads/paper/1a04d6acd90bc133444961d591becacc.pdf

Amankwah-Amoah, J., Khan, Z., & Osabutey, E. L. (2021). COVID-19 and business renewal: Lessons and insights from the global airline industry. *International Business Review*, *30*(3), 101802. doi:10.1016/j.ibusrev.2021.101802 PMID:36568574

Amariles, D. R., & Baquero, P. M. (2023). Promises and Limits of Law for a Human-centric Artificial Intelligence. *Computer Law & Security Report*, *48*, 105795. doi:10.1016/j.clsr.2023.105795

ANA. (2021). Relatório de Gestão e Contas 2020. *ANA - Aeroportos de Portugal*. ANA. https://www.ana.pt/pt/system/files/documents/ana_rgc_2020_pt_website_0.pdf

ANA. (2024). *Vinci Airports – Tráfego até 31 de Dezembro de 2023 [Vinci Airports – Traffic until December 31, 2023]*. ANA – Aeroportos de Portugal. https://pt.newsroom.ana.pt/assets/vinci-airports-trafego-2023-3595-4a6c7.html

ANAC. (2022). *Boletim Estatístico Trimestral N.º 56*. ANAC.

ANAC. (2023a). *Boletim Estatístico Trimestral nº 56* [Quarterly Statistical Bulletin nº 56]. Autoridade Nacional de Aviação Civil. https://www.anac.pt/SiteCollectionDocuments/Publicacoes/BET/BET_56_4TRIM_22.pdf

ANAC. (2023b). *Newsletters de tráfego* [Traffic Newsletters]. Autoridade Nacional de Aviação Civil. https://www.anac.pt/vPT/Generico/PublicacoesINAC/newslettersdetrafego/Paginas/NewslettersdeTrafego.aspx

Andrei, A. G., Balasa, R., & Semenescu, A. (2022, February). Setting up New Standards in the Aviation Industry with the Help of Artificial Intelligence–Machine Learning Application. [). IOP Publishing.]. *Journal of Physics: Conference Series*, *2212*(1), 012014. doi:10.1088/1742-6596/2212/1/012014

Andriotis, K. (2005). Seasonality in Crete: Problem or a way of life? *Tourism Economics*, *11*(2), 207–224. doi:10.5367/0000000054183478

Appelbaum, S. H., & Fewster, B. M. (2003). Global aviation human resource management: Contemporary employee and labour relations practices. *Management Research News*, *26*(10-11), 56–69. doi:10.1108/01409170310784069

Appinventiv. (2023, March 3). *Influence of AI in the Aviation Industry*. Appinventive. https://appinventiv.com/blog/ai-in-aviation/#:~:text=AI%20for%20aviation%20in%20the,implementing%20such%20cutting%2Dedge%20technologies

ARDITI. (2015). Madeira 2020: Estratégia Regional de Especialização Inteligente. *Agência Regional para o Desenvolvimento da Investigação, Tecnologia e Inovação*. ARDITI. https://ris3.arditi.pt/wp-content/uploads/2016/11/RIS3-RAM_2.2.2.1.pdf

Ashford, N., Stanton, H. P. M., & Moore, C. A. (1997). *Airport operations* (2nd ed.). McGraw-Hill.

ASP. (2022). Center for Strategic and International Studies-Aerospace Security Project. https://www.csis.org/programs/international-security-program/aerospace-security-project

ATAG. (2017). *Climate Action Takes Flight*. Beginner's Guide to Sustainable Aviation Fuel.

ATAG. (2021). *Waypoint 2050*. ATARG. www.atarg.org

Automated Airport Staff Scheduling . (n.d.). ZHAW Institute of Data Analysis and Process Design IDP. https://www.zhaw.ch/en/engineering/institutes-centres/idp/research/optimization-and-simulation/automated-airport-staff-scheduling/

Aviation Benefits. (2020). Employtment. *Aviation Benefits*. https://aviationbenefits.org/economic-growth/supporting-employment/

Aviation Week. (2023, April 27th). *Air Serbia To Increase Fleet By Half For Summer Season*. Aviationweek.com. https://aviationweek.com/air-transport/airlines-lessors/air-serbia-increase-fleet-half-summer-season

Aviationbenefits. (2020). *Aviation: Benefits Beyond Borders*. Aviationbenefits. https://aviationbenefits.org/

Azarian, R. (2011). Potentials and Limitations of Comparative Method in Social Science. *International Journal of Humanities and Social Science*, *1*(4), 113–125.

Bae, S. Y., & Chang, P. J. (2021). The effect of coronavirus disease-19 (COVID-19) risk perception on behavioural intention towards 'untact'tourism in South Korea during the first wave of the pandemic (March 2020). *Current Issues in Tourism*, *24*(7), 1017–1035. doi:10.1080/13683500.2020.1798895

Bajaj, R., Sinha, S., & Tiwari, V. (2013). Crucial factors of human resource management for good employee relations: A case study. *International Journal of Mining, Metallurgy &. Mechanical Engineering (New York, N.Y.)*, *1*(2).

Baker, S. R., Bloom, N., Davis, S. J., Kost, K., Sammon, M., & Viratyosin, T. (2020). The unprecedented stock market reaction to COVID-19. *Review of Asset Pricing Studies*, *10*(4), 742–758. doi:10.1093/rapstu/raaa008

Banks, V. A., Plant, K. L., & Stanton, N. A. (2019). Driving aviation forward; Contrasting driving automation and aviation automation. *Theoretical Issues in Ergonomics Science*, *20*(3), 250–264. doi:10.1080/1463922X.2018.1432716

BarOn, R. (1972). Seasonality in tourism – part I. *International Tourism Quarterly*, *4*, 40–64.

BarOn, R. (1973). Seasonality in tourism – part II. *International Tourism Quarterly*, *1*, 51–67.

BarOn. R. (1975). Seasonality in tourism: a guide to the analysis of seasonality and trends for policy making. Economist Intelligence Unit.

Baskas, H. (2023, January 25). Airports turn to AI and other tech tools to hunt for lost bags amid travel meltdowns. *NBC News*. https://www.nbcnews.com/tech/travel/airports-turn-ai-tech-tools-hunt-lost-bags-rcna65335

Bates, T. W., Kahle, K. M., & Stulz, R. M. (2009). Why do US firms hold so much more cash than they used to? *The Journal of Finance*, *64*(5), 1985–2021. doi:10.1111/j.1540-6261.2009.01492.x

Batista, D. A. (2023). *Aeroporto usa inteligência artificial para devolver rapidamente malas e objetos perdidos*. Melhores Destinos. https://www.melhoresdestinos.com.br/inteligencia-artificial-aeroporto.html

Baumann, S., & Klingauf, U. (2020). Modeling of Aircraft Fuel Consumption Using Machine Learning Algorithms. *CEAS Aeronautical Journal*, *11*(1), 277–287. doi:10.1007/s13272-019-00422-0

Baum, C. F., Caglayan, M., Stephan, A., & Talavera, O. (2008). Uncertainty determinants of corporate liquidity. *Economic Modelling*, *25*(5), 833–849. doi:10.1016/j.econmod.2007.11.006

Beaudry, C., & Swann, G. M. P. (2009). Firm Growth in Industrial Clusters of the United Kingdom. *Small Business Economics*, *32*(4), 409–424. https://www.jstor.org/stable/40344561. doi:10.1007/s11187-007-9083-9

Bebeitova, M. (2020). Space Economy and the Concept of Space Mining. *M.A. Thesis, Kocaeli University Institute of Social Sciences*, Kocaeli, Turkey.

Bebel, A. (2014). *Low Versus High Leverage*. LVH.

Beckouche, P. (1996). La France en villes (Félix Damette). Flux, (23), 50-51.

Bélis-Bergouignan, M.-C., Frigant, V., & Talbot, D. (2001). *L'Articulation Global/Local des Modèles Industriels Pharmaceutique, Automobile et Aéronautique*. Institut fédératif de recherches sur les dynamiques économiques. https://www.academia.edu/en/23599595/Global_local_articulation_in_industrial_models_for_phamaceuticals_automobile_and_aeronautics_In_French_

Belobaba, P. P. (2011). Did LCCs save airline revenue management? *Journal of Revenue and Pricing Management*, *10*(1), 19–22. doi:10.1057/rpm.2010.45

Benzler, G., & Wink, R. (2010). From agglomerations to technology-and knowledge driven clusters: Aeronautics cluster policies in Europe. *International Journal of Technology Management*, *50*(3/4), 318–336. doi:10.1504/IJTM.2010.032679

Berthon, P., Pitt, L., Plangger, K., & Shapiro, D. (2012). Marketing Meets Web 2.0, Social Media, and Creative Consumers: Implications for International Marketing Strategy. *Business Horizons*, *55*(3), 261–271. doi:10.1016/j.bushor.2012.01.007

Betiolo, C. R., Rocha, G. C., & Machado, P. (2015). *Iniciativas da Aviação para Redução das Emissões de CO2*. DABR. http://dcabr.org.br/download/publicacoes-tecnicas/Iniciativas_da_Aviacao_para_Reducao_das_Emissoes_de_CO2.pdf

Betts, R. K. (1987). Nuclear Blackmail And Nuclear Balance, (1. Edition). The Brookings Instition, Washington.

Bieger, T., Laesser, C., Wittmer, A., & Wittmer, D. (2012). Big Data in the Aviation Industry: Introduction and Preliminary Results. *Journal of Air Transport Management*, *25*, 1–2.

Bingöl, D. (2016). *İnsan kaynakları yönetimi*. Beta Basım Yayım Dağıtım A.Ş.

Bizarro, T. (2021). Fim do Estado de Emergência em Portugal. *Euronews*. https://pt.euronews.com/2021/04/28/fim-do-estado-de-emergencia-em-portugal

Black, J. (1992). *The British Abroad: The Grand Tour in the Eighteenth Century*. St. Martin's Press.

Blyton, P., Lucio, M. M., McGurk, J., & Turnbull, P. (2001). Globalization and trade union strategy: Industrial restructuring and human resource management in the international civil aviation industry. *International Journal of Human Resource Management*, *12*(3), 445–463. doi:10.1080/09585190122137

Bolbakov, R. G., Sinitsyn, A. V., & Tsvetkov, V. Ya. (2020). Methods of comparative analysis. *Journal of Physics: Conference Series*, *1679*(5), 052047. doi:10.1088/1742-6596/1679/5/052047

Boomerang. (2023). *Why Boomerang?* Boomerang. https://thanksboomerang.com/for-partners

Bouwer, J., Krishnan, V., Saxon, S., & Tufft, C. (2022, March 31). *Taking stock of the pandemic's impact on global aviation*. McKinsey & Company. https://www.mckinsey.com/industries/travel-logistics-and-infrastructure/our-insights/taking-stock-of-the-pandemics-impact-on-global-aviation

Boyd, C. (2001). HRM in the airline industry: Strategies and outcomes. *Personnel Review*, *30*(4), 438–453. doi:10.1108/00483480110393394

Brhane, H., & Zewdie, S. (2018). A literature review on the effects of employee relation on improving employee performance. *International Journal in Management and Social Sience*, *6*(4).

Briguglio, L. (1995). Small island developing states and their economic vulnerabilities. *World Development*, *23*(9), 1615–1632. doi:10.1016/0305-750X(95)00065-K

Brilha, N. (2008). Airport requirements for leisure travelers. In A. Graham, A. Papatheodorou, & P. Forsyth (Eds.), *Aviation and Tourism: Implications for the Leisure Travel* (pp. 167–176). Ashgate Publishing Limited.

British Airways. (n.d.) *About the Club: Executive Club*. British Airways. https://www.britishairways.com/pt-pt/executive-club/about-the-club?source=MNVEXC1about_the_executive_club

Brukardt, R. (2022). How Will The Space Economy Change The World? *McKinsey Quarterly*.

Bruno, G., Esposito, E., & Genovese, A. (2015). A model for aircraft evaluation to support strategic decisions. *Expert Systems with Applications*, *42*(13), 5580–5590. doi:10.1016/j.eswa.2015.02.054

BukhariS. (2011). What is Comparative Study?. SSRN. doi:10.2139/ssrn.1962328

Bulgarella, C. C. (2005). Employee satisfaction& customer satisfaction: Is there a relationship? Retrieved from Çağlar, Ç. (2021). Havacılıkta kurumsal sosyal sorumluluğun iç müşteri tatmini ile ilişkisi: Sektörel bir uygulama. [Havacılık Yönetimi Anabilim Dalı Master, İstanbul Gelişim Üniversitesi, İstanbul].

Business Analytics. (n.d.). *Inteligência Artificial: melhorar a experiência do cliente*. Business Analytics Portugal. http://businessanalytics.pt/inteligencia-artificial-melhorar-experiencia-dos-clientes/

Butler, R. (1994). Seasonality in Tourism: Issues and Problems. In A. Seaton (Ed.), *Tourism: The state of Art* (pp. 332–339). John Wiley & Sons, Ltd.

Butler, R. (2001). Seasonality in Tourism: Issues and Implications. In T. Baum & S. Lundtorp (Eds.), *Seasonality in Tourism* (pp. 5–23). Pergamon. doi:10.1016/B978-0-08-043674-6.50005-2

Butler, R. (2014). *Addressing Seasonality in Tourism: The Development of a Prototype – Conclusions and Recommendations resulting from the Punta del Este Conference*. World Tourism Organization.

Butler, R., & Mao, B. (1997). Seasonality in tourism: problems and measurement. In P. E. Murphy (Ed.), *Quality management in urban tourism* (pp. 9–24). John Wiley & Sons, Ltd.

Büyüközkan, G., Havle, C. A., & Feyzioğlu, O. (2020). A New Digital Service Quality Model and Its Strategic Analysis in the Aviation Industry Using Interval-Valued Intuitionistic Fuzzy AHP. *Journal of Air Transport Management*, *86*, 101817. doi:10.1016/j.jairtraman.2020.101817

Çağlar, Ç., & Türk, A. (2023). Understanding the role of corporate social responsibility on internal customer satisfaction for sustainable business strategy; A qualitative research in the aviation industry. *Journal of Aviation*, *7*(1), 141–146. doi:10.30518/jav.1246801

Calderón, D. J. (2021). Aviation Investment: Economic Appraisal for Airports, Air Traffic Management, Airlines and Aeronautics. England: Ashgate Publishing Limited.

Caniato, F., Kalchschmidt, M., & Ronchi, S. (2011). Integrating quantitative and qualitative forecasting approaches: Organizational learning in an action research case. *The Journal of the Operational Research Society*, *62*(3), 413–424. doi:10.1057/jors.2010.142

Cannas, R. (2012). An Overview of Tourism Seasonality: Key Concepts and Policies. *Alma Tourism - Journal of Tourism. Culture and Territorial Development*, *5*, 40–58.

Cannon, P. S., Angling, M., Barclay, L., Curry, C., Dyer, C., & Edwards, R. (2013a). Extreme space weather: impacts on engineered systems- a summary rep. Royal Academy of Engineering, London, UK.

Cannon, P. S., Angling, M., Barclay, L., Curry, C., Dyer, C., & Edwards, R. (2013b). Extreme space weather: impacts on engineered systems and infrastructure. Royal Academy of Engineering, London, UK. ISBN: 1-903496-96-9.

Carbon Offsetting and Reduction Scheme for International Aviation (CORSIA). (n.d.). *Home*. ICAO. https://www.icao.int/environmental-protection/CORSIA/Pages/default.aspx

Cardoso, P. M. (2023, March 31). Inteligência artificial já está sendo usada em um aeroporto brasileiro. *AERO Magazine*. https://aeromagazine.uol.com.br/artigo/inteligencia-artificial-ja-esta-sendo-usada-em-um-aeroporto-brasileiro.html

Carlson, N. R. (2014). Foundations of behavioural neuroscience [Lexical characteristics of Turkish language] (Trans. Ed. Muzaffer Şahin), Nobel Publications, İstanbul, Turkey.

Carrig, K. (1998). Reshaping human resources for the next century? Lessons from a high flying airline. *Human Resource Management*, *36*(2), 277–289. doi:10.1002/(SICI)1099-050X(199722)36:2<277::AID-HRM8>3.0.CO;2-U

Çelikbilek, Y., & Tüysüz, F. (2020). An In-depth Review of Theory of the TOPSIS Method: An Experimental Analysis. *Journal of Management Analytics*, *7*(2), 281–300. doi:10.1080/23270012.2020.1748528

Cesce (n.d). *Breve historia de la inteligencia artificial: el camino hacia la empresa.* Cesce. https://www.cesce.es/es/w/asesores-de-pymes/breve-historia-la-inteligencia-artificial-camino-hacia-la-empresa

Çetingüç, M. (2016). Havacılık ve Uzay Psikolojisi [Lexical characteristics of Turkish language], Nobel Publications, İstanbul, Turkey.

Chakraborty, K. (2022b). *How Automated Threat Recognition Technology Enhances Airport Security.* Techopedia. https://www.techopedia.com/how-automated-threat-recognition-technology-enhances-airport-security/2/34779

Chang, E. Y. (2020). From Aviation Tourism to Suborbital Space Tourism: A Study on Passenger Screening And Business Opportunities. *Acta Astronautica*, *177*, 410–420. doi:10.1016/j.actaastro.2020.07.020

Chang, S., Wang, Z., Wang, Y., Tang, J., & Jiang, X. (2019, August). Enabling Technologies And Platforms to Aid the Digitalization of Commercial Aviation Support, Maintenance, and Health Management. In *2019 International Conference on Quality, Reliability, Risk, Maintenance, and Safety Engineering (QR2MSE)* (pp. 926-932).IEEE 10.1109/QR2MSE46217.2019.9021222

Chan, W. T.-K., & Li, W.-C. (2023). Development of effective human factors interventions for aviation safety management. *Frontiers in Public Health*, *11*, 1–12. doi:10.3389/fpubh.2023.1144921 PMID:37213611

Chapman, S. C., Horne, R. B., & Watkins, N. W. (2020a). Using the aa index over the last 14 solar cycles to characterize extreme geomagnetic activity. *Geophysical Research Letters*, *47*(3), 1–10. doi:10.1029/2019GL086524

Chapman, S. C., McIntosh, S. W., Leamon, R. J., & Watkins, N. W. (2020b). Quantifying the solar cycle modulation of extreme space weather. *Geophysical Research Letters*, *47*(11), 1–9. doi:10.1029/2020GL087795

Chapman, S. C., Watkins, N. W., & Tindale, E. (2018). Reproducible aspects of the climate of space weather over the last five solar cycles. *Space Weather*, *16*(8), 1128–1142. doi:10.1029/2018SW001884

Chen, T. Y., & Tsao, C. Y. (2008). The Interval-valued Fuzzy TOPSIS Method and Experimental Analysis. *Fuzzy Sets and Systems*, *159*(11), 1410–1428. doi:10.1016/j.fss.2007.11.004

Chen, Y.-H., & Huang, S.-L. (2017). Analysis of Airline Service Personalization and Passengers' Intention. *Journal of Air Transport Management*, *58*, 42–49.

Chen, Y., Xiang, Z., & Li, X. (2019). The Dynamics of Customer Satisfaction with Personalized Recommendations in the Tourism Industry. *Journal of Travel Research*, *58*(8), 1421–1437. doi:10.1177/0047287518786887

Chen, Y., & Zhang, H. (2014). Big Data Analytics for Personalized and Context-Aware Travel Services. *Journal of Hospitality Marketing & Management*, *23*(5), 524–542.

Chung, J. Y. (2009). Seasonality in Tourism: A Review. *e-Review of Tourism Research, 7*(5), 82-96.

Chung, L. H. (2015). Impact of pandemic control over airport economics: Reconciling public health with airport business through a streamlined approach in pandemic control. *Journal of Air Transport Management*, *44*, 42–53. doi:10.1016/j.jairtraman.2015.02.003 PMID:32572319

Chu, T. C., & Lin, Y. C. (2003). A Fuzzy TOPSIS Method for Robot Selection. *International Journal of Advanced Manufacturing Technology*, *21*(4), 284–290. doi:10.1007/s001700300033

Çiçek, B., Bilkay, S., & Aktaş, K. (2023). Pandemi döneminde havacılık çalışanlarının tutumları. *Alanya Akademik Bakış*, *7*(1), 355–374. doi:10.29023/alanyaakademik.1136478

Cohen, E., & Spector, S. (2019). Space Tourism: The Elusive Dream, (1. Edition). Emerald Group Publishing, United Kingdom.

Connell, J., & Taulealo, T. (2021). Island tourism and COVID-19 in Vanuatu and Samoa: An unfolding crisis. *Small States & Territories*, *4*(1), 105–124.

Cooper, C., Fletcher, J., Fyall, A., Gilbert, D., & Wanhill, S. (2005). *Tourism Principles and Practice* (3rd ed.). Pearson Education.

Corluka, G. (2019). Tourism Seasonality – An overview. *Journal of Business Paradigms*, *4*(1), 21–43.

Coşgun, M. (2016). Avrupa Birliği'nde genişleme süreci. In A. Ayata & M. Ercan (Eds.), *Avrupa Birliği ve Türkiye ile İlişkileri: İlişkilerin Siyasi, Askeri, Ekonomik ve Kültürel Çerçevesi* (pp. 21–33).

Coşkun, Ö. F. (2020). Örgütsel sosyalleşme sürecinde kişi-iş uyumundan kişi-örgüt uyumuna yönelik bir model önerisi. *Mustafa Kemal Üniversitesi Sosyal Bilimler Enstitüsü Dergisi*, *17*(46), 605–625.

Costa, L. M. (2022). Determinants of Annual Abnormal Yields of Stocks belonging to the Euro stoxx 50 Index. *European Journal of Applied Business and Management*, *8*(2).

Costa, L., Ribeiro, A., & Machado, C. (2021). Determinants of stock market price: Empirical evidence for the PSI 20. *Ge-Magazine*, (22), 41–53.

Crane, K. W., Linck, E., Lal, B., & Wei, R. Y. (2020). *OECD Measuring the Space Economy: Estimating the Value of Economic Activities in and for Space*. Science and Technology Institute for Defense Analyses., doi:10.1787/c5996201-

Crawford, I. A. (2016). The Long-Term Scientific Benefits of a Space Economy. *Space Policy*, *37*(2), 58–61. doi:10.1016/j.spacepol.2016.07.003

Creswell, J. (2014). *Investigação qualitativa e projeto de pesquisa: Escolhendo entre cinco abordagens. 3*. Penso.

Cüceloğlu, D. (2000). İnsan ve Davranışı: Psikolojinin Temel Kavramları [Lexical characteristics of Turkish language]. Remzi Publications, İstanbul, Turkey.

Cunha, J. M. V. (2015). *Evaluating the privatization of the portuguese national airline-tap* [Doctoral dissertation].

Cunha, L. (2009). *Introdução ao turismo* [Introduction to tourism] 4th ed.). Editorial Verbo.

Dan-Okoro, R., Musa, H. S., & Agidi, V. (2018). Seasonal effects of weather elements on flight operations at Nnamdi Azikiwe International Airport Abuja, Nigeria. *Current Journal of Applied Science and Technology*, *28*(6), 1–10. doi:10.9734/CJAST/2018/41590

Dartmouth. (2023). *Artificial Intelligence Coined at Dartmouth*. Dartmouth. https://home.dartmouth.edu/about/artificial-intelligence-ai-coined-dartmouth

Dasgupta, S. A., Suar, D., & Singh, S. (2013). Impact of managerial communication styles on employees' attitudes and behaviours. *Employee Relations*, *35*(2), 173–199. doi:10.1108/01425451311287862

de Assis, G. S., dos Santos, M., and Basilio, M. P. (2023). Use of the WASPAS Method to Select Suitable Helicopters for Aerial Activity Carried Out by the Military Police of the State of Rio de Janeiro. *Axioms, 12*(1), 77. doi:10.3390/axioms12010077

De Farias Aires, R. F., & Ferreira, L. (2019). A New Approach to Avoid Rank Reversal Cases in The TOPSIS Method. *Computers & Industrial Engineering*, *132*, 84–97. doi:10.1016/j.cie.2019.04.023

De Neufville, R., & Odoni, A. R. (2003). Airport systems: Planning. McGraw-Hill.

De, F. S. M., Russo, R., & Camanho, R. (2015). Criteria in AHP: A Systematic Review of Literature. *Procedia Computer Science*, *55*, 1123–1132. doi:10.1016/j.procs.2015.07.081

Degas, A., Islam, M. R., Hurter, C., Barua, S., Rahman, H., Poudel, M., Ruscio, D., Ahmed, M. U., Begum, S., Rahman, M. A., Bonelli, S., Cartocci, G., Di Flumeri, G., Borghini, G., Babiloni, F., & Arico, P. (2022). A Survey on Artificial Intelligence (AI) and Explainable AI in Air Traffic Management: Current Trends and Development with Future Research Trajectory. *Applied Sciences (Basel, Switzerland)*, *12*(3), 1295. doi:10.3390/app12031295

Delli, K. (2021). Pergunta parlamentar | Impacto da crise da COVID-19 no setor da aviação | O-000033/2021. *Parlamento Europeu*. Europal. https://www.europarl.europa.eu/doceo/document/O-9-2021-000033_PT.html

Demirbaş, E., & Özek, H. (2021). Does feedbaack play a role during the construction of internal customers' psychological capital? *Journal of Global Strategic Management*, *15*(2), 89–106. Advance online publication. doi:10.20460/JGSM.2022.305

Demirel, Y., & Güner, E. (2015). İç müşteri İlişkileri yönetiminin örgütsel vatandaşlık davranışı üzerine etkisi. *International Journal of Alanya Faculty of Business*, *7*(2), 1–14.

Derse, O., & Yontar, E. (2020). SWARA-TOPSIS Yöntemi ile En Uygun Yenilenebilir Enerji Kaynağının Belirlenmesi. *Endüstri Mühendisliği*, *31*(3), 389–419. doi:10.46465/endustrimuhendisligi.798063

Dessler, G. (2013). *Human resource management* (13th ed.). Pearson.

Dettmer, B., Socorro, C., & Katon, H. T. (2002). Marketing de Servicios-Análise Da Percepçâo Da Qualidade de Serviços Através Da Ferramenta Servqual Em Uma Instituiçâo de Ensino Superior de Santa Catarina. *Ciencias Da Administraçao*, *4*(8), 5. https://dialnet.unirioja.es/servlet/articulo?codigo=4014179&info=resumen&idioma=ENG

Deveci, M., Çiftçi, M. E., Akyurt, İ. Z., & Gonzalez, E. D. S. (2022). Impact of COVID-19 pandemic on the Turkish civil aviation industry. *Sustainable Operations and Computers*, *3*, 93–102. doi:10.1016/j.susoc.2021.11.002

Deveci, M., Öner, S. C., Ciftci, M. E., Özcan, E., & Pamucar, D. (2022). Interval type-2 hesitant fuzzy Entropy-based WASPAS approach for aircraft type selection. *Applied Soft Computing*, *114*, 108076. doi:10.1016/j.asoc.2021.108076

Ding, W., Levine, R., Lin, C., & Xie, W. (2021). Corporate immunity to the COVID-19 pandemic. *Journal of Financial Economics*, *141*(2), 802–830. doi:10.1016/j.jfineco.2021.03.005 PMID:34580557

DN. (2020, June 1st). Cronologia de uma pandemia em português. Os três meses que mudaram o país. *Diário de Notícias*. Available at: https://bit.ly/3sBZ4XJ.

Dobruszkes, F., Decroly, J.-M., & Suau-Sanchez, P. (2022). The monthly rhythms of aviation: A global analysis of passenger air service seasonality. *Transportation Research Interdisciplinary Perspectives*, *14*, 100582. doi:10.1016/j.trip.2022.100582

Dodds, R., & Butler, R. (2019). The phenomena of overtourism: A review. *International Journal of Tourism Cities*, *5*(4), 519–528. doi:10.1108/IJTC-06-2019-0090

Doganis, R. (2006). *The Airline Business* (2nd ed.). Routledge.

Doganis, R. (2009). *Flying off course: airline economics and marketing*. Routledge. doi:10.4324/9780203863992

Doğan, S. (2005). *Çalışan İlişkileri Yönetimi*. Kare Yayınları.

Dolnicar, S., & Grün, B. (2014). The Effect of Innovations Relevant to Hotel Performance on Key Customer Outcomes: A Data Mining Approach. *Journal of Business Research*, *67*(9), 1967–1976.

Dormehl, L. (2018). Asteroid Mining is Almost Reality. What to Know About the Gold Rush in Space. *Science Buddies*. https://www.sciencebuddies.org/

Doviak, R. J., Vladislav, M. D., & Zrnic, S. (1999). Aviation Weather Surveillance Systems "Advanced Radar and Surface Sensors for Flight Safety and Air Traffic Management". United Kingdom: The Institution of Electrical Engineers.

Dožić, S., Lutovac, T., & Kalić, M. (2018). Fuzzy AHP approach to passenger aircraft type selection. *Journal of Air Transport Management*, *68*, 165–175. doi:10.1016/j.jairtraman.2017.08.003

DREM. (2021). *Estatísticas do Turismo da Região Autónoma da Madeira - Ano de 2020*. Direção Regional de Estatística da Madeira.

Drobnič, S. (2014). Comparative Analysis. In A. C. Michalos (Ed.), *Encyclopedia of Quality of Life and Well-Being Research*. Springer., doi:10.1007/978-94-007-0753-5_492

Dube, K., & Nhamo, G. (2020). Major global aircraft manufacturers and emerging responses to the SDGs agenda. In *Scaling up SDGs Implementation* (pp. 99–113). Springer. doi:10.1007/978-3-030-33216-7_7

Dube, K., Nhamo, G., & Chikodzi, D. (2021). COVID-19 pandemic and prospects for recovery of the global aviation industry. *Journal of Air Transport Management*, *92*, 102022. doi:10.1016/j.jairtraman.2021.102022 PMID:36567961

Duro, J. A. (2016). Seasonality of hotel demand in the main Spanish provinces: Measurements and decomposition exercises. *Tourism Management*, *52*, 52–63. doi:10.1016/j.tourman.2015.06.013

Duro, J. A., Perez-Laborda, A., Turrion-Prats, J., & Fernández-Fernández, M. (2021). Covid-19 and tourism vulnerability. *Tourism Management Perspectives*, *38*, 100819. doi:10.1016/j.tmp.2021.100819 PMID:34873568

Dymova, L., Sevastjanov, P., & Tikhonenko, A. (2013). A Direct Interval Extension of TOPSIS Method. *Expert Systems with Applications*, *40*(12), 4841–4847. doi:10.1016/j.eswa.2013.02.022

EASA - The European Authority for aviation safety. (n.d.). *Home*. EASA. https://www.easa.europa.eu/en/light

EASA. (2019). European Aviation. *Environment Reporter*, 2019.

Ecer, F. (2018). Third-party logistics (3Pls) provider selection via Fuzzy AHP and EDAS integrated model. *Technological and Economic Development of Economy, 24*(2), 615–634–615–634. doi:10.3846/20294913.2016.1213207

ECO. (2021). Criação de valor com a IA. SAPO. https://eco.sapo.pt/2021/12/15/criacao-de-valor-com-a-ia/

Edelman, D. A., Duggan, L. V., Lockhart, S. L., Marshall, S. D., Turner, M. C., & Brewster, D. J. (2022). Prevalence and commonality of non-technical skills and human factors in airway management guidelines: A narrative review of the last 5 years. *Anaesthesia*, *77*(10), 1129–1136. doi:10.1111/anae.15813 PMID:36089858

EIB. (2021). *The Future of The European Space Sector How to Leverage Europe's Technological Leadership and Boost Investments for Space Ventures*. EIB. https://www.eib.org/attachments/thematic/future_of_european_space_sector_en.pdf

Eichorn, F. L. (2004a). *Applying internal customer relationship management (intcrm) principles for improving business / IT integration and performance*. [Doctoral Thesis, University of Maryland].

Eichorn, F. L. (2004b). Internal customer relationship management (Int-CRM): A framework for achieving customer relationship management from the inside out. *Problems and Perspectives in Management*, *1*, 154–177.

Eilstrup-Sangiovanni, M. (2022). Ordering global governance complexes: The evolution of the governance complex for international civil aviation. *The Review of International Organizations*, *17*(2), 293–322. doi:10.1007/s11558-020-09411-z PMID:35722452

Ekşi İ, G, Boztepe İ, Kurban D, Özcan L, Uçar İ, Bilgin K. B., & Öztürk Ö. (2019). Space and Medicine Where Are We? What Should We Do?. *Med J SDU. 26*(4), 498-504.

Energy Transitions Commission (ETC). (n.d.). *Home*. Etc. https://www.energy-transitions.org/

Eraslan, E., & Balcı, A. İ. (2022). İnsan kaynakları yönetimi ve endüstri ilişkilerinin çatışması noktasında değişen toplu pazarlık düzeylerinin karşılaştırmalı bir analizi. *Niğde Ömer Halisdemir Üniversitesi Sosyal Bilimler Enstitüsü Dergisi*, *4*(2), 164–180. doi:10.56574/nohusosbil.1209232

Erceylan, N., & Atilla, G. (2022). Aviation safety and risk management during COVID-19. In S. Kurnaz & E. Argın (Eds.), *Digitalization and the Impacts of COVID-19 on the Aviation Industry*. IGI Global., doi:10.4018/978-1-6684-2319-6.ch007

Ertel, W. (2009). *Introduction to Artificial Intelligence*. Springer.

Etzkowitz, H., & Leyesdorff, L. (1995). The Triple Helix—University-Industry-Government Relations: A Laboratory for Knowledge-Based Economic Development. *EASST Review*, *14*, 14–19.

EU taxonomy for sustainable activities. (n.d.). Europa. https://finance.ec.europa.eu/sustainable-finance/tools-and-standards/eu-taxonomy-sustainable-activities_en

Eur-Lex. (2018). Regulation (EU) 2018/1139 of the European Parliament and of the Council of 4 July 2018. *Official Journal of the European Union*. https://eur-lex.europa.eu/legal-content/EN/TXT/?uri=celex%3A32018R1139

Eurocontrol (2021). *Aviation Intelligence Unit* (Think Paper #8.). Eurocontrol. https://www.eurocontrol.int/sites/default/files/2021-02/eurocontrol-think-paper-8-impact-of-covid-19-on-european-aviation-in-2020-and-outlook-2021.pdf

Eurocontrol. (2020). *Daily Traffic Variation - States*. Eurocontrol. https://www.eurocontrol.int/Economics/2020-Daily-TrafficVariation-States.html

EUROCONTROL. (2022). *EUROCONTROL Aviation Outlook*, *2050*, 24.

European Commission. (2009, February 11). *The impact of the use of body scanners in the field of aviation security on human rights, privacy, personal dignity, health and data protection*. EC. https://ec.europa.eu/justice/article-29/documentation/other-document/files/2009/2009_05_11_annex_consultation_letter_chairman_art29wp_daniel_calleja_dgtren_en.pdf

European green bond standard. (n.d.). Europa. https://finance.ec.europa.eu/sustainable-finance/tools-and-standards/european-green-bond-standard_en

European Green Deal. https://commission.europa.eu/strategy-and-policy/priorities-2019-2024/european-green-deal_en

European Parliament. (2021). *Le isole dell'unione europea: situazione attuale e sfide future*. Parlamento Europeo. https://bit.ly/3JngAEK

European Union Aviation Safety Agency (EASA). (n.d.). *Home.* EASA. https://www.easa.europa.eu/en/light

Europeu Parliment. (2021). *Le isole dell'unione europea: situazione attuale e sfide future.* Parlamento Europeu. https://www.europarl.europa.eu/RegData/etudes/STUD/2021/652239/IPOL_STU(2021)652239(SUM01)_IT.pdf

Evans, J. E. (2001). Developments in US Aviation Weather R&D. In L. Bianco, P. Dell'Olmo, & A. R. Odoni (Eds.). New Concepts and Methods in Air Traffic Management (vol. 1, pp. 213-224). Berlin: Springer. doi:10.1007/978-3-662-04632-6_13

Faiza, Khalil, K. (2023). Airline Flight Delays Using Artificial Intelligence in COVID-19 with Perspective Analytics. *Journal of Intelligent & Fuzzy Systems*, 1-23.

Farinha, L., & Ferreira, J. J. (2013). *Triangulation of the triple helix: a conceptual framework.* (Working Paper 1). Triple Helix Association.

Farraró, A. V. (2023). *Tourism Issues: Seasonality and Economic Structure.* [Doctoral Thesis], Faculty of Geography and Tourism, Department of Geography, Universitat Rovira i Virgili, Vilaseca, Tarragona, Spain.

Fernandes, C., Peguinho, C., Vieira, E., & Neiva, J. (2019). *Financial Analysis: Theory and Practice – Application within the scope of the CNS.* Syllabus Editions.

Ferrante, M., Lo Magno, G., & De Cantis, S. (2018). Measuring tourism seasonality across European countries. *Tourism Management*, *68*(1), 220–235. doi:10.1016/j.tourman.2018.03.015

Fetzer, T., Hensel, L., Hermle, J., & Roth, C. (2021). Coronavirus perceptions and economic anxiety. *The Review of Economics and Statistics*, *103*(5), 968–978. doi:10.1162/rest_a_00946

FFMS. (2019). Retrato da Madeira PORDATA. Edição 2019. *Fundação Francisco Manuel dos Santos.* Por Data. https://www.pordata.pt/ebooks/MA2019v20190712/mobile/index.html

Fisher, E. G., & Marciano, V. (1997). Managing human resource shortages in a unionized setting: Best practices in air traffic control. *Journal of Labor Research*, *18*(2), 287–314. doi:10.1007/s12122-997-1040-5

Flannery, J. A. (2001). *Safety culture and its measurement in aviation.* University of Newcastle.

Flight Global. (2023). *The pilot survey 2023.* Flight Global. https://www.flightglobal.com/download?ac=91648

Florido-Benítez, L. (2021). The effects of COVID-19 on Andalusian tourism and aviation sector. *Tourism Review*, *76*(4), 829–857. doi:10.1108/TR-12-2020-0574

Fontanet-Pérez, P., Vázquez, X. H., & Carou, D. (2022). The impact of the COVID-19 crisis on the US airline market: Are current business models equipped for upcoming changes in the air transport sector? *Case Studies on Transport Policy*, *10*(1), 647–656. doi:10.1016/j.cstp.2022.01.025 PMID:36157268

Formulário de Contacto – Envie Pedidos, Sugestões Ou Reclamações. (n.d.). TAP Air Portugal. https://www.flytap.com/pt-pt/suporte/fale-connosco

Foster, C. J., Plant, K. L., & Stanton, N. A. (2023). Maladaptation in air traffic management: Development of a human factors methods framework. *Human Factors and Ergonomics in Manufacturing*, *33*(1), 118–146. doi:10.1002/hfm.20974

Friel, P. J. (2019). Space-Based Ballistic Missile Defense: An Overview of the Technical Issues. Laser Weapons in Spac. Routledge, New York. DOI: doi:10.4324/9780429050053

Frigant, V., Kechidi, M., & Talbot, D. (2006). *Les territoires de l'aéronautique: EADS, entre mondialisation et ancrage.* France: Editions L' Harmattan.

Frontur (2021). *Movimientos turísticos en fronteras (FRONTUR)*. Secretaria de Estado de Turismo. https://www.dataestur.es/general/frontur/

Frost, R. (2023, 5th July). Return to travel chaos? Air passengers warned they could face a 'challenging' summer. *Euronews.com*. https://www.euronews.com/travel/2023/07/05/return-to-travel-chaos-air-passengers-warned-they-could-face-a-challenging-summer

FSB Task Force on Climate-related Financial Disclosures. (n.d.). FSB Taskforce. https://www.fsb-tcfd.org/

Furht, B., & Villanustre, F. (2016). Introduction to Big Data. In *Big Data Technologies and Applications* (pp. 3–11). Springer International Publishing. doi:10.1007/978-3-319-44550-2_1

Gabinete Oliveira das Neves. (2017). *Avaliação de resultados e impacto do investimento realizado no aeródromo municipal de Ponte de Sor*.

Gagarin, Y., & Lebedev, V. (1984). *Uzay ve Psikoloji* [Lexical characteristics of Turkish language]. (B. Konukman, Ed. & Trans.). İnkılap Publications.

Gandomi, A., & Haider, M. (2015). Beyond the Hype: Big Data Concepts, Methods, and Analytics. *International Journal of Information Management*, *35*(2), 137–144. doi:10.1016/j.ijinfomgt.2014.10.007

Gao, F., Wang, W., Bi, C., Bi, W., & Zhang, A. (2023). Prioritization of used aircraft acquisition criteria: A fuzzy best–worst method (BWM)-based approach. *Journal of Air Transport Management*, *107*, 102359. doi:10.1016/j.jairtraman.2023.102359

García-cascales, M. S., & Lamata, M. T. (2012). On Rank Reversal and TOPSIS Method. *Mathematical and Computer Modelling*, *56*(5-6), 123–132. doi:10.1016/j.mcm.2011.12.022

Garrigos-Simon, F., Narangajavana, Y., & Gil-Pechuan, I. (2010). Seasonality and price behaviour of airlines in the Alicante-London market. *Journal of Air Transport Management*, *16*(6), 350–354. doi:10.1016/j.jairtraman.2010.05.007

Gates, B. (2021). *How To Avoid a Climate Disaster: The Solutions We Have and the Breakthrough We Need*. Random House Publishing.

Gawande, A. (2009). *Checklist manifesto* (7th ed.). Domingo.

Gemici, E., & Yılmaz, H. (2019). Güvenlik stratejileri ve yönetimi açısından havacılık güvenliği. *Journal of Aviation*, *3*(1), 15–27. doi:10.30518/jav.550123

Gennard, J. (2005). Employee relations. London: CIPD publishing.

Ghorabaee, M. K., Amiri, M., Zavadskas, E. K., & Turskis, Z. (2017). Multi-criteria group decision-making using an extended EDAS method with interval type-2 fuzzy sets. *E+M. Ekonomie a Management*, *20*(1), 48–68. doi:10.15240/tul/001/2017-1-004

Ghorabaee, M. K., Zavadskas, E. K., Olfat, L., & Turskis, Z. (2015). Multi-Criteria Inventory Classification Using a New Method of Evaluation Based on Distance from Average Solution (EDAS). *Informatica (Vilnius)*, *26*(3), 435–451. doi:10.15388/Informatica.2015.57

Gibert, G. R. (2000). Measuring internal customer satisfaction. *Managing Service Quality*, *10*(3), 178–186. doi:10.1108/09604520010336704

Gillet, A., & Tremblay, D.-G. (2021). Working in the air: Time management and work intensification challenges for workers in commercial aviation. *Open Journal of Social Sciences*, *9*(1), 272–290. doi:10.4236/jss.2021.91020

Göker, Ü. D. (2008). The importance of heat conduction and viscosity in solar corona and comparison of magnetohydrodynamic equations of one-fluid and two-fluid structure in current sheet. *Sun and Geosphere, 3*(1), 52-56.

Göker, Ü. D. (2018). Jeomanyetik fırtınaların pilotların kognitif durumlarına etkileri üzerine hipotez [Lexical characteristics of Turkish language]. *Journal of Defense Sciences, 17*(2), 116-138.

Göker, Ü. D. (2012). Magnetohydrodynamic study of shock waves in the current sheet of a solar coronal magnetic loop. *New Astronomy, 17*(2), 130–136. doi:10.1016/j.newast.2011.06.010

Göker, Ü. D. (2023). Short- and long-term changes in the neurophysiological status of pilots due to radiation exposure caused by geomagnetic storms. *Medical Research Archives, 11*(9), 1–17. doi:10.18103/mra.v11i9.4395

Göker, Ü. D., Yazıcı, M., Balcı, G., Köksal, Ö., & Şengelen, H. E. (2021). The statistical analysis of air crash investigations from 1918 to 2019. *Journal of Defense Sciences, 2*(40), 1–32. doi:10.17134/khosbd.1000317

Gomes, D. (2009). *Inteligência Artificial: Conceitos e Aplicações*. Universidade Federal Fluminense. https://www.professores.uff.br/screspo/wp-content/uploads/sites/127/2017/09/ia_intro.pdf

González, V. M. (2013). Leverage and corporate performance: International evidence. *International Review of Economics & Finance, 25*, 169–184. doi:10.1016/j.iref.2012.07.005

Gossling, S. (2020). Risks, resilience, and pathways to sustainable aviation: A COVID-19 perspective. *Journal of Air Transport Management, 89*, 101933. doi:10.1016/j.jairtraman.2020.101933 PMID:32952322

Gössling, S., & Humpe, A. (2020). The global scale, distribution and growth of aviation: Implications for climate change. *Global Environmental Change, 65*, 102194. doi:10.1016/j.gloenvcha.2020.102194 PMID:36777089

Gratton, C., & Jones, I. (2010). *Research methods for sports studies* (Vol. 2). Routledge. doi:10.4324/9780203879382

Grbčić, A., Hess, S., Hess, M., & Krljan, T. (2021). The impact of seasonality on efficient airport capacity utilization. *Scientific Journal of Maritime Research, 35*(2), 215–223. doi:10.31217/p.35.2.3

Green Loan Principles. (n.d.). LSTA. https://www.lsta.org/content/green-loan-principles/

Greene, B. (2004). The Fabric of The Cosmos: Space, Time, and The Texture of Reality. Knopf. (1. Edition). Vintage Books, New York.

Gretzel, U., Sigala, M., Xiang, Z., & Koo, C. (2015). *Recommender Systems in Tourism*. Springer.

Grönroos, C. (2008). *Service Management and Marketing: Customer Management in Service Competition*. John Wiley & Sons.

Gruetzemacher, R., Paradice, D., & Lee, K. B. (2020). Forecasting Extreme Labor Displacement: A Survey of AI Practitioners. *Technological Forecasting and Social Change, 161*, 120323. doi:10.1016/j.techfore.2020.120323

Gu, Y., Onggo, B. S., Kunc, M. H., & Bayer, S. (2021). Small Island Developing States (SIDS) COVID-19 post-pandemic tourism recovery: A system dynamics approach. *Current Issues in Tourism,* (pp. 1–28). Taylor & Francis. doi:10.1080/13683500.2021.1924636

Guillot, A. (2018). What Is RevPar? How to Calculate & Improve RevPAR at Your Hotel? *Amadeus Hospitality*. https://bit.ly/3w9uIg6

Gultepe, I., & Feltz, W. F. (2019). Aviation meteorology: Observations and model. *Pure and Applied Geophysics, 176*(5), 1863–1867. doi:10.1007/s00024-019-02188-2

Gures, N., Arslan, S., & Tun, S. Y. (2014). Customer Expectation, Satisfaction and Loyalty Relationship in Turkish Airline Industry. *International Journal of Marketing Studies*, *6*(April). doi:10.5539/ijms.v6n1p66

Gustafsson, A., Johnson, M. D., & Roos, I. (2005). The Effects of Customer Satisfaction, Relationship Commitment Dimensions, and Triggers on Customer Retention. *Journal of Marketing*, *69*(4), 210–218. doi:10.1509/jmkg.2005.69.4.210

Gustafsson, A., Kristensson, P., & Witell, L. (2005). Customer Co-Creation in Service Innovation. *Journal of Service Research*, *7*(2), 111–124. doi:10.1177/1094670520908929

Hallows, R., Glazier, L., Katz, M. S., Aznar, M., & Williams, M. (2022). Safe and Ethical Artificial Intelligence in Radiotherapy–Lessons Learned from the Aviation Industry. *Clinical Oncology*, *34*(2), 99–101. doi:10.1016/j.clon.2021.11.019 PMID:34922798

Halpern, N. (2011). Measuring seasonal demand for Spanish airports: Implications for counter-seasonal strategies. *Research in Transportation Business & Management*, *1*(1), 47–54. doi:10.1016/j.rtbm.2011.05.005

Hamet, P., & Tremblay, J. (2017). Artificial Intelligence in Medicine. *Metabolism: Clinical and Experimental*, *69*, S36–S40. doi:10.1016/j.metabol.2017.01.011 PMID:28126242

Harris, M. (2016, October). AI-powered body scanners could soon be inspecting you in public places. *The Guardian*. https://www.theguardian.com/technology/2016/oct/25/airport-body-scanner-artificial-intelligence

Harris, D., & Stanton, N. A. (2010). Aviation as a system of systems: Preface to the special issue of human factors in aviation. *Ergonomics*, *53*(2), 145–148. doi:10.1080/00140130903521587 PMID:20099170

Harter, J. K., Schmidt, F. L., & Hayes, T. L. (2002). Business-unit-level relationship between employee satisfaction, employee engagement, and business outcomes: A meta-analysis. *The Journal of Applied Psychology*, *87*(2), 268–279. doi:10.1037/0021-9010.87.2.268 PMID:12002955

Harvey, G., & Turnbull, P. (2020). Ricardo flies Ryanair: Strategic human resource management and competitive advantage in a single european aviation market. *Human Resource Management Journal*, *30*(4), 553–565. doi:10.1111/1748-8583.12315

Hassen, T. B. (2009). Toulouse, l'avion et la ville, de Guy Jalabert et Jean-Marc Zuliani, Toulouse. *Canadian Journal of Regional Science*, *32*(3), 511+. https://link.gale.com/apps/doc/A245543046/AONE?u=anon~f6482c3e&sid=googleScholar&xid=1fd072f9

Hassen, T. B. (2012). Le Système Régional D' ['*Aéronautique à Montréal Entre Dynamiques Territoriales et Sectorielles*.]. *Innovations: Technology, Governance, Globalization*, L.

Hassen, T. B., Klein, J.-L., & Tremblay, D.-G. (2012). Interorganizational Relations, Proximity, and Innovation: The Case of the Aeronautics Sector in Montreal. *Canadian Journal of Urban Research*, *21*(1), 52–78. https://www.jstor.org/stable/26193883

Hendrawati, Erna, I Gede Juanamasta, Ni Made, Nopita Wati, Wiwin Wahyuni, Mira Pramudianti, Nugrahini Wisnujati, et al. (2019). The Role of Customer Service through Customer Relationship Management (CRM) to Increase Customer Loyalty and Good Image the Role of Customer Service through Customer Relationship Management (CRM) to Increase Customer Loyalty and Good Image. *International Journal of Scientific & Technology Research*, *49*, 310.

Henkes, J. A. (2021). Civil aviation in times of pandemic and post-pandemic: A punctual analysis. *Brazilian Journal of Civil Aviation & Aeronautical Sciences*, *1*(5), 1–3.

Henry, L. W. (2016). Leadership, Change, and Public-Private Partnerships: A Case Study of Nasa and the Transition From Space Shuttle to Commercial Space Flight. *IBM Center for the Business of Government*, (pp. 1-51). IBM.

He, P., Sun, Y., Zhang, Y., & Li, T. (2020). COVID–19's impact on stock prices across different sectors—An event study based on the Chinese stock market. *Emerging Markets Finance & Trade*, *56*(10), 2198–2212. doi:10.1080/1540 496X.2020.1785865

Heracleous, L., & Wirtz, J. (2009). Strategy and organization at Singapore Airlines: Achieving sustainable advantage through dual strategy. *Journal of Air Transport Management*, *15*(6), 274–279. doi:10.1016/j.jairtraman.2008.11.011

Heung, V. & Nga-Ching, T. (2016). Personalization of Airport Services: The Role of Passenger Data and Technology. *Journal of Travel Research, 56*(8).

Hewins, I. M., Gibson, S. E., Webb, D. F., McFadden, R. H., Kuchar, T. A., Emery, B. A., & McIntosh, S. W. (2020). The evolution of coronal holes over three solar cycles using the McIntosh archive. *Solar Physics*, *295*(11), 161–176. doi:10.1007/s11207-020-01731-y

Heyden, K. J., & Heyden, T. (2021). Market reactions to the arrival and containment of COVID-19: An event study. *Finance Research Letters*, *38*, 101745. doi:10.1016/j.frl.2020.101745 PMID:32895606

Hinch, T., & Hickey, G. (1996). Tourism attractions and seasonality: spatial relationships in Alberta. In K. Mackay & K. Boyd (Eds.), *Tourism for All Seasons: Using Research to Meet the Challenge of Seasonality* (pp. 69–76). University of Manitoba.

Hooda, S. K., & Yadav, S. (2023). Green Finance for Sustainable Aviation: Stakeholder Perspectives and Systematic Review. *International Journal of Professional Business Review*, *8*(5), e02085. doi:10.26668/businessreview/2023.v8i5.2085

Horiguchi, Y., Baba, Y., Kashima, H., Suzuki, M., Kayahara, H., & Maeno, J. (2017, February). Predicting Fuel Consumption and Flight Delays for Low-cost Airlines. *Proceedings of the AAAI Conference on Artificial Intelligence*, *31*(2), 4686–4693. doi:10.1609/aaai.v31i2.19095

Hosny, A., Parmar, C., Quackenbush, J., Schwartz, L. H., & Aerts, H. J. (2018). Artificial Intelligence in Radiology. *Nature Reviews. Cancer*, *18*(8), 500–510. doi:10.1038/s41568-018-0016-5 PMID:29777175

Huang, M. H., & Rust, R. T. (2018). Artificial Intelligence In Service. *Journal of Service Research*, *21*(2), 155–172. doi:10.1177/1094670517752459

Huang, Y.-T. (2020). Internal marketing and internal customer: A review, reconceptualization, and extension. *Journal of Relationship Marketing*, *19*(3), 165–181. doi:10.1080/15332667.2019.1664873

Huang, Z., Benyoucef, M., & Poon, S. K. (2018). Service Personalization: A Comprehensive Review and Future Research Directions. *Computers in Human Behavior*, *83*, 500–519.

Hunter, L. (2006). Low Cost Airlines. Business Model and Employment Relations. *European Management Journal*, *24*(5), 315–321. doi:10.1016/j.emj.2006.08.001

Hussain, A. (2023). *How artificial intelligence can help airports in the areas of safety and security*. LinkedIn. https://www.linkedin.com/pulse/how-artificial-intelligence-can-help-airports-areas-safety-hussain/

Hylleberg, S. (1992). *Modelling Seasonality*. Oxford University Press. doi:10.1093/oso/9780198773177.001.0001

IAG. (2020). *IAG Flightpath net zero*. IAG.

IATA. (2021). *Outlook for the global airline industry - April 2021 update*. IATA. https://www.iata.org/en/iata-repository/publications/economic-reports/airline-industry-economic-performance---april-2021---report/

IATA. (2022). *Airline Industry Economic Performance – June 2022*. International Air Transport Association. https://bit.ly/3QLM7TL.

IBERIA. (n.d.) *Iberia No Seu Telemóvel - Iberia Portugal*. IBERIA. https://www.iberia.com/pt/pt/iberia-app/

idD Portugal Defense. (2023, September 25). *Factsheet Defence Economy in Portugal*. IDDPortugal. https://www.id-dportugal.pt/wp-content/uploads/2022/10/Factsheet-Economia-de-Defesa-em-Portugal-2022-EN.pdf

INAC. (2012). *Impacto das Transportadoras de Baixo Custo no Transporte Aéreo Nacional* [Impact of Low-Cost Carriers on National Air Transport]. Instituto Nacional de Aviação Civil.

Indeed (2021). *What Is Comparative Analysis and How Is It Used?* Indeed. https://www.indeed.com/career-advice/career-development/comparative-analysis

INE. (2021). Estatísticas do turismo. *Instituto Nacional de Turismo*. https://bit.ly/3K5PFyb.

INE. (2023). *Hóspedes não residentes nos estabelecimentos de alojamento turístico, segundo a NUTS II* [Non-resident guests in tourist accommodation establishments, according to NUTS II]. Instituto Nacional de Estatística.

Instituto de Engenharia. (2018). *A história da inteligência artificial*. Instituto de Engenharia. https://www.institutodeen-genharia.org.br/site/2018/10/29/a-historia-da-inteligencia-artificial/

International Capital Market Association. (2022). *Green Bonds Principles*. ICMA. https://www.icmagroup.org/assets/documents/Sustainable-finance/2022-updates/Green-Bond-Principles-June-2022-060623.pdf

International Civil Aviation Organization (ICAO). (n.d.). *Home*. ICAO. https://www.icao.int/Pages/default.aspx

İpek, S. (2019). Yapay Zekanın Toplum Üzerindeki Etkisi ve Yapay Zekâ (AI) Filmi Bağlamında Yapay Zekaya Bakış. *Uluslararası Ders Kitapları ve Eğitim Materyalleri Dergisi, 2*(2), 203–215.

Isarsoft. (2023a, July). *AI in Airports*. Isarsoft. https://www.isarsoft.com/article/ai-in-airports

İSG. (2010). *Sabiha Gökçen Havalimanı çalışanlarına engelli eğitimi*. ISG. https://www.sabihagokcen.aero/basin-odasi/basin-kupurleri/sabiha-gokcen-havalimani-calisanlarina-engelli-egitimi

İşler, B., & Kılıç, M. (2021). Eğitimde Yapay Zekâ Kullanımı ve Gelişimi. *Yeni Medya Elektronik Der*gisi, 5(1), Ji, P., & Jiang, R. (2003). Scale transitivity in the AHP. *The Journal of the Operational Research Society, 54*(8), 896–905.

Jalabert, G., & Zuliani, J.-M. (2009). *Toulouse, l'avion et la ville. Privat, coll*. Aviation.

Jin, M. J., & Kim, J. K. (2022). Customer Adoption Factors for In-Flight Entertainment and Connectivity. *Research in Transportation Business & Management, 43*(June), 100759. doi:10.1016/j.rtbm.2021.100759

Johnson, J. L., & O'leary-Kelly, A. M. (2003). The effects of psychological contract breach and organizational cynicism: Not all social exchange violations are created equal. *Journal of Organizational Behavior, 24*(5), 627–647. doi:10.1002/job.207

Jordan, P., Pastras, P., & Psarros, M. (2018). *Managing Tourism Growth in Europe: The ECM toolbox*. European Cities Marketing & Toposophy.

Juvan, J., Prezelj, I., & Kopač, E. (2021). Public dilemmas about security measures in the field of civil aviation. *Security Journal, 34*(3), 410–428. doi:10.1057/s41284-020-00240-8

Kallus, K. W., Hoffmann, P., Winkler, H., & Vormayr, E. M. (2010). The taskload-efficiency-safety-buffer tringle-development and validation with air traffic management. *Ergonomics, 53*(2), 240–246. doi:10.1080/00140130903199897 PMID:20099177

Karaman, A. S., Kilic, M., & Uyar, A. (2018). Sustainability reporting in the aviation industry: Worldwide evidence. Sustainability Accounting. *Management and Policy Journal, 9*(4), 362–391. doi:10.1108/SAMPJ-12-2017-0150

Karavardar, G. (2012). Çalışan ilişkileri ve bilgi paylaşımı: Bankacılık sektöründe bir uygulama. *Çankırı Karatekin Üniversitesi İktisadi ve İdari Bilimler Fakültesi Dergisi, 2*(1), 145-156.

Kaynak, İ. (2021). İş stresinin örgüt içi çatışmaya etkisi: Sivil havacılık çalışanları üzerine bir araştırma. *Anemon Muş Alparslan Üniversitesi Sosyal Bilimler Dergisi, 9*(3), 647–658. doi:10.18506/anemon.835175

Kechidi, M., & Talbot, D. (2006). *L'industrie aéronautique et spatiale: d'une logique d'arsenal à une logique commerciale.* HAL. https://EconPapers.repec.org/RePEc:hal:journl:hal-02376465

Kechidi, M., & Talbot, D. (2010). Institutions and coordination: What is the contribution of a proximity-based analysis? The case of Airbus and its relations with the subcontracting network. *International Journal of Technology Management, 50*(3/4), 285–299. doi:10.1504/IJTM.2010.032677

Keding, C. (2021). Understanding The Interplay Of Artificial Intelligence And Strategic Management: Four Decades Of Research In Review. *Management Review Quarterly, 71*(1), 91–134. doi:10.1007/s11301-020-00181-x

Kiracı, K., & Akan, E. (2020). Aircraft selection by applying AHP and TOPSIS in interval type-2 fuzzy sets. *Journal of Air Transport Management, 89*, 101924. doi:10.1016/j.jairtraman.2020.101924 PMID:32989347

Kiraci, K., Tanriverdi, G., & Akan, E. (2022). Analysis of Factors Affecting the Sustainable Success of Airlines During the COVID-19 Pandemic. *Transportation Research Record: Journal of the Transportation Research Board,* 03611981221104462.

Klecha & Co. (2022). *Space Economy Liftoff: Into the Final Frontier.* Klecha & Co. https://www.klecha-co.com/last-research/space-economy-lift-off-into-the-final-frontier/

Klein, J., Tremblay, D., & Fontan, J. (2003). Local systems and productive networks in the economic conversion: the case of Montreal. *Géographie Économie Société, 5*.

Koenig-Lewis, N., & Bischoff, E. (2005). Seasonality research: The state of the art. *International Journal of Tourism Research, 7*(4-5), 201–219. doi:10.1002/jtr.531

Kokény, L., Kenesei, Z., & Neszveda, G. (2022). Impact of COVID-19 on different business models of European airlines. *Current Issues in Tourism, 25*(3), 458–474. doi:10.1080/13683500.2021.1960284

Konert, F. A. A., & Balcerzak, B. T. (2021, June). Legal And Ethical Aspects Of Rules For The Operation Of Autonomous Unmanned Aircraft With Artificial Intelligence. In *2021 International Conference On Unmanned Aircraft Systems (ICUAS)* (Pp. 602-609). IEEE. 10.1109/ICUAS51884.2021.9476822

Koonce, J. M. (1984). A brief history of aviation psychology. *Human Factors, 26*(5), 499–508. doi:10.1177/001872088402600502

Kornienko, A., Kornienko, A., Fofanov, O., & Chubik, M. (2015b). *Knowledge in Artificial Intelligence Systems: Searching the Strategies for Application.* ScienceDirect. https://www.sciencedirect.com/science/article/pii/S1877042814067160?ref=pdf_download&fr=RR-2&rr=81647240fbcd384e

Kotler, P., & Armstrong, G. (2010). *Principles of Marketing.* Pearson Education.

Krafft, J., & Ravix, J.-L. (2000). *Competition and industrial coordination.* Krafft J. (ed.), post-print halshs-00464275. HAL. https://ideas.repec.org/p/hal/journl/halshs-00464275.html

Kraft, S., & Havlíková, D. (2016). Anytime? Anywhere? The seasonality of flight offers in Central Europe. *Moravian Geographical Reports, 24*(4), 26–37. doi:10.1515/mgr-2016-0020

Kramer, A., Friesen, M., & Shelton, T. (2018). Are airline passengers ready for personalized dynamic pricing? A study of German consumers. *Journal of Revenue and Pricing Management, 17*(2), 115–120. doi:10.1057/s41272-017-0122-0

Krasnova, H., Eling, N., Schneider, O., Wenninger, H., & Widjaja, T. (2020). Personalization of Online Services and Its Effect on Customer Satisfaction and Loyalty: The Mediating Role of Trustworthiness. *Journal of Management Information Systems*, *37*(2), 547–585.

Krishankumar, R., Garg, H., Arun, K., Saha, A., Ravichandran, K. S., & Kar, S. (2021). An integrated decision-making COPRAS approach to probabilistic hesitant fuzzy set information. *Complex & Intelligent Systems*, *7*(5), 2281–2298. doi:10.1007/s40747-021-00387-w

Kritikos, M. (2020). *What if AI could improve thermal imaging, to help fight coronavirus?* European Parliament. https://www.europarl.europa.eu/RegData/etudes/ATAG/2020/656299/EPRS_ATA(2020)656299_EN.pdf

Kundakcı, N. (2019). An integrated method using MACBETH and EDAS methods for evaluating steam boiler alternatives. *Journal of Multi-Criteria Decision Analysis*, *26*(1–2), 27–34. doi:10.1002/mcda.1656

Kurnaz, S. (2022). Bibliometric analysis of articles published in the field of aviation: Dergipark academic example. *Management Theory and Studies for Rural Business and Infrastructure Development*, *44*(3), 354–361. doi:10.15544/mts.2022.36

Kurnaz, S., Rodrigues, A., Kholiavko, N., Panchenko, O., & Tarasenko, A. (2022). The perspectives of the air transport market in Turkey during Covid-19 pandemic. *Management Theory and Studies for Rural Business and Infrastructure Development*, *44*(2), 235–243. doi:10.15544/mts.2022.24

Kusumawardani, A. M., & Daniel Tumpal, H. A. (2019). Comparing the Effects of Service Quality and Value-for-Money on Customer Satisfaction, Airline Image and Behavioural Intention between Full-Service and Low-Cost Airlines: Evidence from Indonesia. *International Journal of Tourism Policy*, *9*(1), 27–49. doi:10.1504/IJTP.2019.100078

La Oportunidad de las Finanzas Verdes en el Sector de la Aviación. (n.d.). A21. https://a21.com.mx/rumbo-altura-y-velocidad/2021/02/14/la-oportunidad-de-las-finanzas-verdes-en-el-sector-de-la

Landry, S. J. (2021). Human factors and ergonomics in aviation. In G. Salvendy (Ed.), *Handbook of Human Factors and Ergonomics* (pp. 1667–1688)., doi:10.1002/9781119636113.ch55

Lappas, I., & Kourousis, K. I. (2016). Anticipating the Need for New Skills for the Future Aerospace and Aviation Professionals. *Journal of Aerospace Technology and Management*, *8*(2), 232–241. doi:10.5028/jatm.v8i2.616

Laundal, K. M., & Richmond, A. D. (2016). Magnetic coordinate systems. *Space Science Reviews*, *206*(1-4), 27–59. doi:10.1007/s11214-016-0275-y

Leal, V. (2010b, October). *A Criação de Valor em Portugal.* Instituto Superior Técnico. https://fenix.tecnico.ulisboa.pt/downloadFile/395142108129/DISSERTA%C3%87%C3%83O.pdf

Lee, J. (2019). Effects of operational performance on financial performance. *Management Science Letters*, *9*(1), 25–32. doi:10.5267/j.msl.2018.11.003

Lekakos, G. (2008). Recommender Systems for Large-Scale e-Commerce Applications. *Decision Support Systems*, *45*(4), 892–903.

Leotti, V. B., Coster, R., & Riboldi, J. (2012). *Normalidade de Variáveis : Métodos de Verificação e Comparação de Alguns Testes Não-Paramétricos Por Simulação.* UFRGS. https://lume.ufrgs.br/handle/10183/158102

Leriche, F. (2004). Metropolization et Grands Equipements Structurants. In C. Siino, F. Laumière, & F. Leriche (Eds.), *Presses Universitaires du Mirail.*

Lerner, D. J., & Gorog, J. M. Jr. (2021). How "Rad" is A Trip to Space? A Brief Discussion of Radiation Exposure in Suborbital Space Tourism. *Journal of the American College of Radiology*, *18*(1), 225–228. doi:10.1016/j.jacr.2020.06.020 PMID:33413908

Lim, C., & McAleer, M. (2001). Monthly seasonal variations – Asian tourism to Australia. *Annals of Tourism Research*, *28*(1), 68–82. doi:10.1016/S0160-7383(00)00002-5

Lioutov, L. (2020). *COVID-19: People risk in the airport industry*. ACI. https://blog.aci.aero/covid-19-people-risk-in-the-airport-industry/

Li, X., Zhao, H., Liu, D., & Ma, Y. (2019). Customized Recommendations for Tourism Products Based on LDA Topic Modeling. *Journal of Ambient Intelligence and Humanized Computing*, *10*(1), 173–182. doi:10.1007/s12652-017-0632-6

Lloyd, D. (2000). *Improving employee commitment*. [Department of Education Doctoral Thesis, Concordia University].

López, J., & López, L. (2006). La concentración estacional en las regiones españolas desde una perspectiva de la oferta turística [The seasonal concentration in the Spanish regions from a perspective of the tourist offer]. *Revista de Estudios Regionales*, *3*(1), 77–104.

Lucas, J. (2023, July). *O processo de tomada de decisão através da inteligência artificial*. LinkedIn. https://www.linkedin.com/pulse/o-processo-de-tomada-decis%C3%A3o-atrav%C3%A9s-da-intelig%C3%AAncia-orzzi-lucas/?originalSubdomain=pt

Lucertini, M., Smriglio, S., & Telmon, D. (1997). Network optimization in air traffic management. L. Bianco, P. Dell'Olmo, & A. R. Odoni (Eds.). Modelling and Simulation in Air Traffic Management Berlin. Springer. doi:10.1007/978-3-642-60836-0_5

Lufthansa. (n.d.). *Miles & More - o Nosso Programa Para Passageiros Frequentes*. Lufthansa. https://www.lufthansa.com/ao/pt/miles-and-more

Lukas, B. A., & Maignan, I. (1996). Striving for quality: The key role of internal and external customers. *Journal of Market Focused Management*, *1*(2), 175–187. doi:10.1007/BF00128689

Lusa (2012, September 19). *Embraer investiu 177 ME nas duas fábricas de Évora que já têm quase 100 trabalhadores*. RTP Notícias. https://www.rtp.pt/noticias/economia/embraer-investiu-177-me-nas-duas-fabricas-de-evora-que-ja-tem-quase-100-trabalhadores_n588412

Lyssakov, N., & Lyssakova, E. (2019). Human factor as a cause of aircraft accidents. *Advances in Social Science, Education and Humanities Research, 321*, 130-132.

Machado, M. (2021). *Método de pesquisa qualitativa: O que é e como fazer?* Academica. https://www.academica.com.br/post/m%C3%A9todo-qualitativo-como-fazer

Macit, D., & Macit, A. (2017). Türkiye'de sivil havacılık sektöründe istihdamın mevcut durumu, sorunları ve sorunların çözümüne yönelik öneriler. *Journal of Emerging Economies and Policy*, *2*(2).

MacPherson, A., & Pritchard, D. (2003). The international decentralisation of US commercial aircraft production: Implications for US employment and trade. *Futures*, *35*(3), 221–238. doi:10.1016/S0016-3287(02)00055-1

Madeira.best (2021). Cidades e Municípios da Ilha da Madeira, Cidades e Municípios da Ilha da Madeira. *Madeira Best*. https://bit.ly/3C6Hek7.

Mahtani, U. S., & Garg, C. P. (2018). An analysis of key factors of financial distress in airline companies in India using fuzzy AHP framework. *Transportation Research Part A, Policy and Practice*, *117*, 87–102. doi:10.1016/j.tra.2018.08.016

Makridakis, S. (2017). The Forthcoming Artificial Intelligence (AI) Revolution: Its Impact on Society and Firms. *Futures*, *90*, 46–60. doi:10.1016/j.futures.2017.03.006

Mallick, S. and Rajagopalan, R. P. (2019). If Space is 'the Province of Mankind', Who Owns its Resources? An Examination of the Potential of Space Mining and its Legal Implications. *Observer Research Foundation*. 1-27.

Manca, C., Grijalvo, M., Palacios, M., & Kaulio, M. (2018). Collaborative Workplaces for Innovation in Service Companies: Barriers and Enablers for Supporting New Ways of Working. *Service Business*, *12*(3), 525–550. doi:10.1007/s11628-017-0359-0

Maneenop, S., & Kotcharin, S. (2020). The impacts of COVID-19 on the global airline industry: An event study approach. *Journal of Air Transport Management*, *89*, 101920. doi:10.1016/j.jairtraman.2020.101920 PMID:32874021

Manjunatha Kumar, B. H., Achyutha, P. N., Kalashetty, J. N., Rekha, V. S., & Nirmala, G. (2022). Business Analysis and Modelling of Flight Delays Using Artificial Intelligence. *International Journal of Health Sciences*, (I), 7897–7908. doi:10.53730/ijhs.v6nS1.6735

Manning, R., & Powers, L. (1984). Peak and off-peak use: Redistributing the outdoor recreation/tourism load. *Journal of Travel Research*, *23*(2), 25–31. doi:10.1177/004728758402300204

Martilla, J. A., & James, J. C. (1977). Importance-performance Analysis. *Journal of Marketing*, *41*(1), 77–79. doi:10.1177/002224297704100112

Martin, D. C., Fanson, J., Schiminovich, D., Friedman, P. D., Barlow, T. A., & Wyder, T. K. (2005). The Galaxy Evolution Explorer: A Space Ultraviolet Survey Mission. *The Astrophysical Journal*, *619*(1), 1–6. doi:10.1086/426387

Martín-Martín, J. M., Serdeira-Azevedo, P., Puertas-Medina, R. M., & Guaita-Martínez, J. M. (2023). Análisis comparativo de la estacionalidad turística en dos destinos fronterizos: Algarve (Portugal) – Huelva (España) [Comparative analysis of tourist seasonality in two border destinations: Algarve (Portugal) – Huelva (Spain)]. *Journal of Tourism Analysis*, *30*(2), 26–50. doi:10.53596/r0y74q81

Martins, J. (2015). *Algarve, da Urbanização Turística à Metropolização Sazonal 1960/2013 [Algarve, from Tourist Urbanization to Seasonal Metropolization 1960/2013]*. [PhD Thesis in Sociology], Faculdade de Ciências Sociais e Humanas, Universidade Nova de Lisboa, Portugal.

Martins, P. (2011). *Contibutos para uma história do ir à praia em Portugal [Contributions to a history of going to the beach in Portugal]*. [Master Dissertation, Faculdade de Ciências Sociais e Humanas, Universidade Nova de Lisboa].

Martins, A. M., & Cró, S. (2022). Airline stock markets reaction to the COVID-19 outbreak and vaccines: An event study. *Journal of Air Transport Management*, *105*, 102281. doi:10.1016/j.jairtraman.2022.102281 PMID:36034526

Matei, N., Garcia Leon, D., Dosio, A., Batista e Silva, F., Ribeiro Barranco, R., & Ciscar Martinez, J. C. (2023). *Regional impact of climate change on European tourism demand*. Publications Office of the European Union.

Mathieson, A., & Wall, G. (1982). *Tourism, Economic, Physical and Social Impacts*. Longmann.

McCabe, S., & Qiao, G. (2020). A review of research into social tourism: Launching the Annals of Tourism Research Curated Collection on Social Tourism. *Annals of Tourism Research*, *85*, 103103. doi:10.1016/j.annals.2020.103103

Mccarthy, N., Karzand, M., & Lecue, F. (2019, July). Amsterdam to Dublin Eventually Delayed? Lstm and Transfer Learning for Predicting Delays of Low-Cost Airlines. *Proceedings of the AAAI Conference on Artificial Intelligence*, *33*(01), 9541–9546. doi:10.1609/aaai.v33i01.33019541

McIvor, R., O'Reilly, D., & Ponsonby, S. (2003). The Impact of Internet Technologies on the Airline Industry: Current Strategies and Future Developments. *Strategic Change*, *12*(1), 31–47. doi:10.1002/jsc.618

McKight. P. E. (2010). Kruskal-Wallis Test. The Corsini Encyclopedia of Psychology. Wiley. doi:10.1002/9780470479216. corpsy0491

Mcmullen, M. (1987). Artificial Intelligence in the Airline Industry. *IATA Review. International Air Transport Association*, (2), 16–18.

Meier, M. M., Copeland, K., Klöble, K. E., Matthiä, D., Plettenberg, M. C., Schennetten, K., Wirtz, M., & Hellweg, C. E. (2020). Radiation in the atmosphere-A hazard to aviation safety? *Atmosphere (Basel)*, *11*(12), 1358–1389. doi:10.3390/atmos11121358

Merkert, R., & Swidan, H. (2019). Flying with (out) a safety net: Financial hedging in the airline industry. *Transportation Research Part E, Logistics and Transportation Review*, *127*, 206–219. doi:10.1016/j.tre.2019.05.012

Merkert, R., & Webber, T. (2018). How to manage seasonality in service industries – The case of price and seat factor management in airlines. *Journal of Air Transport Management*, *72*, 39–46. doi:10.1016/j.jairtraman.2018.07.005

Mertens, C. J., Kress, B. T., Wiltberger, M., Blattnig, S. R., Slaba, T. S., Solomon, S. C., & Engel, M. (2010). Geomagnetic influence on aircraft radiation exposure during a solar energetic particle event in October 2003. *Space Weather*, *8*(3), S03006–S03022. doi:10.1029/2009SW000487

Meyer-Waarden, L. (2013). The Impact of Reward Personalisation on Frequent Flyer Programmes' Perceived Value and Loyalty. *Journal of Services Marketing*, *27*(3), 183–194. doi:10.1108/08876041311330681

Michaels, L., & Fletcher, S. (2009). Competing in an LCC world. *Journal of Revenue and Pricing Management*, *8*(5), 410–423. doi:10.1057/rpm.2009.7

Ministry of Tourism. (2021). *Monthly Statistics - December 2020*. Ministry of Tourism - Republic of Maldives. https://www.tourism.gov.mv/statistics/publications/year-2020

Mishra, A. K., & Mishra, D. (2018). Service Personalization in Tourism: A Systematic Literature Review. *Journal of Hospitality and Tourism Management*, *35*, 81–91.

Moghavvemi, S., Sharabati, M., & Wan, K. W. I. (2016). Airline Frequent Flyer Program: Predicting Customers' Satisfaction Using Logistic Regression and Neural Network Models. *Journal of Air Transport Management*, *52*(July), 117–124.

Molchanova, K. M., Trushkina, N. V., & Katerna, O. K. (2020). Digital Platforms and Their Application in the Aviation Industry. *Intellectualization of Logistics and Supply Chain Management*, *1*(3), 83–98. doi:10.46783/smart-scm/2020-3-8

Moreira, M. C. (2015). A New Training Center in Portugal: A Unique Project to Boost the Next Generation of Aviation Professionals. *ICAO Training Report*, *5*(1), 28–30.

Moreira, M. C. (2020). Local governments as enablers of the aviation workforce: A case in Portugal. In *Engaging the Next Generation of Aviation Professionals* (pp. 7–10). Routledge.

Muchanga, A. P. (2014). *The impact of air transport liberalisation on the Portuguese market: low costs vs scheduled airlines: tap, easyjet and ryanair* [Doctoral dissertation].

Muller, R., & Drax, C. (2014). Fundamentals and Structure of Safety Management Systems in Aviation. Aviation Risk and Safety Management Methods and Applications in Aviation Organizations. Switzerland: Springer International Publishing. doi:10.1007/978-3-319-02780-7_5

Mursula, K., Qvick, T., Holappa, L., & Asikainen, T. (2022). Magnetic storms during the space age: Occurrence and relation to varying solar activity. *Journal of Geophysical Research. Space Physics*, *127*(12), 1–36. doi:10.1029/2022JA030830

NASA. (2022). *Astrobotic Technology Reveals Design for Robot to Prospect at Moon's Poles*. NASA. Https://Sservi.Nasa. Gov/Articles/Astrobotic-Technology-Reveals-Design-For-Robot-To-Prospect-At-Moons-Poles/ Access date: 16.12.2022

NASA-CR-194800 (1993). *The National Geomagnetic Initiative*. U.S. Geodynamics Committee Board on Earth Sciences and Resources Commission on Geosciences, Environment, and Resources National Research Council, National Academy Press.

National Transportation Safety Board. (2005). Risk factors associated with weather-related general aviation accidents. Safety Study NTSB/SS-05/01. National Transportation Safety Board.

Negrão, C. (2018). *Influência Da Inteligência Artificial Na Criação De Valor Nos Processos De Negócio Das Organizações*. ISEG. https://www.repository.utl.pt/bitstream/10400.5/19612/1/DM-CSMN-2019.pdf#page16

Neves, A. O., & Marques, R. J. (2017). O Aeródromo Municipal de Ponte de Sor como Motor de Desenvolvimento Local/Regional. In *XI Congresso da Geografia Portuguesa, As dimensões e a Responsabilidade Social da Geografia*, Porto, Faculdade de Letras da Universidade do Porto, Associação Portuguesa de Geógrafos. 78-989-54030-2-8.

Newtral (2020). *Baleares y Canarias, las comunidades más expuestas a la caída del turismo*. Newtral.es. https://www.newtral.es/baleares-canarias-ccaa-expuestas-caida-turismo/20200623/

Niosi, J., & Zhegu, M. (2005). Aerospace Clusters: Local or Global Knowledge Spillovers? *Industry and Innovation*, *12*(1), 1, 5–29. doi:10.1080/1366271042000339049

Niosi, J., & Zhegu, M. (2010). Anchor tenants and regional innovation systems: The aircraft industry. *International Journal of Technology Management*, *50*(3/4), 263–284. doi:10.1504/IJTM.2010.032676

Norori, N., Hu, Q., Aellen, F. M., Faraci, F. D., & Tzovara, A. (2021). Addressing Bias in Big Data and AI for Health Care: A Call for Open Science. *Patterns (New York, N.Y.)*, *2*(10), 100347. doi:10.1016/j.patter.2021.100347 PMID:34693373

O'Connell, J. F. (2018). The Routledge Companion to Air Transport Management. N. Halpern & A. Graham, (Eds.), The Routledge Companion to Air Transport Management. New York: Routledge.

OECD (2008). *Space Technologies and Climate Change: Implications for Water Management, Marine Resources and Maritime Transport*, OECD Publishing. , doi:10.1787/9789264054196-en

OECD (2019). *The Space Economy in Figures: How Space Contributes to the Global Economy*. OECD Publishing. . doi:10.1787/c5996201-en

OECD (Ed.). (2019). *The Space Economy in Figures: How Space Contributes to the Global Economy*. OECD. https://www.oecd.org/innovation/the-space-economy-in-figures-c5996201-en.htm

OECD. (2007). *The Space Economy at a Glance 2007*, OECD Publishing, Paris. . doi:10.1787/9789264040847-en

OECD. (2021). *Economy for People, Planet and Prosperity 2021 Report*. OECD. https://www.oecd.org/sti/inno/space-forum/space-economy-for-people-planet-and-prosperity.pdf

Ogunsina, K., & Delaurentis, D. (2022). Enabling Integration And Interaction For Decentralized Artificial Intelligence In Airline Disruption Management. *Engineering Applications of Artificial Intelligence*, *109*, 104600. doi:10.1016/j.engappai.2021.104600

Oliveira, A. V. M., & Huse, C. (2009). Localized Competitive Advantage and Price Reactions to Entry: Full-Service vs. Low-Cost Airlines in Recently Liberalized Emerging Markets. *Transportation Research Part E, Logistics and Transportation Review, 45*(2), 307–320. doi:10.1016/j.tre.2008.09.003

Önen, V. (2022). İnsan faktörleri eğitimi sorunsallarının tespiti ve buna yönelik geliştirilmiş eğitim modeli ve iyileştirme önerileri. *Journal of Aviation Research, 4*(1), 25–56. doi:10.51785/jar.953657

Operations management. (2023). *The Vital Role of Efficient Operations Management for Startup Airlines*. NY Air Ops. https://myairops.com/blog/2023/09/operations-management-startup-airlines/

Oriental, A. (2021, July 7). Empresários apreensivos com lenta retoma do turismo. *Ano CLXXXVI, 21225*, 6.

OTA. (2021). *O impacto da COVID-19 nas empresas turísticas. Observatório do Turismo nos Açores*. OTA. https://otacores.com/inquerito/o-impacto-da-covid-19-nas-empresas-turisticas/

Ozdemir, Y., & Basligil, H. (2016). Aircraft selection using fuzzy ANP and the generalized choquet integral method: The Turkish airlines case. *Journal of Intelligent & Fuzzy Systems, 31*(1), 589–600. doi:10.3233/IFS-162172

Özgen, H., & Yalçın, A. (2018). *İnsan kaynakları yönetimi: Stratejik bir yaklaşım* (4th ed.). Akademisyen Kitabevi A.Ş.

Özgüner, Z., & Özgüner, M. (2020). Entegre Entropi-TOPSIS Yöntemleri ile Tedarikçi Değerlendirme ve Seçme Probleminin Çözümlenmesi. *İstanbul Ticaret Üniversitesi Sosyal Bilimler Dergisi, 19*(37), 551-568.

Öztürk, L. S. (2019). *Tekstil Sektöründe Önem Performans Analizi Uygulaması ile Üretime Dayalı Stratejik Öncelik Alanlarının Belirlenmesi*. Yüksek Lisans Tezi, Pamukkale Üniversitesi Sosyal Bilimler Enstitüsü.

Pagano, M., Wagner, C., & Zechner, J. (2020). *Disaster resilience and asset prices*. arXiv preprint arXiv:2005.08929.

Paixão, W., Cordeiro, I., & Leite, N. (2021). Efeitos da pandemia do COVID-19 sobre o turismo em Fernando de Noronha ao longo do primeiro semestre de 2020. *Revista Brasileira de Pesquisa em Turismo, 15*(1), 2128, 1-20. doi:10.7784/rbtur.v15i1.2128

Pan, B., Xie, K.-L., & Huang, Z. (2017). An Empirical Study of Online Reviews and Customer Ratings on Booking Likelihood. *International Journal of Hospitality Management, 60*, 58–69. doi:10.1016/j.ijhm.2016.09.003

Paone, M., & Sasanelli, N. (2016). *Aerospace Clusters: World's Best Practices and Future Prospects*. Academia. https://www.academia.edu/33388664/AEROSPACE_CLUSTERS_Worlds_Best_Practice_and_Future_Perspectives

Papadopoulos, E., & Gonzalez, F. (2020). *UAV and AI Application for Runway Foreign Object Debris (FOD) Detection*. IEEE. https://ieeexplore.ieee.org/stamp/stamp.jsp?tp=&arnumber=9438489

Papanikos, G. T. (2020). The impact of the Covid-19 pandemic on Greek tourism. *Athens Journal of Tourism, 7*(2), 87–100. doi:10.30958/ajt.7-2-2

Paraskevas, A., & Nudurupati, S. S. (2015). Customer Customization in Services: A Review and Future Research Directions. *International Journal of Operations & Production Management, 35*(5), 489–516.

Parise, S., & Sheng, M. L. (2021). Customizing Services to Build Stronger Relationships. *MIT Sloan Management Review, 62*(3), 39–47.

Pavić, Z., & Novoselac, V. (2013). Notes on TOPSIS Method. *International Journal of Research in Engineering and Science, 1*(2), 5–12.

Payne, J. E., Gil-Alana, L. A., & Mervar, A. (2021). Persistence in Croatian tourism: The impact of COVID-19. *Tourism Economics, 1354816621999969*. doi:10.1177/1354816621999969

Pedroni, G., Venturini, K., & Cantarello, S. (2019). Discovering the Basic Strategic Orientation of Big Space Agencies. *Space Policy*, *25*(1), 45–62. doi:10.1016/j.spacepol.2008.12.010

Pegasus. (2024). *Olanaklarımız*. Pegasus. https://www.flypgs.com/kariyer-pegasus/olanaklarimiz

Pereira, D., & de Mello, J. C. C. S. (2021). Efficiency evaluation of Brazilian airlines operations considering the Covid-19 outbreak. *Journal of Air Transport Management*, *91*, 101976.

Pérez-campuzano, D., Ortega, P. M., Andrada, L. R., & López-lázaro, A. (2021). Artificial Intelligence Potential within Airlines: A Review on How AI Can Enhance Strategic Decision-making in Times of COVID-19. *Journal of Airline and Airport Management*, *11*(2), 53–72. doi:10.3926/jairm.189

Petroni, G. ve Bigliardi, B. (2019). The Space Economy: From Science to Market. (First Edition). Cambridge Scholars Publishing, United Kingdom.

Petrović, D., Puharić, M., & Kastratović, E. (2018). Defining of Necessary Number of Employees in Airline by Using Artificial Intelligence Tools. *International Review (Steubenville, Ohio)*, (3-4), 77–89. doi:10.5937/IntRev1804077P

Pickvance, C. G. (2001). Four varieties of comparative analysis. *Journal of Housing and the Built Environment*, *16*(1), 7–28. doi:10.1023/A:1011533211521

Pilon, R. V. (2023). *Artificial Intelligence in Commercial Aviation: Use Cases and Emerging Strategies*. Taylor & Francis. doi:10.4324/9781003018810

Pinho, M., & Marques, J. (2021). Business tourism in Porto: An empirical investigation of its potentialities and development challenges. *International Journal of Tourism Cities*, *7*(1), 1–12. doi:10.1108/IJTC-05-2019-0071

Piotrowski, D. (2023). Privacy Frontiers in Customers' Relations with Banks. *Economics and Business Review EBR*, *23*(1), 119-141. https://Doi.Org/10.18559/Ebr.2023.1.5

Pizziol, S., Tessier, C., & Dehais, F. (2014). Petri net-based modelling of human-automation conflicts in aviation. *Ergonomics*, *57*(3), 319–331. doi:10.1080/00140139.2013.877597 PMID:24444329

Plan, A. Financing Sustainable Growth. Retrieved October 16, 2023, from https://eur-lex.europa.eu/legal-content/EN/TXT/?uri=CELEX%3A52018DC0097

Plano de Apoio Ao Cliente. (n.d.). British Airways. https://www.britishairways.com/pt-pt/information/legal/local-requirements/south-korea/customer-service-plan

Popovic, G., Stanujkic, D., & Stojanovic, S. (2012). Investment Project Selection by Applying COPRAS Method and Imprecise Data. *Serbian Journal of Management*, *7*(2), 257–269. doi:10.5937/sjm7-2268

Pordata (2021). Alojamentos Turísticos. *Pordata*. https://bit.ly/3AqMuOp

Pordata (2022). *Tráfego de passageiros nos principais aeroportos: Lisboa, Porto e Faro. [Passenger traffic at the main airports: Lisbon, Porto and Faro]*. Pordata. https://www.pordata.pt/portugal/trafego+de+passageiros+nos+principais+aeroportos+lisboa++porto+e+faro-3248

Porter, M. E. (1990). *The Competitive Advantage of Nations*. Free Press. doi:10.1007/978-1-349-11336-1

Portugal Space. (2020). *Portugal Space 2030 - A Research, Innovation and Growth Strategy for Portugal*. PT Space. https://ptspace.pt/wp-content/uploads/2020/08/PortugalSpace2030_EN_web.pdf

Prentice, C., Hsiao, A., Wang, X., & Sandra, M. C. L. (2023). Mind, Service Quality, Relationship with Airlines. *Journal of Strategic Marketing*, *31*(1), 212–234. doi:10.1080/0965254X.2021.1894216

Publituris. (2022). *Programa de Fidelização Da TAP é o Melhor Da Europa e África Para Os Freddie Awards*. Publituris. https://www.publituris.pt/2022/04/28/programa-de-fidelizacao-da-tap-e-o-melhor-da-europa-e-africa-para-os-freddie-awards

Rabotić, B. (2014). Special-Purpose Travel in Ancient Times: "Tourism" before Tourism? In M. Skakun (ed.), *Proceedings Book of the 2nd Belgrade International Tourism Conference (BITCO 2014): Thematic Tourism in a Global Environment: Advantages, Challenges and Future Developments* (pp. 99-114). Belgrade: College of Tourism.

Rafael, C. (2020). TAP: Tudo Sobre a Principal Companhia Aérea de Portugal. *Melhores Destinos.* https://www.melhoresdestinos.com.br/tap-portugal.html

Ramelli, S., & Wagner, A. F. (2020). Feverish stock price reactions to COVID-19. *The Review of Corporate Finance Studies, 9*(3), 622–655. doi:10.1093/rcfs/cfaa012

Rana, N. P., Chatterjee, S., Dwivedi, Y. K., & Akter, S. (2022). Understanding Dark Side of Artificial Intelligence (AI) Integrated Business Analytics: Assessing Firm's Operational Inefficiency and Competitiveness. *European Journal of Information Systems, 31*(3), 364–387. doi:10.1080/0960085X.2021.1955628

Rashid, T., Ali, A., & Chu, Y. M. (2021). Hybrid BW-EDAS MCDM methodology for optimal industrial robot selection. *PLoS One, 16*(2), e0246738. doi:10.1371/journal.pone.0246738 PMID:33561144

Reilly, B. (2021). Seasons in Italy: Northern European travelers, Rome, and malaria. *Journal of Tourism and Cultural Change, 19*(1), 59–78. doi:10.1080/14766825.2019.1693582

Ren, L., Zhang, Y., Wang, Y., & Sun, Z. (2007). Comparative Analysis of a Novel M-TOPSIS Method and TOPSIS. *Applied Mathematics Research Express, 2007*, abm005.

Reuters (2021). *COVID-battered Malta to pay tourists who visit this summer*. Reuters. https://www.reuters.com/world/europe/covid-battered-malta-pay-tourists-who-visit-this-summer-2021-04-09/

Revista Aeronáutica. (1921). *Aero-Club de Portugal, VIII* (3).

Ribeiro, A., & Quesado, P. (2017). Explanatory Factors of Abnormal Annual Stock Returns. *European Journal of Applied Business and Management, 2017*(Special Issue), 109–126.

Riedle, R. (2006). Importance of CISM in modern air traffic management (ATM). Critical Incident Stress Management in Aviation in Jörg Leonhardt and Joachim Vogt (Eds.). England: Ashgate Publishing Limited.

Riwo-Abudho, M., Njanja, L. W., & Ochieng, I. (2013). *Key success factors in airlines: Overcoming the challenges.*

Roadmap, A. I. (2020). A Human-centric Approach to AI in Aviation. European Aviation Safety Agency, 1.

Rosselló, J., & Sansó, A. (2017). Yearly, monthly and weekly seasonality of tourism demand: A decomposition analysis. *Tourism Management, 60*, 379–389. doi:10.1016/j.tourman.2016.12.019

Rüßmann, M., (2015). *Industry 4.0: The Future of Productivity and Growth in Manufacturing Industries.*

Russo, A. (2014). *Criação de Valor.* Instituto Politécnico De Setúbal. https://core.ac.uk/download/pdf/62696164.pdf

Rust, D. L., Stewart, R. D., & Werner, T. J. (2021). The Duluth International Airport Aviation Business Cluster: The Impact of COVID-19 and the CARES Act. *Research in Transportation Economics, 89*, 101–135. doi:10.1016/j.retrec.2021.101135

Rycroft, M. J., Israelsson, S., & Price, C. (2000). The global atmospheric electric current, solar activity and climate change. *Journal of Atmospheric and Solar-Terrestrial Physics, 62*(17-18), 1563–1576. doi:10.1016/S1364-6826(00)00112-7

Sabuncuoğlu, Z. (2018). *İnsan kaynakları yönetimi*. Bursa: Aktüel 16 Basım Yayım Dağıtım Ltd. Şti.

Sadi, M. A., & Henderson, J. C. (2000). The Asian economic crisis and the aviation industry: Impacts and response strategies. *Transport Reviews*, *20*(3), 347–367. doi:10.1080/014416400412841

Sadullah, Ö. (2018). İnsan kaynakları yönetimine giriş: İnsan kaynakları yönetiminin tanımı, önemi ve çevresel faktörler. In *İnsan Kaynakları Yönetimi* (8th ed., pp. 1–50). Beta Basım Yayım Dağıtım A.Ş.

Sağır, S., Atıcı, R., & Dölek, İ. (2018). Investigation of the severe geomagnetic storm effects on ionosphere at nighttime through ROTI. *Journal of Science and Technology MSU*, *6*(2), 603–609. doi:10.18586/msufbd.493156

Şahin, M., & Çona, A. (2019). İnsan kaynakları yönetimi rol belirizliği-rol çatışması. In M. Sağır (Ed.), *İnsan Kaynakları Yönetimi ve Örgüt İçi Etkileşim* (pp. 219–246).

Salman, A., Kamerkar, U., Jaafar, M., & Mohamad, D. (2021). Empirical analysis of COVID-19 induced socio cognitive factors and its impact on residents of Penang Island. *International Journal of Tourism Cities*. doi:10.1108/IJTC-05-2020-0091

Sánchez, J. G. (2021, November). Roma de Férias – os turistas da antiguidade [Rome on Holiday – tourists from ancient times]. *National Geographic História*, *1*(1), 57–69.

Sánchez-Lozano, J. M., & Rodríguez, O. N. (2020). Application of Fuzzy Reference Ideal Method (FRIM) to the military advanced training aircraft selection. *Applied Soft Computing*, *88*, 106061. doi:10.1016/j.asoc.2020.106061

Sánchez-Lozano, J. M., Serna, J., & Dolón-Payán, A. (2015). Evaluating military training aircrafts through the combination of multi-criteria decision making processes with fuzzy logic. A case study in the Spanish Air Force Academy. *Aerospace Science and Technology*, *42*, 58–65. doi:10.1016/j.ast.2014.12.028

Santana, M., Valle, R., & Galan, J.-L. (2019). How national institutions limit turnaround strategies and human resource management: A comparative study in the airline industry. *European Management Review*, *16*(4), 923–935. doi:10.1111/emre.12177

Santos, M. (2021). *Tecnologias de Inteligência Artificial da Priberam já em funcionamento no aeroporto de Frankfurt*. Ecommercenews PT. https://ecommercenews.pt/tecnologias-de-inteligencia-artificial-da-priberam-ja-em-funcionamento-no-aeroporto-de-frankfurt/

Santos, N., & Moreira, C. O. (2021). Uncertainty and expectations in Portugal's tourism activities. Impacts of COVID-19. *Research in Globalization*, *3*, 100071. doi:10.1016/j.resglo.2021.100071

Saranga, H., & Nagpal, R. (2016). Drivers of operational efficiency and its impact on market performance in the Indian Airline industry. *Journal of Air Transport Management*, *53*, 165–176. doi:10.1016/j.jairtraman.2016.03.001

Sarol, S. D. (2023). Mobile Technology Application in Aviation: Chatbot for Airline Customer Experience. In Technology Application in Aviation, Tourism and Hospitality, 59–72. Singapore: Springer Nature Singapore. doi:10.1007/978-981-19-6619-4_5

Scerri, M., & Grech, V. (2020). The Spanish flu, COVID-19 and Malta's reactions: Contrasts and similarities. *Early Human Development*, *105252*, 105252. doi:10.1016/j.earlhumdev.2020.105252 PMID:33223126

Schieb, P. A., & Gibson, A. (2011). Geomagnetic Storms. Multi-Disciplinary Issues International Future Programme [Lecture Notes], pp. 1-69. CENTRA Technology, Inc., on behalf of Office of Risk Management and Analysis, United States Department of Homeland Security, USA.

Schroer, A. (2023, July). *What Is Artificial Intelligence?* Builtin. https://builtin.com/artificial-intelligence

Schultz, M., Lorenz, S., Schmitz, R., & Delgado, L. (2018). Weather impact on airport performance. *Aerospace (Basel, Switzerland)*, *5*(4), 109–128. doi:10.3390/aerospace5040109

Schulze-horn, I., Hueren, S., Scheffler, P., & Schiele, H. (2020). Artificial Intelligence in Purchasing: Facilitating Mechanism Design-Based Negotiations. *Applied Artificial Intelligence*, *34*(8), 618–642. doi:10.1080/08839514.2020.1749337

Scott, A. J. (1993). *Technopolis: high-technology industry and regional development in Southern California*. Univ of California Press.

Scott, A. J., & Mattingly, D. J. (1989). The Aircraft and Parts Industry in Southern California: Continuity and Change from the Inter-War Years to the 1990s. *Economic Geography*, *65*(1), 48–71. doi:10.2307/143478

Scylla. (n.d.). *How Leveraging AI Helps Optimize Safety and Security for Airports*. Scylla. https://www.scylla.ai/how-leveraging-ai-helps-optimize-safety-and-security-for-airports/

Serrano, F., & Kazda, A. (2020). The future of airports post COVID-19. *Journal of Air Transport Management*, *89*, 101900. doi:10.1016/j.jairtraman.2020.101900 PMID:32834696

Sharma, S., & Mangat, V. (2015). Technology and Trends to Handle Big Data: Survey. In *International Conference on Advanced Computing and Communication Technologies, ACCT*. Institute of Electrical and Electronics Engineers Inc. 10.1109/ACCT.2015.121

Sharma, G. D., Thomas, A., & Paul, J. (2021). Reviving tourism industry post-COVID-19: A resilience-based framework. *Tourism Management Perspectives*, *37*, 100786. doi:10.1016/j.tmp.2020.100786 PMID:33391988

Sharma, V., & Kaur, P. (2019). A study on HR practices in Indian aviation sector. *Think India Journal*, *22*(14), 6875–6882.

Shen, H. (2009). *Organization-employee relationships model: A two sided story*. [Doctoral Thesis, University of Maryland].

Shmelova, T., Sterenharz, A., & Dolgikh, S. (2020). Artificial Intelligence in Aviation Industries: Methodologies, Education, Applications, and Opportunities. In Handbook of Research on Artificial Intelligence Applications in the Aviation and Aerospace Industries (pp. 1-35). IGI Global.

Siddiqui, N. N., & Bisaria, G. (2018). Innovative techniques of motivation for employee retenteon in aviation industry. *Anveshak International Journal of Management*, *7*(1), 136. doi:10.15410/aijm/2018/v7i1/119882

Silling, U. (2019). Aviation of the Future: What Needs to Change to Get Aviation Fit for the Twenty-first Century. In *Aviation and Its Management-Global Challenges and Opportunities*. Intechopen. doi:10.5772/intechopen.81660

Silva, I. M. (2022). *Plataforma made in UPTEC esclarece dúvidas de viajantes nos aeroportos. Notícias* U.Porto. https://noticias.up.pt/plataforma-made-in-uptec-esclarece-duvidas-de-viajantes-nos-aeroportos/

Silva, R. C., & da Silva, A. Q. (2022). Tourism, the aviation sector and the effects of Covid-19 A comparative study on airlines in Brazil: Azul, GOL and TAM. *Hermes Scientific Journal*, (31), 57–75. doi:10.21710/rch.v31i0.629

Sims, N. (2019). *Transforming The Future of Airports with Artificial Intelligence*. Machine Learning and Generative Design.

Sindico, F., Sajeva, G., Sharman, N., Berlouis, P., & Ellsmoor, J. (2020). Islands and COVID-19: A Global Survey. Report. University of Strathclyde Publishing., Available at https://strathprints.strath.ac.uk/75109/, Retrieved July 20, 2022, from.

Singh, A. K. (2016). Competitive service quality benchmarking in airline industry using AHP. *Benchmarking*, *23*(4), 768–791. doi:10.1108/BIJ-05-2013-0061

Sircar, A., Yadav, K., Rayavarapu, K., Bist, N., & Oza, H. (2021). Application Of Machine Learning and Artificial Intelligence in Oil and Gas Industry. *Petroleum Research*, *6*(4), 379–391. doi:10.1016/j.ptlrs.2021.05.009

Škare, M., Soriano, D. R., & Porada-Rochoń, M. (2021). Impact of COVID-19 on the travel and tourism industry. *Technological Forecasting and Social Change*, *163*, 120469. doi:10.1016/j.techfore.2020.120469 PMID:35721368

Smith, J. A. (1998). *The Cold War 1945-1991* (2nd ed.). Blackwell Publishers.

Sobieralski, J. B. (2020). COVID-19 and airline employment: Insights from historical uncertainty shocks to the industry. *Transportation Research Interdisciplinary Perspectives*, *5*(100123), 1–9. doi:10.1016/j.trip.2020.100123 PMID:34173453

Solanki, K. (2020). Analysis of Etihad Airlines human resource management practices & factors that lead to employees motivation. *International Journal of Entrepreneurship*, *24*(1), 1–14.

Soori, M., Arezoo, B., & Dastres, R. (2023). Artificial Intelligence, Machine Learning and Deep Learning in Advanced Robotics, A Review. *Cognitive Robotics*.

Soysal, M., Doğan, G., & Kuzu, L. (2018). Sources of International Law Regarding Space Activities and the Role of the United Nations. *Çukurova University Faculty of Law Journal, 3*(2), 101-133.

Space Economy Academy. (2022). *Top 8 Drivers in Space Economics*. SEAC. https://seac-space.com/top-8-drivers-in-space-economics/ Access date: 03.04.2023

SpacecampTurkey. (2022). Starlink, SpaceX and Elon Musk. https://www.spacecampturkey.com/starlink-spacex-ve-elon-musk Access date: 16.12.2022

Spudis, P. D., & Lavoie, A. R. (2011). *Using The Resources of The Moon to Create a Permanent Cislunar Space Faring System. Proceedings of the American Institute of Aeronautics and Astronautics Space Conference*. Research Gate. 10.2514/6.2011-7185

SREA. (2019a). *Estatísticas do Turismo: janeiro a dezembro 2018*. Serviço Regional de Estatísticas dos Açores. https://srea.azores.gov.pt/Conteudos/Relatorios/lista_relatorios.aspx?idc=392&idsc=6454&lang_id=1

SREA. (2019b). *Estatísticas dos Transportes - 2018*. Serviço Regional de Estatísticas dos Açores. https://srea.azores.gov.pt/Conteudos/Relatorios/lista_relatorios.aspx?idc=392&idsc=971&lang_id=1

SREA. (2020a). *Estatísticas do Turismo: janeiro a dezembro 2019*. Serviço Regional de Estatísticas dos Açores. https://srea.azores.gov.pt/Conteudos/Relatorios/lista_relatorios.aspx?idc=392&idsc=6454&lang_id=1

SREA. (2020b). *Estatísticas dos Transportes - 2019*. Serviço Regional de Estatísticas dos Açores. https://srea.azores.gov.pt/Conteudos/Relatorios/lista_relatorios.aspx?idc=392&idsc=971&lang_id=1

SREA. (2021a). *Estatísticas do Turismo: janeiro a dezembro 2020*. Serviço Regional de Estatísticas dos Açores. https://srea.azores.gov.pt/Conteudos/Relatorios/lista_relatorios.aspx?idc=392&idsc=6454&lang_id=1

SREA. (2021b). *Estatísticas dos Transportes - 2020*. Serviço Regional de Estatísticas dos Açores. https://srea.azores.gov.pt/Conteudos/Relatorios/lista_relatorios.aspx?idc=392&idsc=971&lang_id=1

SREA. (2021c). *Hóspedes, Dormidas e Estada Média por Ilha*. SREA. https://srea.azores.gov.pt/Reportserver/Pages/ReportViewer.aspx?%2fTurismo%2fHospedes+Dormidas+e+Estada+Media+por+Ilha&ilhas=Ilha+Terceira

SREA. (2021d). *Hóspedes, Dormidas e Estada Média por Ilha - Ilha de São Miguel*. SREA. https://srea.azores.gov.pt/Reportserver/Pages/ReportViewer.aspx?%2fTurismo%2fHospedes+Dormidas+e+Estada+Media+por+Ilha&ilhas=Ilha+de+S%C3%A3o+Miguel

SREA. (2021e). *Passageiros Embarcados, Desembarcados, em Transito, por Ilha, Tipo de Voo, Ano e Mês - Ilha da Terceira*. Serviço Regional de Estatísticas dos Açores. https://srea.azores.gov.pt/ReportServer/Pages/ReportViewer.aspx?%2fRelatoriosVarios%2fTransportes-A%C3%A9reos&Ilha=Terceira

SREA. (2021f). *Passageiros Embarcados, Desembarcados, em Transito, por Ilha, Tipo de Voo, Ano e Mês - Ilha de São Miguel*. Serviço Regional de Estatísticas dos Açores. https://srea.azores.gov.pt/ReportServer/Pages/ReportViewer.aspx ?%2fRelatoriosVarios%2fTransportes-A%C3%A9reos&Ilha=S%C3%A3o%20Miguel

SREA. (s.d.). *Estimativas da População Média*. Serviço Regional de Estatística dos Açores. https://srea.azores.gov.pt/ ReportServer/Pages/ReportViewer.aspx?%2FDemografia%2FEstimativas+da+Popula%C3%A7%C3%A3o+M%C3% A9dia&rs:Command=Render

Stahl, B. C., & Wright, D. (2018). Ethics And Privacy in AI and Big Data: Implementing Responsible Research and Innovation. *IEEE Security and Privacy*, *16*(3), 26–33. doi:10.1109/MSP.2018.2701164

Statista (2022). *Government Expenditures on Space Programs*. Statista. https://www.statista.com/statistics/745717/ global-governmental-spending-on-spaceprograms-leading-countries/

Statista (2022). *Valuable Minerals Discovered in Space and Their Values*. Statista. https://www.statista.com/statis-tics/656143/mineral-and-element-value-of-selected-asteroids/

Statista. (2022). *Total Data Volume Worldwide 2010-2025*. Statista. https://www.statista.com/statistics/871513/worldwide-data-created/

Statista. (2023, February 6). *Use of AI at airports 2022*. Statista. https://www.statista.com/statistics/666275/adoption-of-operational-intelligence-capabilities-at-airports/

Stedmon, A., Lawson, G., Lewis, L., Richards, D., & Grant, R. (2017). Human behaviour in emergency situations: Comparisons between aviation and rail domains. *Security Journal*, *30*(3), 963–978. doi:10.1057/sj.2015.34

Steiner, M., Gil, J. A., Ehret, O., Ploder, M., & Wink, R. (2010). European medium-technology innovation networks: A multi-methodological multi-regional approach. *International Journal of Technology Management*, *50*(3/4), 229–262. doi:10.1504/IJTM.2010.032675

STM. (2020). The New Space Age: Space Strategies in Light of Selected Countries' Space Programs in the 21st Century, Cosmic Competition II. *STM Technological Thought Center, Research Report*. https://thinktech.stm.com.tr/tr/yeni-uzay-cagi-21inci-yuzyilda-kozmik-rekabet-ii-secili-ulkelerin-uzay-programlari-isiginda-uzay-stratejileri

Stolzer, A. J., Halford, C. D., & Goglia, J. J. (2008). Safety Management Systems in Aviation. England: Ashgate Pub-lishing Limited.

Suau-Sanchez, P., & Voltes-Dorta, A. (2019). Drivers of airport scheduled traffic in European winter tourism areas: Infrastructure, accessibility, competition and catchment area. *Journal of Air Transport Management*, *81*, 101723. doi:10.1016/j.jairtraman.2019.101723

Suau-Sanchez, P., Voltes-Dorta, A., & Cugueró-Escofet, N. (2020). An early assessment of the impact of COVID-19 on air transport: Just another crisis or the end of aviation as we know it? *Journal of Transport Geography*, *86*, 102749. doi:10.1016/j.jtrangeo.2020.102749 PMID:32834670

Suleymanlı, J. (2022). *An Econometric Model Attempt on Space Economy and Determinants of Space Economy Revenues*. [Ph. D. Thesis, Istanbul University Institute of Social Sciences, Istanbul, Turkey].

Sun, Z., Ma, C., Li, W., & Shen, C. (2014). Flight Operations Quality Assurance Based on Clustering Analysis. *Proceed-ings of the First Symposium on Aviation Maintenance and Management*. Berlin: Springer. 10.1007/978-3-642-54233-6_46

Sundar, S. S., Bellur, S., Oh, J., Xu, Q., Jia, H., & Meduri, S. (2017). User Customization vs. Defaults: The Effect of Defaults and User Expectation Congruence on Perceived Trust in Recommender Agents. *International Journal of Human-Computer Studies*, *98*, 52–65.

Sundar, S., & Sukor, M. (2020). Personalized Services in the Aviation Industry: Challenges and Opportunities. *Journal of Air Transport Management*, *87*, 101856.

Sustainability in aviation. (n.d.). EASA. https://www.easa.europa.eu/en/light/topics/sustainability

Su, X., & Khoshgoftaar, T. M. (2009). A Survey of Collaborative Filtering Techniques. *Advances in Artificial Intelligence*, *2009*, 1–19. doi:10.1155/2009/421425

Su, Y., Xie, K., Wang, H., Liang, Z., Art Chaovalitwongse, W., & Pardalos, P. M. (2021). Airline Disruption Management: A Review of Models and Solution Methods. *Engineering (Beijing)*, *7*(4), 435–447. doi:10.1016/j.eng.2020.08.021

Tajima, A. (2004). Fatal miscommunication: English in aviation safety. *World Englishes*, *23*(3), 451–470. doi:10.1111/j.0883-2919.2004.00368.x

Takeichi, N., Kaida, R., Shimomura, A., & Yamauchi, T. (2017). Prediction of Delay Due to Air Traffic Control by Machine Learning. In a *Modeling and Simulation Technologies Conference* (p. 1323). ARC. 10.2514/6.2017-1323

Tamer, H. Y., & Övgün, B. (2020). Yapay Zekâ Bağlamında Dijital Dönüşüm Ofisi. *Ankara Üniversitesi SBF Dergisi*, *75*(2), 775–803. doi:10.33630/ausbf.691119

Tanrıverdi, G., & Lezki, Ş. (2021). Istanbul Airport (IGA) and quest of best competitive strategy for air cargo carriers in new competition environment: A fuzzy multi-criteria approach. *Journal of Air Transport Management*, *95*, 102088. doi:10.1016/j.jairtraman.2021.102088

Tao, B., Díaz, V., & Guerra, Y. (2019). Artificial Intelligence And Education, Challenges and Disadvantages for the Teacher. *Art Journal*, *72*(12), 30–50.

TCFD. (n.d.). *Recommendations of the Task Force on Climate-related Financial Disclosures*. TCFD. https://www.fsb-tcfd.org/recommendations/

Technical expert group on sustainable finance (TEG). https://finance.ec.europa.eu/publications/technical-expert-group-sustainable-finance-teg_en

Terral, L. (2003). *Les Industries Aérospatiales en Amérique du Nord: Entre Permanences et Recompositions Territoriales*. [Doctoral dissertation, Université de Montréal]. Papyrus database.

Teste de Turing. (n.d.). *Explicando IA*. A to Z FAI. https://atozofai.withgoogle.com/intl/pt-BR/turing-test/

The History of Artificial Intelligence - Spotlight at Stanford Search Results. (1990). Stanford Libraries. https://exhibits.stanford.edu/ai/catalog?f%5Btopic_facet%5D%5B%5D=DENDRAL

Thompson, S., & Smith, G. P. (2009). *Space Policy Development via Macro-Economic Analysis*. NASA. https://www.nasa.gov/pdf/368983main_Applying%20a%20MacroEconomic%20Analysis%20to%20Space%20Policy%202009_06_09.pdf

THY. (2023). *Kurumsal sosyal sorumluluk*. THY. https://www.turkishairlines.com/tr-int/basin-odasi/sosyal-sorumluluk-projelerimiz/

Tiewtrakul, T., & Fletcher, S. R. (2010). The challenge of regional accents for aviation English language proficiency standards: A study of difficulties in understanding in air traffic control-pilot communications. *Ergonomics*, *53*(2), 229–239. doi:10.1080/00140130903470033 PMID:20099176

Tiftik, C., & Yakupoğlu, E. (2023). The importance of aviation safety in terms of human resources management in air cargo transportation. [USBED]. *Uluslararası Sosyal Bilimler ve Eğitim Dergisi*, *5*(8), 125–146.

Timoçin, E., Ünal, İ., & Göker, Ü. D. (2018). A comparison of IRI-2016 foF2 predictions with observations at different latitudes during geomagnetic storms. *Geomagnetism and Aeronomy*, *58*(7), 846–856. doi:10.1134/S0016793218070216

Torkayesh, A. E., Deveci, M., Karagoz, S., & Antucheviciene, J. (2023). A state-of-the-art survey of evaluation based on distance from average solution (EDAS): Developments and applications. *Expert Systems with Applications*, *221*, 119724. doi:10.1016/j.eswa.2023.119724

Tremblay, D., Klein, J., Hassen, B., Tarek, & Dossou-Yovo, A (2012). Les acteurs intermédiaires dans le développement de l'innovation: une comparaison intersectorielle dans la région de Montréal. *Revue d'Économie Régionale & Urbaine*, 431-454. doi:10.3917/reru.123.0431

Tretheway, M. W., & Markhvida, K. (2014). The aviation value chain: Economic returns and policy issues. *Journal of Air Transport Management*, *41*, 3–16. doi:10.1016/j.jairtraman.2014.06.011

Tripathi, G. (2017). Customer Satisfaction and Word of Mouth Intentions: Testing the Mediating Effect of Customer Loyalty. *Journal of Services Research*, *17*(2), 1–16.

Tsurutani, B. T., & Gonzalez, W. D. (1993). The causes of geomagnetic storms during solar minimum. NOAA/ERL/SEL.

Turismo de Portugal. (2021). *Turismo em números - dezembro 2020*. Travel BI by Turismo de Portugal. https://travelbi.turismodeportugal.pt/pt-pt/Documents/Turismo%20em%20Portugal/turismo-em-numeros-dez-2020.pdf

Uğur, N. G., & Akbıyık, A. (2020). Impacts of COVID-19 on global tourism industry: A cross-regional comparison. *Tourism Management Perspectives*, *36*, 100744. doi:10.1016/j.tmp.2020.100744 PMID:32923356

United Nations. (2021). *COVID-19 in SIDS | Office of the High Representative for the Least Developed Countries, Landlocked Developing Countries and Small Island Developing States*. United Nations. https://www.un.org/ohrlls/content/covid-19-sids

UNWTO. (2020). *100% of Global Destinations now have Covid-19 Travel Restrictions, UNWTO reports*. UNWTO. https://www.unwto.org/news/covid-19-travel-restrictions

UNWTO. (2021a). *World Tourism Barometer,* 19(3). UN.

UNWTO. (2021b). *2020*: *Worst Year in Tourism History with 1 Billion Fewer International Arrivals*. UNWTO. https://www.unwto.org/news/2020-worst-year-in-tourism-history-with-1-billion-fewer-international-arrivals

UNWTO. (2022). Word Tourism Barometer – May 2022: Vol. 20. *Issue 3*. World Tourism Organization.

Urrútia, G., & Bonfill, X. (2009). *PRISMA declaration: A proposal to improve the publication of systematic reviews and meta-analyses*. BMJ. https://bmjopen.bmj.com/content/bmjopen/suppl/2013/06/10/bmjopen-2012-002330.DC1/bmjopen-2012-002330supp_PRISMA-2010.pdf

Uslu, S., & Dönmez, K. (2016). Geçmişten günümüze havacılık kazalarının sebeplerindeki değişimler üzerine bir inceleme [Lexical characteristics of Turkish language]. *Journal of Social Sciences*, *3*(9), 222–239. doi:10.16990/SOBIDER.296

Valério, J. (2022). *Inteligência Artificial: A origem [1/7]*. Diferencial. https://diferencial.tecnico.ulisboa.pt/ciencia/inteligencia-artificial-a-origem-1-7/

Valipour, A., Yahaya, N., Md Noor, N., Antuchevičienė, J., & Tamošaitienė, J. (2017). Hybrid SWARA-COPRAS method for risk assessment in deep foundation excavation project: An Iranian case study. *Journal of Civil Engineering and Management*, *23*(4), 524–532. doi:10.3846/13923730.2017.1281842

van der Aa, H., Buil, L., Kabadayi, S., & van der Heijden, H. (2018). The Effects of Chatbot's Conversational Human Voice and Mode of Conversational Voice on Customers' Loyalty. *Computers in Human Behavior*, *89*, 347–356.

Van Rooyen, J., Shrestha, P., & De Beer, E. (2021). Crisis on human resources: Airline companies in Thailand. *Journal of Human Resource Management*, *9*(2), 39–42. doi:10.11648/j.jhrm.20210902.12

Viegas, D. (2015). Aeroporto de Faro foi inaugurado há 50 anos [Faro Airport was opened 50 years ago]. *Jornal do Algarve*. https://jornaldoalgarve.pt/aeroporto-de-faro-foi-inaugurado-ha-50-anos-2/

Vincent, N. C., Bhakar, R. R., Nadarajan, S. R., Syamala, A., & Varghese, J. (2021). Impact of Artificial Intelligence in the Aviation and Space Sector. In *Artificial Intelligence* (pp. 209–229). CRC Press. doi:10.1201/9781003095910-15

Visit Azores (s.d.). *Férias nos Açores — Descubra os Açores durante umas férias em Portugal.* Visit Azores. https://www.visitazores.com/pt/the-azores/the-9-islands/geography

VisitPortugal.com. (n.d.). *Madeira and Porto Santo Guide.* Visit Portugal. https://bit.ly/3SV6eRC.

Wach, K., Duong, C. D., Ejdys, J., Kazlauskaitė, R., Korzynski, P., Mazurek, G., Paliszkiewicz, J., & Ziemba, E. (2023). The Dark Side Of Generative Artificial Intelligence: A Critical Analysis of Controversies and Risks of Chatgpt. *Entrepreneurial Business and Economics Review*, *11*(2), 7–24. doi:10.15678/EBER.2023.110201

Waemustafa, W. (2014). *Customer Satisfaction and Loyalty in the Airline Industry: A Case Study of Malaysia Airlines (MAS) and Air Asia.*

Walker, S., & Cook, M. (2009). The contested concept of sustainable aviation. *Sustainable Development (Bradford)*, *17*(6), 378–390. doi:10.1002/sd.400

Wang, Y., Kevin, K. F. S., & Sparks, B. A. (2014). *What Technology-Enabled Services Do Air Travelers Value? Investigating the Role of Technology Readiness.* Sage. doi:10.1177/1096348014538050

Wang, J., Xiao, F., Dobruszkes, F., & Wang, W. (2023). Seasonality of flights in China: Spatial heterogeneity and its determinants. *Journal of Air Transport Management*, *108*, 102354. doi:10.1016/j.jairtraman.2022.102354

Wang, T. C., & Chang, T. H. (2007). Application of TOPSIS in evaluating initial training aircraft under a fuzzy environment. *Expert Systems with Applications*, *33*(4), 870–880. doi:10.1016/j.eswa.2006.07.003

Wan, M., Liang, Y., Yan, L., & Zhou, T. (2021). Bibliometric analysis of human factors in aviation accident using MKD. *IET Image Processing*, *15*(12), 1–9. doi:10.1049/ipr2.12167

Ward, M., McDonald, N., Morrison, R., Gaynor, D., & Nugent, T. (2010). A Performance improvement case study in aircraft maintenance and its implications for hazard identification. *Ergonomics*, *53*(2), 247–267. doi:10.1080/00140130903194138 PMID:20099178

Wargborn, C. (2008). Managing motivation in organizations: Why employee relationship management matters. [Master of International Management Master, ISCTE Business School].

Watson F. & Williams. (2022). *Get into the Green Scene: Sustainability linked finance in aircraft finance.* Watson Farley & Williams. https://www.wfw.com/articles/get-into-the-green-scene-sustainability-linked-finance-inaircraft-finance/

Weaver, D., & Lawton, L. (2002). *Tourism Management* (2nd ed.). John Wiley & Sons, Ltd.

Weinzierl, M. (2018). Space, the Final Economic Frontier. *The Journal of Economic Perspectives*, *32*(2), 173–192. doi:10.1257/jep.32.2.173

Wensveen, J. G. (2007). Air transportation: A management perspective. England: Ashgate Publishing Limited.

WHO. (2020). *WHO Director-General's opening remarks at the media briefing on COVID-19.* WHO. https://bit.ly/3QLj3fh

Whyte, R. (2004). Frequent Flyer Programmes: Is It a Relationship, or Do the Schemes Create Spurious Loyalty? *Journal of Targeting, Measurement and Analysis for Marketing, 12*(3), 269–80. . doi:10.1057/palgrave.jt.5740114

Williams, A. M., & Shaw, G. (1991). *Tourism and Economic Development. Western European Experiences* (2nd ed.). John Wiley & Sons, Ltd.

Williams, P. D. (2017). Increased light, moderate, and severe clear-air turbulence in response to climate change. *Advances in Atmospheric Sciences, 34*(5), 576–586. doi:10.1007/s00376-017-6268-2

Wink, R. (2010). Structural changes in international aeronautics markets–regional, organizational, and technological dimensions. *Gestion Technologique, 50*(3/4), 225.

Witt, S. F., & Moutinho, L. (1995). *Tourism Marketing and Management Handbook*. Prentice Hall.

World Economic Forum. (2020). *Six Ways Space Technologies Benefit Life on Earth*. Global Future Council on Space Technologies. Briefing Papers, September 2020. www3.weforum.org/docs/wef_gfc_six_ways_space_technologies_2020.pdf

World Intellectual Property Organization. (2023). *Global Innovation Index 2023 – Innovation in the face of uncertainty*. WIPO. https://www.wipo.int/edocs/pubdocs/en/wipo-pub-2000-2023-en-main-report-global-innovation-index-2023-16th-edition.pdf

WTTC. (2021). *Travel & Tourism Economic Impact 2021: Global Economic Impact & Trends 2021 - June 2021*. World Travel & Tourism Council. https://wttc.org/Portals/0/Documents/Reports/2021/Global%20Economic%20Impact%20and%20Trends%202021.pdf?ver=2021-07-01-114957-177

Wu, C., Liao, M., Zhang, Y., Luo, M., & Zhang, G. (2020). Network development of low-cost carriers in China's domestic market. *Journal of Transport Geography, 84*, 102670. doi:10.1016/j.jtrangeo.2020.102670

X2id. (2023). *História da Inteligência Artificial*. X2ID. https://x2inteligencia.digital/2020/02/20/historia-da-inteligencia-artificial-2

Xia, F., Wei, H., & Yang, L. W. (2015). Improved COPRAS Method and Application in Material Selection Problem. *Applied Mechanics and Materials, 707*, 505–508. . doi:10.4028/www.scientific.net/AMM.707.505

Xiong, H., Wu, Z., Hou, F., & Zhang, J. (2020). Which firm-specific characteristics affect the market reaction of Chinese listed companies to the COVID-19 pandemic? *Emerging Markets Finance & Trade, 56*(10), 2231–2242. doi:10.1080/1540496X.2020.1787151

Yang, H. (2007). Airlines' futures. *Journal of Revenue and Pricing Management, 6*(4), 309–311. doi:10.1057/palgrave.rpm.5160105

Yeh, C. H., & Chang, Y. H. (2009). Modeling subjective evaluation for fuzzy group multicriteria decision making. *European Journal of Operational Research, 194*(2), 464–473. doi:10.1016/j.ejor.2007.12.029

Yılmaz, S. (2013). *Space Security* (1st ed.). Milenyum Publications.

Yin, R. K. (2016). *Qualitative Research from Start to Finish* (2nd ed.). Guilford Publications.

Yoshimura, H. (2022). *ICAO CAEP Report that Explores the Feasibility of a Long-term Aspirational Goal for International Civil Aviation CO2 Emission Reductions*. LTAG.

Yu, K. H., Beam, A. L., & Kohane, I. S. (2018). Artificial Intelligence in Healthcare. *Nature Biomedical Engineering, 2*(10), 719–731. doi:10.1038/s41551-018-0305-z PMID:31015651

Zachariah, R. A., Sharma, S., & Kumar, V. (2023). Systematic review of passenger demand forecasting in aviation industry. *Multimedia Tools and Applications*, *2023*(30), 1–37. doi:10.1007/s11042-023-15552-1 PMID:37362707

Zakaria, I. H., Mohammad, N., Abashah, A., Alshuaibi, M. S. I., Othman, A., Ahmad, N., Yaziz, M. F. A., & Akanmu, M. D. (2023). Preparation of Aviation Industry Transition on COVID-19 From Pandemic to Endemic Phase: A Review. *International Journal of Professional Business Review*, *8*(4), e0824. doi:10.26668/businessreview/2023.v8i4.824

Zavadskas, E. K., Turskis, Z., Antucheviciene, J., & Zakarevicius, A. (2012). Optimization of Weighted Aggregated Sum Product Assessment. *Elektronika ir Elektrotechnika*, *122*(6), 3–6. doi:10.5755/j01.eee.122.6.1810

Zeithaml, V. (2008). *Services Marketing : Integrating Customer Focus across the Firm*. 7th ed. Mcgraw-Hill Education.

Zhang, X., & Hu, Y. (2018). Big Data Analytics in the Airline Industry: A Review and Future Research Directions. *Journal of Air Transport Management*, *68*, 1–10.

Zhegu, M. (2007). *La coévolution des industries et des systèmes d'innovation: l'industrie aéronautique*. UQAM.

Zou, L., Reynolds-Feighan, A., & Yu, C. (2022). Airline seasonality: An explorative analysis of major low-cost carriers in Europe and the United States. *Journal of Air Transport Management*, *105*, 102272. doi:10.1016/j.jairtraman.2022.102272

Zsembera, J. (2017). *O turismo nos Açores e a liberalização do espaço aéreo. Análise das perceções das partes interessadas na ilha de São Miguel*. [Dissertação de Mestrado, Universidade Aberta]. Repositório Comum. https://repositorioaberto.uab.pt/bitstream/10400.2/7287/1/TMG/MBA_JanineZsembera.pdf

Zuliani, J., & Jalabert, G. (2005). L'industrie aéronautique européenne: Organisation industrielle et fonctionnement en réseaux. *L'Espace Geographique*, *34*(2), 117–144. doi:10.3917/eg.342.0117

Zupan, J. (1994). Introduction To Artificial Neural Network (ANN) Methods: What They Are and How to Use Them. *Acta Chimica Slovenica*, *41*, 327–327.

About the Contributors

Salim Kurnaz is an Associate Professor at Istanbul Aydın University, with 22 years of experience in aviation. He worked as a maintenance technician, quality control technician and maintenance instructor in the Turkish Armed Forces between 1997-2020. He worked at Joint Force Command (JFCBS) Brunssum/Netherlands between 2010-2013. He received bachelor's degree on Public Management in 2005 and on Aviation Management in 2022 from Anadolu University; master's degree in International Relations from Oklahoma University Oklahoma/USA in 2013 and in Business Management from Malatya Inonu University in 2018. He received his doctorate degree on management Sciences in 2019 from Malatya Inonu University. He continues his studies in the fields of public administration, aviation management, contemporary management systems, strategic management, and behavioral sciences. He is also working as visiting Associate Professor at Kazimiero Simonaviciaus University Vilnius, Lithuania.

António Rodrigues obtained a PhD in Management and Marketing at the University of Seville in Spain. He is currently a professor and researcher at the ISG-Business & Economics School (Lisbon, Portugal). Researcher at the University of Évora (Portugal) in the Post-Doctoral Program in Management, in the project on the materiality and contribution to the SDGs of publicly traded companies in their non-financial reports. He has teaching experience in undergraduate and master's degrees in Aeronautical Management. He is the author of several opinion articles and scientific articles. Professionally, he has experience in the financial, marketing and general management areas. He is certified in Sustainable Finance (ESG Advisor) by EFPA The European Financial Planning Association.

Jorge Abrantes has a PhD in Tourism from the Institute of Geography and Spatial Planning (UL - IGOT). More than 30 years of professional experience in tourism and aviation, mostly in business management and Board roles in companies like TAP Air Portugal, Pestana Hotels & Resorts, White Airways and Turismo de Portugal. Professor of tourism and commercial aviation since 1992, his research areas being related to tourism and transport, innovation in tourism and new accommodation models. Consultant for companies with greater focus in the area of investment projects and business incentive systems.

Ali Davut ALKAN completed his undergraduate education at Atatürk University, Department of Sociology between 2012-2016. He received his master's degree (2019) from Dokuz Eylül University, Institute of Social Sciences in the field of Maritime Safety, Security and Environmental Management. Since 2017, Alkan has been working as a lecturer at Niğde Ömer Halisdemir University, Niğde Social Sciences Vocational School of Social Sciences and continues his doctoral studies in Niğde Ömer Halisdemir University, Institute of Social Sciences, Department of Business Administration, Department of Management and Organization from 2019. Alkan works in the fields of human resources management, strategic management and organizational behaviour.

Ana Cristina Barqueira has a degree in Applied Mathematics and Computation (Probabilities and Statistics area) from Instituto Superior Técnico, a master's in applied mathematics for Economics and Management from Instituto Superior de Economia e Gestão and a PhD in Stochastic Processes and Statistics from Instituto Superior Técnico. She is an adjunct professor at Instituto Superior de Educação e Ciências since 2004, teaching in several degrees and masters. She is a researcher at CEMAT (Center for Computational and Stochastic Mathematics) at Instituto Superior Técnico (Lisbon Technical University) and Senior Researcher at the Centro de Estudos e Investigação Aplicada (CEIA) at ISEC Lisboa. Her research interests include Education, Tourism, Health, Genetics and some Engineering.

Diogo Belejo has been a student at Universidade Lusófona de Humanidades e Tecnologias for the past 4 years, having graduated in Aeronautical Management in 2023. Currently he's taking the first year of his Master's degree in Business Management at the same university.

Beyzanur Cayir Ervural received PhD degree from Istanbul Technical University. She is currently an Associate Professor at Necmettin Erbakan University, Department of Aviation Management in Turkey. Her research interest covers decision-making, supply chain management, fuzzy applications and modelling, data analytics, optimization and forecasting studies. She has numerous publications in this field.

Kübra Cingöz has been working for about 2,5 years as a Research Assistant in Gaziantep University. She completed her master degree in Aviation Management Department and is currently getting her PhD in Kocaeli University.

Vldan Durmaz was born in Eskişehir. She graduated from Anadolu University, Educational Faculty, English Teaching Department in 1988. She had studied as an instructor at Anadolu University, School of Civil Aviation. She had her master degree on Management and Organization and doctorate on Civil Aviation Management at the same university. She has been teaching undergraduate, graduate and PhD courses such as; Air Transportation Management, Airport Management, Airports and Environment, Aviation English at Eskişehir Technical University. She has been attending national and international conferences and studying on the field of management and aviation related to the subject of environmental management systems, airport sustainability, team management, current management applications. She wrote several course and scientific books on strategic management.

Ümit Deniz GÖKER received her Ph.D. on 'Shock Wave Structures in Solar Plasma' and attended a project on 'The Design of Turbopumps Using Liquified Fuel and Cavitation Optimization' from the Ege University, Institute of Natural Sciences, and İstanbul Technical University, Department of Aeronautics and Astronautics Engineering in 2010, respectively; and she has also been in the University of St. Andrews, Institute of Mathematics and Statistics at Scotland, UK as a 'Visiting Researcher' between the years 2007-2008. She later received her Postdoctoral Fellowship on 'Shock Wave Applications in Supernova Remnants' at Bosphorus University, Department of Physics between the years 2011-2017. During her Postdoctoral studies, she visited the University of Sheffield, School of Mathematics and Statistics, Sheffield, UK in 2014. Soon after, she started to work at the National Defense University, Air Force Academy, Faculty of Aviation and Space Engineering as an Assistant Professor between the years 2018-2019, and Associate Professor from 2019 to 2021, and she got her Associate Professor position from the Aeronautics and Aerospace Engineering at the same university in 2019. After she worked in the Topkapı University, Department of Aviation Management from 2021 to 2022, she was at the Czech Academy of Sciences, Department of Solar Physics, Ondrejov, Czech Republic between the years 2022-2023 for her Sabbatical Fellow. Her research interests include Solar Physics, Near-Space Physics, Plasma Physics, Shock Wave Physics, and the Effects of Solar Eruptions, Solar Magnetic Fields on Aviation and Space Flights, and Climate Change.

Lca Piedade has a Doctor in Communication Sciences (organizational and crisis communication), Master in Aeronautical Management and Architect. Has worked in aviation for 36 years, the last 20 of which as Operational Supervisor at Lisbon Airport. Currently a lecturer at Lusófona University. Researcher at the Center for Research in Applied Communication, Culture and New Technologies (CICANT) and CEGIST - Center for Management Studies at Instituto Superior Técnico. Her main research lines are about aviation, communication and crisis communication.

Rui Castro e Quadros, more than 25 years of professional experience (airlines, airports and tourism business), currently he is a BSc Aviation Management Program Director at ISEC Lisbon (and professor) and invited professor at Estoril Higher School of Hotel and Tourism (ESHTE). Research interests focus on air transport, airports, and tourism. He was Executive Director and Member of the Board of Directors of Grupo SATA, Managing Director for Italy Portugália Airlines, where he was responsible for the Italian market and Sales Executive at Iberia, Linhas Aéreas de España, in Lisbon. BSc/MSc in Communication and Post-Graduate in Marketing and Sales; Specialist Title in Strategic Management; and Doctoral Student in Tourism.

Crlos Rouco is an Associate Professor of Human Resource Management in the School of Economic Sciences and Organizations at Lusofóna University, Lisbon. Currently, he is the director of the Department of Air Transport and Airports Management and Director of the Bachelor's degree in Aeronautical Management. He teaches courses on crisis management, business strategy, leadership, human resource management, development and vocational training. He has taught and coordinated several intensive leadership courses (internal regime for 3 and 5 days) for young university students, entrepreneurs, bankers, and firefighters.

Osman Nuri Sunar is an assistant professor at Istanbul Aydın University, Anadolu Bil Vocational School, Department of Transportation Services, with approximately 30 years of aviation experience. Between 1993 and 2022, he worked as an aircraft flight and maintenance technician, quality control, maintenance instructor, flight and maintenance standardization control personnel in various units of the Turkish Armed Forces. He received bachelor's degree on Public Management in 2003 and on Aviation Management in 2020 from Anadolu University; master's degree in Business Management from Kutahya Dumlupinar University in 2008. He received his doctorate degree on Management Sciences in 2021 from Malatya Inonu University. He conducts studies and research in the fields of aviation management, contemporary management systems, strategic management and behavioral sciences.

Carolina Vieira has a degree in Aviation Management and currently studying for a Master's degree in Air Transport Operations. Experience in Safety Operations at ANA Airports of Portugal VINCI Group (Airports).

Index

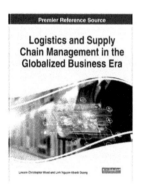

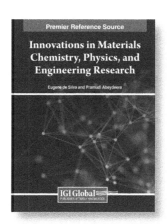
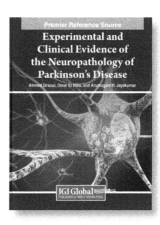

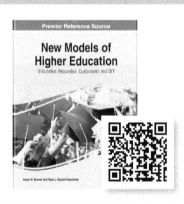

Individual Article
& Chapter Downloads
US$ 37.50/each

Easily Identify, Acquire, and Utilize Published Peer-Reviewed Findings in Support of Your Current Research

- Browse Over *170,000+ Articles & Chapters*

- *Accurate & Advanced* Search

- Affordably Acquire *International Research*

- *Instantly Access* Your Content

- Benefit from the *InfoSci® Platform Features*

THE UNIVERSITY
of NORTH CAROLINA
at CHAPEL HILL

It really provides an excellent entry into the research literature of the field. It presents a manageable number of highly relevant sources on topics of interest to a wide range of researchers. The sources are scholarly, but also accessible to 'practitioners'.

- Ms. Lisa Stimatz, MLS, University of North Carolina at Chapel Hill, USA

9 798369 309087